Paying with Plastic

Paying with Plastic

The Digital Revolution in Buying and Borrowing

David S. Evans
Richard Schmalensee

The MIT Press
Cambridge, Massachusetts
London, England

Third printing, 2001
©1999 Massachusetts Institute of Technology

This book was set in Sabon by Achorn Graphic Services, Inc.

Printed and bound in the United States of America.

Library of Congress Cataloging-in-Publication Data

Evans, David S.
  Paying with plastic : the digital revolution in buying and
  borrowing / David S. Evans, Richard Schmalensee.
    p.   cm.
  Includes bibliographical references and index.
  ISBN 0-262-05062-5 (hc); 0-262-55037-7 (pb)
    1. Credit cards—United States. 2. Bank credit cards—United
States. 3. Electronic funds transfers—United States.
4. Electronic commerce—United States. 5. Consumer credit—United
States. I. Schmalensee, Richard. II. Title.
HG3755.8.U6E94   1999
332.7′65′0973—dc21   99-23902
                                                                   CIP

To our parents,
Richard and Annette Evans
Fred and Marjorie Schmalensee

Contents

Preface

In the last half of the twentieth century, payment cards—credit, debit, and charge cards—have slowly revolutionized how we pay for goods and services. If you bought this book over the Internet, you probably entered the sequence of digits from one of your payment cards. The electrons you set in motion precipitated the movement of money, mostly in the form of binary digits, between you, the merchant, and participants in the sprawling payment card industry. It is increasingly common to find merchants that do not take cash or checks, and increasingly rare to find merchants that refuse payment cards.

Payment cards have also revolutionized how we coordinate the timing of when we purchase goods and services and when we pay for them. The popular media often focus on how credit cards, by making it much quicker and easier to borrow, encourage people to spend beyond their means and get mired in debt. Although removing the hassle from the process of borrowing has allowed some people to borrow too much, credit cards have enabled many more of us to achieve a better standard of living. The millions of people who finance purchases on credit cards want to enjoy life earlier than their current incomes and savings permit. Credit cards enable them to do so.

This book is about the complex industry that lies behind the revolution in how we pay and how we finance. But we have several other stories to tell. One is about how the entrepreneurs behind the payment card industry solved the classic "chicken-and-egg" problem. Consumers do not want cards that merchants do not take, and merchants do not want cards that consumers do not have. Another story is about how the payment card industry was shaped by the highly localized nature of the American banking industry. Credit cards were developed by two bank associations—MasterCard and Visa—which now have thousands of members across the country, ranging from the smallest credit unions to the largest commercial banks. A further story concerns the legal battles that have embroiled these associations, Visa primarily, throughout their existence. These battles have resulted from the collision of associations that have developed a creative and productive mixture of collaboration and competition among its members with antitrust laws that are highly skeptical of any collaboration among competitors.

We bring two perspectives to bear on the payment card industry. First, we examine the evolution of this industry through the lens of economics. We are particularly interested in explaining how economic forces have combined with institutional and technological ones to shape this industry, and in showing how competition works in an industry that does not fit neatly into any of the standard models used by economists. Second, our own introduction to this industry has come in part through consulting work we have done for Visa. We began working for Visa in 1991 when Sears (then the owner of the Discover Card) filed an antitrust lawsuit after Visa refused to let Sears issue a Visa card. We have since worked on several other antitrust matters, including an investigation by the Antitrust Division of the U.S. Department of Justice into competitive practices in the credit card industry that culminated in the Department's suing Visa and MasterCard in October 1998. We believe that the antitrust charges against the credit card associations often stem from a lack of understanding of how competition works in the payment card industry and from a failure to recognize the need for creative solutions to the special problems that affect this unique industry. This book explains how this industry works and argues that it works remarkably well.

Acknowledgments

We are grateful for the help we have received over the years from so many people. We thank Wayne Best, Dominique Fracchia, Tom Layman, Ron Schmidt, Stephen Theoharis, Lamar Smith, and Rob Towne of Visa; Stephen Bomse, Brian Brosnahan, and M. Laurence Popofsky of Heller Ehrman White and McAuliffe; Amanda Adrian, Leah Bartelt, Karin Choo, Daniel Hassan, Terrence Kontos, Melba Largent, Matthew Leder, Miriam Oh, and Bernard Reddy of National Economic Research Associates (NERA). We are extremely indebted to Howard Chang of NERA for many insightful discussions about the economics of the payment card industry and for his significant collaboration on many aspects of this book and to Timothy Classen of NERA for his exceptional research effort. Finally, we are especially grateful to Paul Allen of Visa for providing encouragement, financial support, and many helpful comments over the years. This book, of course, does not necessarily reflect the views of any of the people who have generously provided us with all forms of assistance, nor does it necessarily reflect the views of Visa.

1

Plastic Cards

It was necessary to reconceive, in the most fundamental sense, the nature of bank, money, and credit card; even beyond that to the essential elements of each and how they might change in a microelectronics environment. Several conclusions emerged: First: Money had become nothing but guaranteed, alphanumeric data recorded in valueless paper and metal. It would eventually become guaranteed dots in the form of arranged electronics and photons which would move around the world at the speed of light.

—Dee Hock, former CEO of Visa

Look in your wallet. If you are like most Americans, you have at least one thin plastic card that you often use to pay for things. Take out one of those cards. The card you picked is about 3³/₈″ long by 2¹/₈″ wide, weighs about a fifth of an ounce, has a magnetic stripe on the back, and has your name and a 13- to 16-digit account number embossed on the front. It is called a "payment card." Yours is one of more than 720 million payment cards in the hands of U.S. consumers in 1998.

You can use your payment card—if you have the kind held by most consumers—to pay for your purchases at 4 million merchant locations in the United States and another 11 million merchant locations in other countries around the world. You can pay by presenting the card to the merchant, by reading the account number and other information over the phone, by writing that same information out for mail orders, or by sending the information electronically to the merchant via the Internet. You and other consumers used your payment cards to complete $860 billion worth of payment card purchases in 1997. (We adjust all of the dollar figures in this book so they reflect purchasing power in 1998.)

If you think back to how you paid for things even 30 years ago (provided you are old enough to have been paying for things then, of course), you will realize what an extraordinary revolution has taken place in our payment habits. Back then, people bought almost everything with cash or checks and bought only things they could finance out of their current incomes and savings. Few large retailers, no supermarkets, and hardly any mail order companies accepted payment by plastic. Of course, there were a few exceptions. Some people had charge cards that they used when they traveled or went to a restaurant. But they had to pay their charges in full at the end of each month. Some people had store cards that could be used only at the specific stores that issued the cards. In some cases, consumers could pay off their store card charges over time. Yet in 1977, households on average charged only a little more than $100 per month on their payment cards—about 3.4 percent of the average monthly household income. Today, most consumers pay for at least some purchases with a plastic card, and many of those who pay with credit cards end up financing their purchases. Households used payment cards for an average of $830 of transactions each month in 1997—about 20 percent of the average monthly household income. Most large retailers, supermarkets, and mail order firms take plastic, along with a rapidly increasing number of health care providers and other businesses.

Now try to imagine how you will pay for things ten years from now. Although forecasting is always risky, it seems likely that the ongoing revolution in payment habits will further decrease the use of cash and checks. For instance, more and more consumers have debit cards, which deduct the cost of purchases directly from consumers' checking accounts. Soon, many consumers may have "smart cards." These cards contain a small microchip that can be programmed to provide a variety of services. The electronic purse is one of the first smart services. It allows one to load money onto the chip and draw these funds down to make purchases. In addition, consumers increasingly use the Internet to conduct transactions. Because payment cards are based on computer networks, they provide the natural currency for this burgeoning mode of commerce. Amazon.com, the leading Internet purveyor of books, rarely sees anything other than payment card numbers submitted to its Web site.

The industry behind this revolution is the subject of this book. It is quite extraordinary. To see why, think about what has to happen for you to be able to even use your payment card. The merchant has to want to take your kind of card, so someone has to sell the merchant on the value of accepting that card. The merchant has to have the necessary equipment for processing card transactions, so someone has to provide this equipment to the merchant and service it. This industry had to solve the classic "chicken-and-egg" problem even to have a viable product. What consumer would want to have a payment card if few merchants accepted it? What merchant would want to accept payment cards if few consumers carried them? Far from being just a riddle for kids, this problem required the industry's founders to invest enormous amounts of capital and ingenuity.

The founders developed what economists call a "network joint venture." A joint venture involves cooperation among several independent businesses. The MasterCard joint venture involves cooperation among thousands of financial institutions. Each member issues payment cards, signs up merchants, or does both. The MasterCard joint venture is a network because each member of the joint venture must be able to conduct transactions with each and every other member of the joint venture. The member that issued your MasterCard has to reimburse the member that signed up the merchant whom you paid with your MasterCard. MasterCard and Visa, another joint venture of financial institutions, accounted for 71 percent of all purchases on payment cards in 1997. In no other significant industry do joint ventures play such a preeminent role.

Now think about what happens after you present your card to a merchant. The merchant probably swipes the card through an electronic terminal near the cash register. Within seconds, the terminal connects to a computer miles away and verifies the willingness of the entity that issued your card to pay for your purchase. Over the course of a year, these computers process more than 12 billion transactions between the millions of merchants that take payment cards and the hundreds of millions of consumers that use payment cards. It is a tour de force.

This feat is all the more extraordinary because the computers have so many masters to please. For the network joint ventures, the system has to transfer money to the merchant from the member that signed up the merchant. It has to transfer money from the member that issued the card to the member that signed up the merchant. The member that issued the card must obtain all the information necessary to bill the cardholder. And all along the way, the system works to collect and distribute various fees among the parties that have participated in each transaction.

How this complicated coordination takes place, and how the institutions developed to accomplish this, is a tale in itself. It is an economic and business story of how organizational and technological solutions to complex problems evolve in markets. And it is a story of how those solutions can deviate sharply from the look of competition in other industries, while nonetheless effectively delivering to consumers the benefits of intense competition.

Indeed, it is hard to find an industry that, on the surface, fits as poorly as this one does into the boxes that economists have developed for classifying industries. Firms collaborate through the network joint ventures, yet they compete with each other in issuing cards and signing up merchants. As a result, the industry looks highly concentrated if you inspect the shares of the major card brands, but it looks highly competitive if you look at the shares of individual card issuers. To add to the complexity, Visa and MasterCard have almost exactly the same members, yet they compete with each other for market share.

Then there is the product itself. The payment card provides a means of tender—money—that the merchant and consumer can use to consummate a transaction for some good or service. The payment card provides this service only when the merchant has made a decision to accept the particular kind of payment card (e.g., American Express) that the consumer has in her wallet, and the consumer has made a decision to proffer one of the cards that the merchant takes. Each party to the transaction must agree to use this means of tender. And since both parties to the transaction receive a service from the payment card when it is used, the benefit is joint as well.

Payment cards do not, however, just provide a means of tender. Credit cards—the most common type of payment cards in the United States— enable the consumer to finance a transaction and, in doing so, benefit both the consumer and the merchant. The consumer gets a convenient loan that enables her to better synchronize her earnings and spending. The merchant makes a sale to someone who could not have paid cash and avoids having to offer financing. The average credit card debt across all households was more than $4,400 at the end of 1997. Credit cards have rapidly displaced store credit programs over time. As will be discussed in chapters 4 and 5, credit cards have replaced store cards to the point where outstanding balances on store cards were less than 20 percent as large as the outstanding balances on credit cards at the end of 1997.

Now ubiquitous and intimately part of our lives, payment cards have a fascinating past, present, and future. And their story, not surprisingly, has a cast of lawyers, politicians, and regulators for color, amusement, and diversion from dry economic details. Former New York Senator Alphonse D'Amato helped demonstrate just how important the purveyors of these cards are to the economy. In November 1991, he proposed an amendment to the Comprehensive Deposit Insurance Reform and Tax-payer Protection Act that would have capped credit card rates at four percentage points above the IRS rate for overdue taxes, then 10 percent. When the Senate passed the amendment, the financial markets reacted quickly. The Dow Jones Industrial Average dropped 120 points in one day, at least partly in response to bank executives' prognostications of increased bank failures, decreased credit availability, and depressed spending. The stock prices of two of the largest bankcard issuers declined sharply as Citicorp's common stock value fell almost 5 percent that same day, while MBNA's fell nearly 16 percent. The amendment was dropped, and bank stocks moved back up.

Of less fleeting note, litigation over various aspects of the network joint ventures—MasterCard and Visa—has helped clarify the law concerning joint ventures generally. When the payment card ventures started in the mid-1960s, joint ventures were a relatively uncommon form of business organization. Since then, technological change has created more opportunities for cooperation between independent firms, cooperation that does not require full merger. Also, increased global competition has led more U.S. companies to form alliances with foreign competitors. As a result, joint ventures among high technology firms and between domestic and foreign firms have been occurring at a rapid clip since at least the mid-1980s. Three court cases involving the network joint ventures in credit cards—*Worthen Bank and Trust v. National BankAmericard, Inc.; National Bancard Corporation (NaBanco) v. Visa U.S.A., Inc.;* and *SCFC ILC, Inc. v. Visa U.S.A., Inc.* (generally referred to as the *MountainWest* case)—have resulted in decisions that have had ramifications for all joint ventures.

The evolution of this industry in the face of a web of state and federal regulations and antitrust litigation—actual and threatened—further illustrates the buoyancy of the competitive process. If you ever wondered why your credit card bill comes from South Dakota of all places, you need look no further than the *Marquette* decision, which allowed credit card issuers to get around state interest rate caps by issuing the cards in states without interest rate caps to consumers in states with interest rate caps. South Dakota rolled out the welcome mat for credit card issuers, and jobs that New Yorkers might have filled went to South Dakotans instead. The fact that your local bank hawks both MasterCards and Visa cards is the legacy of the Antitrust Division of the U.S. Department of Justice in the Ford administration. Visa and MasterCard wanted their members' exclusive allegiances, but some members wanted to belong to both associations. Visa asked the Antitrust Division to side with the existing separation of the two ventures. The Antitrust Division declined. Rather than risking expensive, management-consuming antitrust litigation, Visa and MasterCard relented. "Duality"—membership of financial institutions in both associations—soon became almost universal. How these associations have come to compete with each other despite having, in a sense, the same masters is an interesting aspect of this industry's saga. With no obvious sense of irony, the Antitrust Division filed an antitrust lawsuit in October 1998 that seeks to reerect the walls that once stood between these two associations.

There is another mystery. If you live in the United States, the card you use most often is probably a credit card (even if you pay your bill in full every month). If you live in most European countries, the card you use most often is most likely a debit card. Technology cannot explain this difference: both the United States and Europe have access to the same computer and card technology. Solving this mystery will show how the development of industries is shaped by the institutional and legal milieu in which they are born and spend their formative years, although we will also see that the mystery is not as deep as it seems at first.

The Star

The star of our story is the plastic card you pulled out a few minutes ago. At least since the famous line in *The Graduate,* plastic has connoted what is superficial and temporary in modern society. So it is a good idea to give our star a makeover. It is really a peripheral device that gives you, and those you share it with, access to a vast global computer network. From the front, it has some interesting features. Your account number is embossed at the bottom. If you have a MasterCard, the first six digits identify the company that issued the card, the next four digits show region and branch information, the next five digits identify you, and the last digit is just for security. When this embossed information gets pressed on a card slip, it enables the network to find you and the company that issued your card. The name of the company that issued the card is often emblazoned on the front as is the logo of the card brand you have.

But it is the magnetic stripe on its back that really makes it useful, especially as merchants have increasingly installed electronic terminals. That stripe holds most of the key information on your account: your name, account number, expiration date, card type, maybe your personal identification number (PIN), security information, and perhaps other details as well. (Computer chips may replace magnetic stripes in future years.) That information gets sent from your merchant's terminal over telephone lines to a computer. The location and type of the computer depends largely on the brand of your card.

Star Performance

How does a credit card work in practice? Figure 1.1 shows some of the important elements. You go to the Sony store to buy a new DVD player and you want to use your Visa card issued by MBNA (the "issuer"). In the next few seconds this is what happens. The card reader takes data off of the magnetic stripe on the back of the card. It combines this data

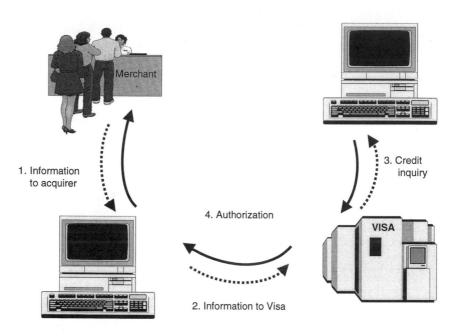

Figure 1.1
How do payment cards work?
Source: Visa U.S.A.

with information about the merchant and the dollar value of the purchase to create an electronic message. It then dials the telephone number of a computer maintained by the merchant's acquirer (the bank that handles transactions for the merchant). Once connected, a message is sent through to the acquirer's computer. This computer reads the message and figures out that you have used a Visa card. It dials up Visa's computer (there are actually two that work in parallel just in case one of them goes down). After reading the message, Visa's computer knows to check with MBNA's computer to see whether you have enough money on your credit line to secure the purchase. If you do, MBNA's computer will send a message back to Visa's computer authorizing the transaction. Visa relays the message back to the Sony store's acquirer, who then sends a message back to the terminal at the store. The terminal prints out the receipt that you sign. Because the entire transaction was captured electronically, the main purpose of the receipt is to help resolve disputes when cards are stolen and signatures are forged. This authorization usually takes just a few seconds. (Some large merchants have a direct connection to Visa's computer and do not go through an acquirer's computer.)

The Sony store then submits a request for payment to its acquirer that, in turn, sends it on to Visa's computer. The Visa computer passes on the request to MBNA's computer, which posts the transaction to your account. Visa's computer consolidates this transaction with all the other Visa transactions and settles accounts among banks. For this purchase, MBNA pays the acquirer, who then pays the Sony store. This process is typically completed within two to three days from the time you made your purchase. The Sony store actually receives only about 98 percent of the amount charged for your DVD player. The remaining 2 percent difference is called the "merchant discount," which is the fee paid to the acquirer for providing its services. The acquirer, in turn, pays about 1.4 percent of the purchase amount to the issuer, in this case MBNA. That 1.4 percent is called the "interchange fee" and is set by Visa; MasterCard has a similar fee. Neither American Express nor Discover need to set interchange fees because they are both the issuer and acquirer on all transactions and keep the entire merchant discount.

Credit cards from other associations, and cards used at other merchants, work in a similar way. Variations may include the identity of the acquirer for the merchant, the entities that actually process the transaction, and the merchant discount, depending on the deal struck. Debit cards also work in a similar way. Instead of sending you a bill for the transaction, however, the bank that issued you the card would deduct the purchase from your checking account.

Some of the intricacies of the credit card transactions arise because issuers such as MBNA participate in both the Visa and MasterCard network joint ventures. They do not operate their own independent card system. If you had presented an American Express card or Discover Card, a few things would have happened differently. The merchant might have a direct line to American Express. In that case, the message created by swiping the card through the reader goes directly to American Express' computer. That computer authorizes (or rejects) the transaction and sends the message right back to the merchant. American Express takes on the role of both merchant acquirer and issuer here, thereby cutting two steps out of the message relay process described earlier. If the merchant does not have a direct line to American Express, the message goes to the merchant's processor, which then transmits the message to American Express. Here, American Express takes on the role of issuer, thereby cutting only one step out of the process. Surprisingly though, with the use of fast computers and reliable telecommunications networks, there is no perceptible difference between the speeds at which American Express, Visa, and MasterCard process transactions.

The Main Characters

Speaking of American Express, Discover, MasterCard, and Visa, they are the major "brands" of payment cards. You can recognize them from their distinct logos. The four brands are also the major operators of payment card "systems." Each system consists of a distinct set of computers and rules for processing transactions, seeking verification, getting approval, transferring funds, and capturing billing information.

American Express is the oldest character here. It started in 1841 as an express company—sort of a cross between bicycle couriers and United Parcel Service. It introduced its first hit product—the travelers cheque—in 1891. Its first charge card—what is now the American Express Green Card—was launched in 1958. It started a credit card—the Optima line—in the late 1980s. Initially a case study in poor product planning, Optima developed into a solid product by the mid-1990s.

Discover is the youngest. Sears Roebuck & Co., which had had an enormously profitable store card, introduced the Discover Card in 1985. Its orange-on-black card became one of the greatest business success stories of the 1980s. By 1991, the Discover Card was accepted by more merchants than the American Express card. In 1993, Sears spun off its investment and credit arm into Dean Witter, Discover & Co. where the card continued to prosper. In fact, just over a decade after its start, Discover was already the third largest issuer of credit cards in the United States. In early 1997, Dean Witter, Discover & Co. and Morgan Stanley Group, Inc., agreed to an $8.9 billion merger, creating the second largest financial services firm in the world.

Visa is the biggest of the players. More than half of the general-purpose payment cards in the U.S. have the blue, white, and gold Visa logo on the lower right-hand corner, and almost all the merchants that take payment cards take Visa cards. Visa started in 1966, although its origins lie in a card first issued by Bank of America in California in 1958.

MasterCard was started at the same time as Visa. It was a star in the 1970s but faded in the 1980s. Cards with the orange-and-red MasterCard balls are second only to Visa in abundance. In 1978, Visa overtook MasterCard in number of cards issued. MasterCard briefly reversed its loss of share in 1992, after embracing novel card programs run by nonfinancial giants like AT&T. But its share of payment card charges has fallen slightly since 1994.

Other Members of the Cast

Although American Express, Discover, MasterCard, and Visa are the main characters in our story, the real action takes place in the constant competitive struggle for the consumer and the merchant. American Express and Discover are in the fray. MasterCard and Visa are too but primarily through their members who vie with each other as well as with American Express and Discover. Let us take a snapshot of the industry in 1997 before the 1998 mergers in banking and credit cards significantly changed the landscape. Table 1.1 shows the top ten bankcard issuers, ranked by the dollar value of transaction volume in 1997. Citibank, MBNA, and AT&T Universal provide examples of the different kinds of large issuers that existed in 1997.

Citibank was the top issuer based on purchase volume on bankcards, with more than 15 percent of total volume. In 1997, it had 24 million Visa cards and 15 million MasterCards in circulation. (In addition to MasterCard and Visa, Citibank also owns two other cards: Diners Club and Carte Blanche. Relatively few of these cards are issued or used in the United States.) Citibank was part of Citicorp, which was the second largest commercial bank in the United States with assets of more than $313 billion in 1997. Like most MasterCard and Visa members, it provides checking account services to consumers along with many other

Table 1.1
The ten largest issuers accounted for less than 65 percent of all MasterCard and Visa credit card volume in 1997.

Rank	Issuer	Charge volume ($ billions)	Share of total issuer volume (percentage)
1	Citibank	103.92	15.16
2	MBNA America	64.13	9.36
3	First Chicago NBD	47.60	6.94
4	Banc One/First USA	42.27	6.17
5	Chase Manhattan	40.24	5.87
6	Household Bank	34.61	5.05
7	AT&T Universal	28.00	4.09
8	US Bancorp	27.02	3.94
9	NationsBank	23.44	3.42
10	Bank of America	22.08	3.22
	Top ten	433.31	63.22
	All issuers	685.41	100.00

Source: The Nilson Report, no. 660, January 1998.

depository and lending services. Payment cards accounted for about 21 percent of Citicorp's overall profits in 1997.

MBNA was the second largest bankcard issuer with more than 9 percent of total volume. It was the fourth-largest issuer of MasterCards (15 million) and the fifth-largest issuer of Visa cards (14 million). MBNA is an example of a relatively recent phenomenon: a "monoline" bank, one created primarily for issuing payment cards. Started in 1981, it had $45 billion of outstanding credit card balances but only $2.5 billion of consumer loans at the end of 1997. Monoline banks were one of the fastest growing kinds of payment card issuers in the early 1990s. MBNA, for example, increased its share of bankcard volume from only 4.5 percent in 1990 to 9.4 percent by 1997.

AT&T Universal was the seventh-largest bankcard issuer in 1997, with about 4 percent of total volume. It was the largest issuer of MasterCards (20 million) and the twelfth-largest issuer of Visa cards (5 million). Started in the spring of 1990, it was the first MasterCard or Visa program run by a major nonfinancial company. The cards were issued through a small bank called Universal Bank, but AT&T controlled all business aspects of the card.

The top ten issuers, shown in table 1.1, accounted for about 63 percent of bankcard volume in 1997. Citibank, MBNA, and AT&T were among the largest bankcard issuers. But they competed with a cast of thousands: the banks that have local or regional card programs. For example, the card program at Old National Bank in Indiana was the 200th-largest Visa and MasterCard program in 1997. But its cardholders had only $69.6 million in credit card volume, amounting to one-hundredth of 1 percent of total industry bankcard volume.

Much changed between 1997 and 1998 as a result of bank mergers and the sale of card portfolios. In 1997, Banc One bought the card portfolio of the large monoline issuer First USA and then announced a merger with First Chicago NBD in the following year. In 1998, AT&T got out of the card business and sold its portfolio to Citibank, which then announced a proposed merger with the Travelers Group. Another monoline issuer was taken over when the Advanta portfolio was purchased by Fleet Bank. And also in 1998, Bank of America (the tenth-largest issuer in 1997) merged with NationsBank (the ninth-largest issuer). In early 1999, another significant development took place when Citibank resigned from Visa's Board of Directors and announced plans to switch allegiance to MasterCard. Citibank stated that Visa brand development efforts benefited smaller issuers who could not build their own brand names. Visa's advertising and marketing were funded, of course, in substantial part by fees paid by the larger members such as Citibank. Citibank wanted to develop its own national and global brand name and wanted to move the Visa logo to the back of the card. Visa was unwilling to relegate its brand, but MasterCard was rumored to be willing to permit this as part of its deal with Citibank.

Supporting Roles

Sort of like the tone-deaf actor who has to have someone dub his singing parts, the payment card firms have found that there are important roles that others perform better. Signing up merchants, selling and servicing card-reading terminals for merchants, switching transactions from the terminals to the correct card system, and doing much of the processing that results in the cardholder's receiving a bill are roles that are now filled by "third-party processors." These processors work on behalf of all the systems to some extent and intensively with many of the members of the Visa and MasterCard associations. You have probably noticed that no matter which card you pull out of your wallet at the merchant, it gets run through the same terminal. This is because the terminals installed by the third-party processors are usually capable of sending transactions to each of the major systems.

First Data Corporation is by far the leading processor in the payment card industry, and it has grown rapidly in recent years by acquiring other processors. Before it was spun off by American Express in 1992, it served primarily as a third-party processor for both acquirers and issuers. Then in 1995, First Data acquired both NaBanco and Card Establishment Services, two of the three largest merchant acquirers in the bankcard industry, making First Data by far the largest merchant acquirer practically overnight. In 1997, First Data handled 8 billion card transactions on behalf of itself as well as other bankcard issuers and acquirers, which included both merchant and cardholder transactions.

The second-leading processor was Total System Services, which handled 3.4 billion transactions in 1997. Total Systems experienced substantial growth as many large banks, including Bank of America, turned over their in-house processing accounts to Total. One of the reasons for Total's success is its TS2, software which helps banks engage in target marketing. In 1996, Total teamed up with Visa to form a joint venture called Vital Processing Services, a full-service merchant processing company. Among its many services, Vital provides electronic authorization and data capture, clearing and settlement processing, and merchant accounting, billing, and reporting.

The Foreign Cast

Payment cards are the closest thing that the world has to a common currency. You can use your Visa card in more than 240 countries and territories at more than 14 million merchants. In 1997, consumers around the world charged more than $2 trillion of transactions on general-purpose payment cards.

Although the major characters described above play the world, there are noteworthy differences. As we mentioned, Europeans rarely use credit cards. In France, for example, there were approximately 26 million payment cards in circulation in 1996. Yet of these cards, less than 3 percent were credit cards; all the rest were debit cards (in the United States, payment cards were primarily credit cards). This story also holds true in other European countries such as Germany, where in 1996 debit cards constituted approximately 83 percent of all general-purpose payment cards.

Additionally, there are credit card brands known elsewhere around the world that remain almost entirely unnoticed in the United States. JCB International, for example, is the leading credit card system in Japan and the fourth-largest international card brand, with more than 4.4 million merchant locations, mostly in the Far East, and $39 billion in charge volume during 1996. In the United States, however, only 500,000 merchants currently accept the card: a pint-sized number when compared to giants like Visa and MasterCard, which are accepted at approximately 4 million outlets around the United States. Many of JCB's merchants cater to Japanese tourists.

The Thirteen Acts

The star, main characters, and other actors will make repeated appearances in following chapters about the tumultuous first fifty years of the payment card industry. Here is a brief synopsis of the action.

From Sea Shells to Electrons (chapter 2) discusses payment cards as the fourth in a sequence of major innovations in how people pay for things, following the development of metallic coins in ancient times, the creation of checks in the Middle Ages, and the spread of paper money during modern times. Payment cards have resulted in the increasing use of digitally represented and electronically transferred money.

Although technological change in computers and reductions in communications costs made this revolution inevitable, it started in the United States at a time when the country had a highly fragmented banking system and a populace heavily dependent on paper checks. These factors have shaped the evolution of the payment card industry in the United States and influenced its evolution elsewhere. *Land of Local Banks, Awash in Paper Checks* (chapter 3) describes the American banking system, which has formed the bedrock of the payment card industry.

The Rise of Payment Cards (chapter 4) traces how a few hundred cards for charging restaurant meals in New York spawned millions of cards for paying for and financing the purchase of goods and services around the world. The combination of payment and financing services on credit cards, along with other key innovations, resulted in the rapid growth in the number of merchants who took the cards and the number of consumers who used them.

Indeed, as we show in *From Gourmets to the Masses* (chapter 5), payment cards have spread through society and have benefited consumers from many walks of life. Only the economic elite had payment cards in the early 1950s; only the poor lack payment cards in the late 1990s. With the spread of payment cards, people can better coordinate their incomes and expenses, smooth income and consumption over their lifetimes, and even more easily start and finance small businesses. (Of course, just as some people eat and drink too much at restaurants or drive carelessly, some people rack up more debt than they probably should.)

Merchants have benefited as well. By providing a convenient payment and financing mechanism, payment cards make buying easier for their consumers. Most of us cringe when the person ahead of us in line pulls out her checkbook and the clerk asks for three forms of identification. Store owners and customers like payment cards because they are fast. *Everywhere You Want to Be* (chapter 6) looks at the growth of payment cards from the merchant side. It explains why merchants take cards and documents the growth and spread of merchant acceptance of payment cards over time.

Chickens, Eggs, and Other Economic Conundrums (chapter 7) is our economist version of intermission. It describes some of the unique economic characteristics of payment cards. Chief among these is the chicken-and-egg problem. No consumer wants a payment card if merchants do not take them. No merchant wants to take payment cards if consumers do not carry them. The solution to this and the fact that the payment card industry has to cater constantly to merchants and consumers have wide-ranging economic implications.

The blood, guts, and gore—to the extent we can offer any—come next. The next several chapters focus on various facets of the payment card industry and examine the competition among the players. *System Wars* (chapter 8) explains how the card systems have competed with each other. It describes two grand wars. American Express' war with MasterCard and Visa looked as though it was going to end in defeat for American Express in the late 1980s. But American Express fought its way back in the 1990s. The other war, between MasterCard and Visa, is less public, because these systems have the same members, but no less serious than that with American Express. Visa had American Express and MasterCard on the ropes in the late 1980s, and the war between these two commonly owned associations continues in the late 1990s.

Issuer Brawls (chapter 9) goes down to the trenches in which the individual issuers of cards fight for consumers. It documents the intense competition and shows how it has benefited consumers through lower prices and greater output. *Puzzles and Paradoxes* (chapter 10) considers some objections that have been offered to this conclusion. Several economists have suggested that competition does not work well in the payment card industry. One author has called the payment card issuing industry a paradox because it looks like a competitive industry but does not work like one.

As with most American industries, competition in the payment card industry takes place not just in the marketplace but in the courtroom as well, usually in the guise of antitrust litigation. *The Antitrust Wars* (chapter 11) describes several major wars that have influenced the shape and evolution of this industry. *Worthen* led to duality. *NaBanco* affirmed the right of MasterCard and Visa to set the interchange fee, a key device for managing the chicken-and-egg problem. *Dean Witter* permitted Master-Card and Visa to keep owners of competing systems out of their associations. After reviewing these cases, we make some suggestions on how the antitrust laws should deal with industries like payment cards in which firms must collaborate as well as compete to provide consumers with the best products and services.

Debit Cards Take Off (Finally) (chapter 12) describes how, after several failed attempts, Visa and MasterCard finally persuaded large numbers of American consumers to carry and use debit cards. People had been talking about debit cards as the next big thing since the early 1970s. It took until the mid-1990s for them to live up to their billing. By then, most consumers had ATM cards that could double as debit cards. An intense advertising and marketing campaign helped Visa persuade banks to issue debit cards and consumers to use them. MasterCard followed suit. The result was that the number of transactions charged to debit cards increased by a compounded annual growth rate of 44 percent between 1996 and 1998.

And They Don't Take Cash (chapter 13) offers some concluding observations and conjectures about what is to come in the ongoing revolution in paying and borrowing.

Increasingly, financial transactions are taking place over electronic networks in which consumers and merchants are represented by series of numbers. Money is just an electronic picture, kept on some computer media, of what you owe or what you have. How long plastic will remain the physical form for recording and transmitting that series of numbers is unknown and completely beside the point. The true revolution, the one that is sure to have long-lasting effects on economic life, is the development of computer networks for exchanging electronic money.

2

From Sea Shells to Electrons

The use of coin, which has been handed down to us from remote antiquity, has powerfully aided the progress of commercial organization, as the art of making glass helped many discoveries in astronomy and physics; but commercial organization is not essentially bound to the use of the monetary metals. All means are good which tend to facilitate exchange, to fix value in exchange; and there is reason to believe in the further development of this organization the monetary metals will play a part of gradually diminishing importance.
—Augustin Cournot, 1838

The manner in which people pay for things has seen few revolutions as fundamental as the spread of electronic money. Coins were the first innovation about 4,000 years ago. Checks were the next about 800 years ago. Paper money came a bit more than a century ago. The payment card, which is just at the half-century mark, is the most recent innovation and just as profound. This chapter traces the history of how we pay for things and then describes the role that payment cards now play in the economy.

What Is Money?

For the early American colonists, sea shells—the Indians' wampum— were the accepted small coinage. Black shells had twice the value of white ones. The Indians, aside from having thought up the currency, were the central bankers as well. They stood ready to redeem shells for beaver pelts, sustaining the purchasing power of the shells. As colonial settlement progressed, the beavers scurried away, so the story goes, and wampum became hard to redeem. Shells were on the way out as the seventeenth century passed.

Rice was money in South Carolina, for a time. Grain, cattle, whisky, and brandy were, at times, also legal tender. But tobacco was a more important and durable currency for our forefathers. It lasted as legal tender in Virginia for 200 years, and in Maryland for 150, until the U.S. Constitution stopped the states from having their own currency. Had it not, perhaps the Federal Reserve Board rather than the Food and Drug Administration would now regulate the tobacco industry.

The currency of early colonial America is, however, a historical aberration. For 2,000 years before the birth of Christ and long after, money was metal. Silver was the usual choice over time, and across Western civilizations copper was used from time to time and occasionally gold, having a good run in Constantinople after the division of the Roman Empire. These rare metals made sense as a currency because they were durable and easy to both transport and store. With the acceptance of metal as exchange, the economy had one of its first "standards."

Although its origin is lost in time, the development of that standard made trade vastly more practical. The next major revolution was the turning of metal into coins of predetermined weight and, therefore, predetermined value. Herodotus, though not one of the more reliable historians, credits this innovation to the Lydians who, he says, "are the first people on record who coined gold and silver into money, and traded in retail."

The Lydians did this in the eighth century B.C., and their invention spread east into the Persian Empire and west to Italy. The Hindus, if their epics are believed, had a decimal system of coins some centuries earlier. The Western Zhou Dynasty in China had developed metallic money between 1000 and 400 B.C. Their copper coins were shaped like a knife, with a hole in the blade and carved descriptions of the coin's origin and value.

Regardless of who gets the credit, the development of coinage was the real origin of money as we know it and the precursor of the paper money and electronic money that followed. Because it was minted by the state—the convention after Alexander the Great was to emboss the head of the sovereign on the coin—the true weight and value of the coin was guaranteed. Coins of varying weights and worth became the "units of account" for conducting exchanges. (For example, the Athenian drachma was based on about sixty-five grains of fine silver from the time of Alexander to the Roman conquest of Greece.) This system made it easier to quote a price that everyone could relate to the costs of others' goods. (The drachma served this purpose far into the period of the Roman Empire.) With coins, the economy had a means of exchange, a unit of account, and a store of value: the three essential characteristics of money.

It took about 2,000 years to have another event of such lasting importance as to call it a revolution in the history of money: the development of checks. Among Westerners, the Italians appear to get the credit for this one. The original invention was the "bill of exchange," developed in Florence around the twelfth century. The bill was a piece of paper issued by a bank that promised the recipient money—at that time, a metal coin—from the bank. With this bill, a trader avoided having to carry heavy coins with him on a long-distance shopping spree and risk their theft. Bills of exchange proved quite handy during the Crusades. (The Chinese actually developed similar bills 500 years earlier, in part because they did not use precious metals for coins, and thus needed a convenient means for consummating more valuable transactions.)

Bills of exchange were also the basis for a revolution in the provision of bank credit. For example, a Florentine trader wants to buy wool in London, which he will sell to a weaver in Venice. The cash-strapped trader goes to his bank. The bank gives him a loan to buy the wool. But rather than giving him coins from its vault, it gives him a bill of exchange. The bill goes to his London supplier, who in turn collects from a branch or agent in London (possibly a certain number of days after the purchase, depending on the type of bill). By this time, the trader has returned from Venice and repays his loan. The bank gets a fee for the loan even though none of its coins actually went anywhere. The innovation here lies in recognizing that "bills of exchange" and their descendants, checks, enable banks to loan out more money than they have in their vaults. (Timing, of course, is everything here. If too many people cash their checks and withdraw their money at the same time, the bank quickly collapses.)

Credit for another crucial revolution goes to the Commonwealth of Massachusetts. In 1690, the Massachusetts government needed to figure out how to pay for an unsuccessful attempt to capture the French fortress in Quebec City. Lacking the Commonwealth's late-twentieth-century enthusiasm for taxing its citizens dry, the colony issued pieces of paper that promised redemption in gold or silver—later. These pieces of paper circulated side by side with gold and silver and were treated as if they were worth the gold or silver they promised. Issuing paper money and postponing its redemption became a regular way for the colonial government to pay for things. (Of course, over time the paper money depreciated in value and Massachusetts really did end up taxing its citizens through this government-induced reduction in the value of their money.) Other colonies caught on as eventually did the rest of the British Empire and later the world. But first the British Parliament, in 1751, put a stop to the use of paper money in New England.

Paper money was, nonetheless, an important innovation. It provided a convenient means of exchange, far lighter and easier to transport than gold or silver coins. It also provided as good a unit of account as anything, although the ultimate unit was still gold or silver. Unfortunately, as a store of value, paper money was subject to the whims of its issuers. They had little incentive to maintain its value by limiting the amount of money printed. That feature was a show stopper in unstable times when governments had to finance wars just about every generation. But by the 1900s most industrialized economies relied on paper money. After 1973, with the fall of the Bretton Woods system that pegged currencies against the U.S. dollar, the price of which was fixed in terms of gold, virtually all industrialized countries abandoned even the pretense that their money was tied to gold, silver, or anything else of intrinsic value.

The adoption of a standard currency for exchange, the introduction of a unit of account through coins with defined values, the development of checking and credit provision, and the creation of paper money were financial innovations that laid the basis for the explosive growth of market economies. Market economies create value fundamentally through exchange between their members. Money vastly facilitates that exchange by reducing the costs of transactions.

Money in America

Although these innovations have affected how exchange is accomplished throughout the world, the mechanics of money vary greatly across countries. In most industrialized countries, money is tangled in a web of gov-

"How will you be paying? Electronic transfer of funds, credit card, check, cash, precious metals, brightly colored shells or livestock?"

ernment regulations and institutional habits—and perhaps none more so than the United States, which is the focus here.

The Continental Congress had no choice but to finance the Revolutionary War by printing paper money. After that, however, paper money was not used as legal tender in the United States until 1862. The Constitution prohibited the states from issuing coins and the national government from issuing paper money. After winning its freedom from the British, the United States began minting a silver dollar similar to the one circulating in the Spanish colonies. The Philadelphia mint skimped a little on the silver, however. This drove the Spanish dollar out of circulation as people reacted to the small weight difference by melting the Spanish dollar and turning the resulting silver in for U.S. currency. This episode foreshadowed instability in the use of money during much of the nineteenth century.

Three key developments shaped the U.S. monetary system into which payment cards would be introduced in the early 1950s. The first was the introduction and gradual spread of paper money. During the 1800s, there was no federally backed paper currency, except when wars led the gov-ernment to finance expenses by printing money. Many state-chartered banks issued notes that circulated like money. Their periodic inability to redeem their notes with gold or silver played a role in the panics that punctuated the 1800s. After the Civil War, paper money issued by nation-ally chartered banks supplanted these notes. By the end of the century, there were many "brands" of paper money in circulation.

The second development was the creation of a strong central bank, the Federal Reserve System, in 1913. The Federal Reserve Act of 1913 authorized the issuance of Federal Reserve Bank notes. This currency, which was secured by direct obligations of the United States, became the standard. By 1920, 69 percent of money (hand-to-hand currency plus cash in bank vaults) consisted of Federal Reserve notes and deposits.

The third development that shaped the U.S. monetary system was the creation of a national check-clearing system by the Federal Reserve Board. Checks drawn against depository accounts became popular after the Civil War. At that time there was no central system, or set of rules, for processing and paying checks. The problem was first remedied in 1914 when Congress authorized the Federal Reserve System to process checks. Then, in 1917, Congress prohibited banks from charging Federal Reserve Charter Banks fees for honoring checks. Checks got a further boost in 1958 from automation when the banking industry developed magnetic ink character recognition (MICR), which we discuss in the next chapter.

As has been the case since 1933, today you cannot redeem your paper money for gold or silver or anything else of intrinsic value. Coins are still made of metal, but if you melted one, you could not sell the metal for the value of the coin. The value of bills and coins comes entirely from the fact that they are widely accepted means of tender. You can exchange them for things you value because other people can exchange the bills and coins you give them for things they value. As such, bills and coins are just aspects of an accounting system that everyone in the economy has signed on to. The "dollar" is the unit of account. So long as the number of dollars each of us (and each business) has is continually tracked and accounted for, no one has to touch a dollar bill or any other piece of paper money.

Cash, Check, or Charge?

In fact, once everyone has a numbered account, all the "money" in the world could reside on a large computer that would transfer units from one account to another as people exchange things of value. That is not where we are today, nor is it necessarily where we will be a century from now, but it is the direction in which we are heading. We are in the middle of a revolution that may not be quite on par with the introduction of coins but is arguably more profound than the introduction of paper money.

Payment cards are at the center of this ongoing revolution. They do not provide a unit of account or a store of value, so they are not the same as money. Instead, they are increasingly essential devices for exchanging virtual money: money that exists only in a system of electronic accounts. It is worth noting that checks provided the first virtual money. Once banks started lending depositors' money and letting people write checks against their deposits, money became intangible.)

Although payment cards are pervasive in today's economy, as a means of exchange they still stand far behind the use of checks. Americans spent $4.2 trillion on personal consumption of goods and services in 1996. Of these expenditures, 57 percent were made with checks, 21 percent with cash, and 22 percent with payment cards. But the share of consumer spending made with payment cards has grown rapidly over time. Back in 1984, the earliest year for which data are available, only 6 percent of personal consumption spending was made on payment cards compared to 58 percent with checks and 36 percent with cash. Figure 2.1 shows a comparison of spending in 1984 versus 1996. It is easy to see from the figure that the increase in card usage came at the expense of cash, not checks.

The growth of payment cards and the relative decline of cash and checks demonstrate an economic fact essential for understanding the evolution of the payment card industry. Payment cards are substitutes for cash, checks, and other means of exchange. The astounding growth of these cards has come at the expense of other kinds of money. That growth, however, has a long way to go; more than three-quarters of consumer purchases are still made with cash or check. Figuring out ways to

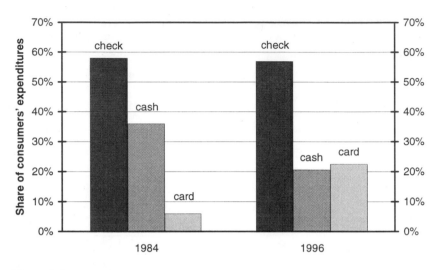

Figure 2.1
Payment cards account for a growing portion of consumers' expenditures.
Sources: The Nilson Report, no. 656, November 1997; "The Use of Cash and
Transaction Accounts by American Families," *Federal Reserve Bulletin,* February
1986.

get this portion of the payment pie is a key competitive challenge for the
current and future purveyors of payment cards and other kinds of electronic money.

Debit or Credit?

The clerk used to ask "Cash, check, or charge?" when you paid for things.
Now, if you say "Charge," the clerk—or the various kinds of display
terminals that increasingly substitute for unskilled labor—may ask,
"Debit or credit?" Even those choices do not exhaust all the possibilities,
for there are three major types of payment cards in circulation now and
another type on the horizon. These cards differ in when and how they
require the consumer to pay for her purchase. Here and throughout the
remainder of this book we focus on "general-purpose" payment cards
that can be used at many merchants, as opposed to store (e.g., Sears) and
gasoline (e.g., Texaco) cards that can be used only for purchases from
the merchant that issued the card.

Charge Cards

With a charge card, you are supposed to pay the issuer upon receipt of your monthly statement. You have nevertheless received a loan because, if you get billed every thirty days and you charge evenly over the month, you get an average of fifteen days before you get billed for an item and then several more days to pay that bill before you get charged interest. Most people write a check to pay off their charge card bill.

The American Express Green Card is the predominant charge card. The typical customer pays an annual fee of $55 plus $30 for each additional card for other family members. For account balances that are more than sixty days late, the customer pays at least $20 and a total amount up to 2.5 percent of the balances. Customers who get "corporate" cards from their company pay somewhat different fees.

Credit Cards

With a credit card, you can pay your charges in full or finance them up to the credit limit that the card issuer has established for you. You still get the same basic loan as with a charge card: the grace period between when you buy an item and when you have to send in a check. But you can extend the term of this loan almost indefinitely so long as you make a minimum payment each month.

The Citibank Visa card is one of the most widely held. The typical customer does not pay an annual fee. In fact, if she pays her monthly bill in full, she pays for nothing but the stamp. But if she does not pay her bill in full, she pays an interest rate—the annual percentage rate (APR)—of 17.9 percent of the remaining balance. If she is tardy in paying her bills, the APR can go up to 21.4 percent. If she uses the card to get a cash advance, she pays 2 percent of the cash amount (but at least $2). Many other Visa cards offer lower rates than those charged by Citibank.

Debit Cards

With a debit card, the payment comes right out of your checking account (what bankers call a demand deposit account, or DDA). The card is issued by the entity that holds your money on deposit (probably a bank, but possibly a money market fund). When you present your card, money is transferred from your account to the merchant's account that day if you enter your PIN or within about two days if you sign a receipt. PIN-based transactions are called "on-line" or "single-message" transactions, and signature-based transactions are called "off-line" or "dual-message" transactions, even though both are made electronically.

The "X-Press Check" card issued by BankBoston is a typical debit card. This card is affiliated with the MasterCard system and is therefore accepted at all locations that take MasterCard. BankBoston, like many banks now, makes this card available to most people who open a checking account with them. If you use this card to make a purchase, your payment to the merchant is taken directly out of your checking account. Some merchants have a "PIN pad": a small terminal through which cards are swiped and PIN numbers are entered. When you use your debit card at a merchant with such a device, the pad typically asks you to select "debit" or "credit." If you select the debit option, the PIN pad prompts you to enter your PIN, and the transaction is an on-line transaction. If you select the credit option, you are asked for your signature, and the transaction is off line. (The credit option is a bit of a misnomer here, although you may get credit for a couple of days.) Of course, at any merchant without a PIN pad, you are asked for your signature and the transaction is off line. Depending on the type of checking account you have, you may be charged a fee (just as you might be charged for writing a check) for using your card. In addition to having the MasterCard logo on it, the card also has the logos of several automatic teller machine (ATM) networks. You can use the card to withdraw money from ATMs affiliated with any of those networks.

ATMs and Smart Cards

The extensive development of ATMs is blurring the line between plastic and cash. There were 187,000 ATMs in the United States in 1998 at which consumers could withdraw money from their checking accounts, and 230 million ATM cards were in the hands of consumers. Like many similar cards, the BankBoston X-Press Check card can be used as both an ATM and a debit card. Some consumers take out cash from the nearest ATM (at the mall, perhaps, or around the corner from a restaurant) and pay with cash rather than plastic. ATM cards enable consumers to minimize the amount of cash they carry in their wallets. Cardholders can withdraw cash as needed, providing an alternative to writing a check or using a payment card.

"Smart cards" or "chip cards" are beginning to provide another plastic substitute for cash. Two types of smart cards are being introduced. Intelligent smart cards contain a little computer with a central processing unit and storage that provides both short- and long-term memory. You can use these cards to download cash from your ATM: you first insert your ATM card to access your account and then insert your smart card to receive your funds in electronic form. You can then spend those funds by inserting your smart card in readers that can transfer your funds to a merchant. (The reader does not have to be at the merchant's location.) For example, the proposed Mondex Internet transaction works like this. You reach a business on-line service that accepts Mondex. After completing your selection, you pay by inserting your Mondex card into a reader attached to a computer. Value from your card is transferred to the vendor over the Internet. Because no central processing is required, Mondex claims that transactions of even a penny are economical.

Memory or stored-value cards are less sophisticated. They have enough computer power and memory to store and transfer a set amount of funds. You can get one of these cards to use at pay phones, vending machines, and subway systems. For example, in Orange County, California, you can pay tolls electronically without ever stopping. As you approach the toll station, you insert your card in a smart-card reader on your dashboard and the toll is electronically deducted from the preset amount on the card. (Hybrid cards combine smart-card technology with the traditional magnetic stripe and bar coding found on payment cards. You can use these for multiple purposes: as an ATM card and a stored-value card, for instance.)

Credit Cards Are King—for the Moment

Most payment cards today in America are credit cards. There were approximately twenty times as many general-purpose credit cards as charge cards and over twice as many general-purpose credit cards as debit cards in 1997. This is the result of robust growth in credit cards over the past decade. Between 1988 and 1997, the number of credit cards grew at almost three times the rate of debit cards (8.1 percent versus

2.8 percent), while the number of charge cards in circulation remained virtually unchanged.

This trend seems sure to change as consumers use debit cards and smart cards more often. In fact, the rapid growth of the number of credit cards masks an interesting fact. When measured by the number of transactions, debit card use at the point of sale grew nearly five times as fast as general-purpose credit card use between 1988 and 1997—49.2 percent for debit card transactions versus 13.1 percent for credit cards—despite the more rapid increase in the number of credit cards. Debit cards are not just a major threat to cash and checks; they compete with credit cards as well. Smart cards have a lot of potential uses, and some of them could sharply reduce the use of small change (for phone calls, subway fare, tolls) as well as checks (Medicaid payments). As the Mondex Internet transaction suggests, smart cards could also easily act as a substitute for credit cards in the burgeoning Internet marketplace.

Credit and charge cards have led a revolution in money for the past twenty-five years. Most of the focus of this book is on credit and charge cards, since their past and present story provides valuable lessons for the future of all electronic-payment cards.

The Role of Payment Cards in the U.S. Economy

Payment Cards Are a Major Means of Exchange

Payment cards have become an essential means of exchange in the economy because they provide consumers and merchants considerable advantages over cash and checks.

Cash is bulky. The typical credit card purchase is slightly more than $75. Two $20 bills, three $10 bills, and five $1 bills weigh just over a quarter of an ounce. A credit card weighs only a fifth of an ounce. Each bill takes up 15.7 square inches, more than twice as much space as a payment card. Multiplied over the number of payments that people make with cards over the course of the month, the convenience of carrying a card instead of cash is clear.

Cash is also easier to steal and harder to trace. In 1995, $850 million of cash was stolen, according to one estimate. There were 84,000 robberies involving purse snatching or pickpocketing in that year. That, in part, is why 80 percent of U.S. adults say they do not like to carry too much cash, and two-thirds say that cash is too easy to lose or have stolen. Fortunately, the proliferation of ATMs has made cash far easier to access than it used to be. As a result, consumers can carry lighter wallets by visiting their local cash machines with greater frequency.

Checks have their own disadvantages. To begin with, checkbooks are inconvenient to carry. The typical checkbook weighs fourteen times more than a payment card. It would take eleven payment cards to fill up the space occupied by a checkbook. Indeed, women are much more likely to carry checkbooks than men because they can put them in their purses. According to one survey of American adults, 55 percent of men but only 28 percent of women prefer not to carry a checkbook.

The other major drawback of checks is that they are often difficult to use outside of your local community. This is in part due to the risk of bad checks. In 1995, approximately one out of every hundred checks presented to a bank for payment was returned. Check verification services have helped a little. But these services verify only that the person to whom the account belongs is not listed on a database of people who have written bad checks, and they charge on average about three cents per check thus verified. Check guarantee services help, too, by taking the risk of a bad check from the merchant. But merchants have to pay somewhere between 1.0 and 2.2 percent of the face value of each check in return for guaranteed payment; riskier merchants may have to pay as much as 5 percent of the face value. Of checks used at stores, about 40 percent are verified and about 5 percent are guaranteed. Interestingly, the growth of debit cards may increase the proportion of bad checks written. Many of the customers who generally do not bounce checks have switched to debit cards, increasing the likelihood that those who still write checks lack sufficient funds to cover them.

Payment cards provide several benefits to merchants. They give customers more payment and financing options and therefore enable consumers to make purchases they otherwise could not make. Aside from reducing the risk of bounced checks, payment cards provide a means of insuring against customer defaults. For example, by having travelers guarantee their reservations with a payment card, hotels can eliminate the risk of loss if those with reservations fail to show up. Car rental

*"Your signature, Your Majesty, as well as your driver's license
and a major credit card."*

companies reduce the risk that customers will abandon or damage a car
by having them secure their rentals with a payment card. Indeed, it can
be quite difficult to rent a car without a payment card.

Mail order sales operations have grown explosively with the aid of
payment cards. Before the advent of payment cards, a customer typically
had to have a catalog, fill out an order form, and mail it with a check
or money order. That was time consuming. Today, a customer calls an
800 number, describes the merchandise, gives a payment card number,
and gets the order in a few days. Payment cards cut several days off the
process and reduce the risk of nonpayment (via, e.g., bad checks or refusal
to pay cash on delivery). In addition, merchants can now sell tickets for
movies, sporting events, plays, and concerts over the phone.

This is not to say that merchants always prefer payment cards to cash or checks when given the choice. Merchants have to pay a percentage on every purchase made with a payment card. These payments average only about 2 percent of transaction value, but they amounted to more than $17 billion in 1996 alone. Merchants could always avoid these charges by accepting cash and checks exclusively; some do just that. However, payment cards are convenient. By accepting them, merchants make shopping more attractive for their potential customers. And if a retailer makes $25 for each additional $100 of sales, he does not have to attract many additional sales through his acceptance of payment cards to make them an attractive proposition. (Chapter 6 discusses this incentive in more detail.)

Finally, payment cards have become the coin for Internet transactions. Not long ago, sending payment card information through the Internet was risky. The Internet sends information between many computers before card data reaches its final destination. Throughout this process, it is possible for information to be intercepted as it passes between the various computers (called servers) that comprise the Web. Criminally inclined minds with access to these servers could easily jot down credit card numbers and go on their own personal spending sprees or sell the numbers to others. Computer-literate thugs can still accomplish this, but recent advances in technology have made the task much harder. When you type in a credit card number and click the "submit" button on your favorite Web merchant site, you now face little risk of having your card number stolen.

Several advances have reduced this risk. Some Web sites are equipped with security features that prevent unauthorized people from seeing anything that travels between your computer and the merchant's computer. Microsoft's widely used browser, Internet Explorer, supports the protocols used by these secured sites. It even lets you know the level of security you are getting with each site. Netscape's Navigator browser implements another encryption technology for security. With these features, criminals either cannot see data on your card or find it scrambled and hard to decipher.

With increased security and wider usage, the Web is supporting many merchants that principally take payment cards. There is now an offshore gambling site (the COSP casino, located in the Cook Islands) that bills bets to your card. Citibank's Jack Nicklaus Visa card gives you extra bonus points when you shop at the Jack Nicklaus pro shop on the Web. Amazon.com, while not yet profitable at the time of this writing, is selling many books that are paid for with payment cards. By the time you read this, much more shopping will take place on the Web, and the virtual stores will not take cash or checks.

Payment Cards Have Become a Major Source of Credit
One major benefit for consumers from shopping with payment cards is that they do not have to pay right away. Credit cards and charge cards enable consumers to defer payment for a few days or weeks, thus helping cardholders better coordinate their earnings and spending. You do not have to have the cash in your wallet or your checking account to buy something you suddenly decide you must have.

Credit cards provide longer-term loans than charge cards and have become a major source of credit in the economy. U.S. consumers owed $453 billion on credit cards at the end of 1997, an average of about $4,400 per household. In 1997, consumers had $1.5 trillion in unused lines of credit at their disposal. This works out to nearly $15,000 per household. Credit cards accounted for 43 percent of consumer debt outstanding (excluding mortgages and home equity loans) in 1997, increasing from 22 percent in 1986 and from 6 percent in 1972.

Many small businesses finance themselves with credit cards. Firms with little experience or credit history—typically firms just starting out and smaller firms—may use credit card "loans" instead of traditional bank loans. Indeed, some banks have actively promoted the use of business credit cards as a cost-effective method of providing credit lines to small businesses. Other banks encourage small business owners to use their personal credit cards to finance their businesses. A 1993 survey found that four in ten small businesses used personal credit cards as a source of financing.

Businesses in the United States have a long history of providing credit to customers for the general purpose of increasing sales. By accepting payment cards, a firm can reap most of the benefits of providing credit to customers without the costs and risks of running its own credit operation.

Although some merchants have developed highly efficient and profitable store card programs—Sears' program has been a major source of company profits—many did not have any particular competence in lending money and discontinued their programs after payment cards became widespread. The spread of payment cards was particularly helpful to small businesses that lacked the capital and volume necessary to operate efficient credit and charge programs on their own.

With the development of inexpensive computer processing, the rise of electronic money was almost inevitable. The mainframe system that Visa installed as its brain in 1973 utilized a computer that processed 1 million instructions per second (MIPS). Visa's system now utilizes a machine that can process 5,000 MIPS. Technological progress such as this has resulted in the proliferation of ATMs, faster authorization and processing of payment card transactions, and the possibility of chip-based smart cards.

The movement away from money as something of intrinsic value and toward money as a unit of account is a revolution that is sure to shape commerce in the next century at least as fundamentally as the spread of paper money has in the past two centuries. The payment card industry is at the center of this revolution. To date, its evolution has depended on the milieu of financial institutions and regulations that existed at the time the payment card was invented and changes in that milieu thereafter.

3

A Land of Local Banks, Awash in Paper Checks

I can't be overdrawn, I still have checks left.
—Anonymous

Most Americans deposit their paychecks at a local bank where they maintain a checking account. Almost 90 percent of all Americans had at least one demand deposit account into which they could make deposits and write checks, according to a 1995 survey. And although innovations in the financial services industry have enabled consumers to write checks against their money market, mutual fund, or stock brokerage accounts, 85 percent of Americans still rely on their local bank as their primary financial institution.

The cornerstone of the typical American's household finances is the checking account at our local bank. From the cable television bill to the home mortgage, we make virtually all of our regular payments by check. Many American women and men carry their checkbooks with them and write checks for a variety of purchases. For example, checks were used for 35 percent of all supermarket and grocery store purchases in 1996. Indeed, in 1996 women used checks for more than 40 percent of all their payment transactions. And although men do not write quite as many checks as women, men used checks for more than 25 percent of their payment transactions in 1996. On average, we write more than 200 checks per year.

We can open a checking account at a plethora of local banks. People who live in the greater Boston area can do so at any of 558 different banks. But when we move from one metropolitan area to another, we usually have to find another bank. Although this is changing as a result of the recent wave of bank mergers, most American banks do not have branches in more than one of our fifty states. BankBoston does not serve Chicago, First National Bank of Chicago does not serve Boston, and neither of them have branches in San Francisco. With many local banks, it is not surprising that in 1997 there were more than 22,000 banks, broadly defined, in the United States—eighty-three for every million residents. There were more than three times as many banks in the United States as radio stations, more than twice as many banks as department stores, and almost twice as many banks as total newspapers published.

Consumer banking in the United States is changing rapidly. Federal and state governments have, over time, relaxed regulations that once prevented banks from setting up branches across the country and that prevented other financial institutions such as brokerage firms and insurance companies from offering banking services. As a result of mergers and acquisitions, the average size of banks has risen and the number of banks has fallen in recent years. At the same time, more and more companies that are technically not banks are providing DDA accounts and other banking services. Banks and other providers of DDA accounts are encouraging consumers to use debit cards rather than checks to make payments against the funds in their DDA accounts.

Yet despite these recent changes, for most of the fifty years since the invention of the general purpose charge card, and for most of the thirty years since the invention of the bankcard associations, the United States has been a land of local banks awash in paper checks. This chapter explains how this unusual banking system developed and its implications for the evolution of the payment card industry. We also take a look at the European experience and see similarities that result from near-universal economic forces as well as differences rooted in idiosyncratic, country-specific factors.

Banking in America

The clear distinction that once existed between traditional commercial banks and other financial institutions has almost vanished. The United States now has a number of types of financial institutions having many, few, or none of the characteristics of the traditional bank. For our purposes, banks are institutions that accept deposits, which are insured by state or federal authorities, and that are empowered to provide a variety of additional financial services including business and consumer loans. (Some state-chartered depository institutions are still insured by their individual states; however, following runs on state-insured thrifts in several states, the vast majority of banks and thrifts are now federally insured.) There are several major types of depository institutions in this country.

Commercial banks are for-profit institutions that typically serve both businesses and consumers. Commercial banks usually take deposits and provide checking accounts and other services to their customers. The merger wave among banks in 1998 created BankAmerica, the country's largest bank holding company, from the merger of NationsBank and Bank of America. The newly formed bank had assets of nearly $600 billion and $345 billion in deposits after the completion of its merger in 1998. Most commercial banks offer a wide variety of banking services to consumers and businesses. For example, among its many other services, Chase Manhattan offers short- and long-term savings accounts, credit and debit cards, foreign currency exchange, and student, home equity, and mortgage loans.

In addition to commercial banks, there are three other types of depository institutions, all of which are often called "thrifts": credit unions, savings banks, and savings and loan associations. Although all depository institutions accept deposits as their main liability, thrifts tend to have longer-term assets and liabilities than commercial banks. Savings banks accept deposits and lend money just like commercial banks, but they generally cater specifically to consumers rather than businesses.

Savings and loan associations (S&Ls) are depository institutions that historically have focused on real estate and housing finance. Before the S&L crisis of the 1980s, S&Ls in aggregate were the most important providers of mortgage funds and the second most important type of financial institution, behind commercial banks. Since the late 1980s, the number and relative importance of S&Ls have declined considerably.

Credit unions, the final type of thrift, are nonprofit cooperatives of members who pool their funds and lend to each other. The members direct all credit union earnings toward low-cost loans and high-interest-rate deposits. The largest credit union in 1998 was Navy Federal Credit Union,

Table 3.1
Commercial banks' share of U.S. bank assets, 1997.

Type of institution	Number of institutions		Total assets	
	Number	Share of total (Percentage)	Assets ($ Billions)	Share of total assets (Percentage)
Commercial banks	9,143	41.3	5,070	78.5
Savings institutions	1,779	8.0	1,037	16.0
Credit unions	11,238	50.7	355	5.5
Total	22,160	100.0	6,462	100.0

Sources: Commercial bank and savings institution data are from Federal Deposit Insurance Corporation, *Statistics on Banking,* 1997, table 104. Credit union data are from National Credit Union Association, *1997 Year-End Statistics,* p. 8.

with more than $10.4 billion in assets and $8.2 billion in deposits. Its members are all in some way affiliated with the U.S. Navy or the Marine Corps. Credit unions provide consumer banking services only to their members. All offer checking and savings accounts and provide consumer loans.

As table 3.1 shows, there were 22,160 federally insured depository institutions in the United States at the end of 1997. ("Savings institutions" in the table comprises both savings banks and S&Ls.) Savings institutions, with average assets of $583 million each, are on average slightly larger than commercial banks, with average assets of $555 million each. Both are considerably larger on average than credit unions, which average only $32 million in assets each. (In addition to the depository institutions described in table 3.1, U.S. residents can patronize a growing number of other financial institutions that provide banklike services. For example, mutual funds such as Fidelity and stock brokerage firms such as Charles Schwab offer check writing services and ATM/debit card usage against funds held in accounts at those institutions.)

Even after the merger wave of 1998, the four largest commercial banks held only 26 percent of total commercial banking deposits. Few other significant industries in the United States are as unconcentrated at the national level as the banking industry. For example, the largest four firms in the brewing industry accounted for 90 percent of industry sales in

1992. In the aircraft industry, the top four firms accounted for 79 percent of sales, and the top four cigarette producers controlled 93 percent of industry sales in the same year.

Indeed, the United States is one of the world leaders in banks per person. We can see this by comparing the average number of banking institutions across countries. The United States has eighty-three banks for every million residents. Canada also has eighty-three, Germany has forty-three, Japan has thirty-seven, the United Kingdom has ten, and France has nine. The United States also leads the world in geographical branching restrictions. Of the nineteen developed countries discussed in a 1997 study by the Office of the Comptroller of the Currency, the United States was the only country with legal branching restrictions. The origins of our highly localized banking system date back more than two centuries.

Small Is Beautiful . . .

In colonial times, America was primarily an agricultural nation. Particularly away from the Atlantic coast, long-distance communications and trade were difficult and risky. Understandably, small business and property owners required the services of conveniently located banks. The local banks that developed tended to be small, just like the towns they served. Larger companies involved in European import and export trade often dealt with the big merchant banks in Great Britain and continental Europe; they had little need for such institutions in America.

Moreover, since colonial times, Americans—or at least their legislators, influenced over the past two centuries by local bank lobbyists and persuaded of the value of local control of lending institutions—have not wanted a banking industry dominated by large national banks. The charter of the first national bank was revoked in 1811 because of state bank opposition. (Banks must obtain a charter from a government, which grants them permission to exist.) A second national bank was chartered in 1816 but was killed in 1836 for the same reason under the populist President Andrew Jackson. In addition, most states either expressly prohibited or implicitly discouraged state-chartered banks from competing with each other by opening multiple branch offices. Later, when national banks finally did emerge, federal regulators ruled that national banks could offer their services from only a single location. The result was an industry with many banks, each serving a single local market.

Early in this century, as the United States industrialized and as transportation and communication improved, profit-motivated bankers began seeking permission to establish branch offices. Some states relaxed their restrictions on within-state banking, and some banks reacted by abandoning their federal charters for "branching-friendlier" state charters. Before this trend turned into an epidemic, Congress reacted by passing the McFadden-Pepper Act in 1927 and the Banking Act of 1933. This legislation delegated authority to the states to establish branching restrictions for all banks within their own territory, and six states immediately outlawed all branch banking within their borders. These laws also effectively prohibited interstate branching. Banks reacted to the latter prohibition by inventing "bank holding companies." (In addition, the Glass-Steagall sections of the Banking Act of 1933 separated the roles of commercial and investment banks by prohibiting investment banks from accepting deposits and prohibiting commercial banks from dealing in the sale of securities.)

Holding companies could own banks operating in several states. But since they were not banks themselves, they were not subject to the interstate banking restrictions of the McFadden-Pepper Act and the Banking Act of 1933. Citibank, in particular, used this device by setting up Citicorp to establish a national network of banks. In 1956, however, the Bank Holding Company Act prohibited this sort of interstate branching, unless both the states involved explicitly permitted it. Not a single state welcomed out-of-state bank holding companies until 1980. As a result, interstate banking was effectively prohibited throughout much of the post–World War II expansion—with the exception of banks that had established branches in other states before the 1956 restrictions.

Although regulators have relaxed branching restrictions in recent years, as we discuss below, past restrictions still cast a shadow on the current structure of U.S. banking. For example, Chase Manhattan Corporation offers consumer banking services only in New York, New Jersey, and Connecticut. BankBoston has branches throughout New England but nowhere else. By contrast, the Bank of Montreal operates throughout Canada, Deutsche Bank throughout Germany, and Sanwa throughout Japan.

The surfeit of U.S. banks is matched by the complex web of laws and regulations—both state and federal—that restrict their operations. The alphabet soup of federal bank regulatory agencies is impressive enough: FRB (Federal Reserve Board), FDIC (Federal Deposit Insurance Corporation), OCC (Office of the Comptroller of the Currency), OTS (Office of Thrift Supervision), and NCUA (National Credit Union Administration). But, in addition, each state has its own collection of supervisors and regulators responsible for its state-chartered banks and banklike institutions.

The nominal objective of this complex apparatus is and has been to maintain the safety and soundness of depository institutions by a variety of means. In the name of safety, regulators have barred U.S. banks from a wide range of activities that foreign banks engage in routinely; these include dealing in stocks and bonds, insurance, and real estate. (Cynics will note that each of these activities has long been performed by a set of specialist institutions with well-oiled lobbying machines.)

Other restrictions have focused directly on prices. If you wanted to open a checking account in the late 1970s, for instance, you could have found several banks that would have given you presents, ranging from a toaster or portable tool kit to a color television, depending, of course, on the size of your account. Why? Because banks were prohibited by Section 11 of the Banking Act of 1933 from paying interest on checking account deposits. Regulation Q of the same act gave the Federal Reserve authority to regulate interest rates on savings deposits. When market interest rates skyrocketed, offering gifts was one of the few methods available to banks to compete for deposits with their nonbank counterparts. A number of innovations, notably money market funds, began to siphon big money from the banks during the inflation of the late 1970s. This flow put pressure on the government to relax restrictions on bank payments of interest. By the mid-1980s, after two major pieces of federal legislation and a lot of regulatory backing and forthing, these restrictions were effectively eliminated. Bank usury laws, which limited loan rates (including those on credit cards) rather than rates on deposits, created similar problems. (These laws and the credit card industry's response to them are discussed in the next chapter.)

The sheer number of U.S. banks, along with the intricate web of laws and regulations that restrict them, has affected the evolution of payment mechanisms in this country. The fact that banks historically served local markets made it difficult for any single bank to develop a payment card that was held by enough consumers and accepted at enough merchants to make it economically viable. As we discuss in the next chapter, Bank of America was able to start one of the most successful proprietary bank-cards—the BankAmericard—because California, its home state, was large and allowed branch banking. It issued cards to many of its existing customers. (This was in the days when credit cards could be sent to people who had not even asked for them.) Bank of America also gained potential new banking customers and renewed connections with existing customers when it solicited merchants to accept the card.

It would have been more difficult for Bank of America to expand outside of California than within. On the cardholder side, it would not have been able to rely on lists of existing account holders and information on their credit history as it did in California. Also, credit bureaus were not available until the mid-1970s to provide outside credit information on card applicants. Creditworthiness was, of course, more important to the credit card business than the charge card business, in which American Express and Diners Club did operate across the country. Because interstate banking was not a realistic option, the potential synergy between offering consumers credit cards and other banking products would not be available. Similarly, on the merchant side, although Bank of America could sign up merchants outside of California, it would not benefit from developing business relationships with those merchants. Thus, Bank of America started its franchise system, licensing banks in other parts of the country to issue BankAmericards. This system eventually evolved into today's Visa system.

. . . But Not Very Efficient . . .

The banking industry is now undergoing rapid consolidation as banks take advantage of legislative and regulatory changes that make it easier for them to expand their geographic reach. The Riegle-Neal Interstate Banking and Branching Efficiency Act of 1994 allowed commercial banks to acquire and operate banks or branches operating in other states as long as the target states concurred. Only Montana and Texas rejected the idea. However, as of mid-1997, twenty-nine states prohibited out-of-state banks from acquiring only the branches of a home state bank. To operate in these states, an out-of-state bank must purchase an entire home state bank, not just a branch or two.

Nonetheless, interstate branching has increased. As banks expanded their geographic scope, the number of commercial banks declined by more than 16 percent between 1994 and 1998, even though total commercial banking assets increased by 24 percent. Several significant mergers have taken place between banks, brokerages, and investment banks in recent years. In 1997, Morgan Stanley merged with Dean Witter Discover. The same year the Travelers Group purchased Salomon, Inc.; it then merged with Citicorp in 1998. NationsBank took over Barnett Banks and later merged with Bank of America in 1998. The First Bank System took over U.S. Bancorp, and First Chicago NBD and Banc One announced a merger in 1998. The merger between the Wells Fargo and Norwest banks was also announced in 1998. The four largest mergers in the banking industry in 1998 involved more than $1.7 trillion of assets, with the Citicorp/Travelers and BankAmerica mergers contributing nearly $1.3 trillion alone. Many credit unions have also merged in the 1990s, though the assets involved were relatively small. The merger of $103 million Alaskan Federal Credit Union with $56 million Denali Federal Credit Union was one of the larger recent credit union mergers.

One economic forecast by the OCC has suggested that by the year 2000, the number of commercial banks (8,984 at midyear 1998) could conceivably decrease to fewer than 8,000. This consolidation, especially mergers among the larger banks, may affect the future of the payment card industry in the United States. Some of the biggest banks may even have outgrown the Visa and MasterCard systems, especially with technological advances making it easier to establish a separate card brand.

. . . And Dependent on Paper

Not only does the United States have a fragmented banking industry, it relies very heavily on paper checks. The personal check remains one of the major competitors to payment cards in the United States. As we saw in the previous chapter, more than 57 percent of consumer payments are made with checks compared with 22 percent by payment cards. Despite the local structure of banking in the United States, a relatively efficient system of check processing developed early in the twentieth century. Banks had to cooperate with neighbors to handle each other's checks. They formed local and regional clearinghouses for processing checks. Many of these clearinghouses decided to honor checks at face value, rather than assessing charges for cashing each other's checks. In 1914, the newly created Federal Reserve Banks started their own clearing facilities. They eliminated all charges for check collection in 1918 to foster the use of their facilities.

Two modern developments have given checks a further boost in the United States. If you pull out a check and look at the bottom, you will see a series of numbers that includes your account number along with numbers that identify your bank. This is the result of MICR (magnetic ink character recognition), which was introduced in 1958 and quickly spread throughout the country. After you cash your check, the bank supplements the MICR code with the amount of the check. As a result, the MICR code at the bottom contains all the relevant information for processing the check. The ability of computers to process MICR-encoded checks has speeded up check processing. Electronic imaging systems are making the check-clearing system even more efficient by reducing the need to maintain paper copies of checks.

Check verification and guarantee services represent another useful development. As discussed in chapter 2, check verification services use databases to identify people with histories of writing bad checks or checks from accounts that have been closed. Check guarantee services, on the other hand, guarantee to pay merchants the full amount of any check they authorize that bounces. To use either sort of service today, a clerk first swipes the check through a terminal, which reads the MICR number. To retrieve personal information on the customer, the clerk then swipes the customer's driver's license through a card reader terminal. If a merchant does not have access to a swiping machine or card reader terminal, the clerk may manually enter the driver's license and MICR numbers.

The check processing system works efficiently at one level. Billions of checks each year get processed quickly. But it is woefully inefficient at other levels. Checks are a debit device: the money comes out of your account only when the check gets presented to your bank, and then only if you have the money in your account. Both you and your bank would like it to take as much time as possible between the time you write the check and the time the money flows from your account. The longer it takes for checks to be presented to your bank for payment, the longer you and your bank can earn interest on the money in your account. Individuals, businesses, and banks all spend resources manipulating the check-clearing system to earn interest or to avoid paying it. The other significant cost of checks arises from the fact that approximately 1 percent of checks are returned to the initial payee, usually because the payor did not have enough funds. This imposes risk on the payee and imposes costs on the check-clearing system, which has to process these returned items. Finally, the check-clearing system is made more expensive because the Federal Reserve System requires banks to return at least an electronic image of the check to the payor.

Checks, along with cash, are the main competitors for payment card transactions. But as we saw in the previous chapter, payment cards have so far made their overall gains mostly at the expense of cash. Displacing check use at merchants therefore presents a potential area of significant growth for payment cards. This can be accomplished in a number of ways. For example, the acceptance of payment cards in supermarkets that started in the early 1990s will likely change consumer habits. New generations of consumers have grown up in a world where payment card use has become increasingly ubiquitous. Also, the recent growth in use of debit cards in the United States is likely to reduce our dependence on checks. Debit cards, after all, access the same deposit accounts as checks. We revisit this issue in chapter 12.

Banks, Nonbanks, and Payment Cards

The changing structure of banking in this country has influenced the character and organization of the U.S. payment card industry from the birth of the bankcard associations to the present. The current revolution in the banking industry could profoundly change the organization of the payment card industry.

Visa and MasterCard in the United States

MasterCard and Visa are major players in the stories to come. As we shall see in the next chapter, they started as associations of banks in part because no single bank had both the geographic reach and the capital to form a nationally accepted payment card. From their inception, these associations have generally limited membership to depository financial institutions. As of 1998, any financial institution eligible for federal deposit insurance can join these associations, unless, as we discuss in detail in chapter 11, they are affiliated with American Express or Discover. (MasterCard, but not Visa, also permits nonfinancial companies to become members.) Thus, essentially all of the depository institutions (commercial banks, savings institutions, and credit unions) discussed in the previous section can join. About one-quarter of them join as full Visa or MasterCard issuers, and that quarter accounts for a significant portion of total banking assets in this country. Indeed, among the fifty largest Visa and MasterCard issuers in the United States are commercial banks whose assets amount to approximately 45 percent of total commercial banking assets.

Of the approximately 14,400 Visa member banks (full-fledged and sponsored issuers) in 1998, 43 percent are commercial banks, 51 percent are credit unions, and 6 percent are savings banks. (We have no data for MasterCard, but the breakdown is probably similar.) The numbers are quite different by dollar volume. Commercial banks accounted for 88.3 percent of outstanding credit card loans at depository institutions in 1997. Credit unions accounted for 7.3 percent and savings institutions for 4.4 percent. (Debit cards and charge cards, which accounted for just over a quarter of total payment card volume in 1997, do not, in general, involve outstanding balances.)

Of the 100 largest bankcard issuers in 1997, ranked by dollar volume, sixty-eight were commercial banks. The largest commercial bank issuer in 1997 (whether measured by outstandings, charge volume, or cards issued) was Citibank. Citibank has a division called "Cards," which includes MasterCard and Visa cards worldwide. It is also the only U.S. bank that issues general-purpose proprietary cards as well: Diners Club, Carte Blanche, and some private-label cards. In 1997, Citibank had 40 million credit or charge cards in circulation in the United States alone.

More than 43 percent of all credit unions, accounting for 88 percent of all credit union members, and more than 90 percent of credit unions with assets of at least $50 million provided credit cards at the end of 1997. These credit unions had issued about 13 million credit cards, and the loans on these cards accounted for 8.2 percent of the $235 billion total outstanding credit union loans at the end of 1997. Eight of the 100 largest bankcard issuers were credit unions in 1997. The nation's largest credit union, the Navy Federal Credit Union, was the nation's forty-third largest credit card issuer in 1997 and the largest credit card issuer among credit unions.

Several large companies that are not financial institutions now have their names on MasterCard or Visa credit cards even though they are not members of either card association. Because they are not eligible for federal deposit insurance, companies such as AT&T, GM, GE, and J.C. Penney have two available methods of issuing their own cards. These companies can either own a bank that belongs to Visa or MasterCard, or alternatively, they can have a contract with a bank that belongs to Visa or MasterCard.

Consider the AT&T Universal Card, before it was sold in 1998 to Citibank. Although AT&T's name appeared on the MasterCards (and Visa cards) obtained through AT&T, Universal Bank was the issuer. AT&T contracted with Universal Bank, which was a MasterCard member. Universal Bank issued MasterCards with AT&T's name on them. AT&T actively participated in making the everyday decisions necessary for the issuance of its cards. It also bought the credit card receivables from Universal Bank on a daily basis and therefore assumed the major financial responsibilities for the business. AT&T made the decisions about soliciting consumers, accepting applications, fixing the interest rate and other card terms, and related matters. Other nonfinancial companies have structured their credit card operations differently, but all have used banks that belong to MasterCard or Visa.

The business of payment cards at banks varies widely. Many banks offer credit and debit cards as one of many customer services, often as part of a package that includes a DDA. For example, a checking account from the Cambridge Savings Bank may come with a MasterCard and a MasterMoney debit card that also functions as an ATM card. In fact,

Cambridge Savings Bank actually issues credit cards to its customers through MBNA and does so primarily as a service to its customers, rather than in an attempt to establish itself as a major issuer.

Some banks specialize in issuing credit cards. These range from institutions such as MBNA, whose primary business is issuing credit cards, to institutions such as Citibank, for which card issuance is one of several important product lines. MBNA takes deposits and makes loans, but its primary business and prime source of income is consumer credit-card loans. In comparison, Citibank's Cards operations, although larger than MBNA's in total, account for only one-fourth of Citibank's total revenues. Even for banks that do not focus specifically on credit cards, credit card loans can be significant. For example, credit card loans account for about 10 percent of BankAmerica's domestic consumer loan portfolio.

Although credit cards were once issued primarily to a bank's own depository customers, many credit cards today are issued to customers of other banks. In fact, 84 percent of credit cards held by U.S. households in 1995 were issued by banks with which the cardholder had no other banking relationship. Most credit cards are issued by banks, such as MBNA or Citibank, that issue credit cards as a nationally marketed product line operationally separate from traditional depository services, or by banks issuing cards on behalf of one of the large nonfinancial companies, such as General Electric or General Motors, that have entered the payment card industry in the last few years. Credit cards remain an important product for banks, but the role of the depository relationship with a customer in selling him credit cards has diminished substantially.

Unlike credit cards, debit cards can generally be issued only to a bank's own depository customers. In 1997, there were 7,931 issuers of either MasterMoney or Visa check debit cards. In practice, this has generally meant that banks included the MasterCard or Visa logo on their ATM card, which then enabled the cardholder to use the ATM card as a debit card at any merchant that took MasterCard or Visa. These cards accounted for 14 percent of all dollars charged on MasterCard and Visa cards in 1997 and are the fastest growing payment card segment.

Nonfinancial companies can issue debit cards if they own or contract with a bank. American Express and Discover, for instance, already solicit customers for debit cards through the Internet and through toll-free numbers. In addition, either company could use a federally chartered savings bank to open depository branches throughout all fifty states. American Express, for example, could use a federal savings bank and its existing network of travel offices across the country—it has offices in all states except South Dakota—to set up a national banking organization and issue debit cards to its depository customers.

In addition to issuing cards, banks also sign up ("acquire") merchants to accept MasterCard and/or Visa. In the earliest days of the industry, member banks typically acted as both issuers and acquirers. Later, most banks came to specialize in either the issuing or the acquiring business. More recently, many banks have decided to contract out important aspects of serving merchants, such as processing transactions through the network and doing the associated paperwork. These third-party contractors who perform these functions have become very efficient, at least partly because they have achieved scale economies by aggregating the business of large numbers of banks. (See chapter 6 for more details.) Many banks still maintain contractual relationships with merchants, but almost all contract out virtually all of the real work to other parties. Currently, few banks are significant players in the acquiring side of the payment card business.

Just as the history of banking in this country has shaped the current state of the payment card industry, changes in banking regulation and the changing structure of the banking industry that has resulted will surely affect the evolution of the payment card industry. Banks are rapidly consolidating and interstate banking is increasing. Many banks are shedding their card portfolios and specializing in other areas, as we discuss in chapter 9. At the same time, consumers are relying on traditional banks less and on mutual funds, brokerage firms, and other financial institutions more for many traditional bank services. Once the exclusive provenance of deposit-taking banks, the payment card industry has seen the rapid development in the last decade of payment card issuers that are not banks or that specialize in issuing credit cards. At the same time, the business of signing up and servicing merchants, once populated almost entirely by banks, has been taken over by nonbank third-party processors (by far the largest is First Data) that specialize in data processing and computer networks.

Visa and MasterCard in Other Industrialized Countries

General-purpose payment cards have spread around the world primarily through the MasterCard and Visa associations. Both are now global associations of banks with international and regional units, although the United States still accounts for a little more than half of worldwide cards issued in both associations. MasterCard International maintains six geographic regions: Asia/Pacific, Canada, Europe, Latin America, Middle East/Africa, and the United States. Each region has its own business committee and decides on local marketing and advertising. Visa International has a similar structure. MasterCard and Visa expanded globally by establishing, or forming alliances with, bank associations in foreign countries. These associations are usually similar to their U.S. counterparts in the sense that they are essentially joint ventures of banks. But the banking structure of each country strongly shapes the character of the domestic association. For example, Visa has only twenty-seven members in Canada. In France, Visa has an affiliation with the Groupe de Cartes Bancaires, but it does not exist as an independent association of banks. Figure 3.1 compares the distribution of Visa card volume among its regions around the world in 1981 and in 1997. Even though Visa experienced tremendous growth in the United States (and Canada) during this period, we see that in relative terms the countries outside of North America have become much more important to the Visa system.

Visa and MasterCard are by far the largest payment card systems worldwide. Of the major general-purpose cards, Visa and MasterCard accounted for 53 and 29 percent, respectively, of global payment card purchase volume at merchants in 1997. American Express accounted for less than 14 percent of global purchases; Diners Club and JCB each accounted for 2 percent. American Express and Diners Club accounted for less than 8 percent and 3 percent respectively of purchase volume outside the United States in 1997, and JCB accounted for less than 1 percent of purchase volume outside Japan.

As an example of payment cards outside the United States, the remainder of this section considers the situation in Europe. There are two main international players in the European payment card industry, Visa and MasterCard. Visa formed alliances with European banks in different countries starting in the late 1960s. MasterCard entered the European

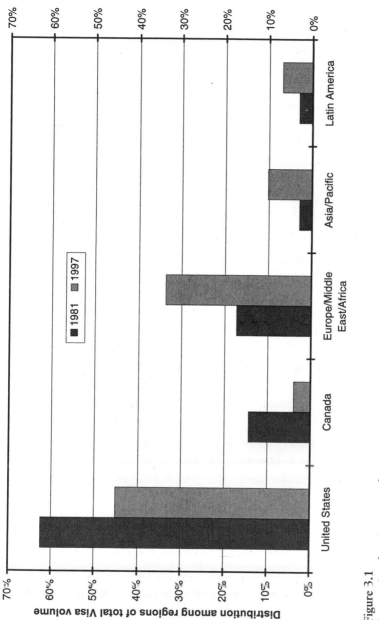

Figure 3.1
International regions are of growing importance to Visa.
Source. Visa International.

market in 1968 by forming a joint venture with EuroCard, an existing European bankcard association. EuroCard, started as a proprietary card system in Sweden in 1964, was purchased in 1978 by a consortium of European banks led by Deutsche Bank and has subsequently developed into a large association of banks across Europe. In 1992, EuroCard merged with Eurocheque, a previously independent payment system that started as a check guarantee system and then evolved into an ATM/debit card network. The new organization was named Europay, with major members such as Deutsche Bank, Barclays, Credit Suisse, and Bank of Ireland. Europay members issue credit and deferred-debit cards that we will refer to as Eurocards. They also issue direct-debit cards generally referred to as edc/Maestro cards (Maestro is used as a debit brand by MasterCard in the United States). Cards (other than edc/Maestro) used to be issued with both MasterCard and Europay logos, and merchants used to display both logos. In 1996, when MasterCard and Europay entered into a new agreement, they created a combined MasterCard/Europay logo that is essentially the familiar MasterCard logo with "Europay" written above the interlocking globes.

MasterCard/Europay and Visa account for the majority of all payment cards issued in Europe. In 1995, MasterCard/Europay and Visa accounted for 32 percent and 20 percent, respectively, of European payment cards issued. (These data include all types of debit and credit cards; they also include cards issued by nonbanks, about 16 percent of all cards.) MasterCard/Europay is the more important debit card system, accounting for 47 percent of European debit cards compared to Visa's 17 percent, with the other 36 percent being domestically branded; this is in large part due to Eurocheque's inclusion in Europay. Visa is the more important credit card system, with almost 60 percent of European credit cards in 1995 compared to MasterCard/Europay's 35 percent.

Diners Club, a distant third, had only 1.3 percent of the market in 1995. American Express had even less, with only half a percent. We discuss the payment card industries in France, Germany, and the United Kingdom later in this chapter. American Express and Diners Club entered all three of these countries in the mid-1960s, but neither has ever developed a major presence. Since the mid-1990s, however, American Express has significantly increased its efforts to expand its international business, as we discuss in chapter 8.

Card use in Europe appears to differ from that in the United States in one fundamental respect. Credit cards grew rapidly in the United States, whereas debit cards languished until the mid-1990s. On the other hand, debit cards grew rapidly in most European countries, whereas even today credit cards are important in only a few European countries. The real difference is not so dramatic, however, because most European debit cards provide some features of U.S. credit cards. Most debit card usage in Europe comes from deferred-debit cards, which deduct charges from a cardholder's account typically once a month. (Deferred-debit cards exist in the United States but are quite uncommon.) In addition, the cardholder's deposit account often has a line of credit associated with it. Although many checking accounts in the United States have lines of credit, they are typically small (perhaps $500 or $1,000) and designed to cover checks against temporary shortages of funds. On the other hand, lines of credit in Germany, for example, are often three times monthly salary and available to individuals on an extended basis. Deferred-debit cards in Europe thus share two significant characteristics with credit cards in the United States. First, they both provide some float for consumers between the purchase date and the payment date. Second, and more importantly, they both provide access to unsecured, revolving credit.

The difference between credit cards and deferred-debit cards with an associated credit line is that with the latter, the cardholder incurs debt only when she has used all the funds from her deposit account. The German debit cardholder is better off than her U.S. counterpart using a credit card in that she never pays 18 percent on her credit card while she has money in her checking account that only pays 3 percent, yet she still has access to credit when her account is depleted. On the other hand, the credit cardholder in the United States is better off in that many different credit card issuers compete in offering her credit cards. She is not limited to obtaining credit from the financial institution with which she does her banking. Indeed, some industry observers have suggested that it was perhaps the desire of banks in some European countries to limit competition among themselves that led to the development of deferred debit over credit.

To see how the European payment card industry compares to the U.S. payment card industry, it is useful to consider France, Germany, and the United Kingdom. Payment card usage is high in the United Kingdom and France, with both countries having payment card volumes of more than $2,500 per capita in 1996; it is lower in Germany, at approximately $1,050 per capita. This compares with just over $3,400 per capita in the United States in 1996. The United Kingdom is the most advanced European country in terms of U.S.-style credit cards. Among bankcards in use in the United Kingdom in 1995, about 30 percent were credit cards, whereas almost 100 percent of those in France were debit cards, and about 84 percent in Germany. Institutional factors have often played important roles in shaping the payment card industry in these countries, as they have in the United States.

The first payment cards in France were issued under the name "Carte Bleue" in 1967 by a group of five major banks. These banks formed a nonprofit association called the "Groupement Carte Bleue" in 1972, which became affiliated with Visa (then BankAmericard) the next year. Visa cards are still issued through Groupement Carte Bleue, with 260 "Blue" issuers in 1996. Visa cards are almost exclusively deferred-debit cards. French banks began to issue credit cards in the mid-1990s, but in 1996 credit cards still made up approximately 1 percent of Visa cards. Europay in France originated with a payment card company started by Sovac, a French finance firm. This enterprise was subsequently purchased by a Swedish financial group in 1973, which then purchased a local French bankcard program run by Credit Agricole (an association of regional French banks) in 1978, and became affiliated with Europay the same year. Although there are now many other EuroCard/MasterCard (EC/MC) issuers, Credit Agricole is by far the largest, accounting for nearly 80 percent of EC/MC cards issued as of 1994. EC/MC cards, like Visa cards, are also mostly of the deferred-debit variety. In 1995, there were about 11 million Visa cards in France, 7 million EC/MC cards, and 5 million domestic payment cards.

French payment cards have two other idiosyncrasies. First, a national card organization called "Groupement des Cartes Bancaires" was created in 1984 largely as a result of government pressure. The group manages and organizes all the technical and administrative facets of the payment card industry. Every bank operating in France participates in the Cartes Bancaires system and is technically a dual issuer, but individual banks tend to have notably stronger affiliations with either Visa or MasterCard/ Europay because they were historically in one camp or the other before Cartes Bancaires. Acquiring is fully dual: an acquirer signs up merchants for all cards issued under the Cartes Bancaires system, including Visa and MasterCard/Europay cards, as well as domestic payment cards. Cartes Bancaires, acceding to the government's wishes, also dictated that all cards be issued as smart cards, with a microchip to prevent fraud, by 1992. Fraud rates did fall substantially as smart cards replaced the old magnetic stripe cards, although this may have resulted in part from other fraud prevention measures also implemented at the same time.

The other French idiosyncrasy is also institutional and government related. Until 1985, the French government, because of a desire to make credit available for business needs, imposed restrictions limiting banks' ability to offer consumer credit. However, operating without similar restrictions, several large finance companies became large suppliers of store cards with revolving credit. The most important of these are Cetelem and Cofinoga, with 5 million and 4 million cards, respectively, in 1996. These cards can be used at many different merchants, unlike store cards in the United States, but merchant acceptance is still at most one-fifth of Cartes Bancaires acceptance and often much less. The intent, at least in the past, was more to allow consumers to use these cards to finance major purchases, such as home appliances, than to popularize store cards as a means of payment. Since 1985, banks have been permitted to issue credit cards but were still discouraged by Cartes Bancaires from doing so and did not start to issue them until the mid-1990s. French banks are also disadvantaged because they do not have as much experience and expertise as the finance companies in extending consumer credit.

In Germany, most debit cards are based on the Eurocheque card, which began as a Pan-European check guarantee card in 1968 that provided customers with the ability to cash checks all across Europe. A consumer would write a paper Eurocheque to pay for her purchase, and the merchant would compare signatures and be guaranteed payment on the Eurocheque (up to a limit of $200 or $250). More recently, PIN-authorized point-of-sale debit capability has been added. The use of the Eurocheque card as an electronic debit card has been increasing but it was still used predominantly as a check guarantee card as of the mid-1990s. By 1996, there were 67 million debit cards in circulation in Germany, almost five times the number of credit cards. Although Germany had one of the highest rates of debit card penetration in 1995, with 7.7 cards for every 10 people, versus 4.1 in France, 4.9 in the United Kingdom, and 8.0 in the United States, Germans did not use their debit cards very much. There were only 1.8 debit transactions per person in Germany in 1995 compared to 32.3 in France, and 2.9 in the United States. (The United States has high debit card penetration but low usage. As we discuss in chapter 12, this is because people hold ATM cards that also function as debit cards, but some ATM cardholders never use them as debit cards.) The dominant payment method in Germany is cash, accounting for more than three-quarters of retail volume. The credit card market is still in its infancy. But as we described above, since debit cards provide access to large lines of credit, they provide access to credit as our credit cards do.

Visa did not play any significant role in the development of the payment card system in Germany until at least the early 1990s. Eurocard development in Germany was heavily influenced by Gesellschaft fuer Zahlungssysteme (GZS), the German banks' jointly owned card transaction processor formed in 1982. Until 1991, GZS was the monopoly issuer (on behalf of its member banks) of Eurocards in Germany and as of 1995 still issued 90 percent of Eurocards there. GZS was still the sole merchant acquirer and the main processor for Eurocards in Germany as of 1996. Europay has become by far the largest card in Germany, accounting for with 92 percent of all general-purpose payment cards in 1996; almost all banks are members of Europay. Visa cards were issued in Germany by Bank of America between 1981 and 1987. The GZS monopoly was successful in resisting Visa's attempts to enter until the late 1980s, when German banks started to become issuers. By 1996, more than half of all German banks were Visa members, although Visa still accounted for only 6 percent of all general-purpose payment cards.

Among all the European countries, the payment card industry in the United Kingdom is perhaps most like the one in the United States: credit cards are commonly used in the United Kingdom, new nonbank entrants came in the mid- to late 1980s, and there are many cobranding and affinity programs (in which a company or organization other than the issuer is involved). Also, debit cards developed late but grew quickly. Credit cards were first issued by Barclays Bank in 1966, which subsequently made reciprocal arrangements with Visa and became a founding member of Visa International in 1974. The other large banks in the United Kingdom formed a cooperative and developed the Access credit card by 1972, which affiliated with MasterCard. Recently, in 1996, MasterCard reached an agreement with the Access banks to remove the Access logo, reissuing cards with a MasterCard logo, and using MasterCard as the acceptance logo at merchant locations. Most banks, including all the major ones, are now dual issuers of Visa and MasterCard. Visa has 60 percent and MasterCard/Access has 37 percent of all general-purpose payment cards in the United Kingdom.

The development of debit brands closely mirrored that of credit brands. Barclays, followed by some other banks, chose to issue a Visa debit card in 1987. A competing group of banks developed a separate brand called Switch, which then became affiliated with MasterCard and its Maestro debit brand. Debit card usage grew rapidly, with the number of debit and credit transactions becoming about the same by the mid-1990s.

What have we learned in our brief tour through Europe? At least four principles seem to hold across different cultures and institutional structures among the countries we have examined. First, residents of developed countries are making more use of payment cards to purchase goods and to finance some of those purchases, whether through credit cards in the United Kingdom or deferred debit cards in Germany or store cards in France. Second, card systems are often started by associations of banks. (We propose some reasons for this in chapter 7.) Even those systems that are started by an individual bank (such as Barclays in the United Kingdom and Bank of America in the United States) eventually become affiliated with many other issuers. Third, although many card systems have developed independently in different countries, strong forces are pushing them to forge alliances: Europay in Europe, Visa and MasterCard globally. MasterCard's recent emphasis on moving toward sole MasterCard branding illustrates the importance of a consistent brand. The Visa and MasterCard brands have probably prospered at least in part because the United States has always been the largest payment card market in the world. And fourth, the European evidence suggests that institutional details do matter, as they have in the United States. French government action led to the prevalence of French store cards as well as France's status as a smart-card pioneer. Europay's dominance in Germany derives from the banks' collective legal monopoly control over Eurocards in the past and the dependence on Eurocheques.

As the end of the millenium approaches, payment cards have become a basic feature of the U.S. economy. Almost all significant financial institutions issue them. Just about every adult has at least one. And almost all major merchants accept them. It is difficult to live without them. Getting this far in the payment system revolution has not been easy, however. It has been a rocky fifty years.

4

The Rise of Payment Cards

Progress always involves risk; you can't steal second base and keep your foot on first base.
—Frederick Wilcox

People have been able to charge purchases for many years. Buy-now/pay-later policies date back at least to Biblical times, although periodically religious and legislative proscriptions against paying interest put a damper on credit buying. Installment credit and revolving credit were pervasive in this country in the nineteenth century. In rural areas, farm equipment was commonly purchased with promissory notes due after harvest. In urban areas, durable goods like furniture were sold on the installment plan.

The simple payment card is not a recent phenomenon either; it has been around since at least the beginning of this century. Hotels, oil companies, and department stores issued cards before World War I. Some large retailers gave cards to their wealthier customers. The cards identified the customers as having a charge account with the store. Metal "charga-plates" with embossed consumer information were introduced by department stores in 1928. In the 1920s, oil companies issued "courtesy cards" for charging gas.

By the end of World War II, letting people use an identification card to charge purchases was no longer a novel idea. Payment cards, however, had a severe limitation back then: they were accepted only at establishments associated with their issuer. With some minor exceptions, no one had issued payment cards accepted across a wide span of unaffiliated businesses. (There were some localized programs, however, such as the cooperative payment card program set up in 1948 by several major New York City department stores. The standard card they established could be used at all participating stores.) As of the late 1940s, the general-purpose payment card—the main character in this book—did not exist. Moreover, most of the existing payment cards required cardholders to pay their bills upon receipt. They did not, in other words, provide credit. This chapter describes the birth of the general-purpose payment card and its development into a product that just about everyone has and uses.

Diners Club and the Birth of the Payment Card

Several key innovations sparked the explosive growth of the payment card industry. The first was made by the founders of Diners Club, who saw the need for a card that would be honored at many different establishments across the country. There are competing stories surrounding the birth of Diners Club, but one version finds Alfred Bloomingdale, grandson of the founder of the department store that bears his name, and Francis McNamara having lunch in Manhattan. They agreed that the idea of offering third-party credit had potential and thought that restaurants in Manhattan, where people were accustomed to using charge accounts, would be a promising beginning. McNamara (later joined by Bloomingdale) started Diners Club in New York in 1950 by giving cards away to consumers and signing up restaurants. When this practice proved successful, Diners Club expanded to other cities and branched out from restaurants to hotels and retail stores.

The success of Diners Club, the first charge card (also known as a "T&E" card, as in "travel and entertainment"), soon attracted other businesses to the nascent payment card industry. Most failed swiftly. Between 1953 and 1954, nearly 100 banks introduced charge cards for use primarily by their own customers and within their own local areas. The pioneers included County Bank & Trust Co. of Paterson, New Jersey; First National Bank and Trust Co. of Kalamazoo, Michigan; and Franklin National Bank of Hempstead, New York. The movement of large department stores to the suburbs in part stimulated these local programs, which helped small local retailers who lacked the charge card or installment programs their larger competitors offered. However, many banks found running a charge card program difficult, and almost half dropped their plans within a short period. None survived as a stand-alone operation.

Between 1948 and 1957, several oil companies attempted—unsuccessfully—to establish universally accepted cards and entered into agreements to accept each other's cards. Thus, Diners Club did not face serious competition until 1958, a watershed year during which American Express, Bank of America, Carte Blanche, and Chase Manhattan Bank all entered the payment card business. (We mostly disregard Carte Blanche in the remainder of the book because it has not played a significant role in the development of the industry; it has a *de minimis* volume of transactions as of the late 1990s, and data are not readily available.)

American Express and Carte Blanche, like Diners Club, were and are charge cards. They provide convenient payment services but truncated credit services. Many consumers, however, clearly wanted to buy merchandise on credit, and most major retailers already offered installment plans (which allowed customers to make major purchases with several payments over time) and revolving credit plans (which allowed customers to buy merchandise against a fixed credit line). Merchants too small to offer such plans were at a competitive disadvantage, though they could always suggest that their customers try to get bank loans. General-purpose charge cards did nothing to change this picture.

By the late 1950s, many banks recognized that there was a market for a card combining payment and credit features. Merchants too small to offer their own credit plans would benefit from having a bank make credit available to their customers. In addition, having a third party arrange and manage credit between consumers and large numbers of retailers offered obvious economies. Further economies resulted from offering payment and charge services in a single card.

In the late 1950s, San Francisco–based Bank of America, then the nation's largest bank, and New York–based Chase Manhattan, then the nation's second largest bank, pioneered the general-purpose credit card. By the end of 1960, forty other large banks had followed suit.

Even though there was demand for credit cards, supplying them was far from a sure way to make money. Extending unsecured credit to consumers, especially those with no other connection to the bank, was a poorly understood departure from standard bank lending practices. By

1962, many bank payment card plans had fled the field, including Chase Manhattan's. Industry estimates placed Chase Manhattan's card-related losses at $43 million by the time it sold its card operations at the end of 1961. Such losses were not just a banking problem, though. American Express considered dumping its money-losing card in the early 1960s.

Banks faced another major problem with their payment card plans: they were restricted from operating across state boundaries and sometimes even from operating across community lines within their home states. Individual banks could not do what Diners Club and its imitators had done. They could not offer a card to consumers and merchants in many cities across the country. Bank of America was the most successful of the bankcard operators, at least in part because it operated a vast branch banking network in one of the largest states, California. Its card was useful to consumers over an extensive, well-traveled area. Some small, local banks established regional joint ventures to gain some of the same advantages that Bank of America had naturally in California.

Although the payment card industry was firmly established by the early 1960s, it was a mere hint of what it is today. (This statement is not disputed, but one symptom of the industry's infancy is that nobody collected useful data until some years later.) As we noted in chapter 1, even as late as 1977, the total charges made by consumers on general-purpose payment cards amounted to only 3.4 percent of total household income. This had grown to 20 percent by 1997. The limited penetration of payment cards resulted from several obstacles, four of which are especially noteworthy:

• Payment cards were useful to consumers only if many merchants accepted them. Conversely, cards were useful to merchants only if many consumers carried (and used) them. Payment card providers had to convince merchants and consumers simultaneously to accept their cards—a difficult and expensive undertaking.

• With the population's increased mobility, payment cards were more useful if they were accepted over wider geographic areas. Such acceptance required a simultaneous nationwide sign-up of merchants and consumers. Few companies had the necessary resources for such a task.

• To establish payment cards' presence quickly, issuers were tempted to dispense them widely to consumers. As companies expanded beyond a known clientele, however, payment cards inevitably came into the hands of people unable to pay their debts. Payment card companies faced a huge financial exposure, and many incurred correspondingly large losses.

• Payment cards were an easy target of fraud. Theft of payment cards became a rampant problem, one that was accentuated by mass mailings of cards.

Over the next quarter-century, the entrepreneurs of the payment card industry would overcome these obstacles through innovation backed by huge financial investments.

The Infancy of the Card Associations

The most serious obstacle to the development of the payment card industry was the need to sign up large numbers of consumers and merchants in a short period of time. This obstacle was overcome through a key innovation, namely, the establishment of a national organization of many payment card issuers under a single umbrella.

In 1966, Bank of America established BankAmerica Service Corporation, a national licensing organization for its "BankAmericard" and "Blue, White and Gold Bands" design service marks. BankAmerica Service Corporation enabled local banks to issue a card that could be used nationally, provided an arrangement for coordinating settlements of accounts between merchant banks and issuer banks, and created a nationally recognized trademark. Through this organization, Bank of America also spread the cost and risk of developing a truly national card. This soon evolved into an international licensing organization and payment system with an internationally recognized service mark.

Following Bank of America's lead, several other banks formed the Interbank Card Association in 1966. At first, banks intended to maintain their individual proprietary card programs, adding only the symbol "i" on the card to stand for Interbank. This symbol turned out to be ineffective for nationwide merchant recognition. Seeking a brand name to rival BankAmericard, Interbank purchased the Master Charge service mark in 1969 from its issuers in California, the Western States Bankcard Association. Interbank changed its name to MasterCard in 1980.

By the late 1960s, the BankAmericard franchise system had become unworkable, resulting in a shift to joint ownership. There were two main

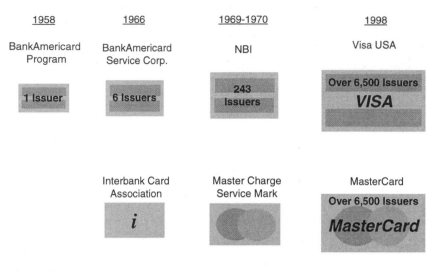

Figure 4.1
Bankcard association membership has grown dramatically over time.

reasons for the shift. First, the infrastructure set up by Bank of America had become increasingly inadequate for handling growing numbers of franchisees and transactions. Though Bank of America could potentially have fixed these problems within the existing franchise system, the discontent these problems fostered provided an impetus for change. Second, the franchisees had also grown and become more important to the system. As such, they wanted a voice in its future direction. In 1970, Bank of America spun off its credit card licensing organization to an independent, nonstock membership corporation: National BankAmericard, Inc. (NBI). NBI had 243 charter members, including Bank of America, Bankers Trust and First Chicago, as well as community and regional banks. NBI changed its name to Visa U.S.A. in 1976. Visa and MasterCard, as we will refer to them from now on, gave local banks a means of competing with the national charge cards offered by American Express, Carte Blanche, and Diners Club. By the end of the 1960s, more bank credit cards than charge cards had been issued.

Visa and MasterCard grew quickly, in part because of the innovative organizational structure they adopted. (Figure 4.1 summarizes their growth and evolution.) Both evolved into associations with virtually open membership policies. From the mid-1970s, any financial institution eligible for federal deposit insurance that did not issue American Express or Discover/Novus cards could become a member of Visa or MasterCard. Starting in the mid-1980s, retailers, investment firms, insurance companies, automakers, and other firms discovered a way to issue their own general-purpose payment cards through financial institutions eligible for membership, as discussed in chapter 3. Using this method, companies such as AT&T were able to enter the card industry.

The card associations themselves were run by boards of directors. The directors were elected by member banks, which were allocated votes based on the volume of various products they offered. The boards of directors then appointed management, which was responsible for certain centralized functions: developing operating regulations, coordinating transactions processing and interchange payments between members, developing system-wide innovations such as interchange technologies, promoting the association brand through advertising and other means, and coordinating other system-wide matters, such as fraud control. Individual members, however, were solely responsible for setting card interest rates, fees, and special features, and for signing up merchants and cardholders. This structure resulted in card systems that fostered competition between members while centralizing those aspects of the system that jointly benefited all members. (More on the organization of the associations appears in chapters 7 and 8.)

Allowing new members to join the associations had two opposing effects on existing members. On the one hand, new members attracted new cardholders and new merchants to the networks, participants the existing members might not have reached. These new cardholders and merchants increased the value of cardholder and merchant accounts for existing members. Besides sharing in the interchange revenues, members benefited because the cards they had already issued would now be more widely accepted. Adding more cardholders and merchants to the network increased the value of the payment services the network offered.

Although the growth in membership in the card associations had positive effects for the members as a whole, it also meant that new members competed with existing members for cardholders and merchants. This increase in competition reduced the profitability of existing members' portfolios. It also reduced the return existing members received from their investments in the card brands.

In the early years of the associations, the benefits from adding new members were clearly far more important than the increased competition they produced. Members were dispersed across the country, and there was little national competition. Relatively few consumers had cards, and relatively few merchants accepted them. Adding members primarily increased the value of the card brand. However, as the market became more saturated, the net benefits of adding new members decreased.

For several reasons, Visa and MasterCard initially had little trouble finding banks to issue cards. First, the card plans that had survived the earlier phases of the industry were profitable. Second, banks were afraid of being left behind. Many banks issued cards either to preempt or counter their competitors' plans. Third, there was a growing belief that credit cards were a stepping stone to the "cashless society." Credit cards were therefore a form of research and development, leading to the day when electronics would replace cash and checks. Fourth, cards created an opportunity for cross selling. One banker said: "[A] charge card plan is a great opportunity for cross-selling. It's not only an additional bank service for your present customers . . . but it's a powerful lead-in for new customers." Many banks even felt that they could not offer their retail customers an acceptable menu of banking services unless they operated a card plan. One banker predicted that "[i]n time to come, the lack of a credit card could be likened to a place of business without air-conditioning." (In the early 1990s, entry into payment cards also involved cross selling. Many of the industrial companies that started cards during this period marketed them in association with other products: e.g., GM and its cars, AT&T and its long-distance service, GE and its appliances.) Developments in existing technology provided a fifth reason for banks to enter the field. Advances in computers clearly made credit card plans more attractive.

Nevertheless, success did not come easily or quickly. In 1971, *American Banker* reported: "[T]he top managements of many of the nation's large credit card–issuing banks, though, are becoming increasingly disillusioned with the negative profit contribution of their card programs and are questioning whether they can afford to stay in the business." Wells

Fargo lost nearly $28 million between 1967 and 1970; Bankers Trust lost more than $21 million in 1969 and more than $11 million in 1970; Citibank lost more than $11 million in 1970; Riggs National Bank lost more than $4 million in 1970 (as always, these figures are in 1998 dollars); losses, fraud, and theft forced Harvard Trust to leave the business the following year. In 1970, charge-offs for all bankcard plans exceeded $425 million. (Charge-offs are defined as payment card debts on which the consumer has defaulted that are judged to be uncollectable, in many cases because the consumer has gone bankrupt. Charge-offs do not include amounts uncollectible because of fraud.)

Early Policy Issues: Duality and Usury

By the start of the 1970s, the essential features of the payment card industry were in place. The industry consisted of two major kinds of cards: charge cards provided payment services, and credit cards provided both payment and credit services. Charge cards were provided primarily by American Express, Diners Club, and Carte Blanche. Credit cards were provided primarily by two bank associations: Visa and MasterCard. During the 1970s, however, the payment card industry changed considerably in response to a number of factors: roller-coaster economics (six-month Treasury bill rates climbed from 4.5 percent in 1971 to 11.4 percent in 1980), natural changes that come with the growth of any industry, and changes in the rules of the game.

Duality

Until 1974, banks were associated with either Visa or MasterCard, but not both. Visa prohibited MasterCard-issuing banks from issuing its cards or handling its merchant paper. In July 1971, one of Visa's charter members, the Worthen Bank and Trust Company of Little Rock, Arkansas, filed an antitrust suit claiming that Visa's prohibition was essentially an illegal group boycott. This case was eventually settled out of court. In an effort to reduce its exposure to similar lawsuits, Visa asked the Antitrust Division of the U.S. Department of Justice in 1974 for a business clearance review—in effect, a letter of approval for a rule that would prohibit dual membership by card-issuing and agent banks. After a year of consideration, the Division declined to grant clearance on the grounds that there was insufficient information. Faced with an ambivalent Antitrust Division and the possibility of expensive litigation, Visa removed all restrictions on dual membership in mid-1976. The age of what has become known as "duality" began, and members of each system rushed to join the other. (Chapter 11 discusses this episode in more detail.)

Competition among issuers increased sharply as new members scrambled to sign up consumers for their second card, and, as Lewis Mandell wrote in his book on the development of the credit card industry, "[a]lmost overnight, aggregate credit lines for customers rose [$36 billion] nationwide." As part of promotional efforts to sign up merchants quickly, members even reduced merchant fees, but soon raised them to their old levels.

Over time, almost all member institutions have chosen to join both associations, and the increasing overlap in membership has led to some decline in competition between the two systems. According to Donald Baker and Roland Brandel:

Apparently, the difference in interchange fees set by the two organizations was much greater before duality than since. In addition, most dual cardissuers apply similar finance charges to both cards . . . [whereas] before duality, different issuers competed with each other in offering different cards and sometimes calculated finance charges differently.

This result is not surprising. Any firm with a vested interest in both systems considers the effect of its MasterCard program on its Visa program's profits and vice versa. Those conflicting profit interests get translated into management decisions through the cooperative ownership of each association.

Considerable competition developed over time, though, for at least two reasons. First, the associations were managed independently, thereby fostering competition between the two management groups (despite, perhaps, the ultimate desire of the member-owners to limit competition). Second, the financial importance of Visa and MasterCard varied across members, and many members have come to specialize in one brand while still maintaining some presence in the other. These specialized members have an incentive to push one system over another and thereby press their favored system's management to compete against the other system.

(Chapter 8 discusses the implications of duality for competition between the systems in considerably greater detail.)

Marquette and the State Usury Laws

As mentioned earlier, usury laws and other restrictions on the charging of interest have impeded the provision of credit throughout history. In the United States, many states imposed ceilings on interest rates that could be charged on loans. In times of low inflation, these ceilings were a manageable problem for payment card issuers, but as inflation rose following the 1973 Arab oil embargo, they became more onerous. The rate of inflation jumped from 4.2 percent in 1972 to a peak of 9.4 percent in 1981.

Card issuers must pay for the money they use to finance their credit card receivables (i.e., the money they have paid to acquirers but not yet collected from cardholders). The rate of interest for this money—the card issuers' cost of funds—increased from an average of 4.7 percent of outstandings in 1972 to an average of 12.4 percent of outstandings in 1981. It then decreased to an average of 8.0 percent in 1992. For a card issuer, the spread between the interest rate consumers pay and the cost of funds is a major source of revenue. This spread has been small, and even negative in some years.

Beyond making payment card lending unprofitable during times of high inflation, usury laws also circumscribed the bankcard issuers' ability to market their cards on a national or regional basis. Interest rates that were acceptable in one state were not in another. To compensate for the lower profit margins on lending, issuers had to tailor other aspects of their cards to compensate for this difference. Issuers in states with lower interest rate ceilings raised their credit criteria for the applicants who would receive their cards, imposed fees, and used alternate methods for calculating interest charges. Thus, in the absence of usury laws, there would have been far less variation across states with respect to interest rates, fees, card features, and the availability of credit.

Usury laws hurt card issuers and cardholders alike. The inability to issue cards with uniform terms throughout a region or the nation as a whole deprived some issuers of scale economies. Those card issuers who did market in multiple states (e.g., Continental Bank of Chicago and

Citibank) also probably incurred higher costs because they had to market cards and process bills under multiple terms and conditions. Although usury laws benefited consumers who could obtain cards with favorable rates, they harmed many other consumers who could not get credit cards at all.

A 1978 Supreme Court ruling clarified the application of such usury laws and helped create a national market for payment cards. Marquette National Bank of Minnesota challenged the right of First of Omaha Service Corporation, a subsidiary of First National Bank of Omaha, to apply interest rates higher than the Minnesota rate ceiling to its Minnesota credit card customers, even though the rates were permissible under Nebraska law. The Supreme Court sided with First of Omaha. In *Marquette National Bank v. First of Omaha Service Corp.*, the Court ruled that as a national bank, First National Bank of Omaha "may charge interest on any loan at the rate allowed by the laws of the State where the bank is located." The Court also said that a bank's "location" refers to the state in which the bank is chartered, regardless of the states in which it solicits customers.

The *Marquette* decision led to three major developments. First, nationally chartered banks began moving their credit card operations into states with less-restrictive usury laws. Citibank, for example, moved its credit card operations from New York, which at the time had an interest rate cap of 12 percent on balances greater than $850, to South Dakota, which had raised its interest rate ceiling to 19.8 percent. Second, in an attempt to attract or retain such movable card operations, several other states began to modify their usury laws. By 1988, the majority of states still had some form of an interest rate cap on credit card loans, but many had raised their ceilings. Third, less balkanization from state credit restraints set the stage for the marketing of payment cards on a nationwide basis. Several other factors, including changes in marketing laws, were also important in the development of nationwide issuance. Citibank led the way in the early 1980s. By 1992, more than 100 issuers marketed their cards nationally. By permitting a national market, *Marquette* probably enabled issuers to realize scale economies in marketing and processing costs, and thus to make payment cards more readily available to consumers across the country.

The 1980s Spending and Debt Spree

At the start of the 1980s, the payment card industry consisted, in order of charge volume, of Visa, MasterCard, American Express, Diners Club, and Carte Blanche. (Citibank, which is also a member of Visa and MasterCard, purchased Diners Club in 1981 and Carte Blanche in 1978.) Visa and MasterCard were separate associations of almost the same group of banks. The payment card industry was well established, but it had faced financial difficulties during the 1970s. These difficulties culminated in severe losses during the 1980–82 recession, when issuers faced both a high cost of funds and mounting defaults on card payments as the economy plummeted.

Coming out of the recession, however, the payment card industry faced a better environment. Interest rate ceilings were no longer as serious a problem as they had been. The cost of funds fell dramatically after the 1980–82 recession, and it has remained low ever since. Moreover, many states eliminated or relaxed their usury laws. In any event, after the *Marquette* decision, most banks could impose national interest rates without regard to individual state ceilings. To compensate for the loss of interest income resulting from the deposit requirements imposed in 1980, many banks started charging annual fees for cards. (The new deposit requirements compelled creditors with more than $3.75 million in consumer credit outstanding to place 15 percent of all unsecured credit into special deposits with the Federal Reserve System.)

The payment card industry grew dramatically over the remainder of the 1980s, during one of the longest peacetime economic expansions in U.S. history. Between 1982 and 1990, the total amount of consumer credit outstanding rose from $620 billion to $950 billion, and average consumer credit outstanding per household increased from $7,370 to $10,085.

In this period, overall consumer spending rose as well, from $3.3 trillion ($39,780 per household) in 1982 to $4.6 trillion ($49,050 per household) in 1990. Furthermore, during this period, restaurant spending increased from $116 billion ($1,400 per household) to $212 billion ($2,250 per household). These increases meant greater opportunities for consumers to use payment cards.

Not surprisingly, the increased demand for payment and credit services, combined with a more favorable financial environment for payment card issuers, generated an enormous increase in the supply of payment card services. The usual competitive responses of entry and expansion accounted for this growth.

Many banks and near-banks (such as credit unions) joined the Visa and MasterCard associations in the 1980s. Between 1981 and 1991, about 4,200 financial institutions became members of the Visa association. (Legislation that made more institutions eligible for deposit insurance expanded the pool of possible entrants.) Moreover, during the 1980s, Visa and MasterCard dramatically increased the number of merchants accepting their cards. From 1980 to 1990, the number of U.S. merchants accepting Visa increased by nearly 40 percent. By 1991, more than 2.5 million merchants accepted Visa cards. MasterCard experienced similar growth in merchant acceptance.

Credit and charge card issuers expanded their business during this time by issuing more cards and increasing cardholders' credit lines. The total number of credit and charge cards more than doubled, from 140 million in 1983 to more than 300 million in 1992; the total dollar value of transactions increased from $175 billion to $460 billion over the same period; and the total outstanding balances increased from $60 billion to $227 billion.

Affinity cards were a major innovation in the field in the 1980s. In 1978, Visa introduced affinity programs that, for the first time, allowed a nonmember's name or logo to be displayed on the face of the card. In 1985, faced with an apparently saturated payment card market, both Visa and MasterCard began allowing new affinity programs. After only one year, 296 clubs, charities, professional associations, and other nonfinancial organizations had developed Visa and MasterCard affinity programs. MBNA alone had 4,500 affinity card programs in early 1998, ranging from the Sierra Club to the National Hockey League. Affinity cards are also known as "cobranded" cards, with the latter term generally used for cards involving for-profit companies (which typically have brand names).

The 1980s also saw the launch of the Discover Card by Sears Roebuck & Co.'s Dean Witter subsidiary, and American Express' introduction of a credit card to complement the charge card it had been issuing all along. The signature orange-and-black Discover Card was first introduced in 1985 and rose to stardom almost overnight. Less than two years after its release, there were already 22 million cards in circulation—more than Citicorp had accomplished after two decades—and $5 billion in receivables, ranking it third among all credit and charge cards in the United States.

A year later, in 1987, American Express launched the Optima card and for the first time entered the credit card business. However, what American Express initially thought would be a successful competitor to MasterCard and Visa quickly turned into a disaster. Default rates skyrocketed and losses soared, costing the company hundreds of millions of dollars. Not until the early 1990s was American Express finally able to solve the card's problems and profit from Optima as it had initially expected.

Whereas Visa, MasterCard, Discover, and American Express were poised for further growth in the 1990s, two of the pioneers of the payment card industry, Diners Club and Carte Blanche, had become minor players, with a combined share of less than 2.5 percent of payment card transaction volume.

The 1990s and the New Millennium

Soon after AT&T announced its release of a no-fee-for-life credit card in March 1990, other nonfinancial companies such as General Motors, General Electric, and Ford jumped in. Cobranded entry by these and other nonbanks has resulted in a wave of consumer enhancements on their cards, ranging from discounts on long-distance calls to rebates on a new car.

Many of these nonbanks entered the credit card business with the intention of increasing volume in their traditional lines of business. AT&T, for instance, entered in part to preserve its base of customers: "We saw our relationships with 22 million calling-card customers in jeopardy," stated Paul Kahn, head of AT&T Universal Card Services Corp. In addition to augmenting their lines of business, however, many of these companies grew into credit card giants. In 1997, four of the top twenty-five credit card issuers were nonbanks that either did not exist or were not among the top fifty issuers in the United States in 1990.

One important industry trend in the 1990s has been the increased issuance of securities backed by credit card receivables. Issuers have used securitization of existing card portfolios to fund future growth. These card-backed bonds are typically structured like corporate bonds, with no principal being repaid until the bonds reach maturity, typically in three to five years. The bonds are backed by but do not pay out the actual stream of payments by cardholders. The cardholder accounts also still belong to the issuer. In 1990, only about 1 percent of total card balances were securitized. This share increased dramatically to more than 50 percent of total balances by 1997. This trend has been particularly important for monoline issuers that have no significant assets from consumer deposits. As we discuss in chapter 9, the outright sale of credit card portfolios has also grown in importance during the 1990s.

American Express rebounded from years of stagnant or declining growth during the late 1990s. For the first time since 1988, American Express increased its market share during 1997, expanding its share of transaction volume from 16.2 percent to 16.8 percent. By combining increased merchant acceptance with new perks for its cardholders and expanding into credit cards, American Express has been trying to shed the strictly upper-class image it has held for so many years and in fact once cultivated. (See chapter 8 for more details.) Reversing the downward spiral was not easy. To gain wider acceptance, American Express lowered its merchant discount from 3.22 percent in 1990 to 2.73 percent in 1997. (This was still higher than the rates charged by Visa, MasterCard, and Discover, however.) American Express developed relationships with corporations like Delta Airlines and Calloway Golf to provide their customers with premiums that ranged from airline miles to discounts on golfing paraphernalia. American Express also focused on the international market, signing up issuing banks in more than thirty countries around the world (but not, as we discuss in chapter 8, in the United States).

If the 1970s was the decade that launched credit cards into stardom, the 1990s will be known as the decade that made the debit card (the subject of chapter 12). Between 1990 and 1998, the number of on-line debit card transactions (i.e., transactions that require a PIN to be entered at the point of sale) increased rapidly from 12.4 million during June 1990 to 150 million during June 1998. Similarly, the total number of off-line debit transactions (i.e., those requiring the cardholder's signature upon authorization) increased nineteenfold between 1990 and 1997. (As we discuss in chapter 12, much of the action took place starting in the mid-1990s.) Between 1990 and 1997, the number of banks issuing off-line debit cards increased from 1,100 to more than 5,500. Many now offer their customers the opportunity to combine their ATM card with a Visa check card or MasterMoney card. Debit cards have quickly grown into a significant substitute for both cash and credit, and an estimated 230 million debit cards were in the hands of consumers in 1998.

The popularity of the Visa and MasterCard brands, combined with heavy advertising, especially by Visa, was an important force behind the debit card surge. Visa, for instance, signed personalities such as Bob Dole, former senator and unsuccessful presidential candidate, to appear in its Visa check card commercials. Consumers can use their Visa check cards or MasterMoney cards at any of the merchant locations that accept Visa or MasterCard. These off-line debit cards are also attractive for merchants, because they require no further investment beyond traditional credit card processing machines: they use the same transaction processing technology as signature-based credit cards do.

Risk, Innovation, and Investment

It is very easy to underestimate the risks entrepreneurs face in the creation of new products and industries. The enormous prosperity of certain new ventures often overshadows the uncertainty and fear of failure that can stifle many companies at their inception. When we evaluate a successful industry, we tend to forget the failures, bankrupt entrepreneurs, and still-born industries that dot economic history. We marvel at winners such as Visa in payment cards, MCI in long-distance telecommunications, and Compaq in personal computers. But we forget the National Retail Merchants Association, which failed in its effort to build a competing payment card system (discussed later in this chapter); Datran, which lost more than $250 million in an unsuccessful long-distance telephone venture; and RCA, which had to write off $1.7 billion of losses trying to compete with IBM in mainframe computers.

In the early days of the payment card industry, entrepreneurs and investors faced enormous uncertainties. Operating costs, competition, and regulation were all unknown. Furthermore, entering this industry required a large investment that entrants could never recover if they left the industry (what economists call a sunk cost). The pioneers of the payment card industry therefore bore considerable financial risk.

Risks of Starting and Operating a Payment Card Business

The credit card business was, from the beginning, very different from banks' traditional types of lending. Instead of the conventional personalized approach to credit management, credit card lending relied on a more systematic and objective (i.e., computerized) approach. Before the arrival of the bankcard, banks usually extended credit only after interviewing the prospective client and verifying his creditworthiness. But bankcard credit is based on a larger scale, mass-marketing approach.

A bank wishing to offer credit cards could not start out small while it learned the business. *The American Banker* reported in 1966: "Credit cards are not something a bank can 'feel its way into.' They require a big splash of publicity, much careful planning, aggressive selling and perhaps above all, the courage to continue as the losses mount."

Mass marketing was needed to solve the chicken-and-egg problem mentioned earlier. Consumers can use credit cards only if merchants accept them; merchants will sign on to a card plan only if many of their customers use the card. The banks initially broke this impasse with mass mailings of free, unsolicited credit cards. The mailings got the cards to the consumers, providing a sufficient cardholder base to attract merchants.

But mass mailings had a price. Given the volume of customers who were to receive the cards, banks could perform no more than a basic credit check and could not provide secure delivery. High levels of fraud and delinquent accounts resulted. In 1960, for example, Bank of America's losses from fraud and defaults amounted to 15 percent of its credit card transaction volume, or nearly $44 million on a volume of $290 million.

Most banks tried to guard against misuse and fraud by establishing "floor limits." Charges over the floor limit had to be approved. In the early days, this involved calling the merchant bank's credit center. Many banks also relied on computer printouts of cardholder activity that allowed them to identify unusual patterns of use. Many provided participating merchants with "hot lists" of suspicious accounts. Each of these methods had limitations. The earliest computer analyses drew their data from sales slips, which were available only after the purchases. It could take weeks for the number of a suspicious account to appear on a hot list. Even then, unscrupulous users could avoid scrutiny simply by keeping their purchases below the floor limits.

Problems with theft and fraud also proved stubborn. Merchants mailed in slips for nonexistent purchases. Cards were stolen from homes and mailboxes, as well as directly from the manufacturers. The mass mailings proved especially susceptible to theft, particularly when cards were sent in bundles of brightly colored envelopes. One mail theft of about fifty cards cost Wells Fargo more than $800,000. A healthy black market in stolen cards developed, and soon there were indications that organized crime was involved. Even as the banks developed methods to combat existing fraud, criminals developed new scams, such as altering cards with an iron, or shaving off and rearranging the embossed letters and numbers.

The problems posed by interchange exacerbated banks' difficulties. Interchange required that banks clear each other's charge slips in the same way that they cleared each other's checks. Even in the early years, nearly 50 percent of all transactions in some systems involved an interchange, which not only could significantly increase the flow of paper but also complicated the process of authorization. It made fraudulent use more tempting, because the cards could be used throughout an increasingly wide region, one that eventually became international. It also made fraud prevention much more difficult because the bank would have to patrol an entire region or country, not just its local market. The geographic breadth of the interchange systems hampered authorization for some time; rapid national transaction authorization systems did not develop until the 1970s. However, the development of these systems and of other credit card technologies was itself a risky process. (In the early 1990s, a Visa executive stated that some projects [about 10 to 20 percent] were abandoned after the first steps proved them to be impractical or problematic. R&D projects had even less chance of success. An R&D program was held to be successful if one in ten projects succeeded.)

Member banks had to work out a set of operating rules for interchange. For example, the member banks had to decide whether the merchant, the merchant's bank, the cardholder, or the cardholder's bank would assume liability for fraud or defective goods. These policies had to comply with the federal Truth in Lending Act and similar state laws limiting cardholder liability. The banks also had to agree how to divide the revenues from the merchant discount between the merchant's bank and the cardholder's bank. Joining an interchange involved negotiating these and other details, even including the appearance of the members' cards.

Issuers faced another major risk in uncertainty over the availability and cost of funds to support their credit card lending. The credit card industry grew substantially during the 1960s despite periods of tight money. By the early 1970s, increases in the cost of funds eroded card plan profits. Because interest rates had previously been stable for a long time, this volatility in the cost of funds came as quite a shock to most bankers. Usury laws that prevented issuers from increasing their finance charges exacerbated the negative impact of the increase in the cost of funds.

Competitive Risks

Issuers of credit cards faced another challenge: competition—from other issuing banks as well as from retailers, oil companies, American Express, and other payment card plans. Bank credit card programs also faced competition from other payment mechanisms, such as check-credit plans, checks, and cash. How would methods of payment evolve? Who would reap the fruits of the industry? Neither question had a certain answer.

An additional significant obstacle facing the bank credit cards was the resistance of large retailers. Retailers had pioneered many features underlying the banks' card plans, including the card itself. The retailers, however, brought a completely different approach to their card plans. For retailers, a credit program was not just a payment system: it was a way to attract business and to build customer loyalty. Not surprisingly, many larger retailers refused to accept bank credit cards, and most held out into the 1970s. Not until the Visa–J.C. Penney accord of 1979 did bank credit cards crack one of the Big Three department stores (Sears and Montgomery Ward being the remaining two). In the earliest years, retailers' lack of cooperation was enough to force some plans out of business.

Competition with retailers grew even fiercer when, in 1971, the National Retail Merchants Association (NRMA) decided to pool its members' resources and set up a joint charge plan that would have the size to compete with the credit cards. In describing the plan, Ira G. Kaplan said to merchants:

You are deluding yourself . . . if you believe that submersion of identity into bankcard systems is in your future best interest. [The aims of the banks and the aims of the retailers are] diametrically opposed. [The] danger for the retailer is the submersion of his identity, image and even his very existence to the banks.

At the time, credit card issuers had no reason to believe that the NRMA would ultimately fail. In fact, in Sweden, Inter Conto did successfully develop a private-label card for smaller retailers. Even in 1998, retailers' cards retain a strong presence. Most large retailers, including Sears, Montgomery Ward, Macy's, and Nordstrom's, are still successfully issuing cards. This suggests that retailers' inclination to extend credit to their customers is not a trivial force in determining the evolution of payment methods. In fact, outstanding balances on store cards were nearly one-fifth the level of outstanding balances on general-purpose credit cards in 1997.

Further competition for credit card plans came from the charge card plans such as Diners Club and from the gasoline cards offered by the oil companies. Both types of plans differed in focus from bank credit cards. The charge cards were aimed at the traveling businessperson and usually did not offer deferred payment. Oil cards were used to attract customers to a single brand. Nonetheless, both competed with bankcards for certain types of business. Many of the same restaurants and stores accepted credit cards and charge cards, and oil companies, in an attempt to reduce losses and further promote their product, extended their card plans to cover other goods and services. In addition, in 1966, American Express, Carte Blanche, and Diners Club set up franchise programs with many banks whereby the card systems operated the plans, but the banks offered lines of revolving credit in association with the cards. American Express had more than 200 such plans by 1968.

A final competitor for the credit card was the check-credit plan. In a typical program, a bank issued a line of credit to a special checking account. The customer could then write checks against this account. A variant was to provide the customer with a line of credit to cover overdrafts on an ordinary checking account. Check-credit plans often included a check guarantee card that the customer could use as identification.

Check-credit plans generally proved more flexible and less expensive to operate than card plans. Clearing checks was faster and less expensive than clearing credit card billing slips. Advocates of check-credit plans in the United States also pointed to their widespread acceptance in Europe.

Although check-credit plans eventually proved to be considerably less successful than credit cards, the *Federal Reserve Bulletin* in 1973 reported that "at one time [they] were thought to provide an attractive alternative to credit cards, especially for smaller banks that could not afford to operate a full credit-card plan." Several major banks, including Chase Manhattan and Los Angeles' Security-First National, promoted check-credit plans as well. In fact, in 1967, more banks offered check-credit plans than credit cards, and the two services had comparable outstanding balances. Soon, there was even a national check-credit plan, the Bancardcheck, licensed by Boston's First Financial Marketing Group.

Regulatory and Legal Risks

Credit card entrepreneurs faced additional uncertainty over how the federal and state governments would regulate the industry and how the courts would resolve a variety of issues raised by the spread of credit cards. Before the *Marquette* decision, it was not clear that a bank's credit card operation could apply the interest rate allowed in its home state to customers living in other states with more stringent regulations.

Furthermore, MasterCard and Visa have faced almost continual high-stakes antitrust litigation since the early 1970s, as we discuss in more detail in chapter 11. In the mid-1980s, NaBanco challenged the interchange fee, which is critical to the management of the credit card associations. Competing card systems have tried to use the antitrust laws to gain access to the MasterCard and Visa brands. Sears tried this in the early 1990s (and filed an antitrust lawsuit), and American Express tried in the mid-1990s (and helped spark a U.S. Department of Justice investigation).

In the early 1980s, Nordstrom attacked a rule that requires merchants to accept all cards with the association's logo—Visa's honor-all-cards rule—as did a group of large retailers led by Wal-Mart in the late 1990s. Each of these lawsuits threatened key aspects of the business in addition to exposing the associations to huge antitrust damage awards. (Sears, for example, sought $1 billion in its lawsuit; Wal-Mart and other retailers are likely to seek an even larger sum in theirs.) Cases such as these mean that issuers remain uncertain about the future regulatory environment in which they will conduct business.

Financial Risk

Over time, the operating, market, and regulatory uncertainties the payment card industry faces have decreased, but only gradually. Even today, a new payment card venture faces considerable risks. Will the cardholders be good credit risks? American Express experienced unexpectedly high default rates when it introduced the Optima card in 1987. Will competition from existing or other new programs make the venture uneconomic? AT&T's unexpected and highly successful entry into the credit card market endangered the economic viability of some bankcards. Yet AT&T is no longer in the credit card business: it sold the business to Citicorp after its card became unprofitable, partly as result of increased consumer defaults. Finally, will state or federal legislation concerning interest rate caps or fees prevent the venture from earning a competitive rate of return?

More than four decades after the birth of Diners Club and a quarter century after the start of the bankcard associations, the financial markets still consider payment cards a risky business. Issuers invest considerable sums of money in attracting new cardholders and developing loan portfolios. Many cardholders default on their unsecured credit card loans, as American Express learned after launching its Optima Card. Carlos Lapuerta and Stewart Myers, after studying profitability and riskiness of credit card issuers, concluded that the monoline banks—those that primarily issue credit cards—tend to be riskier investments than either the stock market as a whole or even banks in aggregate.

In the face of these uncertainties, the pioneers of the payment card industry made enormous investments to sign up consumers and merchants, to promote the use of payment cards, and to develop the interchange systems necessary for crediting and debiting the various participants in the payment card transaction (the consumer, the merchant, the issuing bank, and the acquiring bank). In all likelihood, these investments would have been lost had the business failed. (That is less true today, because markets for selling credit card portfolios are well developed.) Thus, the payment card entrepreneurs made sizable sunk-cost investments in an industry that, for many of its early years, had a very doubtful future.

Summary

To become a viable product, the payment card had to become more advantageous to consumers and merchants, at least for some transactions, than standard methods of payment such as cash or checks. It had to be more desirable than other new payment methods, such as the check-credit plans prominent at one time. The payment card also had to be superior to any alternative payment methods that might develop before payment card ventures had an opportunity to earn back their investments with an adequate rate of return.

Even if one could have been certain that the payment card would succeed, it was far from clear in the industry's early stages whether banks, retailers, or other firms would become the major issuers of payment cards. Were banks to become important card issuers, it was unclear whether individual banks, small groups of large banks, large groups of banks, or another configuration would perform most of the issuing. It is still not clear how payment cards and payment methods will evolve and, consequently, how past investors in this business will fare.

The payment card industry has grown enormously in its first half century. But the growth has been episodic and nonlinear. It had a slow steady build until it was about seventeen, accelerated in spurts until its mid-thirties, then had explosive growth through its forties. Its further expansion must come from weaning more consumers from paying with cash and checks and convincing sellers that have not generally taken payment cards to rely on them. Nonetheless, its achievement to date is impressive. It has gone from hawking cards to selected Manhattan gourmets to providing cards to individuals within all demographic groups across the nation and from handling a few restaurants to servicing millions of merchants.

5

From Gourmets to the Masses

Nothing so cements and holds together all the parts of a society as faith or credit, which can never be kept up unless men are under some force or necessity of honestly paying what they owe to one another.
—Cicero

Credit card issuers have increased the range of consumers to whom they are willing to extend credit by using complex credit scoring techniques. Consequently, credit has been democratized and payment cards are now used throughout society—by college students and retirees, by the unemployed and hopeful entrepreneurs, by some of the poorest households and most of the wealthiest, and by members of both genders, and of all racial and ethnic groups. Credit cards have led the way in taking a product that was originally targeted to well-off restaurant goers in Manhattan and making it available to the masses. Only 16 percent of households had credit cards in 1970, and half of them were among the top 25 percent of households in terms of income. By the 1980s, all but the poorest households had ready access to credit cards. Meanwhile, American Express has repositioned itself from being a card for the country club set—"Membership Has Its Privileges"—to one used by regular guys like Jerry Seinfeld, one of their major television pitchmen in 1998. In addition to credit cards like Visa and MasterCard and charge cards like American Express, debit cards have become available to most people who have checking accounts at their local bank or thrift.

In this chapter, we document the growth of credit cards—the type of payment card that has had the greatest impact on how consumers pay for and finance purchases—and their diffusion across many segments of American society. We explain how payment cards have enabled people to make less use of cash and checks, thereby enabling them to keep less of their wealth in checking accounts, wallets, and piggy banks that earn them little or no interest. We go on to show how the basic economic features of credit markets explain why some consumers and firms face liquidity constraints: they can't borrow all they'd like to at prevailing interest rates. Then we examine how credit cards have relaxed these constraints and provided an extremely convenient and readily available source of financing for consumers and small businesses. Lastly, we consider the proposition—sometimes advanced by our fellow economists over lunch—that consumers who use debit cards or finance purchases on credit cards are irrational.

Much of the research reported in this chapter is based on the Survey of Consumer Finances (SCF), which the Federal Reserve Board has conducted since the end of World War II. The SCF is a highly regarded and often-cited source of information on the saving, spending, and financing habits of American households. The SCF started including detailed questions on credit card use in 1970; the last SCF for which data were available for our research was conducted in 1995.

As with most surveys, the SCF has both strengths and weaknesses. Its chief strength is that it provides data on the use of payment cards from a representative sample of households, along with extensive detail on those households. Its main weakness is that people give survey takers information that is not always reliable. Not surprisingly, for instance, people tend to understate the amount of debt they have. So the SCF is not the best source of data on, for example, the total credit card debt of the American public; Visa and MasterCard have more reliable information. There are inconsistencies between the numbers reported in this chapter and those in other chapters on, for example, the average charge volume per household, but the SCF is the best source available for making comparisons among different segments of the population.

The Growth and Diffusion of Credit Cards in the American Economy

Growth in Credit Card Use

Between 1970 and 1995, the percentage of households with at least one credit card more than quadrupled, from only 16 percent to more than 65 percent. And households increased the use of their cards. When credit cards first hit the market even the small group of people who had them did not use them very much. The average monthly household charge was $125 (as always, in 1998 dollars) for the elite households that had credit cards in 1970. The average monthly household charge was $500 for the many households that had credit cards in 1995. The ratio of average household credit card charges to household income went from just under 4 percent in 1970 to more than 16 percent in 1995.

Among households that had credit cards, average monthly balances—the amount of money the household owed on its credit cards—increased from less than 1 percent of household income to just over 5 percent of household income between 1970 and 1995. That increase resulted from two factors. The fraction of households carrying balances rose somewhat, from almost 40 percent in 1970 to almost 60 percent in 1995. And households who held balances held bigger ones: average balances for these households more than quadrupled between 1970 and 1995. (They grew from $700 in 1970 to just over $3,000 in 1995. As mentioned above, however, households understate the amount of debt they have. The percentage increases, however, are accurate if people understated debt by the same degree in 1970 as in 1995.) Figure 5.1 shows the growth in the percentage of households with at least one credit card and the growth of household charges as a percent of household income for 1970–95.

The Diffusion of Cards across Income Classes

In 1970, households that had a credit card were usually members of the economic elite. At that time, the median household income of households with at least one credit card was 47 percent higher than the median household income of households overall. Indeed, based on income, the typical household with credit cards was in the top 25 percent of all households. In 1995, households that did not have credit cards were on the economic fringes of society. The median household income of households with no cards was 50 percent lower than the median household income of households overall. Approximately 70 percent of households without cards in 1995 had incomes under $23,000, and more than 40 percent fell below the poverty line. (We based the poverty line, which depends on both household size and income, on guidelines reported by the U.S. Department of Health and Human Services. In 1995, for example, the poverty

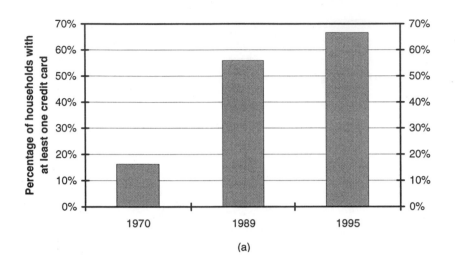

(a)

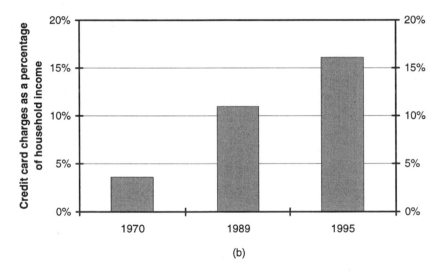

(b)

Figure 5.1
a) Ownership of credit cards increased from 1970 to 1995.
b) Usage of credit cards also increased from 1970 to 1995.
Source: Surveys of Consumer Finance, 1970–95.

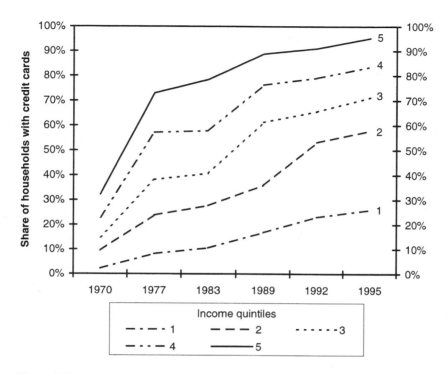

Figure 5.2
Credit card ownership has increased sharply across all household income levels.
Source: Surveys of Consumer Finance, 1970–95.
Note: Income is lowest for households in quintile 1 and highest for households in quintile 5.

line was $10,400 for two-person households and $16,300 for four-person households.)

To see how card holding has diffused across income classes, we have divided households into five equal-sized income classes (quintiles) for each year from 1970 to 1995. (In 1970, for example, 20 percent of all households had income below $15,060, so that is our first income class for that year. Twenty percent of households had incomes above $53,660, and that is our fifth income class for that year.) Figure 5.2 shows the breakdown of card ownership over time by income quintiles. Credit card ownership grew sharply in each quintile over the period depicted.

To see how credit cards have become more widely available to consumers over time, we have compared the percentages of various

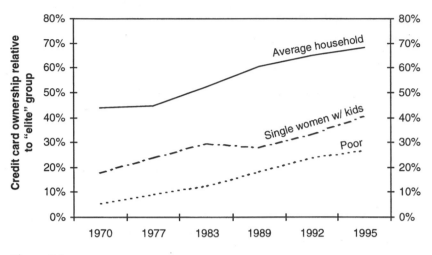

Figure 5.3
Card ownership by less-privileged households has increased dramatically relative to that of the "social elite."
Source: Surveys of Consumer Finance, 1970–95.
Note: Households in the "Poor" group are in the lowest income quintile. "Elite" group consists of white, college-educated men with their own business whose household income is in the top quintile.

socioeconomic groups that have payment cards. We started out by identifying an "elite" group that consists of households headed by white, college-educated, self-employed men whose household income was in the highest quintile (about 50 percent of such households had credit cards in 1970 compared to 16 percent of all households). We then created ratios of the percentages of each group holding credit cards to the percentage of the "elite" group holding credit cards. Thus, a ratio of 0.50 for, say, all households, means that all households are on average half as likely to have credit cards as households in the elite group. Figure 5.3 shows the ratios over time for several socioeconomic groups. Poor households—defined as those in the lowest income quintile—were only 6 percent as likely to have credit cards as the elite group in 1970. By 1995, they were more than 25 percent as likely. The average household was only 44 percent as likely to have credit cards as the elite group in 1970 but almost 70 percent as likely by 1995. Single women with children, a group with a higher than average proportion of households that face economic difficulties, were less than 20 percent as likely as the elite group to have credit cards in 1970 and approximately 40 percent as likely by 1995.

Payment Cards and the Transactions Demand for Money

Although now pervasive, payment cards still lag far behind cash and checks as a means of exchange. Americans spent $4.1 trillion on personal consumption of goods and services in 1996. As we noted in chapter 2, of these expenditures, 57 percent were made with checks, 21 percent with cash, and 22 percent with payment cards. But the share of consumer spending made with payment cards has grown rapidly over time. In 1984, the earliest year for which data are available, only 6 percent of personal consumption spending was made with payment cards, compared with 58 percent with checks and 36 percent with cash. These data suggest that the growth of cards came largely at the expense of cash. However, it is important to recognize that the figures for checks are dominated by payments for mortgages, rent, and other large bills that people could not have put on their credit, debit, or charge cards during the years we are considering. Most of the increase in payment card use and the decline in cash and check usage has occurred at merchant locations where people pay for goods and services in person.

The growth of payment cards at the expense of cash and checks demonstrates an economic fact that is essential for understanding the payment card industry. Payment cards are substitutes for cash, checks, and other means of exchange. Economists have argued that people hold cash and checking deposits for two primary reasons. The "transaction" motive arises because households receive income in lumps—a biweekly or monthly paycheck, for example—but make purchases almost continuously. Households therefore have to figure out how much money to keep on hand from their periodic incomes to pay for purchases. In addition to keeping income and spending in sync, people have a "precautionary" motive for holding liquid assets. We all experience unpredictable demands for means of payment. Such demands can range from an unexpected chance to go to Paris at a discount to a serious family emergency.

Most consumers now have the choice of using cash, checks, credit cards, or charge cards for many of their day-to-day transactions. (Debit cards were not important payment devices for the 1970–95 period discussed in this chapter.) There are costs associated with using each type of payment method. The major cost of holding cash is the opportunity cost: consumers do not earn interest or dividends on cash in their wallets. Checks are bulky to carry and inconvenient, but many consumers earn at least some interest on their checking account balances. Payment cards are cheap for people who pay their balances off at the end of the month: they get an interest-free loan as a result of the 25- to 30-day grace period offered on most cards and pay only the card's annual fee, if any. Payment cards are more expensive for people who carry balances: they pay interest from the time of the transaction and at rates that typically exceed the rates on other consumer loans, such as automobile loans or home equity loans. On the other hand, carrying balances provides benefits as well: it enables consumers to coordinate better the timing of income and consumption.

Payment cards provide a way for households to satisfy their transaction and precautionary demands for money. We would therefore expect the proliferation of payment cards to reduce the demand for cash balances (cash in hand or in checking accounts). Of course, consumers still have to have money in their checking accounts to pay their payment cards bills. However, consumers can reduce their need for cash balances in two ways. They may hold funds in higher-yielding assets until it comes time to pay their card bills. For example, they can write a check from a money market account or transfer money from savings to checking. Also, they can synchronize their income flow with bill payment: when their paycheck arrives they can channel funds to bill payments and high-yielding financial assets, thereby minimizing their need for checking account deposits during the month.

One study, based on 1983 data from the SCF, found that credit card ownership was associated with lower levels of checking deposits. A 10 percent increase in the probability of holding a card was associated with a reduction in checking deposits of 8 percent and money fund balances of 11 percent. Another study, using data from a single bank, found that credit card possession led to a significant reduction in the amount of money people had in their checking accounts. More generally, payment cards may reduce the need for a whole range of liquid assets—savings and money market accounts, certificates of deposit, or Treasury bills— besides checking accounts. Surprisingly, little empirical work has been done to test for and chart such effects.

In recent work, David Blanchflower, David Evans, and Andrew Oswald have looked into effects of payment card ownership on liquid assets using the 1983–95 SCFs, a much larger and more detailed source of information than was employed in previous studies. They examined the effect of payment cards on checking account balances as a percentage of total financial assets, holding constant other factors that could affect cash balances (such as income, age, and education). Table 5.1 summarizes the results. The first column reports the reduction in checking account balances (as a percentage of financial assets) for each type of payment card. (It also reports whether these results are statistically significant, indicated by an asterisk next to the estimated changes. An estimate is said to be statistically significant if, roughly speaking, one would observe such a large coefficient by chance less than 5 percent of the time.) The results show that, with the exception of store cards, holding payment cards has a large and statistically significant effect on checking account balances. For example, a household with a bank credit card would have a checking account balance, measured as a percentage of its total financial assets, that would be approximately 3.5 percentage points lower than a comparable household with the same total assets, but which had no credit cards. A household that has each of the cards in the table would have a checking account balance (again measured as a percentage of its total financial assets) more than 5.5 percentage points lower than the same household that held no payment cards. The second column of the table translates these differences into dollar terms.

Overall, households that had bank credit cards held about $815 less in checking account balances than otherwise similar households that did not have bank credit cards in 1995; that is about 22.5 percent of average checking account balances of about $3,625 for the SCF sample of households in 1995. Although these kinds of dollar differences appear large at first glance, they are not really surprising. In a world where consumers did not have the option of using credit cards, they would have to use checks a great deal more than is common in the late 1990s. Such people would, in turn, have to keep much larger checking account balances.

Table 5.1
Payment card ownership tends to reduce checking account balances significantly.

Payment card	Reduction in checking account balance as percentage of all financial assets	Amount by which owning payment cards reduced checking account
Bank credit card	3.5%*	$ 815*
Charge card	1.1*	550*
Gas card	1.1*	326*
Store card	0.0	0
Total reduction	5.6*	1,691*

Source: Surveys of Consumer Finance, 1983–95.
* Statistical significance at the 5 percent level.

By reducing the need for cash balances, payment cards provide a potentially enormous benefit to consumers. According to the SCF, approximately 66 million households owned credit cards. Based on our estimates
shown in table 5.1, each of these households have reduced their average
checking account balances (measured as a percentage of total financial
assets) by 3.5 percentage points. For cardholding households (whose median total financial assets are $23,300), this 3.5 percentage point decrease
translates to roughly $54 billion in reduced checking account balances.
If these households invested those reduced cash balances in bank savings
accounts, which had an average interest rate of 3.1 percent in 1995, they
would have earned accumulated interest of $1.7 billion in 1995. One
might argue that people who carry balances actually come up short because they have to pay card interest rates that exceed the rates on their
savings accounts. But the SCF shows that approximately 44 percent of
cardholders carry no balance on their credit card, and more than 50 percent claim they always or almost always pay off their balances. These
households clearly benefit from their use of payment cards.

Credit Cards and Liquidity Constraints

Most households find that their incomes increase until the head of the
household (and other wage earners) reach middle age and then level out

and possibly decline toward the retirement years. Since this relationship has held for many generations, we believe that most younger people understand it and, accordingly, expect that their incomes will rise over time. With that expectation, it is reasonable for younger people to try to enjoy life a bit more by borrowing against the higher levels of income they expect to earn in their middle years. During those same middle years, though, they also need to save for retirement, when their incomes will likely be relatively low.

All this indicates that people, in effect, try to spread their lifetime wealth around so that their levels of well-being are more similar over the years than their annual incomes would allow. Unfortunately, although people have an incentive to engage in this behavior and can do so to some extent, several obstacles make it hard to move income over one's lifetime. Most importantly, it is difficult to borrow against future income. Lenders have little security for loans based on personal income: people can escape liability by filing for personal bankruptcy. Long ago, lenders could indenture (temporarily enslave) people who failed to make good on loans. Fortunately, the advance of civilization has eliminated indenture and slavery.

Two other problems tend to result in lenders' being wary of anybody looking for a loan. Both stem from what economists call "asymmetric information": borrowers know more about the likelihood that they will repay than do lenders. First, lenders face an "adverse selection" problem. The most avid customers for debt tend to be the least creditworthy, and no lender ever knows enough to judge creditworthiness perfectly. Thus when borrowing rates increase, those who are certain to repay their loans are more discouraged from borrowing than those who face financing difficulty or whose desire to charge greatly exceeds their ability to pay. The people to whom a lender does not want to lend are exactly the ones who are most eager to borrow. In addition, lenders also face a "moral hazard" problem. When a consumer procures a large loan, it allows him to borrow more than in the past or take other risks, thus increasing the likelihood of default.

As a result of adverse selection, moral hazard, and the fact that lenders cannot take future earnings (human capital) as effective collateral, lenders in all credit markets sensibly engage in "credit rationing": they limit the amount they provide to individual borrowers. Sometimes that limit is zero. When these limits affect individual borrowers, they face "liquidity constraints." A household is usually said to be liquidity constrained when lenders refuse to make it a loan or offer it less than the amount it wishes to borrow at the going interest rate. A variety of studies have suggested that roughly 20 percent of American households are liquidity constrained. As might be expected, constrained households are typically younger than average, are less wealthy, and have smaller accumulated savings.

We would expect that credit cards would relax these liquidity constraints. Banks provide secured and unsecured lending through a variety of distribution vehicles. (With secured loans, the lending institution can legally attach the physical (e.g., house, car) or financial (e.g., bank deposits) assets that secure the loan if the borrower fails to repay the loan. With unsecured loans, the lending institution can still seek repayment but the process is harder and more complex.) Credit cards have proven to be a popular and effective vehicle for banks to extend unsecured credit to consumers and a convenient way for consumers to borrow money from banks. Banks have benefited from the credit card infrastructure developed by the bank associations and by various businesses that have developed to service bankcard programs. (These are discussed in the next chapter.)

Of course, credit cards by themselves do not provide a panacea for liquidity constraints. Credit card issuers, like all lenders, limit their exposure to the moral hazard and adverse selection problems by rationing credit. But over time, credit card issuers have expanded the range of consumers to whom they are willing to extend credit and have increased the amount of credit available over time by developing and using sophisticated credit screening tools. These are rules for deciding which credit card applications should be rejected (i.e., receive a zero credit line) and, among those accepted, for deciding how large a credit line each one should be given. In addition, payment card issuers update judgments of their customers' creditworthiness as they observe their customers' behavior over time.

Considerable advances have been made in credit-scoring techniques, which rely on past behavioral data to identify problematic cardholders. One system used by many of the largest issuers analyzed 5 million credit files from each of the credit bureaus over the course of a year to develop profiles from those files that resulted in bankruptcy. These profiles can be compared to those of current cardholders and applicants. More than 300 characteristics were studied, such as frequency of cash advances and types of merchants frequented (i.e., casinos), to refine the identification of risky behavior. Another system, developed by Fair, Isaac & Co. (a third-party firm that was one of the originators of credit-scoring techniques), studied the patterns of bankruptcy cases over two years and found that issuers need to recognize spending and payment patterns more than six months prior to an actual bankruptcy to prevent significant losses. Such patterns include an initial increase in average monthly spending with a subsequent increase in revolving balances as early as eighteen months before bankruptcy. Interestingly, average monthly spending eventually declines closer to the bankruptcy filing date, while balances continue to increase over the entire period.

Issuers are using credit-scoring models to predict cardholder behavior more accurately before a card is issued. This has permitted banks to avoid issuing credit to applicants who present extremely high credit risks as well as allowing for expansion of the possible cardholder base by more carefully considering a wider range of variables. Credit scoring provides a more comprehensive picture of a card applicant's credit history by considering patterns over a longer time frame and quantitatively analyzing numerous factors to eliminate the subjectivity that plagued credit decisions in the past. As the market for issuing credit cards to persons with unblemished credit histories has become saturated, aggressive issuers have been able to expand their card operations by issuing to customers with problematic credit histories (often referred to as "subprime" accounts). Although these customers represent higher levels of credit risk, they are also often willing to pay higher fees and interest rates in return for the convenience of credit cards. More sophisticated credit-scoring models have enabled banks to differentiate between high-credit-risk customers and to take into account likely borrowing behavior in predictions of customer-specific profitability.

The development and increasingly widespread use of credit-scoring techniques was one of the drivers behind the spread of credit cards from upper-middle-class to lower-middle-class households. And together with intense competition among issuers, it was one of the contributors to the

Table 5.2
By 1995, younger households had a higher portion of their income as credit card balances than older households.

| | Credit card balances as a percentage of household income | | | |
Age group	1983	1989	1992	1995
18–24	2.9%	20.4%	28.0%	50.0%
25–49	9.7	24.0	30.2	41.1
50–64	10.1	16.6	21.8	35.2
Over 64	4.2	6.6	19.9	17.0

Source: Surveys of Consumer Finance, 1983–95.

dramatic increase in the amount of credit available to households during the 1990s. According to the SCF data, the total amount of credit available to households increased from $515 billion in 1989 to $900 billion in 1995.

By making credit more widely and more easily available, credit cards have relaxed liquidity constraints for many consumers and have made it easier to borrow against future earnings. In 1995, households whose head was under the age of 25 had household balances that amounted to 50 percent of their monthly household incomes; those with heads between the ages of 25 and 49 had household balances that amounted to 41 percent of their monthly household incomes; those with heads between the ages of 50 and 64, 35 percent of their monthly households incomes; and those with heads over the age of 64, 17 percent of their monthly household incomes.

Interestingly, this relationship has changed considerably over time, as we show in table 5.2. Prior to the 1995 SCF, balances as a percentage of household income for households whose head was under the age of 25 were lower than those for households whose head was between the ages of 25 and 49, and quite substantially lower in 1983, in fact. However, younger households have increased their balances as a percentage of income more rapidly than older households. We suspect that this increase has resulted from the increased availability of credit cards to younger households over time. (We have not reported results prior to 1983 because the only data available prior to 1983 were for 1970, when credit cards were just getting established. The general relationships re-

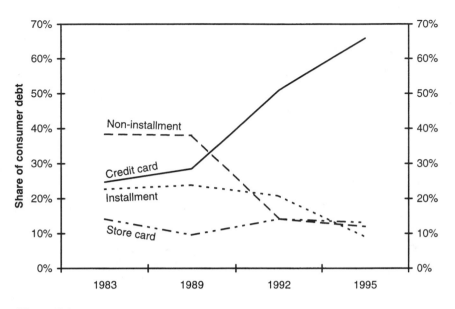

Figure 5.4
The substitution of credit card debt for other forms of consumer debt has risen over time.
Source: Surveys of Consumer Finance, 1983–95.
Note: Consumer debt includes credit-card, store-card, installment and non-installment debt. It excludes housing, household improvement, and motor-vehicle related loans.

ported in table 5.2 also hold after controlling for differences in education, gender, and other demographic characteristics.)

Given that households have increased their credit card borrowing over time in the aggregate, it is not surprising that credit cards have displaced other forms of credit. Many households that used to rely on large department stores or consumer finance companies for short-term loans are now relying on their credit cards. In figure 5.4 we present shares of four types of consumer debt: credit card debt, store card debt, installment debt, and noninstallment debt. (The term "installment debt" describes consumer loans that have fixed payments and a fixed term. Both installment and noninstallment debt consist of consumer loans for household durable goods; hobby, recreation, and entertainment goods; savings and investments; special expenses such as education, tax, and medical expenses; home durable goods; and other miscellaneous personal needs.)

Besides credit card debt, we chose the other three types of debt depicted in the figure because they most closely compete with credit card debt in the consumer debt market. Thus, we have excluded housing and motor vehicle debt from this discussion, because few, if any, people purchase houses, motor homes, or automobiles with their credit cards. Figure 5.4 shows that since 1983, credit card debt has grown to account for 60 percent of all consumer loans outstanding (exclusive of mortgage and automobile loans), while other types of competing debt have lost substantial share. Credit card debt constituted, on average, 17 percent of households' total consumer debt in 1970. By 1995, households' credit card debt on average had almost doubled, to 32 percent of households' total consumer debt (inclusive of mortgage and automobile loans). This growth indicates consumers' substitution of credit card loans over other sorts of consumer loans.

Credit Cards and Entrepreneurship

When Jeannette Lee started Sytel, Inc., in 1987, her government clients often took months to pay her. To get by, she relied on roughly fifteen credit cards. She reached the credit limit on each of them. But, by 1996, her company had placed sixty-fourth on the Inc. 500 list, the small business equivalent of the Fortune 500. She now has 250 employees and draws a $200,000 annual salary. Business successes like this have over time helped the U.S. economy grow and create jobs. Of the 1.5 million new jobs created in 1995, more than 70 percent of these were created in small business–dominated industries. The small business segment of the U.S. economy accounted for about half the private gross domestic product in 1995. Small businesses provide most workers with their first jobs and initial on-the-job training in basic skills and employ 54 percent of the private workforce.

Stories like Jeannette Lee's abound. They illustrate two key facts about small businesses. First, the fact that many entrepreneurs borrow on their personal credit cards suggests that financing a business is difficult: entrepreneurs often face liquidity constraints. Entrepreneurs tend to resort to credit cards for financing when other loan sources are scarce. Second, the ability of entrepreneurs to use personal credit cards shows that this source of financing provides an increasingly large pool of capital for small business start-ups. According to the SCF, the amount of credit card financing available to the American public was $900 billion in 1995. That pool of credit was equally available to people to start their own businesses as it was to buy stereo equipment. Indeed, $140 billion of credit card financing was available to households headed by someone who already owned a business in 1995.

Of course, stories about how credit cards helped people start successful businesses do not show that credit cards are an important source of financing any more than stories about how people started successful businesses in their garages show that having a garage is key to business prosperity. This section examines the role of credit cards in financing small businesses. In addition to examining the SCF data, we use the *1993 National Survey of Small Business Finances* (NSSBF). The NSSBF provides detailed information on the use of credit cards by small businesses in 1993. Together, these data sources provide a broad and deep picture of how small businesses use credit cards. (This discussion does not consider the use of payment cards, such as the American Express Corporate Card, that do not provide revolving credit.) The SCF data provide information on households headed by individuals who have their own business; these self-employed individuals may have a sole proprietorship, own their own corporation, or belong to a partnership. Most all self-employed individuals operate very small businesses. The NSSBF data provide information on businesses that have fewer than 500 employees.

Small Business Financing

If you wanted to start a business, where could you obtain financing? First, you could dig into personal savings. If your coffers are only half full, you might look to friends, family, or a local bank for a start-up loan. Once your application for a bank loan has been denied by at least two banks, you might try to obtain a loan guaranteed by the Small Business Administration (SBA). If you were operating a more sophisticated business, you might also try obtaining equity investments from venture capital firms or other investors. In 1997, $11.5 billion of venture capital was provided to American businesses.

Obtaining capital from any of these sources is difficult because lenders always want to be certain their funds will be repaid. Lending to businesses is inherently risky but lending to small businesses is especially so. Most small businesses fail within a short span of time. In fact, less than half of new firms remain in operation five years after their birth.

Although friends and family do not necessarily require a high rate of return on their loans, they are often financially unprepared to lay out the large sums of money necessary to get a business off the ground. Most requests for venture capital are denied: venture capital firms fund approximately one out of every 100 or 200 proposals they receive. To even consider obtaining a traditional loan from a bank or funds from a venture capital firm, borrowers must be able to prove they are a good risk. To obtain funds, businesses must be prepared to provide several years of financial statements, information on existing debts and accounts receivable and payable, lease details, projected future income streams, and signed personal financial statements. Technology-based firms must make a case for future profits, often long before they have anything to sell. To receive a loan backed by SBA, borrowers must be able to prove their good character as well as their expertise and commitment to business success. To obtain a loan backed by SBA, borrowers are expected to contribute a large portion of their own funds to prove their dedication to the venture at hand.

As in all lending markets, adverse selection and moral hazard lead business lenders to ration credit: to limit the amount that individual businesses can borrow or to make no loan to certain businesses at all. A number of studies have documented the existence of liquidity constraints for small businesses (in addition to the consumer studies mentioned above). A study by David Evans and Boyan Jovanovic found that people with more assets were more likely to start businesses, and they presented some evidence that wealthier people were not more likely to start a business just because they were better entrepreneurs. Two subsequent studies have strengthened their argument by showing that people who receive inheritances are more likely to start and continue small businesses. Surveys indicating that obtaining financing is one of the major obstacles in establishing a small business buttress this evidence of liquidity constraints. Indeed, evidence from the 1995 SCF suggests that one-third of all self-employed respondents who had applied for loans in the previous five years were either denied credit or not granted all the credit for which they had applied.

The Use of Credit Cards by the Self-Employed

The self-employed have benefited from credit cards in the same way other consumers have. Credit cards provide a convenient payment mechanism and a convenient and easily accessible method for borrowing. They also enable the self-employed to choose among a very large group of banks that offer credit cards. It would be very unusual for a small business owner in California to obtain an unsecured business loan from a bank in Maryland. It is very common, however, for a small business in California to obtain a credit card from a bank in Delaware (e.g., MBNA) or one of many other distant states and to have a credit line available on that card that he can use to finance his business.

The SCF provides information on the use of credit cards by households and whether or not the household was headed by a self-employed individual, but provides no information on whether the card was actually used for business purposes. However, the NSSBF reports that 41 percent of small businesses in 1993 used their owners' personal credit cards to finance the business. Therefore, the availability of credit cards and credit lines to small business owners is important. Also, it is possible to infer the increased use of credit cards by small business owners by comparing them to wage workers with similar characteristics.

By 1995, approximately 7.7 million self-employed households had a credit card. These households accounted for more than three-quarters of all self-employed households. They reported having borrowed $19 billion against those credit lines. Although data on available credit in 1970 is not available, it is clear that credit card borrowing has increased dramatically over time. The average credit card loans outstanding for households headed by a self-employed worker was $97 in 1970 and approximately $2,565 in 1995—an increase of more than 2,500 percent.

Of course, the fact that the self-employed now have access to a large volume of credit on their personal cards does not tell us whether and to what extent they use that credit. To help address this issue we have compared credit card use by the self-employed with that by employees. We

Table 5.3
Self-employed households have more credit card ownership and carry higher balances than wage-worker households.

Year	Effect of self-employment	
	Additional cards	Additional balances
1970	−0.09	$−247
1977	0.03	−101
1983	−0.07	56
1989	0.19*	1,280*
1992	0.37*	933*
1995	0.25*	1,806*

Source: Surveys of Consumer Finance, 1970–95.
*Statistical significance at the 5 percent level.

compared people who work for themselves (the self-employed) and people who work for someone else (wage workers).

Table 5.3 reports the additional number of cards and additional balances held by self-employed workers compared with those for similar wage workers between 1970 and 1995. In 1995, compared to households headed by wage workers, self-employed households had on average one-fourth of a card more and carried almost $2,000 more in balances than wage worker households. This was not always so. In 1970, for example, self-employed households were likely to have slightly fewer cards and to carry somewhat smaller balances than similar wage worker households (although the differences were not statistically significant).

Credit Card Use by Firms with Fewer than 500 Employees
We now turn to an analysis of the use of personal and business credit cards by businesses with fewer than 500 employees. As with the preceding analysis, this one focuses only on cards that provide a credit line and excludes charge cards like the American Express Corporate Card. But it also includes a type of card we have not discussed before: the business card, which is offered by American Express, Visa, and MasterCard. Banks provide credit to small businesses through this card as well as

through other traditional bank lending. For example, if you opened up a small business in the Boston area and banked with the Bank of Boston, you would probably receive an application for a loan as well as an application for a business credit card with a line of credit. As a result, small business owners can finance business purchases on either their personal credit card or on a business credit card.

Our analysis is based on data drawn from the NSSBF conducted during 1994–95 for the Board of Governors of the Federal Reserve System and the U.S. Small Business Administration. It provides information on business financing and owner characteristics for approximately 4,600 firms with fewer than 500 employees. The NSSBF asked several questions about credit cards and distinguished between personal credit cards (those issued to one of the owners of the business) and business credit cards (issued to the business itself). The following NSSBF questions were used to determine the incidence of credit card use:

• Did the firm use business credit cards to finance business expenses during 1993?
• Did the firm use owners' personal credit cards to finance business expenses during 1993?

Table 5.4 summarizes the incidence of personal versus business credit card usage by the characteristics of the firm and its owner. In the sample, 40.7 percent of firms' owners used their personal credit cards to help finance business operations. A smaller but still sizable 28.9 percent used business credit cards. And 15.5 percent used both sorts of cards. Overall, 54 percent of the U.S.'s small firms used some kind of credit card in 1993 to pay for business expenses.

Table 5.4 further shows that credit card use is spread across many types of small firms. Note that businesses that faced serious or somewhat serious credit market problems (52.5 and 47.3 percent, respectively) were most likely to use personal credit cards for financing. Firm size was also a significant determinant of whether the owner used his or her personal card to finance business expenses. Figure 5.5 shows personal and business card use in relation to firm size. Bigger firms were more likely to use business credit cards and less likely to use personal credit cards. Business credit cards were especially important in firms with at least five

Table 5.4
Many types of small businesses used credit cards in 1993.

Type of firm	Type of card used for business		
	Personal	Business	Both
All	40.7%	28.9%	15.5%
White owned	40.8	28.9	15.2
Minority owned	40.2	27.7	17.1
Not in business in 1990	41.5	22.5	12.4
Firm age less than 5 years	42.1	22.9	12.8
Firm age between 5 and 20 years	41.6	29.9	15.5
Firm age 20 years or more	36.3	29.2	16.5
Exporter	51.9	45.0	25.2
Sole proprietor	42.5	22.9	13.8
Partnership	35.0	25.0	14.2
S corporation	45.3	34.8	19.6
C corporation	36.4	34.7	15.3
Manufacturing	38.8	32.0	16.9
Nonmanufacturing	41.8	27.9	15.0
Firm faced			
Serious credit market problems	52.5	30.2	20.7
Somewhat serious credit market problems	47.3	34.9	20.9
Not serious credit market problems	36.3	26.7	12.7

Source: National Survey of Small Business Finances, 1993.

employees. Use of personal credit cards was particularly prevalent in businesses that had fewer than five workers.

   One might also expect that by providing a readily available source of financing, the availability of credit cards would make it easier for businesses to expand. By smoothing good periods and bad, credit cards may also sustain firms and, in the long run, help turn a small employer into a large employer. Indeed, Blanchflower, Evans, and Oswald have found that firms with business credit cards grow more quickly than do firms without business credit cards. Part of this correlation almost surely arises because more successful firms are more likely to be approved for business

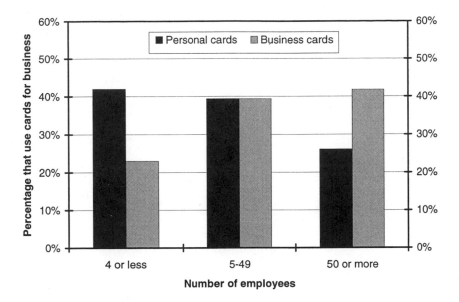

Figure 5.5
Smaller firms rely more on personal cards and larger firms rely more on business cards.
Source: National Survey of Small Business Finances, 1993.

credit cards. But the faster growth may also result from business credit cards' helping to make capital more readily available to smaller firms.

But Are Payment Cards Really a Good Deal?

The question is often raised as to whether payment cards are really a good deal. Consumers obviously think so. Almost every adult has at least one. Most people who have credit, debit, and charge cards use them to pay for things. And many people who have credit cards use them to finance purchases. But some economists attempt to make a case that consumers use these cards irrationally.

Most consumers who finance purchases with credit card loans could find a cheaper source of financing. They are probably earning a lower rate of return on their savings—even, in most years, if it is invested in the stock market—than the interest rate they are paying on their credit card debt. They could also probably obtain cheaper loans by obtaining a personal loan from their bank or, even better, a home equity loan.

Consumers who buy things with their credit or charge cards but pay their balances off at the end of the month, on the other hand, are getting an extremely good deal. They have gotten an interest-free loan from the card issuer for the time between buying something and paying for it, an average of about two weeks. The interest savings (what is often called the "float" in this context) does not usually amount to much, but a penny saved is a penny earned.

In fact, credit and charge cards are such a good deal for people who pay their bills on time that, some would argue, only a fool would pay with a debit card instead of a credit card. With a debit card, the money comes out of your checking account within a couple of days (and possibly in a couple of minutes, as we discuss in chapter 12). You give up the float that you could earn if you paid with a charge or credit card, and obviously you would not need to finance if you had the money in your checking account to begin with.

Yet in our experience, many financially savvy people use debit cards and finance purchases with credit cards. It is hard to believe that these individuals, along with the millions of perhaps less savvy cardholders, are unaware of the costs of using their cards or are wasting money on purpose. More likely, consumers perceive costs and benefits from using various payment and financing devices that go beyond the simple interest rate comparisons discussed above.

For example, consumers incur a variety of costs in securing alternative sources of financing for purchases. It takes time to apply for loans, time during which special purchase opportunities may be lost. Consumers have to obtain an application, provide more financial information than they ordinarily have to provide for a credit card application, and possibly make one or more personal visits to the bank. They then obtain a loan that is less flexible than that provided through credit cards. Unlike credit card loans, other loans often have fixed terms and payments. These transaction costs could easily swamp the available interest savings. Consumers may also have sound reasons for financing on their credit cards rather than drawing down their savings. Because of liquidity constraints, they may want to have a cushion of savings to cover unexpected decreases in income (resulting from, say, job loss) or increases in expenditures (emergency medical expenses, for example).

Perhaps more importantly, consumers may find that assigning particular roles to credit and debit cards helps them manage their finances. If we sought only to maximize free float and minimize our interest expense, we would choose credit cards over debit and repay the balance in full each month. But real people have trouble keeping track of those balances during the month and resisting the ever-present temptation to use future income to enjoy life a bit more today. They need ways to manage their monthly and lifetime finances that do not require lots of calculations. One response to this problem is to use debit instead of credit. Surveys have found that many people do not like to pay for groceries with a credit card. They pay for groceries with debit cards (or cash or checks) because they want to resist the temptation to eat more than they can afford. Other people prefer debit cards over credit cards because they like the convenience of paying with plastic but do not want to get into the habit of spending more than their incomes allow.

Many of our economist friends are troubled by this "irrational" behavior. But of course, it is no more irrational than any other manifestation of consumer preferences that differ from our own. Some might argue that consumers who charge vintage French wines on their American Express cards are far more irrational than consumers who pay for six-packs of beer with their debit cards.

Another common complaint about credit cards is that they entice people to accumulate too much debt. This complaint is partly paternalistic. Some people dislike borrowing just as other people frown on eating meat. Neither preference is wrong, but we would argue that neither should be imposed on others.

This complaint, however, also points to a problem for which there is no easy solution. Credit card issuers have strong financial incentives to prevent cardholders from getting overextended. They incur significant losses each year from people who cannot pay their bills. And, unlike issuers of secured loans such as those for houses or automobiles, credit card issuers have no collateral and limited recourse for collecting bad debts. Credit card issuers could reduce the number of households that become overextended by tightening the criteria for granting credit. That, however, would reduce the amount of credit available to many households that want to borrow and will repay the loans. No conceivable improvements in credit-scoring techniques could enable issuers to distinguish households that, because of bad luck or bad intentions, will accumulate more debt than they can afford from households that can and will repay. As with many products, some consumers will abuse credit cards. It is a cost of doing business for card issuers and a cost of continuing to enjoy the benefits of credit card financing for cardholders.

It is useful to stop and think about how different household finances were in the 1950s from what they are in the 1990s. If you headed a typical household in the 1950s, you were very dependent on your weekly paycheck and your savings. You kept money in your checking account to pay for weekly expenses and maybe a reserve for emergencies, and you probably had a passbook savings account in which you accumulated money to pay for durable household goods and other large items. You had to keep a good cushion of cash in your checking and savings account, because you may have had nowhere else to go to pay for unexpected expenses or to handle sudden drops in your income. If you were young and starting a family, you would have to wait to buy things that would make your life more enjoyable even though you knew you had a good income coming in over time. If you wanted to buy a refrigerator, or start a business, or finance a vacation, you could not obtain financing without a fair amount of difficulty.

The nostalgic may long for the days when men were men and people did not spend money they did not have. But if you head a household in the 1990s, you are generally better off than your 1950s counterpart, even with the same real income. Payment cards have broken two chains on your personal finances. You are not chained to your weekly paycheck. Credit and charge cards provide you with some flexibility in the timing of transactions. You are also not constrained by your current annual income. You can more easily buy things you are going to enjoy over several years even though you cannot shell out the full purchase price today.

Of course, you would have none of these benefits if you had payment cards but no one accepted them for payment. Why merchants accept them is a subject to which we now turn.

6

Everywhere You Want to Be, Not Everywhere They Want to Be

In God we trust; all others must pay cash.
—Anonymous Merchant

You have finally realized your lifelong ambition of opening a hardware store in Fargo, North Dakota. In addition to figuring out which brands of sledgehammers and duct tape to stock, you have to decide how you are going to let people pay and then arrange to implement each of the payment mechanisms you decide to accept. Should you take checks in addition to cash? If so, should you sign up with a check verification or check guarantee service? Which, if any, brands of payment cards should you take? Should you use your local bank to arrange for all of your payment processing needs, if indeed it has the capacity to do that, or should you contract with one of the many businesses that specialize in helping merchants with electronic payments?

You cannot answer these questions without considering what forms of payments your customers would like to use and how your competitors are answering these questions. Chances are that you will not bother accepting the JCB card. Fargo hardware stores are not a common stomping ground for Japanese tourists, so unless local consumers start carrying JCB cards, you may not even want to waste the decal space on your door. Perhaps you are not certain whether to take American Express cards because they are more expensive to accept than other payment cards. But if all of the other hardware stores in Fargo take American Express, you may reconsider. Consumers who wanted to put that chain saw on their American Express Green Card may shop elsewhere if you tell them that you do not take that means of payment.

If you are like most retail merchants today, however, you will almost certainly accept MasterCard and Visa, and you may accept American Express, Discover/Novus, Diners Club, and Carte Blanche as well. Thus if you're a consumer, payment cards are almost everywhere you want to be, especially if you want to be at an establishment that is somehow connected to travel and entertainment or retail trade. Payment cards are not everywhere *they* want to be, though. Cash and checks are still the primary means of payment for many transactions in the economy.

This chapter discusses the merchant side of the payment card industry. We first describe the players who affect the merchant's decisions to take particular types of payment cards and discuss one of the fundamental rules of payment card systems: all merchants signing up for a brand must accept all cards issued under that brand. We then examine the benefits and costs of accepting particular payment mechanisms and describe how merchant acceptance and the portion of payments made with payment cards has changed over time.

Who Are the Players?

Many different actors play a role in the merchant's decision to accept payment cards and his choices of how to handle payment card transactions. The payment card systems set the ground rules for signing up merchants, such as deciding who can enter into contracts with merchants and prescribing some terms of those contracts, and provide the authorization and settlement systems on which the merchant relies. The systems' fee structures are important determinants of the prices that merchants pay for processing payment card transactions. Banks were initially the major acquirers for payment card transactions for MasterCard and Visa. Over time they have subcontracted more and more of their tasks to third-party firms that act as processors (third-party processors) and as acquirers (independent sales organizations). Acquirers and third-party processors install devices manufactured by terminal manufacturers. These include electronic card readers and PIN pads.

Payment Card Systems

American Express and Discover each have their own direct sales forces to solicit merchants to accept their payment cards. American Express uses Centurion Bank, and Discover uses Greenwood Trust. They contact merchants, conduct advertising and other marketing activities, distribute terminals, and process transactions. American Express also provides merchants with proprietary terminals that connect directly to its authorization system. Starting in the early 1990s both systems began to use outside firms (independent sales organizations or ISOs) to sign up small and medium-sized merchants to accept their payment cards. Both systems operate their own computer systems and backroom operations necessary for completing the essential processing steps of any card transaction. They also perform their own research and development regarding processing innovations.

MasterCard and Visa perform four closely related functions. First, they set the ground rules for who can contract with merchants and what the merchants' obligations are. Second, they operate the authorization and settlement systems that acquirers and third-party processors must access to process payment card transactions. Third, they establish fees, including the interchange fee that places a floor on the prices that merchants pay to their acquirers for processing payment card transactions. Fourth, they develop and encourage system-wide innovations in transaction processing.

Bank Acquirers, Third-Party Processors, and ISOs

In combination, a variety of businesses provide the following merchant-side services:

• signing up merchants and managing the relationship with the merchant
• installing terminal equipment
• providing authorization services when customers present their cards
• keeping track of transactions and providing reports to merchants based on these data
• transferring funds to the merchant on a daily basis to cover card purchases (also known as clearing and settlement)
• responding to merchant problems with card processing

• providing specialized services such as analyses of purchasing patterns at the merchant

Some acquiring banks conduct all aspects of merchant acquiring, from signing up the merchant to transaction processing and customer service. Other banks serve as the customer's point of contact but outsource the processing function to third-party processors. Still others serve solely as the depository institutions where clearing and settlement occur; this is especially likely when an ISO or third-party processor is the active party in the merchant relationship.

Bank Acquirers Only members of the systems can enter into contracts with merchants for acquiring, although member banks can work with third-party firms to do so. In the early days of the bankcard systems, you had to go to a bank (and it was probably your local bank) to obtain acquiring services. However, the acquiring business evolved over time, especially after 1990. It was difficult for banks to stay in the business as technological requirements increased required capital expenditures on computer equipment. Acquiring had become more of a high-tech industry than a financial business by the mid-1990s. Scale economies had become so important in processing that large bank acquirers or large third-party firms did the bulk of the processing. Whereas some banks outsourced their processing requirements to these third-party firms, most eventually just left the business.

Third-Party Firms Two types of third-party (nonbank) firms have played an important role in the growth of the merchant acquiring business. Many banks that were in the acquiring business subcontracted one of the major aspects of acquiring—actually processing the transactions—to third parties. An industry segment grew from this, populated by firms known as third-party processors. By processing transactions for many acquirers and their merchants, third-party processors capture significant scale economies. Third-party processors also process transactions on the issuing side of the business. In the early days of the industry there was a niche for third-party firms to acquire small merchants that were often not serviced by bank acquirers. Any such nonbank acquirer is known as an "independent sales organization" (ISO). Typically, a large third-party firm will act as both a third-party processor and as an ISO, depending on the bank for which it is working. These terms are used somewhat interchangeably, although some industry people tend to reserve the term "ISO" for the firms that continue to focus on smaller merchants.

As we have said, third-party firms now control most of the processing business. Many now do everything from signing up the merchant to installing and maintaining equipment to processing transactions. Many of the banks that stayed in the acquiring business are acquirers in name only: their name is on the contract with the merchant, and they handle settlement and clearing, but the merchant's important relation is with a third-party firm. Today, most ISOs work on behalf of multiple systems to sign merchants. The terminals they sell are capable of diverting transactions to any of the major payment card systems. Moreover, although a merchant still needs to sign separate agreements for each payment card system, she typically needs to deal with only one ISO for billing and settlement. By 1997, nonbanks and banks involved in joint ventures with nonbanks controlled 60 percent of the acquiring market when measured by charge volume.

A Giant in the Making   By far, the biggest player in the acquiring business is First Data Corporation. First Data, either alone or as part of joint ventures with various banks, handled 38 percent of all Visa and Master-Card merchant volume in 1997. First Data's history reflects many of the important changes in the acquiring business over the past decade. It was founded in 1971, and its first move was to take over processing duties for the Mid-America Bankcard Association, a bankcard processing cooperative. During its first nine years, First Data took over two additional regional bankcard processing associations. American Express purchased First Data in 1980 when First Data was providing transaction processing services to more than 100 financial institutions and processing 250 million transactions annually. After the acquisition by American Express, First Data was able to take over the processing duties for several more regional bankcard associations, including the Eastern States Bankcard Association in 1988. First Data was not, however, involved in processing

American Express transactions. By the time American Express sold off most of its equity in First Data in 1992, First Data was processing transactions for 1 million merchants.

In 1995, First Data acquired NaBanco and Card Establishment Services (formerly the merchant acquiring unit of Citibank), the first and third largest merchant acquirers at the time, respectively. This catapulted First Data to the number-one position in both merchant acquiring and processing, far ahead of all of its competitors. First Data then entered into a number of joint ventures with major banks including Wells Fargo, NationsBank, and Banc One. As part of these joint ventures, First Data transferred a large portion of its merchant accounts to its partners. These transfers helped address the concerns of First Data's processing customers that First Data was now a direct competitor in the acquiring business.

In 1997, First Data and its partners accounted for fourteen of the top fifty merchant acquirers, including three of the top ten, as can be seen in table 6.1. First Data's largest joint venture partner, Chase Manhattan, was the largest merchant acquirer overall in 1997, and First Data (exclusive of its joint venture contracts) was the third-largest acquirer. Table 6.1 also shows the increased importance of nonbanks in acquiring as well as the significant increase in concentration between 1988 and 1997.

First Data is also the leading processor on the issuing side, processing more than one-third of all Visa and MasterCard accounts. First Data's access to both cardholder and merchant data allows it to offer some of the "closed-loop" services American Express is able to offer (discussed in more detail in chapter 7). Suppose First Data is the processor for your Visa card. First Data is also likely to be involved with more than a third of the merchants you frequent. It therefore has a lot of information on you and your favorite stores, certainly more information than an issuer that is not involved in the merchant business. First Data might offer, for example, to let a new bookstore offer discounts to cardholders within the same city who have purchased books in the last six months. The prominence of First Data in both the issuing and acquiring business has led some to suggest that it has the potential to become a competing payment card system. Although it does not have any name recognition among cardholders, it is well known among merchants and has an impressive processing infrastructure in place.

Table 6.1
Acquirer concentration has increased significantly over time.

Rank	Company	1988 Volume ($ millions)	Share of volume (percentage)	Company	1997 Volume ($ millions)	Share of volume (percentage)
1	National Processing Co.	21,093	8.5	Chase Manhattan*	94,943	15.5
2	NaBanco (NB)	14,936	6.0	National Processing Co.	74,809	12.2
3	Citibank	14,805	6.0	First Data Corp. (NB)	64,711	10.6
4	Bank of America	9,433	3.8	Paymentech (NB)	46,223	7.6
5	National Data Corp. (NB)	7,861	3.2	BA Merchant Services	29,080	4.8
6	Citizens Fidelity	7,730	3.1	National Data Corp. (NB)	22,915	3.8
7	Security Pacific National	6,289	2.5	Fifth Third Bank	21,417	3.5
8	First Interstate Bancard	5,765	2.3	U.S. Bancorp	20,104	3.3
9	Wells Fargo	5,241	2.1	First of Omaha	16,902	2.8
10	Banc One	3,878	1.6	Banc One*	16,520	2.7
	Top 10 acquirers	97,029	39.0		407,624	66.7
	Top 50 acquirers	161,134	64.8		594,662	97.3
	All bankcards	248,796	100.0		611,039	100.0

Source: The Nilson Report, no. 446, February 1989; no. 663, March 1998.
Note: (NB) indicates nonbank acquirers and asterisks indicate First Data joint venture partners.

Terminal Manufacturers

Card terminals have come a long way from the little box that would dial up the payment card system in the early 1980s. In the late 1990s, large merchants have sophisticated electronic cash registers connected to a variety of devices including a card reader, a bar code scanner, perhaps a PIN pad, and the store's payment system, which sends out authorization requests. Some of the larger merchants even have direct connections, for example, to Visa or an on-line debit system. Terminal manufacturers are also poised to enter emerging markets, such as smart cards and Internet transactions. In fact, in 1997, Hewlett-Packard acquired VeriFone, the leading payment card terminal manufacturer with a 55 percent share, to take advantage of potential synergies in facilitating Internet commerce. The terminal business is highly concentrated, with the second- and third-largest firms (HyperCom and Verifact/Roswell) accounting for most of the remainder of sales in the industry in the United States.

A Typical Retail Acquiring Relationship

To get an understanding of the relationships among these players, consider which firms you might deal with if you decided to accept Master-Card, Visa, American Express, and Discover/Novus at your hardware store in Fargo, North Dakota, in 1998. You can find yourself an acquirer through the Yellow Pages (under something like "Credit Card & Other Credit Plans") or on the Internet. Or the acquirer might find you and try to sell you on the benefits of card acceptance. Your acquirer might end up being a bank or an ISO. In any case, you really only have to deal with the acquirer. You might sign separate contracts to accept Visa, Master-Card, American Express, and Discover/Novus, but you can get all your transactions consolidated on one report from the acquirer, although you may receive payment separately from American Express and Discover/ Novus. You might find it a bit strange that a Visa/MasterCard bank would be interested in selling you on American Express and Novus, but the acquiring business is about getting transaction volume regardless of the payment card system involved.

The acquirer is also quite happy to sell you the equipment needed for accepting payment cards: anything ranging from a simple card reader to a fully integrated cash register system to computer software for managing your accounts. You will also have the option of leasing the equipment. The acquirer will want information from you, such as your financial history, your firm's financial and business history, and some references. In the past, it might have taken a month for your application to be approved, but with advances in technology, an acquirer representative can show up at your store, verify that it indeed seems to sell hardware, and transmit your application through her laptop to headquarters. You can be approved within minutes if everything checks out.

Honor All Cards

"Honor all cards" is the first commandment of the payment card industry: any merchant that joins a payment card system must accept for payment all of the cards that carry that system's mark. Each of the major payment card systems has this rule. Visa's version is known as the honor-all-cards rule, and we use this term here to refer to all such rules. Merchants are not allowed to pick and choose which Visa cards they wish to accept. They can't, for example, accept only Gold Visa cards, out-of-state Visa cards, or Citibank Visa cards. Nor are merchants permitted to accept only Visa credit cards and to decline Visa debit cards.

All payment card systems have honor-all-cards rules for a simple reason: payment card systems are in the business of providing uniform acceptance of their card brands. A payment card system creates a brand, advertises and promotes it, and offers that brand as an acceptance mark that is used by a wide range of "different" cards. That is the business model followed by American Express, Novus, and the on-line debit systems, as well as Visa and MasterCard. Payment card systems, even when they were small or in their infancy, have always required their respective merchants to honor all cards.

To be successful, payment card systems have to develop a mark that informs consumers that their cards will be accepted at merchants displaying that mark and that consumers can expect a particular level of service (rapid authorization, for example) at those merchants. They also have to develop a mark that informs merchants that transactions by consumers who have cards displaying that mark can be processed through the payment card system associated with that mark. There are obvious scale economies from investing in a single mark. For example, American Express has invested in creating a brand image that conveys information to merchants and consumers about the American Express authorization system, the types of merchants that are likely to accept American Express cards, and the other benefits of the card. It is efficient for American Express to spread the costs of developing that brand image across as many cards as possible.

Although it is conceptually possible for a card system to develop multiple acceptance marks for use by each card type, that would be a very costly and confusing way to run a system. Consider American Express, which started with its charge card but has since developed a plethora of card offerings, including the Optima card and the Delta SkyMiles card. American Express' cardholders simply have to look to see if a particular merchant "takes American Express," not whether it takes the particular card variant that the consumer has. Of course, there might be a few merchants that, for example, would like to take the Green Card but not the Optima card; those merchants might in fact choose not to take American Express at all because of their inability to take one card but decline the other. But American Express decided that the value of having a consistent acceptance mark for its brand far outweighs the potential loss of a few Green Card merchants for American Express.

Honor-all-cards rules provide a cardholder with the assurance that her card will be accepted at merchants displaying her card's acceptance mark. That assurance gives her valuable information, and it reduces the amount of time she has to spend searching for a merchant that takes the particular payment method she possesses. One of the fundamental business purposes of any payment card system is to provide that assurance to cardholders. In the case of Visa and MasterCard, this is something that none of its members individually could do. Without this guarantee, the value of the card brand for cardholders and merchants would be severely diminished.

Honor-all-cards rules also reduce transaction costs and staff training for merchants. Merchants can display a small set of logos that inform consumers about which cards they accept. They can train their staffs to process cards that have these particular logos. Without these rules, merchants would have to provide information that they accept (or do not accept) variants on each card. They would also have to train their staffs concerning which variants to accept and which not. The decision by particular merchants not to take certain types of cards (Green Card vs. Gold Card, Citibank vs. MBNA, debit vs. credit) issued by a given payment card system would have external effects. In particular, it would reduce cardholders' assurance that their cards will be accepted at merchants that display the system's logo and thereby would impose a cost on consumers.

The Economics of Merchant Acceptance

Why do some stores accept virtually any payment method consumers might want to use, while some stores do not accept checks and some do not accept credit cards? Why do some Federal Express locations refuse cash? Why do some stores accept cash but not take bills over $20? Why do some stores accept checks but require the customer to sign up in advance for check-writing privileges? Why do some stores accept credit cards only when the customer buys more than $5 or $10 worth of goods? We try to provide some answers to these questions by examining your decision on what payment methods to accept at your hardware store in Fargo.

The Costs and Benefits of Taking Plastic

You will almost certainly take cash. You could go through a formal analysis of this choice, but you know that there are lots of customers who want to use cash in hardware stores, especially for smaller purchases. Almost everyone that can take cash (e.g., mail and telephone order retailers cannot) does take cash. (One of the few exceptions we are aware of is Federal Express at its smaller locations.) But you will take cash although you might think about whether to accept bills over $20. If you find out that counterfeit bills are not a big problem, you will probably go ahead and take $50 or $100 bills.

Your decision now comes down to whether to take credit cards or checks or both. You might consider installing a PIN pad and taking on-line debit or offering store credit to repeat customers, but for simplicity, let us ignore those possibilities. Also, let's say you have decided that checks are worthwhile, perhaps at least for North Dakotans with photo IDs. (In making that decision, of course, you might well go through an analysis similar to the one we describe now for credit cards.)

So you are now thinking about whether or not to accept credit cards for payment. Accepting credit cards has two primary effects on your profits. You may get some additional sales. Some of your customers may not be carrying cash or their checkbooks when they stop by your store, or they may avoid your store altogether because they like to pay with plastic.

The amount of these additional sales depends on the importance your customers place on paying with credit cards. Consumers are more likely to want to pay with credit cards for large transactions, because they are less likely to have sufficient cash on hand and are more likely to want to finance the purchase. Figure 6.1 shows the share of payment methods consumers use for transactions of different sizes. Cash is commonly used in small transactions but not for large transactions. The opposite is true for the use of credit/charge and checks, which fits in with our intuition that these payment methods are more desirable for larger transactions.

The value of the additional sales you get from accepting credit cards depends on how much you mark up the goods and services you sell. For a given level of additional sales, you will care much more about making additional sales if you make a $20 profit on a $40 sale than if you make a $2 profit on a $40 sale. So we would expect merchants with high markups to care more about getting incremental sales, which means they are likely to be willing to take whatever payment methods their customers want to use.

Of course, you also have to consider the potential cost of accepting credit cards, the second effect on your profits of accepting credit cards. There are fixed costs incurred in setting up credit card acceptance, including purchasing a card reader, setting up phone lines, and staff training. (Of course if, for example, you already take Visa and MasterCard, then the additional start-up cost of accepting Discover is relatively small because Discover transactions can be processed using the same equipment.) You incur these costs regardless of your volume of credit transactions, so you must have a large enough volume of credit transactions to cover

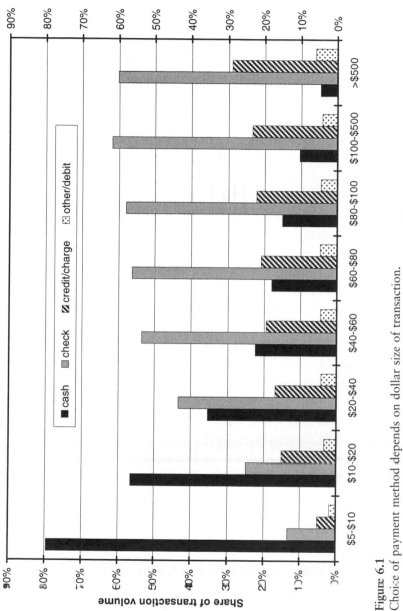

Figure 6.1
Choice of payment method depends on dollar size of transaction.
Source: Calculations based on data from Visa's Payment Systems Panel Study, 1996.

these costs. In addition, there are variable costs of credit acceptance, including the merchant discount, checkout time to process the card, and backroom processing. The details vary by merchant, but let's assume you have concluded that credit card transactions cost you more than cash transactions. (If it were the other way around, there would be no question that you should take credit.)

Weighing these benefits and costs of taking cards yields some interesting conclusions. You are more likely to take credit cards if you stand to gain significant sales. For example, you are more likely to take credit cards at your hardware store than your friend might at his convenience store because you sell big-ticket items like riding mowers. You may decide, however, to accept credit only on transactions above $5 or $10. Consumers are likely to be willing to use cash as an alternative for small transactions, so you may not lose sales from this policy.

You are more likely to take credit cards if you make significant profits from incremental transactions. More generally, higher-margin merchants are more likely to take credit cards and other payment methods. This is quite intuitive: the merchants that gain the most from additional sales the card brings are the most likely to take them.

Finally, you are less likely to take credit cards if their fixed and variable costs are high relative to the costs of other payment methods that your customers might use. This last observation, when applied to other payment methods, helps explain some generally observed phenomena. For example, the fact that many stores do not accept $50 or larger bills for payment is probably because those bills are more likely to be counterfeit and perhaps more likely to be stolen by employees, thus making the cost of accepting large bills significantly higher than the cost of accepting smaller bills. Another example is the difference in check acceptance policies. In many small towns, checks are commonly used because everyone knows one another and the risk of fraud is negligible. In many inner-city neighborhoods, it is almost impossible to find a store that accepts checks because of concerns about bad checks. Many supermarkets accept checks only from consumers who have applied for and received check-writing privileges because the stores believe the cost of accepting those checks is sufficiently low.

No Man Is an Island

We have described so far a simple version of the factors you are likely to consider in deciding whether to take a particular payment method at your hardware store. But the benefits and costs of taking cards also depend closely on what other merchants choose to do. If a Japanese tourist wants to buy a tool belt, cannot find another hardware store in Fargo that takes his JCB card, and has cash, you do not have much motivation for letting him pay with the more expensive (to you) plastic. On the other hand, if being the only JCB merchant in town guarantees that all Japanese tourists will flock to you and Fargo has a significant number of Japanese tourists, maybe you will take JCB, especially since your local customers don't have JCB cards, so they won't switch from cash to JCB. In either case, this means that your decision to take the JCB card depends primarily on the decision of all other hardware stores in Fargo whether to take the card.

Based on our Japanese tourist example, we can divide potential card users into two groups: "incremental" and "switcher" customers. (This categorization is oversimplified but useful.) The incremental customers buy only from stores that accept cards. The switcher customers do not base their choice of stores on whether cards are accepted but use their cards if the store they choose happens to take cards. Incremental customers increase the value of card acceptance and switcher customers decrease the value of card acceptance. Let's now consider how your decision to accept cards depends on your competitors.

Suppose, as a simple example, there are 10,000 incremental consumers who want to use credit cards for payment at the ten hardware stores (including yours) in Fargo. If all the other hardware stores take credit cards, then you would get 1,000 additional customers, on average, from credit acceptance. You weigh this against the costs imposed by your switcher customers, who would otherwise use, say, cash. In addition, there are the fixed costs of taking cards. If the profits on sales to the additional 1,000 customers are sufficient to offset the costs of credit acceptance, then all of the hardware stores will decide to take credit. This is the case in many merchant segments as of the late 1990s.

Suppose, however, that profits from the 1,000 additional customers do not cover the extra payment costs. Then some merchants will not accept credit. But as the number of hardware stores that do not take the credit card increases, the volume of incremental sales rises for those that do. If, for example, only five of the hardware stores take credit, then they split the 10,000 customers among themselves and receive 2,000 additional customers each. If only one hardware store takes credit, then it gets all 10,000 additional customers itself in our admittedly simple example. Even if it would not be profitable for all ten stores to take cards, it seems likely that at least one might find it worthwhile to be the store that does. (In our example, we are treating all hardware stores as identical, so it is difficult to determine which ones in particular would decline credit. In reality, differences in payment-processing costs among hardware stores as well as differences in the importance of credit to their customers are important in determining which stores will accept credit.)

Our example might suggest to you that if all of your competitors take cards, then card acceptance is less valuable to you than if none of them did. And you would be correct that if everyone takes cards, there is more competition for the incremental customers. But there is one important consideration left. The fact that all of your competitors take cards suggests that, based on their experience, they have decided that profits from incremental customers in the hardware business are more important than costs imposed by switchers. If everyone takes cards, it is probably profitable for you to do so as well, unless, of course, you would do substantially less well with incremental customers than your competitors.

There is also a dynamic aspect of competition among merchants. Suppose you choose to become the first hardware store in Fargo to accept cards. Perhaps customers did not seriously consider the possibility of using credit cards to buy hardware prior to your decision. But after you started to take cards, customers started to get used to the idea and perhaps came to expect that they could use cards at hardware stores. Customers that were initially switchers, or would not even have used cards at all, might begin to behave more like incremental customers. They might ask your competitor why she, unlike you, does not accept cards. Purchasing habits and expectations might change so that most if not all hardware stores would end up accepting cards. Thus some merchant categories have shifted fairly quickly from a situation in which few merchants took cards to one in which most merchants took cards, although decreases in interchange fees and merchant discounts have driven some of these shifts.

For some merchant types, the value of credit acceptance is on balance so great that all stores accept credit. And, in fact, credit acceptance is nearly universal in most merchant categories. On the other hand, a few merchant categories, mostly ones such as convenience stores or fast food restaurants where transaction amounts are small and speed is important, have little or no credit card acceptance.

More and More Merchants Take Payment Cards

Over time the benefits to merchants of taking payment cards have increased and the costs have decreased. As a result, payment cards have spread from one merchant to another and from one type of merchant to another. Nevertheless, all payment cards (including store cards) accounted for only 23 percent of the dollar value of consumer payments for goods and services in 1996.

Changes in the Costs and Benefits of Accepting Payment Cards

Several forces have decreased the costs to merchants of taking payment cards and increased the benefits. The cost of authorizing and settling payment card transactions has declined as a result of decreases in the costs of telecommunications and computer processing. Following the breakup of AT&T in the mid-1980s, the Consumer Price Index (CPI) for interstate toll calls declined by 25 percent from 1984 to 1998. The price of computer processing has declined with the rapid technological development in computing. The CPI for information processing was cut in half from 1990 to 1998, and the Producer Price Index (PPI) for computers decreased by 66 percent over the same period.

It is easy to forget how cumbersome credit cards used to be. Suppose you were a consumer trying to use your BankAmericard in the late 1960s. Let's say you found a BankAmericard merchant—they weren't that common then, particularly outside California—and found something you wanted to buy. If it was inexpensive it would be below the floor limit, which meant the merchant would not need to call for authorization. The merchant would still have to look up your card in a thick bulletin of stolen or fraudulent cards. If you were buying something over the floor limit, the merchant would have to call to get the transaction approved. Remember, the merchant was guaranteed payment, but only if he followed all the BankAmericard procedures. Calling for authorization in those days meant actually calling up BankAmericard, being connected to the issuer, and getting approval. If it was late in the day you might be out of luck if your issuer's authorization center had closed.

It wasn't that easy for the merchant to get paid either. You signed a paper slip on which your card had been imprinted. These slips were consolidated by hand and sent to the acquirer. The acquirer then sorted these slips manually. BankAmericard in those days had about eighty issuer "endpoints" to which card slips were sent to be distributed to issuers, so slips were sorted into up to eighty piles to be mailed separately. Some banks used expensive mainframe computers to help keep track of the slips and to do some of the basic accounting. When the issuers received the slips, they would have to enter the information to bill their cardholders and to pay the acquirers into their accounting systems. Such a transaction-processing system was naturally prone to both errors and fraud.

Beginning in the early 1970s, the payment card systems invested in developing electronic systems for authorization and settlement. Over the next two decades, the development of these systems involved installing computers and developing software that could assist with authorization and settlement. It also entailed encouraging merchants to install electronic card readers that could read the relevant card and transaction information and send this information over telephone lines to a series of computer switches and computer processors. The reduction in telecommunication and computer processing costs during the 1990s has helped reduce the fees that merchants incur for payment card transactions (more on this below). It has also reduced the time it takes to process a transaction, and this has therefore decreased the amount of time store clerks need to spend on this chore and made paying with plastic more convenient for consumers.

Technological improvements in communications, processing equipment, and computer processing speed have also enabled acquirers and third-party processors to realize scale economies in processing transactions. Unlike the issuing side of the business, which consists of thousands of competing members with no one firm holding a dominant share, high concentration has come to characterize the acquiring business. This consolidation has driven costs down and resulted in an acquiring business in which participants make razor-thin margins but on high volumes of business. Scale economies in processing, reductions in computer and communications costs, and technological improvements in processing equipment and procedures has resulted in sharp reductions in merchant discounts over time.

Comprehensive data on merchant discounts over time are not available. However, it is possible to document the decline in several ways. When Diners Club was first introduced, its merchant discount was 7 percent. The entry of American Express almost a decade later helped reduce the merchant discount to 5 percent for most merchants. By 1991, the American Express merchant discount was 3.25 percent, compared to just below 2 percent for MasterCard and Visa and 1.6 percent for Discover. As of 1998, a typical merchant pays a merchant discount of nearly 2.75 percent for American Express, about 1.8 percent for MasterCard and Visa, and 1.6 percent for Discover. (The merchant discounts for on-line debit cards are considerably lower, as discussed in chapter 12.)

Figure 6.2 shows the average merchant discount on Visa transactions minus the interchange fee. This *net* merchant discount is the average increment charged by Visa acquirers on Visa transactions. The sharp decline in figure 6.2 reflects increases in processing efficiency. It does not reflect decreases in costs the merchant bears in processing transactions, which have almost certainly occurred.

The percentage cost to merchants of accepting payment cards has declined absolutely over time. It has also probably fallen relative to the cost of taking alternative forms of payment. Although the development of electronic cash-counting machines and improved cash registers has reduced the cost of taking and processing cash transactions somewhat, cash affords limited opportunities for computer-based or communications-based improvements in processing. Check processing has improved over time as a result of the developments described in chapter 2, but as with cash, the nature of the beast limits what computers and high-speed data links can do.

Finally, the benefits to merchants of taking payment cards have increased dramatically over time. More and more consumers have at least

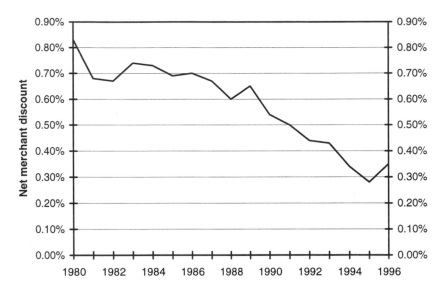

Figure 6.2
The net merchant discount rate for Visa transactions has declined sharply over time.
Source: Visa U.S.A.
Note: Net merchant discount is the merchant discount rate net of the interchange fee.

one payment card, and many consumers like to pay with their charge, credit, or debit cards. Merchants can make more sales by catering to consumer demand for paying with plastic. As more merchants have recognized this opportunity for increased sales, other merchants have recognized that their failure to compete in this dimension will cost them sales. Payment card acceptance has grown organically as payment cards have become more valuable to consumers and merchants alike.

The Growth of Merchant Acceptance
During the 1950s, acceptance of charge cards spread to restaurants, hotels, and other travel and entertainment-type businesses. After the entry of American Express, tourist-oriented retail stores increasingly took charge cards. With the introduction of MasterCard and Visa in the late 1960s, more retail stores began taking bankcards. The first merchants to sign up tended to be smaller: the big merchants had their own store card

"We now take three major credit cards."

programs and viewed the bankcards as competitors for that business. The small merchants, however, often saw the bankcard systems as a blessing, especially if they had tried to run their own billing systems. For a reasonable fee, the bankcard systems would guarantee payment and take the billing and collection hassles out of the hands of the merchant.

Not until 1979 did the first major nationwide department store chain, J.C. Penney, decide to accept bankcards. The major department stores were still concerned that bankcard acceptance would harm their proprietary store cards. Retailers felt that store cards were an important tool in maintaining customer loyalty. But as J.C. Penney's CEO said, "[w]e recognized that we had 15 million active accounts, while all Visa members have 35 million active accounts. . . . It seems logical to expect that a good number of people who don't carry our card but who have Visa accounts would use Visa cards in our stores if they had the chance."

Some department stores, such as Montgomery Ward, followed J.C. Penney's example but by the mid-1980s there were still major stores that did not accept bankcards. In particular, many of the more upscale retailers, such as Bloomingdale's and Macy's, accepted American Express because it was perceived as a prestige card but were uncertain about the value of bankcard acceptance. In 1986, Visa and MasterCard aimed marketing campaigns at the thirty top department stores that did not accept bankcards. Among their selling points were that acceptance would result in incremental sales and that bankcards were less expensive than American Express. By the end of 1987, fourteen of those thirty stores had signed up. And a few years later, virtually all department stores accepted bankcards.

In the 1990s, the payment card success story was their penetration into supermarkets. Discover, quickly followed by Visa and MasterCard, sought acceptance at supermarkets in the late 1980s, initially without any great success. By 1991, only about 5 percent of supermarkets accepted credit cards. In April 1991, Visa created a special interchange fee of 1.0 percent for supermarkets (compared to an average of 1.4 for other merchants) as an incentive for acquirers to sign up more supermarkets. MasterCard followed Visa's lead and announced plans to match Visa's interchange fee, effective April 1992. Discover followed suit by lowering its discount rates to supermarkets. American Express also began a sales effort directed toward supermarkets and significantly lowered its discount rates to supermarkets. In the next few years, the dam broke. Nearly 70 percent of supermarkets accepted bankcards by 1996, and well over 90 percent accepted them two years later. Even American Express rapidly increased its acceptance at supermarkets, from about 25 percent in 1995 to about 60 percent in 1997.

Why did supermarkets demonstrate almost herdlike behavior in taking payment cards in the 1990s? The price was right: the lower merchant discounts certainly helped persuade these low-margin businesses to take plastic. But it is also instructive to consider the sales pitches that all of the payment card systems were making to supermarkets. The systems made three important arguments, and they all tie in to our earlier discussion of choice of payment methods. First, they asserted that credit acceptance would bring incremental sales, due either to consumers buying

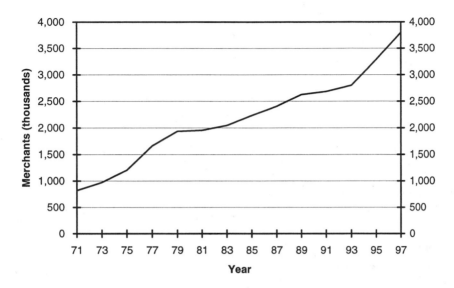

Figure 6.3
The number of Visa merchant locations quadrupled between 1971 and 1997.
Source: Visa U.S.A.

goods at supermarkets that they might buy at other types of stores that accepted credit or, as more and more supermarkets accepted credit, supermarkets that declined to accept credit would lose customers that wanted to use credit. Second, the systems asserted that credit acceptance would generate a "higher-margin basket mix." Some surveys suggested that purchases by credit customers contained a larger mix of higher-margin sales such as health and beauty products. So, the card systems argued, supermarkets would both get incremental sales and make a higher profit on those sales. Finally, the systems asserted that credit was really pretty quick to use at the checkout lane. One study found that credit was faster than checks but slower than cash. This, the card systems argued, in combination with the lower merchant discounts meant that card acceptance was really not that costly.

The number of merchants that take at least one payment card has increased over time. But as the above chronology suggests, growth has occurred in fits and spurts. Figure 6.3 shows the number of merchant locations accepting Visa cards over time. The number of MasterCard merchants, at least since duality began in 1975, has been virtually the same as for Visa. From 1981 to 1997, the bankcard systems nearly doubled their merchant base, but this growth was clearly not uniform over the period. After the merchant base more than doubled during the 1970s, growth slowed significantly as fewer of the most obvious merchant segments were left to sign up. However, as the systems turned to ISOs, which signed up a lot of smaller merchants, and with the rapid expansion of cards into supermarkets, there was a sharp upturn in merchant growth in the 1990s.

Discover, which started operations in 1985, had by the end of 1987 signed up 730,000 merchants to accept its cards. Ten years later more than 3 million merchants accepted the Novus line of cards in which Discover was the primary brand. Whereas Discover resisted the temptation to use ISOs for signing up merchants longer than the other systems, American Express in 1994 began entering into partnerships with third-party service providers to remain competitive with the bankcards. At its inception in 1958, American Express claimed 17,500 merchant locations, which grew to more than 80,000 within the first four years of the card. In 1994, when it had 1.4 million domestic locations, American Express stopped officially reporting its merchant location data. As its market share languished during the early 1990s, American Express realized it needed to expand its merchant base drastically, but it also realized the costs of hiring an extra thousand employees solely for that purpose. Thus, the company turned to ISOs and other third-party acquirers. By 1997, American Express' External Sales Agent (ESA) program was responsible for signing up nearly 70 percent of its new merchants added each year. The number of merchant accounts added annually to the American Express merchant base increased from 50,000 to 400,000 after the creation of the ESA program. At the same time, American Express began to diversify its merchant base away from its strong focus on travel and entertainment merchants to other categories such as supermarkets, gas stations, and other "lowbrow" merchants. From 1995 to 1997, American Express more than doubled its merchant coverage at supermarkets, and from 1991 to 1998 the company increased the percentage of its cardholders' general-purpose plastic spending that its merchants could accommodate from 73 to 95 percent.

By 1996, payment cards had established themselves as an essential payment mechanism among most merchant segments. At gas stations, more than 35 percent of the dollar value of transactions took place using credit cards, and debit cards accounted for another 7 percent of volume. At apparel shops, department stores, electronics outlets, and many other retailers, credit cards had become the dominant form of payment.

Most consumers now have access to payment cards that provide them with a convenient payment method, a means of reducing the amount of cash and checking account balances, and an easy way to borrow money. Most merchants also have access to payment cards that enable them to offer a convenient device that consumers want and to avoid the cost of providing loans to consumers. To create these conveniences, the payment card industry has had to solve some difficult economic problems. Indeed, although the peculiar nature of banking and checking in this country has profoundly influenced the evolution of the payment card industry, many of the institutional arrangements developed over the past fifty years have been in response to fundamental economic conundrums that beset this industry. Some of these arrangements were needed to solve the chicken-and-egg problem—or what economists refer to as "positive network externalities." Others were needed to minimize the costs of coordinating business dealings between a large number of players—what economists call "transactions costs."

7

Chickens, Eggs, and Other Economic Conundrums

A successful credit card program requires the participation of . . . thousands of store owners, who have to be recruited with the promise that there will be enough cardholders to make accepting the card . . . worth their while. At the same time the bank is recruiting merchants, though, it must also recruit cardholders—promising them that there will be enough merchants signed up to make carrying the card worth *their* while. It was a chicken-and-egg dilemma. Which came first, the customers or the merchants?
—Joseph Nocera, *A Piece of the Action*

Your payment card is simple to use, but that simplicity required the solution of complex technical and economic problems. When you use your MasterCard or Visa card, the activities of several participants in the marketplace have to be coordinated to complete your transaction, even though some of these market participants may be direct competitors in important respects. These participants usually include the bank that issued your card, the merchant, the bank that services the merchant, a third-party processor that handles the paperwork, and the card system that has its logo on your card. These entities are all parts of a payment card "network."

Payment card networks have a combination of economic characteristics that separate them from other industries, even other industries based on networks. This has posed interesting problems for industry participants, who have in turn responded with novel solutions. In this chapter, we lay a foundation for our later analysis by discussing four key economic characteristics of the payment card industry.

First, the last card you used is different from all the others in your wallet and from at least some cards that your friends have. Payment cards offer many combinations of features; some issuers provide a wide range themselves. Citibank alone has six different cards that you can apply for over the Internet. As in many industries, competing payment card products differ in significant respects, and nonprice competition is critical: the industry exhibits "product differentiation."

Second, as we noted above, payment cards are provided through a network industry in which participants are linked economically in unusual ways. Payment cards are useless to consumers unless merchants accept them, but merchants have no reason to accept cards unless consumers carry them and want to use them. This poses a chicken-and-egg problem for any payment card system, as we have discussed in earlier chapters. The problem is more complex for multiparty systems: when a bank persuades a merchant to accept MasterCard, for instance, it benefits other banks' MasterCard customers as well as its own.

Third, at least one of your cards probably has either the MasterCard or Visa logo on it. That means that the card issuer belongs to one of these two joint ventures. Although joint ventures in general are becoming more prevalent and important, especially in technology-intensive industries, the size and scope of the MasterCard and Visa not-for-profit joint ventures make the payment card industry unique. And the unique aspects of these joint ventures have, in turn, posed interesting and difficult management problems.

And fourth, some payment cards are charge cards and others are credit cards. Charge cards have two sources of revenue: cardholder fees and merchant fees. Credit cards have those same two sources of revenue plus a third source: finance charges when cardholders carry unpaid balances. The extra pricing flexibility provided by this third revenue source for credit card issuers has posed a major challenge to charge card issuers in the United States.

Product Differentiation

One bushel of red #2 winter wheat is just like another, as are two truckloads of sulfuric acid. In markets like these, no buyer is willing to pay a premium for the output of any individual seller, so that all products sell for the same price, and competition is all about price and cost. Economists say these are markets for "homogeneous" products; the business management literature tends to call them "commodity" markets.

On the other hand, you probably cannot name even two restaurants that are exactly alike, particularly when you take into account differences in location. Nobody thinks automobiles are homogenous products either. In markets like these, prices of competing products can differ somewhat because buyers do have preferences, and advertising, location, product design, and research are often important dimensions of competition. In these markets, we say that products are "differentiated."

Prevalence and Importance
A little reflection reveals that markets in which products are perfectly homogeneous are rare. In most consumer markets, in particular, buyers do not consider all competitors' products to be identical. A quick trip to the supermarket reveals that packages of such apparently standardized products as baking soda, salt, sugar, and flour are carefully labeled so that buyers can identify the producer. And different producers charge different prices at least some of the time. On the other hand, there is a visible difference between the flour section and the breakfast cereal aisle. Along the cereal aisle, many different brand names are displayed on boxes stressing unique features ranging from oddly shaped marshmallow bits for the young at heart to high fiber for those with a more mature outlook on things. Many of these brands are heavily advertised, particularly on Saturday mornings. An economist might be justified in ignoring product differentiation in baking soda, salt, sugar, and flour, but ignoring the important product differentiation in breakfast cereals would miss the essence of the business.

At first blush, these distinctions might seem irrelevant to the payment card industry. After all, all payment cards permit the user to buy something and to avoid paying for it for at least a few days. And all credit cards make it possible to borrow on the spur of the moment to finance a purchase. This sounds a lot more like salt than like cereal, suggesting that the payment card market does not have important product differentiation. That would be an easy assumption to make, but it would be wrong.

In fact, a closer look at the payment card industry reveals a great deal of heterogeneity among consumers and issuers. And this heterogeneity generates important product differentiation. Differences in consumers' demands for credit are an important source of heterogeneity. Some consumers use their payment cards mainly as a convenient substitute for cash and checks; they write one check at the end of each month instead of many during the month and always pay their card bills in full. In the industry, these people are called "transactors" or "convenience users." Others use payment cards as an important source of credit, permitting them to take out an instant loan when they encounter something expensive they want to buy or a trip they want to take. These consumers are called "revolvers." Revolvers pay finance charges; transactors do not.

Not all consumers can be neatly classified as either transactors or revolvers, of course. Some consumers may behave like transactors for some groups of purchases and revolvers for others. For example, many consumers have both transaction-oriented cards (e.g., the American Express Green Card) and finance-oriented cards (e.g., credit cards with low interest rates). Also, some American Express cards carry a companion line of credit that the cardholders can draw upon to spread payments over time. Nonetheless, the transactor/revolver classification is useful.

The transactor/revolver dimension is not the only one along which consumers differ, of course. Some consumers are willing to pay an annual fee for a card that permits them to earn frequent flyer miles, whereas others particularly enjoy using cards with the logos of their favorite college or pro sports team. Some regularly use their cards to obtain cash advances; others never do so. Similar differences exist with respect to all the many features that payment cards provide (or elect not to) and the many sorts of fees that they impose (or elect not to).

On the other side of the market, some banks issue cards primarily as a service to their depositors; others market aggressively on a national basis and try to segment the markets by offering a range of products, each tailored to a different set of interests. Table 7.1 shows differences between a sample of "typical" programs for top issuers as of January 1998. Many of these specific cards may no longer exist by the time you read this, but there will likely be other, similarly diverse offerings available. Some card products are aimed at transactors and thus must rely heavily on annual fees (because transactors generate little or no income from finance charges), whereas other products are aimed at revolvers and can waive annual fees entirely (because finance charges provide sufficient revenue).

A few of the other dimensions along which payment cards differ are the following:

- method of calculating interest charges
- amount of credit provided
- service fees
- interest rates
- special card features

We discuss each in turn.

Method of Calculating Interest Charges   Methods used to calculate interest charges vary substantially from one card program to another. The most important areas of variation include the length of the grace period, the method for calculating the outstanding balance, the type of compounding used for calculating finance charges, and the way the effective date of a transaction is defined.

To illustrate, it is useful to compare the Discover Card with the Citibank Visa card. A Discover cardholder who charges less than $1,000 in annual purchases has a fixed rate of 19.9 percent, whereas a cardholder who charges more than $1,000 annually has a fixed rate of 17.5 percent. The Citibank card, on the other hand, charges a variable rate equivalent to the prime rate plus 9.4 percent (17.9 percent total as of August 1998). Both cards increase their interest rates if accounts fail to remain "in good standing," to 21.9 percent for Citibank and 22.5 percent for Discover. Though grace periods can vary significantly in the marketplace, both these cards offer grace periods of approximately 25 days for repayment of balances for purchases. This means cardholders have a minimum of 25 days between receiving a bill and paying off the balance or some portion thereof before interest is charged on the average daily balance, unless the balance was not paid in full the previous month.

Citibank and Discover differ dramatically in how they compute interest on outstanding balances. Citibank calculates interest charges based on its cardholder's average daily balance and applies a monthly periodic interest rate, whereas Discover uses what is known as a "two-cycle average daily

Table 7.1
Payment cards characteristics varied across issuers in 1998.

Company	Special card name	Interest rate	Grace period (days)	Annual fee	Late fee	Over-limit fee	Cash advance fee
Citibank		Pring + 9.4%	20–25	0	$25	$25	2.5%, $2 min.
MBNA		15.90%	25	0	$20	$20	2%, $2 min.
Chase Manhattan	Wal-Mart MasterCard	14.48%	25	0	$25	$25	3%, $3 min.
First USA	National Audubon Society Visa	13.99%	25	0	$20	$20	2%, $10 min.
Wachovia Bank	Prime for Life	Prime rate	20	$88	$24	$24	4%, $3 min.
Household Bank	GM Card	Prime + 10.4%	25	0	$25	$25	3%, $3 min.
First Chicago NBD		Prime + 7.9%	20–25	0	$20	$20	2.5%, $2.50 min.
AT&T Universal		10.3% + 5-day average of 30-day rate for commercial paper	25	0	$20	$20	2%, $2 min., $20 max.
Advanta		Depending on invitation, 12–18%	0	0	$25	$25	4%
Capital One		The greater of LIBOR + 10.18% or 15.9%	25	0 if a balance is transferred, otherwise $20	$25 max.	$25 max.	2.5%, $2.50 min.
Bank of America	America West FlightFund Visa	Prime + 9.9%	21	$45	$20	$20	3%, $2 min.
Banc One		14.99%	25	0	$20	$20	2%, $2 min., $20 max.

NationsBank		Prime + 2.9%	20–30	$19 if card used 3 or more times/yr. and have additional relationship account w/ NationsBank, otherwise $39	$20	$20	2.5%, $2.50 min.
		Prime + 5.9%	20–30	0 if card is used 3 or more times/yr. and have NationsBank checking account, otherwise $19	$20	$20	2.5%, $2.50 min.
		Prime + 9.9%	20–30	0 if use card 3 or more times/yr., otherwise $19	$20	$20	2.5%, $2.50 min.
First Union National		Prime + 5.9%	25	0	$29	$29	2.95%, $2.95 min.
Wells Fargo		Prime + 11.55%	20–25	0 first year, thereafter $18	$25	$25	3%, $3 min.
Bank of New York	Gold Visa	13.49% if balance > $2500, 15.49% if balance < $2500	25	0	$29	$29	3%, $3 min.
Chevy Chase Bank	Standard	18.90%	25	0 first year, thereafter $28	$25	$25	3%, $4 min.
American Express Green Card		NA	NA	$55	Greater of $20 or 2.5%	No limit	2%, $2.50 min. with Express Cash enrollment
Discover		Prime + 8.9%	25	0	$20	$20	2.5%, $2 min.

Source: Company Web pages and employee quotations, January 1998.
Note: Prime rate was 8.5 percent at time of writing.

balance" method and compounds interest daily. The difference is that in addition to a cardholder's average daily balance for the current month, Discover also uses the balance on your card from the prior month to calculate your total average daily balance, if the previous month's bill was not fully paid. Citibank simply uses your average daily balance for the current month.

To see the effect of the two-cycle method, let us say a consumer spends $1,000 on her new credit card on January 1 of a particular year for which she receives a bill on January 6. On January 31, because she is short on cash, she simply sends in the minimum required payment, say $100. On February 1, the consumer spends another $1,000, but this time, at the end of February, she pays off her entire balance. What are her total interest charges over this period?

If the consumer owned a Citibank card, she would owe interest on the average daily balance during February, since that is the first billing cycle during which the full balance had not been paid. (Note that the average daily balance in February includes February charges. Some cards do not include new purchases in calculating average daily balances.) If she owned a Discover Card, however, she would not only owe interest on her average daily balance during February, but she would also owe interest for the average daily balance during January. The two-cycle method differs from the average daily balance method in that it takes into account purchases made in both the current month and the previous month if last month's balance was not paid in full. Assuming for simplicity that interest rates for both cards are identical at 18 percent, total interest accrued on a Citibank card in this example would be $28.50, but total interest accrued on a Discover Card in this example would be $44.90. (To get a monthly interest rate, 18 percent divided by 12 equals 1.5 percent. Citibank's charges are then calculated by taking 1.5 percent times $1,900, the average daily balance during February. Discover's charges include additional daily compounded interest on the average daily balance of $1,000 during January.) Compared to typical cardholder usage, this example likely exaggerates the difference in interest expense between the two methods. If average balances remain fairly constant over time, the difference in interest charges between the methods would decline.

The Amount of the Credit Line   All credit cards come with a limit on the amount that the cardholder can charge. (We discussed the reasons for this in chapter 5.) Larger credit lines increase the dollar volume of transactions that can be charged over a billing period and the total dollar amount that can be financed. All other things being equal, cards with larger credit lines are more valuable to consumers but riskier for issuers. An issuer may attempt to differentiate its card offers by extending relatively higher lines of credit than other issuers to similarly creditworthy applicants. The development of "platinum" bankcards in the mid-1990s resulted in offers of relatively higher credit lines, sometimes with promises of $100,000 credit limits. By 1998, 15 percent of households held platinum credit cards and mail offers of platinum cards accounted for more than 50 percent of all card offers. However, the "preapproved" offers for $100,000 credit lines rarely translated into actual extensions of such limits, and the average credit limit on platinum cards was only $7,800.

Service Fees   Card issuers sometimes impose service fees on their cardholders, including late fees, over-limit fees, and cash advance fees. In 1983, service fees per account for Visa and MasterCard averaged about $3 annually, and annual fees per account were about $17 (as always, in 1998 dollars). In 1989, before the entry of AT&T and other large nonbanks into issuing of Visa and MasterCard, service fees per account had risen to about $9 annually, but annual fees per account had fallen to about $15. Average service fees per account exceeded annual fees in 1993. In 1996, the relative levels of service fees and annual fees were almost mirror images of those in 1984: average service fees had grown to about $16 per year, whereas annual fees had fallen to about $4.

Service fees also tend to vary from issuer to issuer. As table 7.1 shows, late fees can range from $20 to nearly $30, and fees for cash advances may range from 2 to 4 percent of the transaction value, with minimum fees ranging from $2 to $10. As with prices in general, discussed in more detail below, service fees are adjusted both to reflect related costs (e.g., the costs of making cash advances or, more subtly, the increased default risk associated with late payments) and to help cover common costs (e.g., the costs of maintaining the computer systems).

Card Features   Many issuers offer services besides payment and credit. These services, which can be valuable for some cardholders, became increasingly popular during the early 1990s as competition for cardholders intensified. For example, Discover offers a cash-back bonus based on the volume of purchases. Some issuers offer discounts on products sold by affiliates of the card issuers (e.g., AT&T, GM, and GE). Still other issuers, such as Citibank, offer discounts on products they sell that are based on points accumulated through card use. Some issuers offer travel insurance; others reward users with frequent flyer miles. Many major cards allow the cardholder to skip a payment periodically. Other common enhancements include warranty extensions, purchase protection, price protection, collision damage on rental cars, rental discounts, travel rebates, and credit card registration. Minimum payments, the availability of cash advances, and interest charges on cash advances vary across different card plans.

Cards that provide credits for frequent flyer programs have become very popular. In 1987, Citibank offered the first card that was tied to one of the airline frequent flyer mile programs. Charges on Citibank's Advantage card gave the cardholder points in American Airlines' Advantage program. Most airlines now have one or more broadly similar affinity cards with credit card issuers. One of the more popular programs is the American Express Rewards program. Charges on the American Express card give the cardholder points that can be used on several airlines.

Affinity partnerships such as the airline miles program have become increasingly popular since the late 1980s. The American Express Delta Airlines Optima card has the largest cobranded airline program, with an estimated 2.8 million cards issued by the end of 1997. Affinity programs come in all shapes and sizes. There are Star Trek cards that have scenes from the show imprinted across the front of the card. There are cards that carry the logos of professional sports teams. There are also charity cards that contribute a small percentage of your purchases to a designated charity. While the sponsoring companies establish consumer loyalty and name recognition, consumers are able to earn rewards for card usage or to carry a card bearing a logo with which they identify.

Some Implications

The payment card industry, then, offers a variety of products, with a range of features and pricing strategies, to consumers with different tastes. In an industry like this, competition is about more than who can offer the lowest price. In fact, as we have seen, any card carries with it a whole system of prices: an annual fee (perhaps) and one or more interest rates, along with rules for when interest is charged, as well as fees for such things as late payments and cash advances. Issuers and payment card systems compete by developing and offering new features and novel packages of existing features, coupled with carefully designed pricing systems.

Because it is difficult for consumers to learn about and compare alternative card products, issuers and payment card systems spend a good deal on marketing, notably on advertising and direct-mail solicitations of prospective customers. According to one industry source, Visa spent $227 million on advertising in 1996; MasterCard, $102 million; American Express, $169 million; and Discover/Novus, $108 million. In total, the systems spent more than $600 million on advertising their cards in 1996. In addition, individual MasterCard and Visa issuers attempted to differentiate themselves through advertising. In 1996, Citibank outspent all other issuers by far, with advertising expenditures of more than $60 million.

Perhaps not all of these advertising messages provide information in any narrow sense. One could argue that you learn at least a little the first time you hear "It's Everywhere You Want to Be," "Master the Possibilities," "And They Don't Take American Express," "Membership Has Its Privileges," and "It Pays to Discover," but nobody can argue that you learn anything the hundredth time. But marketers tell us even the hundredth time helps build and reinforce a favorable brand image.

A second important feature of markets with product differentiation is that because competing products are not perfect substitutes, individual sellers have some pricing discretion, even when there are many competitors. In the textbook example of a perfect market, with absolutely no product differentiation, if a farmer tried to sell her truckload of red #2 winter wheat for even a penny above the going market price, she would not find a single interested buyer. Similarly, neither Goldman Sachs nor anybody else can sell Treasury bills for even a tiny fraction of a penny above their going market price.

On the other hand, ice cream shops in Cambridge, Massachusetts, can raise prices a bit without losing all their customers, even though there are many places in Cambridge to buy ice cream and competition for the business of Harvard and MIT students is intense. The key is that ice cream shops differ in location, selection, service, and a host of other ways, and customers' locations and tastes also differ. Most ice cream gourmets would not boycott their favorite vendor to save a few pennies, particularly if it meant walking several blocks. Credit card issuers are more like ice cream stores in Cambridge than like wheat farmers or Treasury-bill dealers: if a bank raised its late-payment fee by a few percent, for instance, it would likely retain most of its customers.

A final important feature of markets with product differentiation is that at any given time, no matter how intense competition is, some sellers may be receiving supracompetitive profits—profits higher than could be earned on average by investing in other businesses with the same risk. When competition is intense, such profits are the returns on innovation in features, operations, or marketing that competitors cannot immediately imitate. The restaurant business offers a good example. Competition in this business is intense in most large cities, but at any one time a few restaurants are always fully booked well in advance. Why are those restaurants doing so well while others fail? Generally because they offer something to consumers—such as exceptional service, an elegant ambiance, an extensive wine list, or simply well-prepared food—that competitors, for some reason, cannot immediately imitate. Over time, however, it becomes easier to imitate or even surpass, and profits of this sort become harder to sustain. The turnover in leading payment card issuers, discussed further in chapter 9, suggests that any supracompetitive profits in this industry are of this same sort.

Although some of these departures from the ideal of perfect competition that many of us learned in Econ 101 may seem odd, they are not signals that anything is amiss. Product differentiation arises in the payment card industry and in many others because competing sellers work hard to tailor their offerings to appeal to differences in tastes, not because something evil is going on. Because their tastes differ, consumers would almost certainly be less well served if there were only a single flavor of payment card and all competition focused on price.

Economics of Network Industries

Many industries are based on networks: collections of nodes and links between these nodes. Graduates of the MBA program at MIT's Sloan School form a social network: each graduate is a node, and these nodes are linked by correspondence and conversations. The telephone system is a huge network. Each telephone (and customer) is a node, and telephone wires and switches connect these nodes. And the payment card system is a network. The nodes consist of the cardholders, the merchants who take the cards, and the entities that issue the cards and acquire transactions. The nodes are linked through wires (generally telephone lines), switching devices, and the postal service.

Network industries often share an interesting and important economic property: consumers of their outputs benefit when an increasing number of other consumers also use these products. E-mail over the Internet is more valuable the more people who can receive and send it. Similarly, your Visa card is more valuable to you the more merchants accept it; accepting Visa cards is more attractive to a merchant the more consumers carry them.

Basic Concepts of Network Economics

The existence of a "network externality" (or "spillover") is the first and most important characteristic of any network industry, including the payment card industry. There is a network externality when the value existing users get from the network increases when another user joins the network. The new user therefore has an effect that is "external" to her. That effect can arise *directly* from increasing the size of the network. For example, if Mr. Jones may at some point want to e-mail a document to Ms. Smith, then Mr. Jones benefits when Ms. Smith gets access to the Internet. The same is true for telephones, communications software, fax machines, and other networks that people use to communicate with one another.

Network externalities can also arise *indirectly*. That happens when additional network users spur the demand for complementary products. If more people buy VHS VCRs, for instance, more video stores will carry VHS tapes. And if more people carry Discover Cards, more merchants will take Discover Cards. Discover Cards will become more valuable to both cardholders and to merchants.

This indirect network externality creates the classic and important chicken-and-egg problem for the payment card industry. Merchants are reluctant to accept a card that consumers do not carry and use, and consumers are reluctant to carry (and cannot use) a card that merchants do not accept. A payment card system can survive only if it has a critical mass of both cardholders and merchants. The problem is even more complicated for the bankcard associations: if Bank A issues more Visa cards, the merchant customers of Bank B will be made better off, and Bank B will benefit.

Network externalities result in "increasing returns" in consumption. The more customers a network gets, the more valuable the network becomes on average to each customer because of direct or indirect externalities. To some extent, that is true in many industries: a Diet Pepsi lover benefits when more people drink Diet Pepsi because more soda machines will stock Diet Pepsi. The difference is quantitative: a defining characteristic of network industries, in the sense we are using the term here, is that increasing returns are important enough to determine industry structure and market behavior fundamentally. Increasing returns in consumption have profoundly influenced the payment card industry, but not the diet soda industry. In the economics literature, "network externalities" and "increasing returns" are sometimes used almost interchangeably. It is useful, however, to distinguish between the technological attribute of industries that make them a network (network externalities) and the consequence of those externalities (increasing returns).

Increasing returns are closely related to a third key concept, "positive feedback." The more customers a network gets, the more attractive that network becomes to other customers. That makes it easier for the network to attract another customer. That customer makes it even easier for the network to attract the next customer, and so on. Positive feedback is especially important on the merchant side of the payment card industry.

As more consumers have a particular card brand and more merchants take that card brand, it becomes harder and harder for other merchants not to take that card brand. Merchants risk losing sales to consumers who want to use that card brand and can easily do so with competing merchants.

Obviously, if increasing returns are important at all network sizes, a network becomes most valuable when everyone has joined it. Even when network externalities are exhausted at smaller network sizes, network industries tend to have only a handful of competing networks. There is only one network of fax machines, all conforming to standards that enable them to communicate with each other. There is only one Internet. There are four important payment card networks in the United States, but all are compatible with point-of-sale card readers that conform to a common standard. When network externalities are important, multiple networks that do not interconnect can survive only if they are offering consumers substantially different services. In the case of payment cards, multiple networks exist in part because these networks offer consumers and merchants somewhat different products.

Business Behavior and Public Policy

The economics literature has highlighted a number of particular problems that firms in network industries face. Some of the efficient solutions to those problems have historically raised antitrust concerns.

It is generally appropriate, for instance, to worry that cooperation between competitors may reduce competition without providing offsetting efficiency gains. In network industries, however, the probability that cooperation will yield efficiency gains is higher than in most other sectors. Joint ventures and other business alliances are often very useful in network industries. Providing network services often requires more capital and expertise than any single firm has, and joint ventures may facilitate vital cooperation. Joint ventures can permit competition and innovation in areas important to consumers but not essential to the cooperation needed for the joint-venture members to interact with each other.

Without cooperation through joint ventures, U.S. banks, which have only recently been able to operate across state lines, would have encountered substantial difficulties in establishing national (let alone international) payment card systems to challenge Diners Club. Over time, Visa and MasterCard have negotiated complex rules for processing transactions that allow them to offer services competitive with the proprietary systems of American Express and Discover. The bankcard systems clearly could not function without extensive cooperation among firms that compete vigorously along a range of dimensions, but the value of cooperation in this case plainly does not imply that all possible forms of cooperation should always be permitted in network industries. (We return to this subject in chapter 11, in which we discuss the application of the antitrust laws to the bankcard associations.)

In one important respect, many network industries are like public utilities: often their fixed costs are a large proportion of their total costs. For public utilities, fixed costs are often the costs of owning and maintaining expensive fixed assets. A payment card network has several sources of fixed costs. First, it obviously needs to build and maintain the infrastructure to process transactions, which includes the physical electronic system as well as the set of rules and regulations governing members. In addition, a successful general-purpose payment card system likely needs to be national in scope. This necessitates a considerable investment in advertising and promotion to develop a brand name. Individual system members also incur considerable costs in building a merchant base and a cardholder base, both of which are essential. For example, in the mid-1990s it cost banks about $53 on average to sign up a cardholder. The existence of joint ventures in the payment card industry helps limit the duplication of network fixed costs.

The fact that many modern network industries are undergoing rapid technological change further complicates how we analyze these industries for antitrust purposes. Especially in their early stages, network industries can be chaotic and dangerous places for firms. Missteps early on can be fatal. And since only a few competing networks, and perhaps only a few competing firms, may survive, because of increasing returns, the stakes can be enormous. It is not surprising to see very aggressive competition early on in network industries, since the only way to solve the chicken-and-egg problem is to invest heavily in market penetration. Competitors in network industries may rationally sell below cost for a substantial period, hoping to "make it up on the volume" later on. The difficult early years of the payment card industry, which we discussed in chapter 4, illustrate this practice well. Many of the early entrants into this business lost substantial amounts of money and exited quickly. Moreover, even the firms that eventually became successful in the payment card industry experienced difficult times in the industry's early years. American Express almost sold its card operations in the early 1960s (see the next chapter for more details), and Bank of America was essentially forced to relinquish its hold on the BankAmericard that it had founded.

In network industries, as in industries with important scale or learning economies, we also tend to see temporary dominance of one or a few firms or networks. There is a temptation to think that such dominance will be permanent. But most network industries are not like manufacturing industries, in which ownership of capital-intensive capacity or key proprietary technology may give rise to long-lived dominance. As we shall see, the shares of payment card networks and individual issuers have varied considerably over time.

Just as economies of scale or scope can be exhausted at some level of firm size or output diversity, the magnitude of network externalities can decrease as a network grows and can reach zero at some point. Exhaustion of network externalities can result from congestion or from intractable management problems associated with running large, complex networks. Similarly, where national coverage of a joint venture is valuable, as in payment systems, attainment of such coverage may exhaust network economies. The natural limits on network externalities together with product differentiation explain why multiple networks can survive in the same industry. Payment cards illustrate this, as do long-distance telephony (three major carriers—AT&T, MCI, and Sprint—and many smaller ones), and wire services for news (AP, Reuters).

Some Economics of Joint Ventures

The Visa and MasterCard joint ventures are far more complex than ordinary firms in important respects. They involve thousands of independent firms, each with its own shareholders, strategic objectives, and internal management problems. In addition, each of the two associations has its own staff of employees who work for it directly and thus work indirectly for the thousands of member banks and their millions of shareholders.

Economic Roles of Joint Ventures

Joint ventures are by no means a new mode of organization. But joint ventures, along with other forms of interfirm cooperation, have become much more common in the last quarter-century. Joint ventures are organized for at least five reasons: to conduct research and development, to produce a good or service, to market a good or service through advertising and other promotional efforts, to exchange information, and to establish standards. The MasterCard and Visa joint ventures engage in all five of these activities to some degree. Both associations conduct research and development concerning technology for processing cards as well as new types of card products. Each association produces at least some of the attributes—for example, the brand name, the processing system—that characterize the payment cards its members issue. MasterCard and Visa both engage in extensive advertising and brand promotion. Both associations also collect information from members and share this and other information with members. And finally, MasterCard and Visa have both established standards (e.g., the card design, the design of terminals to read the cards) for their members.

We observe both joint ventures and single firms functioning as payment card systems. American Express and Discover, the major single-firm systems, are often referred to as "closed-loop" systems because all transaction data is captured within the system. Because a single owner has contracts with all cardholders and merchants that belong to its system, it sees and captures all of the data that flow between the cardholder and the merchant. It authorizes and settles all transactions. Figure 7.1 shows the flow of funds and information in a closed-loop system.

By contrast, the Visa and MasterCard joint ventures, known as "open-loop" systems, must transmit data among thousands of members. When the participant who signed up the cardholder differs from the participant who signed up the merchant, the transaction between the two is processed through a centralized authorization and settlement system. That system

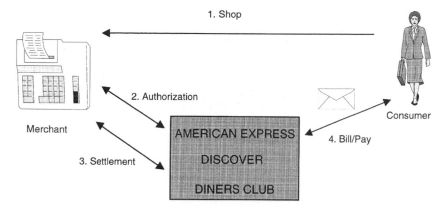

Figure 7.1
In a closed-loop system, the owner authorizes and settles all transactions.

receives the details of the transaction and transmits them to the issuer, and it executes the transfer of charges between the issuer and acquirer. Each issuer independently sets the prices (fees and finance charges) for the cards it issues, and each acquirer independently sets the prices (fees and merchant discount) for the merchants it services. The only significant price the system sets is the interchange fee, which determines how the issuer and the acquirer divide the costs and revenues of a transaction that could not have happened without both of them. (The economic role of the interchange fee is described below.) Since the acquirer has to pay the issuer an interchange fee for each transaction, that fee sets a floor under the merchant discount. Figure 7.2 shows the flow of funds and information in an open-loop system. We now consider the advantages and disadvantages of these two types of payment card systems.

Open-Loop Advantages
Banks came together in the MasterCard joint venture and later transformed the BankAmericard franchise system into the Visa joint venture because doing so offered several economic advantages. Most obviously, network externalities made wide geographic coverage valuable to payment card systems, but particularly in the industry's early years, limitations on capital availability and restrictions on the geographic scope of

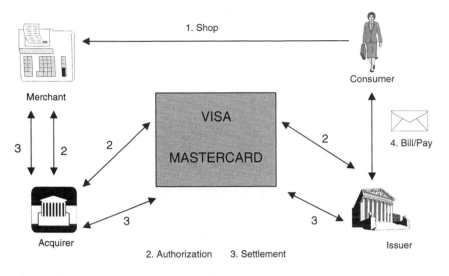

Figure 7.2
An open-loop system requires coordination among many different parties.

banks' activities made it difficult for an individual bank to obtain such coverage on its own. Although national issuers and acquirers did emerge, beginning in the 1970s, they did so only after MasterCard and Visa had become nationally recognized brands and widely accepted among merchants. Discover's entry in the mid-1980s was easier because it was easy for merchants to take another card brand on existing terminals; it would have been much harder if merchants had had to install separate equipment. On the other hand, the fact that American Express managed to build a national card brand on its own early in the industry's history suggests that it might have been possible, if not necessarily economical, for Bank of America or another large bank to have done the same.

The open-loop structure has had some other advantages as well. First, it enabled the banks involved to exploit scale economies in the development of brand images. Second, it helped the banks to pool their resources so that computer systems for handling billions of transactions annually could be developed and maintained economically. Much of the complexity of these systems, however, was necessary precisely because of the open-loop structure. Closed-loop transactions are typically just routed between the merchant and the card system, which has all of the information on the cardholder. Open-loop systems, on the other hand, need to maintain complex authorization and settlement systems.

The former BankAmericard franchise system (discussed in chapter 4) provided these last two advantages, but it lacked two other features of the open-loop systems. As we have noted, growth in any one bank's merchant or consumer base tends to benefit other banks, particularly those operating in other geographic regions. In a franchise system, a natural tension exists between the franchisees and the franchisor about who captures these benefits, whereas in a joint venture it may be possible to treat participants in a symmetric way. More generally, the joint venture form can also help reduce the transactions costs necessary for accomplishing certain business objectives. A joint venture provides an organizational form that enables the participants to use both formal and informal contracts for interacting in various dimensions. A joint venture results in an integration between the firms, along at least some business dimensions, that in turn results in informal contracts (e.g., a joint management making decisions) replacing formal contracts (e.g., a contract that dictates the actions taken and compensation received by each firm in a franchise system). In the complex, uncertain, and rapidly changing credit card business, the system of franchise contracts governing the BankAmericard enterprise proved inflexible and unworkable.

Open-loop systems can also have some advantages when it comes to system expansion. Expansion can take place whenever any of the individual members of the open-loop systems perceive profit opportunities, without any approval from centralized management. Any member of the system can implement issuer-level innovations without the need to obtain a consensus. For example, American Airlines initially approached American Express with its idea to offer an airline miles card. (The idea was—and is—that every \$1,000 charged on the card would yield the consumer some fixed number of frequent flyer miles.) In what now appears to have been a blunder, American Express decided it was not interested. American Airlines eventually partnered with Citibank to offer the first airline miles card, and it was hugely successful. The ability of each individual member of an open-loop system to develop features on its cards provides a degree of flexibility and responsiveness to market conditions that might be difficult to replicate within a closed-loop system.

Open-Loop Disadvantages

In some respects, it is amazing that the MasterCard and Visa joint ventures not only have endured but have come to play leading roles in the payment card industry. Joint ventures are relatively fragile organizations. One study estimated that 60 percent of business alliances fail. In no other major industry are large, long-lived joint ventures nearly as important as they are in payment cards.

Many of the difficulties that joint ventures face as a way to organize business activity do not exist or are less severe for fully integrated firms. Moreover, the solutions that joint ventures implement to deal with these obstacles are, by the very nature of joint ventures, often rules or regulations that have to be written down and explicitly enforced. To the extent that single firms face similar problems, they resolve them internally and, generally, much less visibly.

Divergent Objectives   Even though Visa members realize they all benefit from the existence of Visa, they are still independent entities with separate profit motives. Although Visa members would agree on the importance of making Visa a successful payment card system, they likely have different ideas about what they want Visa to do. As evidenced by Citibank's switch to MasterCard, an important area of conflict is over the relative importance of the system brand image versus the images of the member banks. After all, one of the main roles of the bankcard systems is defining the brand through advertising, promotion, and innovation. One can only imagine the debates within Visa and MasterCard over advertising and research budgets, for instance. Is money better spent on another network television campaign, for instance, or in improving fraud detection systems? Large, national issuers such as Citibank want to develop their own brand image and advertising, and they likely prefer a smaller role for Visa and MasterCard than do small, local issuers.

Another illustration of divergent interests are major cobranding agreements (for example, with organizations such as the NFL or merchants such as Wal-Mart) in which the bankcard associations sometimes pay millions of dollars for an exclusive Visa or MasterCard program. These deals directly benefit the particular bank involved and the bankcard association, but their value to other member banks is less clear. The other issuers receive some benefit from the greater success of the card brand, but the deals also put them at a competitive disadvantage relative to the banks that get the cobranding agreements.

Externalities   Open-loop members can take actions that directly impose costs and benefits on other members, such as using direct mail to sign up new cardholders or increasing efforts to sign up new merchants. Whereas some actions of this sort benefit the entire system, others would not be taken by a closed-loop system because they would be detrimental to the system as a whole. But in an open-loop system, individual members may choose to take actions that harm not only other individual members but also the system as a whole. In general, they have no reason to be concerned with the spillover or externality effects of their actions on other members and the system.

The natural objective for a joint venture as a whole is to maximize the total value that all members receive, and to that end it will want to impose rules that deter an individual firm from taking actions that are detrimental to the system as a whole, such as free-riding on others' investments, and that encourage individual members to enhance the venture's assets beyond the point at which they individually benefit. These problems do not arise to nearly the same extent for a closed-loop system, in which everyone ultimately reports to a single management team charged with maximizing profits for the firm as a whole.

It is easy to cite examples of activities that would be profitable to individual bankcard issuers but detrimental to the system involved. For instance, Visa recently faced an antitrust action from one member that wanted to issue a Visa card that would earn the cardholder points in an American Express rewards program. This card program, Visa contended, would have allowed American Express to use the Visa brand to build loyalty to its own brand and would have allowed the Visa member to gain from letting American Express free-ride on the collective efforts of all other Visa members. Visa was successful in its defense of this case. Visa has also had to bar card programs that were designed with questionable taste and that would have undermined the overall value of the Visa brand. For example, one issuer proposed a card affiliated with the Hooters chain of restaurants, which offers food served by buxom waitresses in tight, skimpy outfits. Of particular concern was the design of the card, which included an inappropriate juxtaposition of the eyes of the owl that serves as the Hooters brand symbol with certain parts of the female anatomy. Though the Hooters card might well have been successful enough with certain cardholder segments to make significant profits for the issuing bank, Visa decided it would have been detrimental to the system as a whole.

Open-loop systems also need rules that provide incentives for members to increase the value of the joint venture even when they do not individually benefit. As we discussed above, most Visa and MasterCard transactions involve a different acquiring and issuing bank. The acquirer's actions in signing up merchants and the issuer's actions in signing up cardholders have significant externality effects. Visa and MasterCard both implement an interchange fee that the acquirer pays to the issuer. The interchange fee is proportional to the size of the transaction. It varies depending on the type of merchant and the merchant's processing equipment but averaged about 1.4 percent of dollar volume in 1998. The interchange fee can be an important tool for open-loop systems in dealing with the externality problem.

One way to see how this works is to reflect on the impact of changes in interchange fees on the issuing side of the business. Since, as we show in chapter 9, competition in issuing is very intense by any measure, changes in consumer costs should also reflect changes in interchange fees. Thus, an increase in these fees will raise acquirers' costs and, accordingly, cause them to raise merchant discounts, but it will also lower issuers' costs (by providing an offsetting stream of revenue) and because of competitive pressures lead them to reduce costs to consumers. The effect of a change in interchange fees is not to increase the total cost paid by merchants and consumers together (and thus not, as some have charged, to exploit any potential monopoly power the system might have) but to allocate that total cost between merchants and consumers.

Why would a payment card system as a whole be interested in shifting costs between merchants and consumers? Start with the assumption that the system's economic value depends, roughly, on the product of the number of consumers who carry the card and the number of merchants who accept it. This assumption implies that acquirers' efforts become more valuable to the system the more successful issuers have been and vice versa. Now suppose that a system has a lot of merchants but not many cardholders. Under these conditions, raising merchants' prices somehow and lowering cardholders' will likely increase the system's value. How can this be done when issuers and acquirers price independently? Answer: by raising the interchange fee.

The same basic argument applies when one thinks about fixed costs, like issuers' advertising or, in a related context, investment in ATMs. It is reasonable to think that the value of ATM networks is more sensitive to investment in ATMs, done by acquirers, than in any marketing likely to be done by card-issuing banks. It thus makes sense that ATM systems would be interested in encouraging investment in ATMs, and they in fact use interchange fees to do this. In ATM systems, in contrast to payment card systems, interchange fees flow from issuers to acquirers.

In contrast to all this, a closed-loop system's CEO can directly maximize the system's profitability and efficiency because she, in principle, controls all prices and investment decisions. When she sets the merchant discount, for example, she can factor in that merchant discount's effect on the value of her system's card to cardholders. Discover, for example, decided it was important to enter the supermarket segment and offered lower merchant discounts to supermarkets. Visa and MasterCard, on the other hand, took more time to set a lower interchange fee for supermarket transactions, although it was effective once set. Interchange is also a much blunter instrument for taking into account the effect of merchant penetration on consumers and consumer penetration on merchants. Discover chose to offer a low, flat per-transaction fee to the Sam's Club discount stores, probably because Discover felt the special deal was necessary in this particular case. It is much more difficult for Visa and MasterCard, using the interchange fee, to create incentives for their members to make similar deals. And indeed, most Sam's Club stores do not accept Visa and MasterCard.

Another advantage of a closed-loop system is that it captures all information about all transactions because it provides both cardholder and merchant services. Although open-loop systems as a whole (inclusive of issuer and acquirer) capture the same information, the systems are structured so that the issuer and acquirer retain much of it. The acquirer captures information about the transaction and the merchant that it does not share with other members of the system, and the issuer captures information about the cardholder that it likewise does not share. Participants do not share this information because it is valuable for competing with one another. The last thing an issuer wants is to reveal information about its cardholders that would help other issuers decide which ones to target and how to appeal to them.

Their richer information resources make it easier for closed-loop systems to design and offer special promotions and targeted marketing initiatives. American Express computers maintain and update weekly a profile of 450 attributes, such as age, gender, and purchasing patterns, on every cardholder. These profiles enable American Express to send out information about home health care products, for example, only to people of a certain age and with a certain pattern of medical charges on their card. Likewise, having identified your predilection for Italian food, American Express might run a joint promotion with a new Italian restaurant in your neighborhood that offers you a free bottle of wine if you charge your dinner there with your American Express card.

Organizational Problems   In addition to externality problems, joint ventures face a range of unique organizational difficulties that have no exact counterparts in other organizational forms. First, by its very nature, a joint venture requires that all parties give up some control over portions of their operations. This is hard for any firm to do, especially if its new partners are its former, or even current, competitors. To interact successfully these firms must come to trust one another, a requirement that a 1992 *Fortune* article claimed to be the "biggest stumbling block to the success of alliances." Differences in national culture and in how business is conducted make trust particularly difficult to establish in international joint ventures.

Visa and MasterCard have faced many of these problems. This is hardly surprising with memberships including banks of different sizes, from different geographic regions, and with different strategic focuses for their card programs. Small-town bankers were initially outraged, for instance, when Citibank and others began using direct mail to "invade their territories," attempting to sign up cardholders. In the 1990s,

MasterCard attracted a disproportionate share of card programs run by non-financial firms and monoline banks, while Visa remained more identified with traditional commercial bank issuers. Among the ten largest bankcard issuers based on charge volume in 1997, six were traditional commercial banks, and the other four were either monolines or non-financial firms. Though all six traditional banks issued more Visa cards than MasterCards, three of the four monoline/nonfinancial firms (MBNA, Household, and AT&T Universal) issued primarily MasterCards.

Decision making in the open-loop systems is generally more cumbersome than in the closed-loop systems. Because members' interests do not always coincide, all have an incentive to create checks and balances to protect themselves, even though this necessarily slows the decision-making process. For example, the Visa Board of Directors has to authorize all projects costing more than $1 million. Consequently, Visa management has to obtain the board's approval for significant business initiatives. To obtain this approval, Visa management needs to build a consensus among board members that these initiatives will benefit them as well as other members. Generally, Visa management consults extensively with members, especially Board members, before proposing significant business initiatives to the Board. This approval process makes it difficult for Visa management to pursue projects that do not benefit a broad spectrum of members. For example, until recently First Bank was the only substantial issuer of Visa's Corporate Card. It was difficult for Visa management to devote significant resources to its Corporate Card program until a substantial number of other issuers became interested in it. In contrast, members of the Board of Directors at American Express do not represent competitors in the payment card industry and are concerned only with whether management decisions benefit American Express.

Interdependent Pricing

As we noted earlier in the chapter, charge card systems receive revenue from two sources: merchant fees and cardholder fees. Credit card systems receive revenue from those same two sources, but also have a third source of revenues: finance charges paid by cardholders. This additional pricing variable has proven to be important in the system wars we describe in the next chapter.

The business economics of charge and credit cards are fundamentally different. Figure 7.3 demonstrates this difference through a breakdown of revenues for the two types of systems. We see that bankcard issuers receive a bulk of their revenues from finance charges, whereas American Express receives most of its revenues from the merchant discount. In addition, card fee revenues are substantially more important for American Express than for the bankcard issuers.

If you think of charge and credit cards only as providing different, competing bundles of financial services to consumers, you might think that there is nothing special about this situation. Charge cards provide cardholders with "payment services," and credit cards also provide "lending services." (Or more precisely, by permitting the cardholder to wait longer before paying his bill, they offer a greater range of lending services.) In many markets, different firms offer distinct bundles of goods or services. Mortgage companies typically provide only mortgages, for instance, whereas banks usually provide mortgages and a host of other products. Under competition, consumers would be charged a price for each bundle that covers the long-run service-specific incremental costs of providing all services in that bundle. Firms would select bundles of services to offer based on economies of scope in production and distribution or because some consumers prefer to buy bundles of various sorts. (Loosely speaking, economies of scope arise when broadening the product line reduces per-unit costs, holding product-specific volumes constant. In contrast, economies of scale arise when increasing product-specific volumes reduces per-unit costs, holding the product line constant.) Things are not quite this simple in the payment card industry. Providing payment card services to consumers and merchants involves significant joint costs.

Figure 7.3
(a) Merchant discount fees dominate American Express' revenue.
Source: 1997 American Express Annual Report.
Note: Figures represent share of total card-related revenue.
(b) Finance charges dominate bankcard issuers' revenues.
Source: Credit Card News, April 1, 1998.
Note: Figures represent shares of issuer revenues.

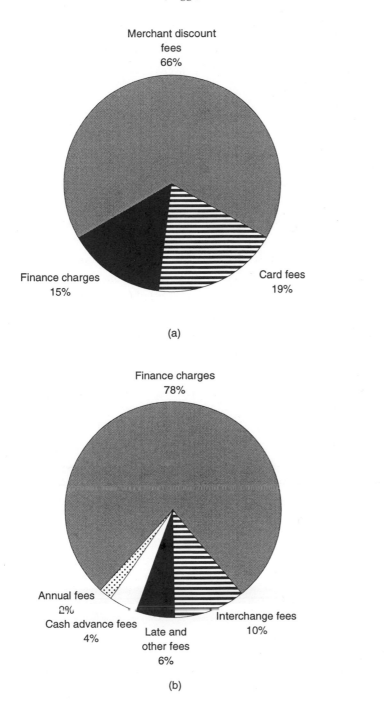

(a)

(b)

(A cost is "joint" if it is incurred for more than one product. To take the classic case, producing leather and beef involves the joint cost of raising the cattle.) To stay in business, a firm must cover its joint costs as well as its service-specific incremental costs.

To see the importance of joint costs in payment cards, consider a charge card system: the provision of credit is not an issue, and the system provides only a payment mechanism for consumers and merchants. Consumers would not want a charge card without a merchant base, and merchants would not want a charge card without a cardholder base. Therefore, in some sense, all of the costs of a charge card system are joint. For example, the cost of mailing a cardholder statement is incurred as a result of providing payment services to both the merchant and the cardholder. If the charge card system did not have to worry about what its competitors were charging, it would find it most profitable to charge higher prices to (and thus recover most of its costs from) the parties that are less sensitive to price. Merchants are arguably less price sensitive than cardholders on average.

As we discussed in chapter 6, merchants may find it profitable to accept a payment method even if it is more expensive than other payment methods as long as they gain sufficient additional sales as a result. Indeed, the merchants that account for the vast majority of all payment card charges accept all of the major card brands, even though their merchant discounts typically differ. (Though many merchants do not take American Express or some of the other cards, these merchants are typically small and collectively do not account for much volume.) And once they have accepted any one of these card brands, merchants must accept all cards bearing that brand. Consumers, on the other hand, shop among the major card brands and, even when they have multiple brands in their wallet, can substitute among the card brands as well as cash and checks. Consumers, with more substitution possibilities, are likely to be more sensitive to differences in prices among cards than merchants. Given these likely differences in price sensitivity, it is not surprising that American Express receives more than three times as much revenue from merchant discounts as from cardholder fees.

Credit card systems involve an additional layer of complexity. In addition to providing transactions services for merchants and cardholders, a credit card system also extends credit to cardholders. By making possible purchases that might otherwise be postponed or abandoned, this benefits not only the system's cardholders but also the merchants they frequent. And in addition to merchant discounts and cardholder fees, the system now has a third source of revenue: finance charges. The fact that there are two broad types of cardholders—transactors, who pay off their balances and revolvers, who tend to carry balances—makes pricing decisions more complex. Assuming that they are broadly rational, transactors should pay more attention to cardholder fees, and revolvers should pay more attention to finance charges.

For the charge card system, we argued that the costs of providing transactions services to consumers and merchants were joint, because there was really only one product. But for credit card systems, each of the two main products—the facilitation of transactions and the extension of credit—clearly could in principle be provided separately. At the same time, however, it is equally clear that credit card transactions are important in the provision of credit card loans, and that credit card loans are important in the production of many credit card transactions. Thus, the costs of providing transactions services in a credit card system are at least partly joint between those services and the extension of credit.

Credit card systems can maximize profits (and cover service-specific and joint costs) through the merchant discount (which the open-loop systems influence through the interchange fee), interest rates to cardholders, and fees to cardholders. They have chosen to collect a larger portion of their revenues from finance charges. This pattern may arise in part because of their view that the overall demand for credit is relatively insensitive to interest rates, a view supported by at least one empirical study and considerable folklore within the industry.

Now let's put the two kinds of systems together in the same marketplace. The strategy for recovering joint costs followed by credit card systems constrains the pricing of the charge card systems. The charge card systems face competition from credit card systems that can offer lower annual fees to revolvers to hold and use their cards and can offer lower discounts to merchants to accept their cards because they can recover some of their joint costs from finance revenue.

When we discuss American Express in the next chapter, we will see that American Express historically attempted to recover a large fraction of its costs from merchants, whose demand for accepting American

Express cards from the elite customers American Express had recruited was apparently relatively inelastic. This strategy began to unravel in the late 1980s for two reasons. First, the credit card companies offered lower prices to merchants and to transactors than American Express. Second, as more consumers had credit cards, the cost to merchants of declining to take American Express cards decreased. Consumers could use their credit cards instead.

This chapter has introduced several important economic aspects of the payment card business that shape both the nature of competition and the structure and operation of the two large joint ventures. On reflection, it probably is not surprising that it took the industry so long to achieve its present importance—and it probably is surprising that the Visa and MasterCard joint ventures perform as well as they do. These uniquely large joint ventures have evolved considerably over the last quarter-century. They have had to improvise and learn from their mistakes as they have grappled with a set of unique managerial and operational problems they faced.

The multilevel competition in the payment card industry, on which the next five chapters focus, also has unique elements. We first consider competition among the major card systems (American Express, Discover, MasterCard, and Visa). The competition between MasterCard and Visa is especially interesting because both systems have essentially the same members. Intense competition also takes place among the thousands of issuers of MasterCards and Visa cards even though these issuers collaborate through the bankcard associations. (Competition is also intense between acquirers and the other companies that engage in processing, but as we discussed in chapter 6, few MasterCard and Visa member banks are important players in this competition anymore.) And finally, competition is increasing among MasterCard, Visa, and many of the regional ATM networks for debit card transactions. An interesting dimension of this level of competition arises because many debit card transactions can be routed through several different networks, giving rise to efforts to persuade consumers or merchants to route transactions through a particular network.

8

System Wars

When opponents present openings, you should penetrate them immediately. Get to what they want first, subtly anticipate them. Maintain discipline and adapt to the enemy in order to determine the outcome of the war. Thus, at first you are like a maiden, so the enemy opens his door; then you are like a rabbit on the loose, so the enemy cannot keep you out.
—Sun Tzu, *The Art of War*

It started in Boston—a skirmish that turned into a rebellion that routed one of the great payment card systems. Boston was in recession in the winter of 1991. Unemployment in the metropolitan area was the highest since 1982, and personal income had fallen back to 1987 levels. In part because of defense cutbacks, the high-technology industry in Boston and the surrounding Route 128 corridor was in a slump. Housing prices had declined 24 percent since their peak in 1987. With your job at risk and your home equity sinking fast, would you dine at Jasper's, an expensive seafood restaurant near Boston's waterfront? The recession had hit Jasper's and other premier restaurants in town hard. They tried to trim expenses to stay afloat.

Some restaurants found the fees they had to pay to American Express especially irksome. Every time a patron whipped out her American Express card to pay her check, the restaurant saw an average of 3.25 percent of its revenues slip away. That is what American Express took off the top of the bill as its merchant discount. If the patron pulled out a Visa or MasterCard, the restaurant would lose only 2 percent of the check. And if she pulled out cash or a check, the restaurant would lose nothing, although it would have to handle the cash and worry about theft and losses from bad checks. Of course, the restaurant might lose some customers if it did not accept American Express. The big question was: How many customers would it lose?

In the winter of 1991, Jasper White, the owner of Jasper's, and other restaurateurs asked American Express to shave its merchant discount, just as they had gotten discounts and concessions from other suppliers. American Express refused. It is not hard to see why. Merchant fees accounted for 60 percent of its revenues from the American Express card. Shaving its merchant discount by half a percentage point would cost American Express at least $445 million annually and eliminate its charge card profits. The only way it could make up that revenue would be to raise its annual fees, but that increase could easily drive cardholders away, since the annual fee of $64 (as always, in 1998 dollars) for American Express' lowest-priced Green Card was already three times the average for Visa and MasterCard. Moreover, American Express argued that the valuable cardholders it delivered to merchants justified its merchant fee. With its "Membership Has Its Privileges" advertising campaign and other brand positioning efforts, American Express had sought to cultivate elite customers used to high spending. At the beginning of the uprising, one of American Express' marketing executives explained to a Boston interviewer, "Especially in troubled times, if there's one segment that continues to spend, it's American Express cardholders."

Perhaps they would keep spending, but they didn't have to use their American Express cards to do so. By the early 1990s, most American Express cardholders had one or more MasterCard or Visa credit cards. American Express cardholders could use those credit cards at almost all the places that took American Express charge cards, including the rebellious Boston restaurants, and many more places that did not take American Express cards because of the high merchant fees. The threat of losing high-spending American Express cardholders was less credible than it used to be. As one of the ringleaders of the Boston revolt says he put it to American Express: "You guys don't get it. This isn't the eighties anymore. Times have changed."

Visa and Discover soon took advantage of American Express' plight. Visa offered to pay any legal expenses the Boston restaurants incurred in their fight with American Express. Discover, the newest payment card system, sent a marketing team to Boston offering a merchant discount of 1.5 percent—less than half that charged by American Express—and thereby raised its merchant acceptance rate at Boston restaurants from 23 to 78 percent.

The infamous "Boston Fee Party" was underway. By April 1991, more than 250 Boston restaurants were threatening to drop the American Express card. (Only a few, including Jasper's and Biba—another upscale Boston eatery—actually dropped it, however.) Soon restaurants across the country were threatening to drop the American Express card. Although the Boston restaurateurs represented only a small fraction of the 120,000 restaurants that took the American Express card nationwide, the press was merciless. *The Boston Globe* wrote a scathing piece critiquing the elitist attitudes of American Express and its cardholders. Faced with mounting pressure, American Express relented. It announced that it would negotiate merchant discounts individually with merchants. That soon led other merchants, including Land's End and U-Haul, to seek discounts.

American Express lowered its merchant discount dramatically over the next few years. Between 1990 and 1996, its average merchant discount fell from 3.22 percent to 2.74 percent. Of course, American Express did not drop its merchant discount solely because of the rebellion in Boston. For several years, Visa's television advertisements had attacked American Express. The staccato stories of consumers paying for frolics with their Visa cards always ended with "And They Don't Take American Express." American Express was accepted in many fewer locations than Visa because of its higher merchant discount. Indeed, if you believed the Visa advertisements, anyone who dropped American Express would be in very fashionable company. American Express' share of combined charge and credit card transaction dollars had dropped from more than 24 percent when the advertisements first aired in 1985 to less than 21 percent in 1991 when the Boston Fee Party took place.

The Boston Fee Party was one of the key battles in the system wars that have raged since 1958 when American Express introduced its charge card to challenge Diners Club, then the dominant payment card. These wars have provided long-run benefits to consumers and merchants through lower prices, faster service, and enhanced features. American

Express decreased its merchant discount as a result of competition from Visa and the other systems. Visa, MasterCard, and Discover gave consumers alternatives to the American Express card for charging purchases. And they gave merchants other ways to allow American Express cardholders to charge. Visa gave consumers information that American Express cards were not as useful as Visa cards because they were not accepted at as many locations. American Express was forced to become more competitive with the other systems by lowering its merchant discount. That helped expand American Express' merchant base and made its cards more useful to its cardholders. That, in turn, placed more competitive pressure on MasterCard and Visa to stem any loss of charge volume to American Express.

Much of this happened as a result of competition among payment card *systems* rather than among payment card issuers or payment card acquirers. For American Express, Discover, and Diners Club, the issuing, acquiring, and systems functions are integrated into a single entity. When American Express makes decisions about merchant discounts, it naturally thinks about the impact of these decisions on its profits from both cardholders and merchants. Likewise for Discover and Diners Club. But the situation is fundamentally different for MasterCard and Visa. In these associations, individual members engage in issuing and acquiring, and the associations determine brand positioning, the interchange fee that helps determine merchant discounts, and system-wide innovations such as quicker transaction processing. It was advertising by the Visa *system*— not by member issuers—that caused American Express to lower its merchant discount. By lowering its merchant discount and expanding its merchant base, American Express reduced the spread in value between its cards and *all* cards issued by individual members of the MasterCard and Visa systems.

This chapter focuses on two major series of battles in the payment card industry to illustrate how systems competition affects cardholders and merchants. The first half of the chapter examines the rise of American Express, its precipitous fall, and its recent efforts to reestablish itself. Here the war is between the preeminent charge card system and the credit card systems. The second half concentrates on competition between and within MasterCard and Visa. The fact that these two systems have the

Table 8.1
Comparison of the five major credit and charge card systems, 1997.

System	System type	Entry date	Cards issued (millions)	Transaction volume ($ billions)	Merchant outlets (millions)
Closed-Loop					
American Express	Charge	1958	20.3	131.5	1.9
	Credit	1987	9.3	20.6	1.9
Novus (Discover)	Credit	1985	47.8	57.3	3.2
Diners Club	Charge	1950	1.4	9.2	1.4
Open-Loop					
Visa	Credit	1966	240.7	436.4	3.8
MasterCard	Credit	1966	164.5	248.9	3.8

Sources: The Nilson Report, nos. 663, 664; 1998 *BankCard Update*, Ram-Research.

same member-owners makes the war between them particularly interesting. Before turning to these two wars, we review the important players and discuss the key competitive weapons that these systems can wield.

Who Are the Warriors?

Five primary payment card systems have fought in the system wars. Table 8.1 shows how these systems compared in 1997, a half-century or so after Diners Club first staked out this industry. Visa was the largest with 89 million cardholders, more than 240 million credit cards issued, and $436 billion in U.S. credit card transaction volume in 1997. By the late 1990s, Diners Club had become a minor system, with only 0.6 percent as many cards issued and 2.1 percent as much transaction volume as Visa—and most Diners Club cards were corporate cards. Figure 8.1 shows how the card systems' shares have changed in recent years.

In chapter 7, we described two important dimensions along which these systems differ. First, some are open-loop systems in which a changing cast of independent firms participate, whereas others are closed-loop systems that involve only the system owner. Second, some offer charge

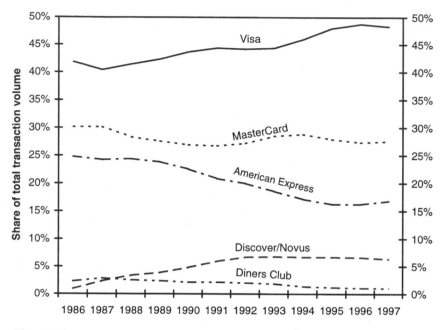

Figure 8.1
Major credit and charge card shares of dollar values of transactions, 1986–97.
Sources: 1999 Faulkner & Gray *Card Industry Directory* and Visa U.S.A.

cards and others, credit cards. Table 8.1 shows where the current payment card systems are on these two dimensions. The strengths and weaknesses of these different system types have played a significant role in the changing fortunes of the major systems.

Diners Club was the first payment card system. It faced little competition until American Express' entry in 1958. By 1960, American Express had a higher volume of charges than Diners Club. The open-loop credit card systems—MasterCard and Visa (their names were different at the time; see chapter 4)—entered in 1966. By 1975, Visa and MasterCard combined had three times as much annual charge volume as American Express. Visa became the largest payment card system in 1979 and has held that position ever since. Discover, a closed-loop credit card system, entered in 1985, was larger than Diners Club by 1988, and had approximately 38 percent as much transaction volume as American Express by

1997. JCB, the fourth-largest credit card issuer in the world, attempted to break into the U.S. market for individual and corporate credit cards in 1991 but failed to garner significant market share. By 1994, JCB had narrowed its focus to merchant outlets at destinations popular with Japanese tourists and to issuing cards to affluent international travelers.

The Weapons of War

Many weapons have been used in the competition between the systems. Before we describe how these have been used in the various battles, it is helpful to take a brief inventory.

Advertising

If you have watched any television in the past twenty years, you have seen many advertisements for each of the leading payment card systems. Industry estimates suggest that the four major card systems (Visa, MasterCard, American Express, and Discover/Novus) spent more than $460 million on television advertising in 1996 alone. Visa (the system, not the individual issuers) spent $160 million on television advertising that year; American Express spent $133 million on television advertisements (mainly on payment cards, but also on some other American Express products such as travelers cheques); MasterCard spent $90 million; and Discover spent $81 million.

Through the years, the leading payment card systems have engaged in extensive advertising and marketing campaigns. These advertisements provide information about the characteristics of the payment cards issued by the system. For example, Visa with its "Visa—It's Everywhere You Want to Be" campaign has highlighted that many merchants take its card. And although that is true, it is equally true for MasterCard. Nationwide, 3.8 million merchants accepted Visa and MasterCard in 1997, whereas only 1.9 million accepted American Express, and 3.2 million took Discover/Novus. In addition, each bankcard issuer engages in its own marketing efforts to differentiate itself from other bankcard issuers. Discover's "It Pays to Discover" campaign advertises the fact that its card has a cash-back bonus feature. And American Express has different ads for the different brands that it offers. For example, for its charge card, American Express advertises the fact that it doesn't charge high interest on revolving credit like its bank competitors. For its Optima family of credit cards, American Express advertises the benefits that each card carries.

The advertisements also try to persuade consumers that they should be using a particular card by linking that card to other consumer preferences. For example, for many years American Express tried to persuade consumers that by having the American Express card they were part of an elite club: "Membership Has Its Privileges." American Express did not have to be as concerned about its customers' creditworthiness as did credit card companies that offered credit lines that exposed them to long-term risks of default. People who held American Express charge cards had to pay their bills every month, so American Express faced less risk of default than did issuers of credit cards. In addition, many American Express cardholders held corporate cards, the charges for which were reimbursed by their employers. But as we saw in chapter 7, many of the "elite" American Express charge cardholders were deadbeats with their new American Express Optima credit cards.

Innovations
The systems also compete with each other through innovations that enhance the product for merchants or consumers. We mentioned two of the major consumer innovations in chapter 7: the affinity card and the airline mile cards. But perhaps the most important series of innovations that have taken place over time have involved improvements in processing transactions. These improvements have sharply reduced the time that consumers and merchants have to wait to consummate a transaction. They have also improved the accuracy of authorizations and thereby reduced fraud. Since the early 1970s, Visa and MasterCard have each pushed to make improvements to their systems, often competing for superiority. The complexity of coordinating transactions among thousands of issuers and acquirers is almost overwhelming. But the bankcard system that finds the most efficient solutions to this processing nightmare will also reap significant benefits. We discuss below the role of technological choices in the war between Visa and MasterCard.

Merchant Acceptance

The closed-loop systems maintain central control over the process of signing up merchants, although they have contracted out most of the work to third parties in recent years (as we discussed in chapter 6). Members of the open-loop systems sign up merchants, although in recent years the banks, too, have made increasing use of specialist acquirers operating under contract. Through the interchange fee, the open-loop systems control acquirers' incentive and ability to sign up merchants.

In deciding whether to accept payment cards from a particular system, one of the major considerations for merchants is how much they will have to pay off the top for each transaction. In the closed-loop systems, the system determines the merchant discount rate or rates, and the system can negotiate with merchants individually, as American Express did in response to the Boston Fee Party. Hence closed-loop systems can use the merchant discount strategically to encourage certain merchants (or classes of merchants) to take the system's card.

In the open-loop systems, in contrast, the system determines the interchange fee applicable to each transaction. This fee places a floor under the corresponding merchant discount, but the actual discount is set by individual acquirers. Although the open-loop systems thus have less control over merchant discounts, they can set different interchange fees for different classes of merchants to accomplish system goals and to engage in strategic behavior relative to the other payment card systems. The lower supermarket interchange fee offered by both Visa and MasterCard, discussed in chapter 6, is an important example of this.

The Rise and Decline of American Express Cards

The First Hundred Years

The changing fortunes of American Express in the payment card industry illustrate the competitive interaction of the systems and the strategic use of the weapons described above. American Express had been in business for more than 100 years before it entered the payment card industry. It started in 1850 with the merger of two express mail companies. The first of these was founded in 1841 when Henry Wells and his investor Crawford Livingston started Livingston Wells to deliver mail more quickly and more reliably than the Post Office to residents of the cities in New York. William Fargo joined them and extended their routes to Chicago.

Seeing their success, John Butterfield, the owner of most of the stagecoach routes in western New York, founded a competing company. In 1849, he and James Wasson founded Butterfield, Wasson & Co., and their entry triggered a price war. As there were no antitrust laws then, and because the price war was costly to the two combatants, a truce was called and a merger was soon consummated. In March 1850, Wells and Butterfield met in Buffalo and signed the Articles of Association of the American Express Company.

The owners of the new company were not happy for long, however. Fargo wanted to start an express route in California, then booming from the Gold Rush. Butterfield vetoed the idea, Wells and Fargo left American Express, and Wells Fargo & Co. was born in 1852. (Wells Fargo eventually became one of California's largest banks. It was the thirteenth-largest issuer of MasterCard and Visa cards in 1997, based on charge volume of $11.4 billion and 6.5 million cards issued.)

American Express went on to develop an express mail and cargo service. The company formed cooperative relationships with the railroads and other express companies that serviced regions outside its territory. It made its mark during the Civil War period, reliably delivering packages and mail between Union troops and their families. American Express became a highly profitable firm offering a vital service.

Attempting to seize profit opportunities, other firms entered the express business. The most formidable competitor to American Express for a time was the Merchants Union Express (MUE), which was formed in 1866. MUE waged a fierce price war against American Express, and losses ensued for both companies. As it had done before, American Express merged with this difficult competitor in 1867.

As the post–Civil War expansion of the rail network linked what had been regional markets into national markets, it became more important to move money across the country. But cash was too easily stolen. In the absence of a national bank, it fell upon the mail services to devise a mechanism for the safe transportation of funds. The U.S. Post Office developed the money order, which was simply a kind of check. Postal money orders soon became a popular way to move funds to the western frontiers and back again. American Express introduced a competing money order product.

Money orders were not a very good substitute for cash, however. They were generally used to transfer a fixed amount of money, either for deposit in a distant bank or for the purchase of goods at a previously agreed upon price. They therefore lacked the flexibility of cash. They were also subject to theft and counterfeit. To help solve these problems, Marcellus Flemming Berry, an American Express employee who had also designed its money order product, invented the travelers cheque. As today, the American Express Travelers Cheque could be obtained in a variety of denominations so that it could substitute for cash. The purchaser signed the check when it was issued and then again when it was cashed. The dual signatures reduced the possibility of losses due to theft. The American Express Travelers Cheque quickly became one of the company's signature products after its introduction in 1891. As Americans started traveling abroad in increasing numbers, they took American Express Travelers Cheques, which they could cash at a growing network of American Express offices in Europe.

To enhance the value of its travelers cheques, American Express engaged in marketing efforts to solicit banks and other merchants throughout Europe and the United States to accept its cheques. The company argued to merchants that most Americans traveling in Europe would carry its cheques in place of other forms of credit. In addition, American Express promised to reimburse merchants for the full amount of the cheques without discounting and insured the merchant against consumer fraud. Eventually, most merchants here and abroad accepted American Express Travelers Cheques almost as readily as cash. The travelers cheque became wildly successful for American Express and started a path of fundamental change for the company.

Whether intentionally or not, American Express had found a novel way to make money. A consumer gives American Express money equal to the face amount of the travelers cheques plus a percentage commission on this face amount. In addition to keeping this commission, American Express earns interest on the float: it can invest the value of the cheques until they are used and the merchant returns the cheque to American Express for redemption. Even better, some fraction of travelers cheques are held by consumers for long periods of time—a consumer has some left over after a trip to France, for example, and decides to hold on to them until she goes abroad again—and some are never cashed at all. By 1997, on sales of more than $25 billion, American Express had an average of $6 billion in travelers cheques outstanding. American Express has typically invested the nonseasonal, or fixed, portion of these outstanding balances in long-term tax-free bonds and the more cyclical portion of outstandings in short-term bonds. In 1997, American Express earned a yield of 9.2 percent on the outstanding travelers cheques, for revenues of approximately $550 million. Despite challenges by Citibank, Visa, MasterCard, and some Japanese and Swiss banks, American Express has maintained its market leadership in travelers cheques. In 1997, American Express issued approximately 50 percent of all travelers cheques worldwide.

Banks were instrumental in increasing distribution of travelers cheques and reaching consumer segments that otherwise would have been ignored. This was largely a matter of convenience. Consumers were used to going to their depository institutions for money orders and other financial services, so banks were a natural place to buy travelers cheques.

The business model for travelers cheques parallels that for payment cards in two important ways. First, American Express faced the chicken-and-egg problem. For travelers cheques to be a useful payment mechanism for consumers, merchants had to be willing to accept them. For merchants to be willing to accept travelers cheques, however, enough consumers had to want to use them for the merchant (or the merchant's bank) to incur the cost of redeeming them. Second, American Express found that it could profit from consumers' seeming financial carelessness. It is usually more costly to hold travelers cheques between trips than to put the money into an interest-bearing account, though it does save time.

The Rise of the Green Card

The Birth   A hundred years after its foundation in Buffalo, American Express was the world's largest travel agency and operated the world's largest private mail service, while generating gross profits of $146 million and netting $8.40 per share of outstanding stock. Between its cheques and its travel offices, it was profiting enormously from the boom in international travel following the end of the Second World War. The number of American Express travel agencies grew from fifty at the end of the war to nearly 400 ten years later. The company sold approximately $12.5 billion of travelers cheques in 1955 and claimed to control 75 percent of the travelers cheque business worldwide.

The same year that American Express turned 100, Diners Club was founded. Diners Club initially introduced a charge card with an annual fee of $19 (as always, in 1998 dollars) targeted to restaurants. This closed-loop payment card system also generated revenues from a 7 percent merchant discount. Diners Club soon expanded to other travel and entertainment segments such as hotels, restaurants, and florists. After four years, it raised its annual fee for cardholders to $28. By 1958, it had an annual charge volume of more than $450 million and earned gross profits of $39 million from merchant discounts and cardholder fees. By 1960, Diners Club had signed up 1.25 million cardholders.

American Express considered buying Diners Club in 1956 but rejected the idea. The next year, it decided instead to enter the charge card industry on its own. It had 17,500 merchant locations and 250,000 cardholders when it started on October 1, 1958. Setting a tone that would carry it through the 1980s, it initially set its annual fee 20 percent higher than Diners Club, thereby suggesting that it was the more "exclusive" card. But it set the initial merchant discount slightly lower: 5 to 7 percent for restaurants and 3 to 5 percent for hotels and motels. As with most (if not all) new payment card issuers, it was unprofitable at first. (Chapter 10 explains why.) Part of its problem was inexperience. American Express had not issued credit before. And even though it was offering a charge card, it was in effect extending a loan from the time of purchase until the charge card bill was paid. Some customers did not pay when the bill was due, and American Express was initially ineffective at getting prompt payment. By 1961, with losses mounting, it considered selling the business to Diners Club but decided that such a sale might not pass muster with the Justice Department. Instead, American Express hired George Waters, later known as the "Father of the Card," to run its card operations. Waters started putting pressure on customers who had not sent their payments in on time. And he raised the annual fee to $38 and then to $47.

Despite the increased fees, the American Express payment card system grew. There were 900,000 cardholders that could use their cards at 82,000 merchant locations by the end of 1962, the first year that the card operation posted a small profit. The number of cardholders and their charge volume continued to rise rapidly, with more than 3 million cardholders and approximately $7 billion in charge volume generating an estimated $50 million of net profits by 1969. The charge card soon became the company's single most recognizable product. Even in the wake of competition by banks, which instituted licensing programs in 1966 that eventually came to be known as Visa and MasterCard, the American Express card flourished. By 1977, American Express had 6.3 million cardholders in the United States who generated $20 billion in charge volume.

Don't Leave Home Without It   By the middle of the 1970s, the American Express card was well established throughout the country. It had become the dominant card in the travel and entertainment sector, with more than five times as many cards issued as Diners Club, its closest competitor in the T&E category. Many upscale restaurants, hotels, rental car companies, stores that relied on tourists, and other travel and entertainment–related businesses accepted the American Express card.

Why would these merchants have accepted a payment mechanism that cost them approximately 5 percent off the top of each transaction? One reason is immediately obvious. These merchants were not operating in the perfectly competitive industries described in introductory economics textbooks. One of the basic features of perfect competition is that all consumers are charged a given price for a particular good or service, and that price equals the cost of providing another unit of that good or service. (This quantity is known as the "marginal" or "incremental" cost.) The fact that American Express cardholders were usually paying the same price as customers paying cash shows that the merchant was receiving two different prices for the same thing. (Some merchants, such as gas stations, did penalize charge customers, but almost all soon found the extra revenue not worth the hassle.) Cash was a less expensive medium of payment than charge cards. (The relative cost of checks is less clear.) The fact that merchants could still make money after they had given American Express 5 percent of the purchase price shows that prices before paying the merchant discount, the prices received from cash customers, were above marginal cost.

Merchants selling for more than marginal cost are better described by the modern economic models discussed in chapter 7 in which sellers have some market power (i.e., some ability to raise price above marginal cost) because they are differentiated from their competitors by location and/or product differences. These differentiating factors don't necessarily ensure high or even adequate profits. In fact, an average of approximately 15,000 retailers (0.73 percent of all firms) failed annually from 1992 to 1995. Merchants have fixed costs of operation, and they fail if the profits from pricing above marginal cost are insufficient to cover those fixed costs. Differentiation carries with it some control over price, but it does not guarantee the ability to cover all costs or even to meet the next payroll.

If American Express cardholders would have bought the same amount from a merchant using cash, the merchant would have had little incentive to accept American Express cards and take a lower effective price from American Express cardholders. But if American Express cardholders would have shopped elsewhere or would have bought less if they could not use their card at a merchant, it could be profitable to take the card. For example, suppose a restaurant had an incremental profit margin of 40 percent and American Express was more expensive by 1 percent. Even if thirty-nine out of forty American Express cardholders would have patronized the restaurant even if it did not take American Express cards, the additional profit from the one who would not is sufficient to make it profitable to take the card. (It makes 40 percent on the incremental customer and loses a total of 39 percent—1 percent each—on the others.) Moreover, American Express cardholders were more likely (certainly in the days before ATMs) to have limited cash or out-of-town checks, because they often used their cards while traveling.

Of course, as we discussed in chapter 6, whether it made business sense for any particular merchant to take the American Express card depended on what other merchants were doing. At one extreme, if only a few merchants were taking the American Express card, a merchant could gain a competitive advantage over his rivals by taking the card. He could capture sales from people who had the cards and wanted to use them. At the other extreme, if most merchants were taking the American Express card, a merchant who did not would risk losing sales to his rivals who took the card. Consumers would just shop elsewhere. As more consumers had the American Express card, in some industries virtually all merchants decided to take the card (hotels and upscale restaurants) and in other industries (gas stations and supermarkets, until recently) virtually all merchants decided not to take the card. The successful development of the American Express card illustrates the role of spillovers or externalities in the growth of payment card systems. As more merchants accepted the card, the value of the card increased and more consumers were willing to pay the annual fee for the card and use it. As more consumers had the card, more merchants realized they could gain additional sales by taking the card. And as more merchants in an industry took the card, more merchants realized they would lose sales by not taking the card.

By the mid-1970s, American Express had developed a prestigious payment card. Its cards were used by the economic elite and widely accepted by travel-related businesses, upscale restaurants, and upscale stores. Card membership was highest for well-off households and lowest for the poorest households. In 1978, almost 50 percent of households with annual incomes greater than $55,000 had American Express cards. American Express would burnish this image in the next decade. In 1975, it started its classic "Don't Leave Home Without It" advertising campaign, which emphasized the value of the card for charging purchases at merchant locations around the world. During the following year, American Express began running its "Do You Know Me?" television advertisements. The "Do You Know Me?" ads featured American Express cardholders who were famous for something but whose faces were not well known to the public. One of the classic advertisements featured William Miller, an obscure congressman who had been chosen to run for Vice President with Barry Goldwater in 1964. The pitch was that unless you're better known than William Miller, carrying an American Express card would enhance your prestige.

But by the late 1970s, most consumers did not need to have an American Express card to charge their purchases. In 1978, only thirteen years after they had started in earnest, the bankcard systems had signed up more than 100 million cardholders and convinced more than 1.8 million merchants to take their cards. Consumers charged nearly $100 billion worth of goods and services on MasterCard and Visa cards in 1978, more than three times as much as was charged on American Express cards in that same year. Nevertheless, American Express was able to build its business by continuing to focus on upscale merchants and upscale cardholders. At the start of the 1980s, American Express had a merchant discount that was almost 50 percent higher than that charged by Visa and MasterCard: 3.6 percent versus 2.5 percent. And it charged cardholders an annual fee of $60 for its standard Green Card and $85 for its Gold Card. By 1984, the Gold Card fee had been raised to $96, and American Express' net profits from its charge card business alone were estimated to total $370 million.

Believing that consumers and merchants would continue to pay a premium for a "prestigious" card, American Express mounted a new advertising campaign in the mid-1980s to emphasize the elite nature of its card products. "Membership Has Its Privileges" hit television viewers in 1987. This campaign was particularly puzzling because the 1980s were rapidly becoming the "value" decade, epitomized in the card business by the entry of Discover with its cash-back feature in 1985.

And They Don't Take American Express

By the late 1980s, several developments weakened the business model that had served American Express extremely well since the inception of its charge card thirty years earlier. First, many consumers had bank credit cards that were widely accepted and could do roughly as much as American Express charge cards. Consumers could easily do without their American Express cards. You could charge purchases at almost all the U.S. locations that took American Express cards and at many that did not. As with American Express cards, you could pay for the charges on the next billing cycle. In addition, however, the credit cards let you take out an instant loan at any time to finance purchases. Second, because most American Express cardholders also had MasterCard or Visa cards, the business case for merchants to take American Express cards weakened. In 1991, for example, almost 90 percent of American Express cardholders also had either a MasterCard or Visa card.

Third, the pricing strategies adopted by the open-loop credit card systems like Visa severely constrained the pricing strategies available to closed-loop charge card systems like American Express. As we discussed above, the credit card issuers who made up these systems had incentives to keep card fees low to get cards in the hands of consumers from whom the companies could realize profits from lending. And although the economic determinants of the merchant discount/interchange fee are quite complex, as we discussed in chapter 7, the credit card systems at least appear to have been much more interested than the charge card systems in gaining wide merchant acceptance. So American Express faced stiff competition in the two pricing dimensions available to it: cardholder fees and merchant discounts.

On the other hand, American Express still maintained several advantages over credit cards. Spending limits could be more flexible, because American Express cardholders were advanced credit only for about thirty days. And American Express had used its central access to all relevant data to develop a popular corporate card that businesses had widely adopted for their employees.

Visa capitalized on American Express' problems with the "It's Everywhere You Want to Be" advertising campaign that featured "And They Don't Take American Express" as the tagline. These commercials started airing in 1985 and were still being used in various forms in the late 1990s. Consumer perceptions of the different card brands changed remarkably after the advertisements started airing. At the beginning of 1985, about 35 percent of consumers thought Visa was accepted at more merchants, compared with 28 percent for American Express. By the late 1980s, Visa's numbers had increased to 45 to 50 percent while American Express' were below 20 percent. By the mid-1990s, nearly 70 percent of consumers said Visa had the greater merchant acceptance and only 5 percent of consumers said American Express.

Fortuitously or not, the share of payment card transactions made with American Express charge cards started falling shortly after the Visa advertisements were televised. The American Express charge card share had been roughly steady at just over 25 percent during the early 1980s. Since the Visa advertisements started airing, the American Express charge card share has fallen steadily. Between 1985 and 1996, American Express saw the share for its charge card drop from more than 24 percent to 16 percent. The consumer survey evidence suggests that this loss was partly attributable to the Visa advertisements.

Of course, other factors were also at work. Between 1985 and 1990, households, had on average increased the number of credit and charge cards at their disposal from two to three; that figure would increase to 4.7 by 1997. However, this growth was not evenly distributed between American Express and the bankcards. From 1990 to 1997, the average number of Visa and MasterCards per household grew by nearly 80 percent while the average number of American Express cards per household increased by just over 5 percent. For most consumers who had American Express cards, there was no obvious advantage to paying with their American Express cards rather than with one of the other payment cards in their wallet. If you were not sure you wanted to pay off your charges at the end of the month, you would not want to pull out your American Express card. (There were two major exceptions: corporate cardholders and credit-constrained cardholders who had more credit available on their American Express cards than on their other payment cards.) If you were sure you were going to pay off your charges at the end of the month, you would write the same check no matter which card you used. Moreover, even in this situation, the case for not using your American Express card grew stronger over time. By 1987, many other card issuers started offering incentives to charge on their cards. Discover offered cash back at the end of the year depending on charge volume, and several Master-Card and Visa issuers awarded frequent flyer miles or other incentives to charge on their cards.

The crux of the problem American Express faced was not the Visa advertisements or even the rise of cards that rewarded consumers for using them. Rather, it was the conflict between the business economics of credit and charge cards discussed in chapter 7. Credit cards could do everything that charge cards could do and more. And credit card systems had competitive incentives to charge a relatively low price for the service that both types of cards provided: charging purchases. In addition, American Express failed to recognize the early signs of the "value" decade and was not responding to consumers' growing desire for economy. As a result, the spread of credit cards naturally limited the growth of charge cards and constrained the prices that charge card systems could obtain from consumers.

The spread of credit cards also increasingly constrained the merchant discounts that charge card systems could sustain. As more American Express cardholders had bankcards in their wallets and had reduced incentives to use their American Express cards, merchants had less reason to pay American Express a premium merchant discount. The incremental sales resulting from accepting American Express cards, while also accepting the three credit card brands, almost certainly declined during the 1980s. That in turn reduced the number of merchants willing to accept American Express charge cards at any given merchant discount level and constrained the prices that American Express could charge merchants. The Boston Fee Party was a very public manifestation of the tightening of this constraint by the early 1990s.

A New Business Model

American Express was in serious trouble in a number of areas by the early 1990s. Its flawed introduction of the Optima credit card in 1987 had resulted in large losses from unexpectedly high charge-offs, adding to other severe losses at its Travel Related Services division. The Boston Fee Party had generated a lot of bad publicity, as had scandals involving senior management. Several commentators argued at the time that it was questionable whether American Express could survive for long.

After Harvey Golub replaced James Robinson as the Chief Executive Officer of American Express in 1993, American Express began to make a number of radical changes in its business strategies to compete with the credit card systems. First, it introduced a variety of credit card–based products under the Optima logo. Several of these products were designed to compete with the increasingly popular affinity cards issued by the bankcard systems. The introduction of the Membership Miles program also allowed American Express' charge cardholders to earn frequent flyer miles from a variety of airlines. Second, American Express's advertising shifted from emphasizing the elitist nature of its card to emphasizing the comparative advantages of its card products over those the other systems offered. Third, it reduced its merchant discount and increased its investment in expanding merchant acceptance. Fourth, it attempted to increase its distribution of cards by forming alliances with banks that belonged to the bankcard systems. Finally, it appears that American Express attempted to weaken the bankcard systems by making strategic alliances with selected members of those systems and by encouraging members of the bankcard systems to oppose system strategies that adversely affected American Express. We concentrate on this last change in the remainder of this section.

In the mid-1990s, as part of its alliance strategy, American Express embarked on a plan to distribute its cards through banks that belonged to the MasterCard and Visa systems. As of late 1998, however, American Express has not implemented the plan in the United States because both bankcard associations have adopted rules that prohibit members from issuing the cards of American Express, Discover, or other systems "deemed to be competitive." But MasterCard and Visa did not adopt similar rules in Europe, in part because of the threat of antitrust action by the European Commission. As of mid-1998, American Express had formed alliances with more than forty banks (most with Visa or Master-Card affiliations) in thirty countries throughout the world, including Australia, Brazil, France, Greece, Israel, Korea, South Africa, Spain, Switzerland, Turkey, and the United Kingdom. These banks have issued or will issue American Express cards. The relationship with the Bank of Hapoalim, Israel's only major MasterCard issuer, is one example of these alliances.

In American Express' partnership with Bank Hapoalim, which began in 1995, the initial card solicitations aimed to persuade Hapoalim's own MasterCard customers to use American Express as a premium brand. In the first year of this partnership, Bank Hapoalim issued some 80,000 American Express cards, an astounding percentage increase in American Express' Israeli customer base, which previously had consisted of only a few thousand cardholders. In addition, the partnership helped American Express increase its merchant base, thereby encouraging further usage by tourists (particularly from the United States) who visit Israel each year.

In 1998, American Express announced an alliance with Credit Suisse in Switzerland. This was particularly noteworthy because it was the first time American Express had become involved in supporting a Visa or MasterCard portfolio. American Express and Credit Suisse formed a joint venture to handle all of Credit Suisse's card marketing, including its Visa and MasterCard programs. In addition, American Express discontinued its independent marketing efforts in Switzerland and put its card portfolio into the joint venture.

Banking relationships were important for American Express' expansion efforts outside the United States. In Europe, for example, the payment card industry is subject to strict regulations that, in many countries, prohibit direct mailing of card solicitations. That restriction makes entry harder than in this country. In addition, the payment card industry is more concentrated in many foreign countries than in the United States, with a small number of large banks accounting for the preponderance of payment card issuing. In Canada, for example, six national banks accounted for 86 percent of all charge volume on MasterCard and Visa cards in 1997. In the United States, on the other hand, the top six issuers accounted for 49 percent of all charge volume on MasterCard and Visa credit cards in 1997. Importantly, bank brand identities are considerably stronger in Canada than in the United States, and Canadian bankers can use strong customer relationships to cross sell a variety of banking products effectively.

In the United States, in contrast, credit card issuers make extensive use of direct-mail advertising, and banking and credit card relationships are much less closely linked. For example, in the United States, at least five out of six cardholders do not have their checking accounts at the same bank that issued them their card. Many credit card issuers solicit customers nationally, whereas banks almost always solicit depository customers only locally or regionally. Moreover, unlike that of most foreign countries, it is relatively easy to enter the U.S. banking industry. As we discussed in chapter 3, American Express could expand its banking business nationally.

It is therefore less clear why American Express has sought banking alliances in the United States and has complained that the refusal by MasterCard and Visa to allow such alliances violates the antitrust laws. (Indeed, American Express' complaints helped launch a multiyear investigation of the credit card industry by the Antitrust Division of the U.S. Department of Justice. This investigation culminated in the filing of a lawsuit against Visa and MasterCard in October 1998 that seeks to prohibit MasterCard and Visa from prohibiting its members from issuing for American Express. This same lawsuit seeks to end dual memberships in MasterCard and Visa.) It appears that American Express has sought to reduce, at least indirectly, the extent to which the bankcard systems compete with American Express. At a speech given at the 1996 Credit Card Forum, for instance, American Express Chairman Harvey Golub stated that Visa is "actually run for the benefit of a relatively few banks and the association staff—rather than in the interests of all of its members." He argued to the bank members in attendance that Visa had failed the majority of its members by:

• "Spending money that you've contributed on things that don't particularly benefit you;
• Subsidizing a few individual banks who compete against you; and
• Deciding what products you can and can not offer to *your* clients."

Chairman Golub then proceeded to discuss four Visa practices that he argued were not in the interests of many banks. Perhaps not coincidentally, all have or are intended to have substantial effects on American Express: (1) Visa's advertising attacks on American Express' merchant coverage; (2) Visa's payments to support cobranded cards; (3) Visa's lowering of interchange fees, which forced down American Express' merchant discounts; and (4) Visa's development of corporate and purchasing card systems, travelers cheques, Visa Travel money, and home banking.

As we discussed in chapter 7, the bankcard systems already have difficulties making effective collective decisions because member banks have different incentives and compete with each other. Chairman Golub's remarks sought to exploit some of the inherent fragility in the bankcard systems' joint venture organizations. Incentive differences would be increased and the bankcard systems would become less cohesive organizations if some issuers—and not others—were also to issue American Express cards. For example, it is extremely unlikely that banks that issued both Visa and American Express products would want Visa to compete aggressively against American Express. Those issuers would likely want Visa to stop advertising against American Express, limit downward pressure on American Express' merchant discount, and stop funding development of products designed to compete with products available from American Express.

In addition to the potential gains to American Express from reducing system-level competition that were suggested by Chairman Golub, it seems almost axiomatic that banks issuing American Express products would have reduced incentives to use their bankcards to compete as aggressively against American Express. It follows that the more successful American Express might become in convincing Visa members to issue its American Express cards, the greater the reduction in competition from Visa issuers against American Express.

The members of the bankcard systems compete vigorously with one another in the United States. The bankcard systems have nonetheless remained relatively cohesive because certain common objectives make at least some members better off without making other members worse off. A common interest in maintaining the value of the system brand is one of the major sources of cohesion. Increasing the size of the merchant and cardholder base is another, related common objective. Brand positioning and marketing at the system level potentially further both goals.

Visa's "It's Everywhere You Want to Be" advertising campaign provides an important example. This campaign put competitive pressure on American Express to reduce its merchant discount and increase its merchant base. Indeed, American Express Chairman Harvey Golub recently remarked "[W]e did lower prices at American Express. But, at the same time we lowered our costs by an even greater amount. We became more competitive and we vastly increased merchant coverage." This competitive pressure benefited both the merchants through lower discounts and American Express cardholders, whose cards could now be accepted in more locations.

Enabling member banks to issue American Express cards would reduce the cohesiveness of the bankcard systems. It would clearly pit banks that issued both Visa and American Express cards against those issuing only Visa cards. The joint issuers would have profit incentives to oppose brand positioning or other investments that would hinder their American Express card franchise. The Visa Board of Directors in Europe in 1997, for example, included Lloyds Bank, National Westminster Bank, Credit Lyonnais, and Deutsche Bank, all of which had partnerships with American Express. The joint venture formed by American Express and Credit Suisse, for example, makes joint decisions for the two issuers. This may be tolerable within Visa Europe because member banks compete less intensively with each other in the credit card business (as, indeed, in other businesses), so that system cohesiveness is less precarious. In the United States, however, it is difficult to imagine that Visa would have conducted its highly successful advertising campaign against American Express with the same intensity if American Express had had similar representation on Visa's U.S. Board. American Express thus devised a strategy that not only would provide additional distribution for its cards, at least outside of the United States, but would also weaken its major system competitors.

Thus far, it appears that American Express's new business model, and the strategies that went along with it, have worked. After ten years of decline in the United States, American Express had a leveling off of its share of charge volume in 1996 followed by an increase of 0.6 percent (60 basis points) in 1997. The number of merchants that accept American Express cards increased by approximately 30 percent between 1995 and 1997, compared to only 16 percent for Visa and MasterCard. Also, net profits at American Express Travel Related Services (TRS), the division of American Express that controls its card operations, increased from $1.14 billion in 1995 to $1.37 billion in 1997, an average annual growth of nearly 10 percent.

The Bankcard Battles

Visa's main target in its "It's Everywhere You Want to Be" advertising campaign was not American Express. It was MasterCard. MasterCard was Visa's closest competitor at the start of this campaign. It was the second-largest payment card system with 29 percent of all charge volume in 1984, the year before the Visa campaign started. Moreover, surveys indicated that consumers viewed MasterCard and Visa as almost indistinguishable in important respects. Of course, that view was just about right. Both card brands were accepted at essentially the same locations, and they provided very similar services. American Express, on the other hand, was a much smaller system competitor, offered a charge card rather than a credit card, and had developed the reputation as the "high-quality" brand.

Visa wanted to differentiate itself from MasterCard. To do so, it focused its advertising on comparisons to American Express that attempted to enhance Visa's prestige by invoking and challenging American Express' position as the industry leader in upscale markets. As Visa's advertising agency put it to a committee of Visa members responsible for advertising, they would use American Express as a "straw man" with MasterCard as the ultimate target. Visa executives even discussed the "halo effect" of positioning American Express as Visa's primary competitor, instead of MasterCard. This strategy also allowed Visa to extend its market coverage into the travel and entertainment arena that had long been the domain of American Express, while MasterCard was left to expand its already mature retail sector.

The apparent effects of Visa's advertising campaign on consumer perceptions of MasterCard are striking. Prior to the advertisements, when consumers were asked which card brand was accepted at more merchants, 35 percent said Visa and 28 percent said MasterCard. By 1994, almost three times as many consumers said Visa as said MasterCard (69 percent versus 25 percent) even though MasterCard and Visa were accepted at almost the exactly same locations in the United States. Before the advertisements, when consumers were asked which card brand was the best overall card, 40 percent said Visa and 35 percent said MasterCard. Seven years after the advertisements started airing, 59 percent of consumers said Visa and only 22 percent said MasterCard.

The effects of Visa's advertising on MasterCard's share of charge volume are hard to quantify. It is difficult to separate the effects of the advertising from the effects of many other dimensions of competition between the two systems, as well as competition from other systems. In particular, a major market event took place in the payment card world contemporaneous with Visa's advertising campaign: the entry of Discover in 1985. Discover grew to capture about 6 percent of all credit and charge card volume by 1991. Over the same period, Visa maintained or slightly increased its share, while MasterCard's declined by 2.6 percentage points, a fairly substantial loss relative to its 29.5 percent share in 1986. It is probably an oversimplification to say that Discover's success came at the expense of MasterCard, but that's what the raw data seem to suggest. If consumers had viewed Visa and MasterCard comparably, there would have been no reason to expect that Discover would be more successful in taking share away from MasterCard than from Visa. And Visa's advertising campaign likely played a significant role in Visa's ability to maintain its share in the face of Discover's entry.

Visa's advertising strategy was particularly effective because it left MasterCard little room to respond. "MasterCard Is Everywhere, Too" probably would not have helped, and at the time there were few real differences between MasterCard and Visa to which MasterCard could draw the consumer's attention. MasterCard relied on celebrities to tout its product in its "Master the Possibilities" campaign that began running shortly after Visa's "It's Everywhere You Want to Be" campaign started. When Visa began positioning itself as a player in the travel and entertainment market, MasterCard decided to focus on traditional bankcard markets such as department stores. However, in 1987, MasterCard changed advertising agencies and shifted its marketing focus to stress its position in the premium gold card market. In 1988, it unveiled its "Choose the Card that Makes a Difference" advertising campaign, which claimed that MasterCard was the leading system for gold cards. This was a clear attempt to heighten consumers' perception of the prestige of carrying a MasterCard to counter Visa's marketing attempts to enhance its reputation in upscale market sectors.

The most intriguing aspect of Visa's strategy is that it was used at all. Remember, as a result of duality MasterCard and Visa had virtually the same members. And these members usually issued both cards. Table 8.2 reports the shares of Visa and MasterCards for the ten largest issuers (measured by total cards issued) of bankcards in 1986. Most of these issuers had significant shares in both programs. For example, 25 percent of the transaction volume handled by the ten largest issuers of Visa cards in 1986 came from MasterCards they also issued. Therefore, to the extent that Visa took share away from MasterCard it might appear that Visa's strategy was, in effect, just moving share from the MasterCard column to the Visa column at its member banks. Why would banks spend their money to do this?

The remainder of this section explores the nature of competition between the two bankcard systems under duality. To understand how, why, and to what extent the two commonly owned bankcard systems compete

Table 8.2
The top ten bankcard issuers in 1986 had significant shares in both Visa and MasterCard.

Rank	Issuers	Cards issued (thousands)	Share of cards issued		Total charge volume ($ millions)
			Visa (percentage)	MasterCard (percentage)	
1	Citibank	15,400	84	16	16,496
2	Bank of America	11,000	82	18	11,227
3	Chase Manhattan	7,800	80	20	8,019
4	First Chicago	6,756	77	23	7,715
5	Manufacturers Hanover	6,750	40	60	5,270
6	Marine Midland	4,400	50	50	2,749
7	Chemical Bank	4,150	45	55	3,359
8	Maryland National	3,400	15	85	4,199
9	Wells Fargo	2,800	28	72	2,979
10	Banc One	2,500	90	10	1,932

Source: The Nilson Report, no. 406, June 1987.

with each other, we begin by explaining how the management and control of the bankcard associations differs from most business organizations. We then examine how common ownership affects the incentives of the members to allow the managements of both associations to compete with each other. Finally, we examine some of the major ways in which MasterCard and Visa have engaged in systems-level competition.

Management and Control in the Bankcard Associations

When you buy American Express Travelers Cheques at your local bank, you are dealing with a distributor of American Express products. When you buy a hamburger at your local McDonalds, you are dealing with a franchisee of McDonalds, Inc. In both these cases, the "upstream" entity—American Express or McDonalds—determines the product sold, largely determines its image and how it is priced, and earns substantial profits. When you obtain a Visa or MasterCard from a bank, however, absolutely none of this applies.

Neither Visa nor MasterCard earns profits. As a legal matter, both are ordinary, for-profit corporations but they neither retain profits nor distribute them to their member banks. This is remarkable enough to bear repeating: the corporations that own two of the most valuable trademarks in the world are operated on a break-even basis. The associations have their own employees, but they are owned by the banks that issue their cards and are supervised by boards of directors composed of representatives of those banks. Economically, these associations operate much less like independent manufacturers than like input-supply cooperatives, such as a grain elevator jointly owned and used by a group of farmers.

Similarly, the bankcard associations do not determine the products provided at retail, though they do invest in developing new products and features that member banks may elect to offer. The associations design and operate the worldwide computer networks that make using credit cards so easy, and the designs of these networks necessarily affect card issuers' abilities to offer certain product features. If, for instance, a network does not send to issuing banks the detailed information that large corporations receive when their employees use American Express corporate cards, issuing banks will be unable to offer credit cards that compete with the American Express corporate card. Over time, these systems have become more capable, both expanding the range of products that can be offered and enhancing the efficiency with which existing products can be delivered.

Visa and MasterCard also maintain regulations that govern the interchange process. The regulations specify how fraud and other security issues are handled; how the risk of nonpayment is apportioned; how the costs of running the system are shared; and a variety of other details that must be specified for the operation of a highly decentralized network. Most of these regulations are needed to forestall disputes that would otherwise arise in a system of independent members who compete with each other. These regulations also deal with externalities among association members. The structure of these regulations may also affect the sort of features that may be offered. Nonetheless, within the constraints computer system design and operating regulations necessarily impose, the associations place no restrictions on the features individual issuers offer, and a wide variety of feature packages are in fact offered. Moreover, a good deal of work on the development of new products and features is done by individual issuers, not by the systems.

Similarly, though the bankcard associations do affect the broad images of their brands, individual issuers, interested in differentiating their own offerings, also play a crucial role. The associations focus on aspects of their brand images that apply to their entire membership. Thus, for instance, the associations collectively adopt rules and guidelines dealing with the appearance of their members' cards. These rules have become more relaxed over time but still reflect the importance of maintaining brand image. As we described in chapter 7, Visa rejected a proposed Hooters cobranded card for this reason. In addition, of course, the Visa and MasterCard associations invest in advertising to shape their brand images. But individual issuers also invest heavily in image advertising and other marketing efforts. Citibank alone invested $65 million in 1996 to promote its line of credit cards. The result has been that a large fraction of the country knows that "It's Not Just a Visa, It's a Citibank Visa." (This will presumably change given Citibank's new allegiance to Master-Card.) In addition, individual issuers' cards differ in features and in service quality. Thus issuers, to an important extent, determine their cards' images and reputations, to a much greater extent than, say, the local

McDonalds, or even the local Ford dealer shapes the image and reputation of its products. And a wide variety of images and reputations can accordingly coexist within the associations.

Things are a little bit more complicated when we turn to pricing. Although it is true that the associations do not directly determine prices issuing or acquiring banks charge, they do collectively set fees that affect those prices. The fees paid to the associations to cover their costs play a relatively small role. The interchange fee is much more important, about ten times the size of the membership dues and fees. The interchange fee puts a floor under the merchant discount. Indeed, since the acquiring side of the business is fairly competitive, one can expect changes in merchant discounts to generally reflect changes in interchange fees. In large part for this reason, it was argued in the *NaBanco* case, discussed in detail in chapter 11, that collective determination of the interchange fee is little more than cartel price fixing. As we argued in chapter 7, however, the interchange fee in fact allocates total cost between issuers and acquirers to align incentives and benefit the system as a whole.

Because a large number of independent members control the bankcard associations, thinking of the associations as single entities masks several levels of complexity. At the first level, banks' preferences, as they apply to particular Visa or MasterCard decisions, are unlikely to coincide. American Express' Harvey Golub was probably right, for instance, that large numbers of Visa members, most likely the smallest banks, will probably not receive much benefit if Visa develops a corporate card that can compete successfully with American Express. On the other hand, such a product could be quite valuable for some other banks. Decision making at the level of the Visa board is inevitably political, in the very general sense that it involves reaching a collective decision despite differences in individuals' preferences.

At a second level, it is important to recognize that no part-time board of directors can ever fully control an organization's full-time employees, if only because the employees are inevitably much better informed about key details of the operation and of their own actions. Thus, the bankcard associations' staffs inevitably have significant independence. On the other hand, since the staffs are better informed in important respects, and since it would be impractical in any case to have the board make all decisions,

the association staffs have been explicitly given a fair degree of auton-
omy. As we mentioned in chapter 7, Visa management can initiate routine
projects, costing up to $1 million, without board approval. Manage-
ment largely determines the board's agenda and thus shapes debate at
board meetings. And although Visa has a number of advisory committees through which member banks can offer opinions on, among other
things, marketing strategy, these committees have no authority to make
decisions.

We thus have a complex version of what is called the "principal-agent"
problem in law and economics. In the simplest version of that problem,
a single individual, the principal, attempts to negotiate a contract with a
second individual, the agent, that will provide the agent with the strongest
possible incentives to serve the principal's interests. Most commonly it
is assumed that the principal is interested in profit. The agent, of course,
has different interests. For example, a CEO (the agent) may be more interested in creating a huge corporation so she can feel important than in
running a smaller but more profitable enterprise. Alternatively, the agent
may be more averse to risk than the principal. The problem is complicated
because the agent is better informed about the state of the world and/
or about her own actions than the principal; the principal must rely on
imperfect indicators of performance (like profit or market share) to determine what reward the agent deserves for her actions. Here the problem
is further complicated in the case of the bankcard associations because
there are multiple, competing principals (the issuing banks) as well as
many individuals on the association staffs.

Incentives for System Competition with Overlapping Membership
Perhaps the oddest feature of the bankcard systems, in the United States
at least, is that essentially all members of one system are also members
of the other. This state of affairs, called "duality," has held since the
Worthen case (introduced in chapter 4 and discussed in more detail in
chapter 11) in the mid-1970s. If the relation between bankcard associations and issuing banks were an ordinary manufacturer-retailer relation,
there would be nothing noteworthy here: it is hardly unusual for retailers
to sell competing brands. Novelty arises because the associations are nonprofit entities owned and controlled by the banks, so that every bank has,

in principle, some say in the conduct of both associations. Because it is relatively rare to have two important competitors under common control, it is natural to ask whether duality has reduced competition at the system level and harmed consumers. We look first at the theory and then at the evidence. Neither is without ambiguity, but together they suggest better performance than one might expect at first blush.

It is first important to note that more competition between Visa and MasterCard is not necessarily in consumers' interest for two basic reasons. First, in most situations involving "ordinary" firms, increasing competition in effect transfers monopolistic profits to consumers in the form of lower prices and/or higher quality. But the bankcard associations do not earn profits, monopolistic or otherwise. Competition at the system level can be increased only if the associations raise prices to merchants and consumers (by raising fees charged to acquirers and issuers) and invest the proceeds in more advertising and/or research and development (R&D). Second, although economic theory provides relatively clear standards by which to judge whether prices are too high or too low, there are no such standards for advertising or R&D. Economic theory simply offers no basis for arguing that consumers would generally be better off if Visa and MasterCard spent more—or less—on advertising or R&D. Under many plausible circumstances, competition drives firms to spend too much money on advertising, especially the kind of advertising that does not provide useful information to consumers, and on R&D, especially R&D that just duplicates what a competitor is doing or has done. Although you might not be surprised that advertising is sometimes bad, you probably find the notion that R&D spending could be bad as quite counterintuitive. The problem is not that R&D has undesirable effects—it rarely if ever does—but rather that firms sometimes have incentives to spend more on R&D to compete with their rivals than would make sense from the point of view of society as a whole. It is good to invest in developing a better mousetrap, but it would be a waste if every company in the United States began racing to be the first to market the first all-titanium, Pentium-driven mousetrap.

In recent work, Jerry Hausman, Greg Leonard, and Jean Tirole have shown that in at least one important circumstance, duality would in theory not affect the associations' R&D spending. Suppose that each system's R&D aims entirely at reducing its members' costs of operating within that system (these costs would, of course, include credit losses and charge-backs). Suppose also, in rough conformity with the facts, that each member's contribution to system R&D spending is proportional to the size of its card program. Finally, suppose for the moment that the members perfectly control the associations. Then whether or not they belong to another bankcard association, the members of any one association are, in effect, seeking to minimize the sum of their per-unit costs of doing business and of supporting R&D. They will choose the level that minimizes this sum, whether or not they are also members of another bankcard association. This cost-minimizing level is also the socially optimal level.

In fact, Hausman, Leonard, and Tirole argue that if the principal-agent problem discussed above is serious, duality can actually encourage innovation. They note first that duality can help mitigate the principal-agent problem. Banks that are members of both associations can more easily compare the performance of the associations' staffs and can thus more effectively provide incentives for good performance. Moreover, to the extent that each staff's compensation is related to its association's market share, banks' ability under duality to switch business from one association to another provides a natural mechanism by which banks can readily reward good performance. Moreover, Hausman, Leonard, and Tirole show that banks' ability under duality to switch business in response to successful innovation can, under some reasonable assumptions, increase spending on system-level cost-reducing innovation, as the associations compete for market share.

These models capture important elements of reality and demonstrate that the effects of duality on incentives and performance are not simple to disentangle. It appears difficult to quarrel with the argument that duality helps banks solve the principal-agent problem they face, and the work by Hausman, Leonard, and Tirole seems to us to show that there is no reason to think that duality reduces system-level spending aimed at reducing costs. On the other hand, it is easy to extend their analysis to show that spending on advertising or product development by one association that would increase that association's demand and reduce its rival's presents a more complex picture. There is no simple relation between actual and socially optimal levels of such spending under any market conditions. If the banks perfectly control the associations, then duality will reduce spending of this sort. This may make consumers better off or worse off. On the other hand, if association staffs are free to determine spending levels, and if they are rewarded based on relative market shares, duality, by making it easier for banks to switch business from one association to the other, may lead to increases in this spending. This, too, may make consumers better off or worse off.

Actual Competition between MasterCard and Visa

If, as a matter of theory, duality has a complex and, in important respects, ambiguous effect on competition at the system level, it is of particular interest to ask whether there has been vigorous competition in practice. As a matter of common sense, if not of rigorous theory, the more intense the competition that has been observed, the less likely it is that ending duality would substantially increase competition. (It follows from the discussion above that this sort of evidence cannot help one decide whether duality is pro- or anticonsumer. However much competition one observes in practice, it could be excessive or deficient in theory.)

Although it is hard to quantify the intensity of system-level competition between MasterCard and Visa, it is not hard to find significant examples of actions taken by one system that have disadvantaged the other. The level of competition appears to have increased in recent years as the two associations' membership profiles have diverged. MasterCard has become more identified with nonfinancial and monoline issuers. Seven of the thirteen members of MasterCard's U.S. Region Business Committee (its version of Visa's Board of Directors) in mid-1997 were these nontraditional issuers, compared to only two out of twenty for Visa's Board.

The main formal constraint the two systems impose is that bank members may not serve on the U.S. Board of Directors (or U.S. Region Business Committee) of both Visa and MasterCard. The daily operations of Visa and MasterCard are run by the separate management and staff of the two systems. They do not interact except on certain fraud and security issues, and on very limited operational issues, where information sharing would seem socially desirable. For example, Visa and MasterCard staff meet periodically to align their procedures for processing charge-backs (transactions disputed by the cardholder) so that members do not need to learn two different sets of procedures. It is also noteworthy that Visa's senior management have pay incentives that depend not only on Visa's market share relative to American Express but also on its share relative to MasterCard.

Since the early 1970s, Visa and MasterCard have each pushed to make improvements to their systems, often competing for superiority. In 1973, for example, Visa launched its authorization system (BASE I), followed shortly thereafter by its clearing system (BASE II). Following Visa, Master-Card launched its own systems (known as BankNet and I-Net).

MasterCard chose to implement a decentralized transaction processing system in contrast to Visa's centralized system. Visa uses three central global supercenters, whereas MasterCard uses a decentralized system with more than fifteen sites in the United States alone. The Visa and MasterCard systems were two very different technological solutions to the same problem. MasterCard chose its decentralized plan in part to save on telecommunications costs, which were substantially more important in the early 1970s than they are in the late 1990s. MasterCard also thought that decentralization would limit the risk of major system failure because it was unlikely that many sites could fail at the same time. The downside for MasterCard was that decentralization makes it harder to offer some kinds of services. All Visa transactions pass through the central Visa system; the same is not true for MasterCard. MasterCard's decentralization makes it harder to develop some innovations that depend on access to a central database. Visa is at an advantage relative to Master-Card in this respect. The closed-loop systems, American Express and Discover, in turn have similar advantages relative to Visa.

Competition through system-enhancing improvements has continued over time. In 1992, for example, Visa introduced PaymentService 2000 (PS 2000). PS 2000 provides for more information to be passed through on authorization messages, including the full detail from the magnetic stripe on the back of the card, which allows the issuer to check the card's validity. This reduces fraud losses. In addition, PS 2000 allows the message authorizing a transaction to be matched with the message requesting payment on a real-time basis. This innovation has reduced costs both to issuers and acquirers by vastly increasing the efficiency of what normally used to be a three- to ten-day process. MasterCard, on the other hand, still has no comparable process in its system.

PS 2000 is an interesting example of Visa's innovative activity because, unlike BASE I and BASE II, it was not a solution to an immediate problem. In fact, members were somewhat resistant to PS 2000 because its implementation would require that they upgrade their processing systems. Visa staff tell us that they wanted to develop PS 2000 for three major reasons. First, this was a way to use the advantage of Visa's centralized system over MasterCard's decentralized system: if Visa successfully lowered charge-back rates this would increase Visa's appeal, relative to MasterCard, for issuers. Second, PS 2000 would help enhance the data on some of the transactions sent to issuers and allow Visa to minimize some of the closed-loop advantages of American Express in the corporate market. For example, American Express' superior data-capturing allowed them to provide more detailed year-end summaries of charges for cardholders than Visa could at the time. And third, reduced charge-backs due to the implementation of PS 2000 would make debit transactions more attractive for issuers, making Visa's debit card more competitive.

As we discussed above, both Visa and MasterCard use advertising as a competitive weapon at the system level. Since comparative advertising itself is rare, the absence of any between Visa and MasterCard is not surprising, especially since there are more differences between Visa and American Express than there are between Visa and MasterCard. Furthermore, other than the Visa and American Express advertising campaigns, there has been almost no comparative advertising between pairs of card systems (e.g., Visa versus Discover, or MasterCard versus Discover, or MasterCard versus American Express, or American Express versus Discover).

Marketing plays a vital role in issuing members' brand decisions when they choose between Visa and MasterCard, particularly for cobranding deals with retailers and other merchants. Accordingly, Visa and Master-Card each spend tens of millions of dollars each year on their marketing activities, trying to attract cobranding deals and bidding for banks' business. Vigorous marketing has been rewarded: for example, both Sears and Wal-Mart decided in 1996 to issue a cobranded card with Master-Card rather than Visa because of the substantial difference in association support and fees.

Over the past twenty-five years, Visa and MasterCard have competed on product and feature innovation, often releasing new product features at separate times. In 1991, for example, Visa bought Interlink as a complement to its on-line debit program; MasterCard did not respond for more than two years. Additionally, partly in response to MasterCard's receiving more upscale business, Visa launched a premium card in 1982, a precursor to Visa Gold, in an attempt to appeal to a more upscale segment of customers. There is evidence of competition for features in other areas: MasterCard, for example, has recently begun to market against Visa on card features such as purchase protection plans, which Visa removed as a required feature of its gold cards in 1996.

Finally, some of the fastest-growing products offered by MasterCard and Visa—the debit cards (Visa check and MasterMoney), which accounted for 14 percent of the systems' transaction volume in 1997, an increase of 50 percent from the previous year—are provided on a nondual basis. Banks do not issue both Visa check and MasterMoney cards as a result of an agreement that the systems reached with a group of states that had filed an antitrust lawsuit. Together with the increasingly divergent memberships of the two associations, the growth of nondual products is likely to further increase the degree of competition between the two systems over time. As mentioned above, however, the Justice Department filed a lawsuit in October 1998 to end duality.

The wars between the systems have involved strategic moves using principally advertising, innovation, and other methods of product positioning. And the fact that MasterCard and Visa have the same members has further complicated these wars. This is not a textbook model of competition. Yet systems competition has been vigorous in its own way. Consumers have benefited from the competition to increase merchant acceptance and to improve authorizations. Merchants have benefited from declining merchant discounts and increasingly efficient authorization and settlement of accounts. The battles among issuers to win consumers, on the other hand, are about as close to the textbook model of competition as we ordinarily see in the real world.

9

Issuer Brawls

And while the law [of competition] may be sometimes hard for the individual, it is best for the race, because it ensures the survival of the fittest . . .
—Andrew Carnegie

Although the advertising jabs between the card networks make for amusing diversions during the *X-Files,* what ultimately determines who wins is which issuer gets you to carry its card and to use it when you shop. Vigorous competition among issuers for your spending and credit fueled the rapid expansion of payment cards by putting downward pressure on prices and upward pressure on features and service. Chapter 12 deals with the recent emergence of debit cards; here we focus on credit and charge cards. Because of data availability at the time of writing, we concentrate on competition among issuers as of 1997. The possible impact of the bank merger wave of 1998 is discussed briefly at the end of the chapter.

Who Are the Players?

If you can afford to buy this book, you probably get frequent requests in the mail to sign up for a new card (for which you may have even been preapproved). Your magazines and newspapers are studded with advertisements for more new cards with yet more new features, complete with handy application forms for your convenience. And when you stand in line at your bank or at many other locations, you are faced with a pile of applications for new cards. Solicitations now come from four distinct kinds of card purveyors, three of which issue cards through one or both of the bankcard networks: single-issuer networks, monoline banks, depository institutions, and nonfinancial companies. Of the top fifty issuers (based on charge volume) in 1997, there were three single-issuer networks, five monoline banks, thirty-two depository institutions, and ten nonfinancial companies. These fifty issuers accounted for approximately 90 percent of credit and charge card transaction volume.

Single-Issuer Networks

Among the fifty largest issuers, the single-issuer networks accounted for approximately 27 percent of the dollar value of transactions on credit and charge cards in the United States in 1997. American Express was the largest issuer of cards in the United States, based on dollar volume. Its charge cards accounted for approximately 87 percent of its transaction volume; its Optima credit cards accounted for approximately 13 percent. Novus, the other major single-issuer network (which issues Discover and Novus cards), issues only credit cards and is the fourth-largest issuer based on charge volume. Diners Club, now operated by Citibank, is a third single-issuer network, but its transaction volume made up only 1 percent of total credit and charge card volume in 1997.

Depository Institutions

Depository institutions—banks or near-banks such as credit unions that offer checking account services to consumers and, generally, a range of related services—account for the largest portion of payment card charge volume: 45 percent of the charge volume of the top fifty issuers in 1997. (We have excluded from the calculations in this paragraph banks that principally provide credit cards and offer limited depository services; they are covered by the discussion of monoline banks below.) Of the top ten issuers in 1997, four were depository institutions. These included Citibank—the largest bankcard issuer, whether measured by dollars outstanding, number of cards issued, or dollars charged—Chase Manhattan, First Chicago NBD, and US Bancorp. Although active depository institutions account for a large percentage of charge volume, they account for an even larger fraction of issuers. As we discussed in chapter 1, many of these depository institutions have relatively minuscule card programs.

Although most MasterCard and Visa cards are issued by banks that offer checking account and other consumer banking services, most of these cards are issued to consumers who do not purchase those services from the issuing bank. In fact, in 1995, only 16 percent of all MasterCard and Visa cards were issued to cardholders who had at least one other banking relationship with the issuing bank.

Monoline Banks

The term "monoline" is simply a name used to refer to an issuer that engages wholly or primarily in issuing credit cards. Although some monoline issuers are chartered as credit card banks (some with charters that do not allow them to accept consumer deposits), others are chartered as standard depository institutions. MBNA, for example, is a nationally chartered bank just like Citibank. However, MBNA is often referred to as a monoline, since issuing credit cards is its primary business.

Among the fifty largest issuers, monoline banks accounted for approximately 16 percent of charge volume in 1997. Moreover, two of the five monoline banks among the fifty largest Visa and MasterCard issuers in 1997 were also among the ten largest credit and charge card issuers. MBNA had the largest program of the monolines and was the second largest Visa and MasterCard issuer, based on charge volume. The other leading monolines in 1997 were First USA, Capital One, Advanta, and Providian.

Nonbanks

In 1997, two of the ten largest issuers were nondepository institutions affiliated with giant nonfinancial corporations that entered the payment card industry in the early 1990s. Household Bank, which issues the General Motors card, was in eighth place and AT&T Universal was in ninth place. Although both the GM and AT&T cards were issued through separate financial intermediaries, the programs were closely managed by the nonfinancial companies whose trademarks reside on the cards. Together, nonbank issuers accounted for about 12 percent of the charge volume among the top fifty issuers in 1997.

Figure 9.1 shows the breakdown of charge volume by the four types of players. Depository institutions, monoline banks, and nonbanks in this

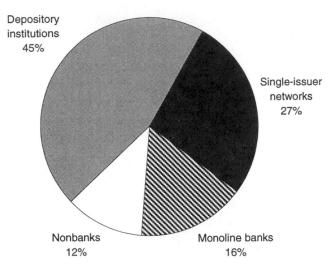

Figure 9.1
There are a variety of issuer types.
Source: The Nilson Report, no. 660, January 1998.
Note: Issuer shares are based on total charge volume for the fifty largest credit and charge card issuers.

sample, all of which issue only through the MasterCard and Visa associations in the United States, accounted for approximately 73 percent of the top fifty issuers' charge volume that year.

Product Differentiation and Market Segmentation

Competition among these payment card issuers takes place in card acceptance and card usage. Each issuer tries to get consumers to take its card, either in addition to or in place of cards from other issuers. Each issuer then tries to get consumers who have its card to charge more purchases on it and, for credit cards, to carry greater balances. Issuers are trying to get consumers to switch their payments from cash and checks as well as other payment cards.

Several factors on the demand side and the supply side of the payment card industry drive competition in acceptance and usage. On the demand side, the diversity of consumer tastes for making payments in various ways, and for obtaining financing for those payments with unsecured loans, shapes payment card products. On the supply side, competition is driven by differences in expected profits from providing services to consumers whose various usage patterns and levels of credit risk are uncertain prior to issuing them a card and may change during their card ownership. These factors affect the revenues received and the costs incurred over the course of the relationship between the issuer and the cardholder.

Consumer Demand

Transactors and Revolvers   Consumers obtain two primary services from payment cards: the ability to pay for goods and services (payment services) and the ability to finance those purchases for some period of time (credit services). Consumers differ in their demand for payment and credit services. As we noted in chapter 7, it is useful to think of consumers as being either transactors, who pay their balances in full every month, or revolvers, who use their cards as an important source of credit and thus regularly incur interest charges.

Transactors and revolvers obviously have different sensitivities to annual fees and finance charges. Transactors would prefer low annual fees, but revolvers would prefer low interest rates. Transactors are generally higher-income consumers who charge more than average; they comprise roughly a third of cardholders but account for about half of charge volume. According to one survey, more than 40 percent of cardholders with incomes greater than $87,000 pay their bills in full each month compared with less than 25 percent of cardholders with incomes less than $17,500.

Service fees (such as late fees, over-limit fees, and finance charges on cash advances) provide revenues to issuers but are likely to be largely invisible to most consumers trying to choose between different credit card plans. Most consumers seldom incur these fees, except possibly finance charges on cash advances. Such service fees made up only about 10 percent of issuers' revenue in 1997, whereas finance charges on revolving balances made up more than 75 percent of revenues. As a result, consumers would typically have little reason to consider these fees when choosing between cards from different issuers. If consumers (rationally) place little weight on these fees, issuers will not be able to appeal to different customer segments by reducing them. We have yet to see an advertising campaign by an issuer that features the slogan "No Late Fees!"

Competing Payment Mechanisms   Payment cards compete with each other to provide consumers with a noncash method for making payments and obtaining loans. Cards also compete with other payment methods, such as cash and checks, to secure space in consumers' pockets. From wampum to electronic funds transfers, consumers' choices of payment methods are virtually limitless. How then, do consumers decide which payment method they will use? Why, for example, has the use of payment cards grown so rapidly in the United States in recent years?

Institutional, legal, and cultural factors are generally thought to influence the use of particular payment methods across countries. One such factor deals with consumers' varying attitudes toward credit and loans across countries. Other factors include countries' payment systems infrastructures as well as their crime rates. A high crime rate tends to encourage consumers to carry less cash. One factor, however, strongly encourages consumers to use payment cards for their transactions: convenience.

Simply put, payment cards are much easier to carry around and use than are most of the other payment methods. A study performed by the Gallup Organization examined consumers' attitudes toward different payment systems. Nearly one-half (46 percent) of U.S. adults agreed that writing checks at store checkout counters is inconvenient. Similarly, almost half of all Americans (46 percent) also agreed that it takes too long to pay by check in a store. More than 70 percent agreed that it is annoying when merchants do not accept checks. More than three-quarters of U.S. adults responded that they do not like to carry too much cash. Two-thirds agreed that cash is too easy to lose or have stolen. The list of reasons why cash and checks are inconvenient is long. Payment cards allow consumers to carry less cash and checks, to keep track of their expenditures easily, and to free themselves from running to the bank each time they run out of cash.

Economics of Supplying Payment Card Services

Successful card issuers have offered card features to get consumers to take their cards and then to use them. To see how they can do so profitably, it is useful to look at the revenues issuers receive and the costs they incur.

Issuer Revenue Payment card systems receive revenues from two sources: merchants who accept their cards and consumers who use their cards. Systems receive merchant discounts from merchants in exchange for immediate payment of cardholders' charges. These discounts are generally calculated as a percentage of transaction volume, but they may also include transaction-specific amounts. Credit and charge card systems also receive fees from cardholders in exchange for a bundle of transaction services and credit; these include annual fees, finance charges, and various other cardholder assessments. These fees may or may not vary with card usage. Annual fees generally do not vary with usage. Finance charges are related to outstanding balances, which may be only loosely related to charge volume; for example, a consumer at her credit limit owes finance charges but cannot make additional charges. Service fees (such as late fees), on average, go up with volume, but there is no necessary link between volume and these fees; a given cardholder who increases volume may or may not find it slightly more difficult to pay her bills on time.

As we discussed in the last chapter, the relative importance of merchant discounts, cardholder fees, and finance charges differs dramatically between the open-loop systems and the closed-loop systems. As we also noted there, in the bankcard systems interchange fees (generally set as a percentage of transaction value) serve to transfer some fraction of merchant discounts from acquiring banks (who set the merchant discounts that merchants pay) to issuing banks. (No such fees exist in closed systems because the issuer and acquirer are the same entity.) In the case of MasterCard and Visa, finance charges provide the preponderance of issuer revenues (78 percent).

It is hard for issuers to forecast individual cardholders' spending and financing patterns, and therefore the revenue received from merchants and cardholders is uncertain. Cardholders who charge little generate little merchant-related income. Cardholders who pay their bills every month do not produce any interest income; indeed, these cardholders get interest-free loans during the grace period. Pricing payment cards is an intricate and risky process because cardholders may be either transactors or revolvers, and because their patterns of behavior are not known in advance. Eliminating the annual fee, for example, might attract more cardholders, and finance charges earned from revolvers might offset the

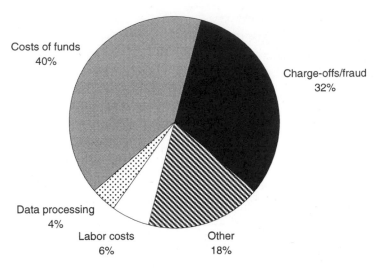

Figure 9.2
The major components of issuers' costs are costs of funds and charge-offs/fraud.
Source: Visa U.S.A., *Profit Analysis Report,* quarter ending September 30, 1996.
Note: This figure displays only costs on the issuing side of the business. Shares
are percentages of total issuer costs.

corresponding loss in fee revenue. However, no-fee cards appeal dispro-
portionately to transactors, for whom the annual fee is the only regular
card cost.

Issuer Cost   Operating a payment card program entails a variety of
costs. In addition to the system-level costs discussed in the previous chapter, other costs are specifically associated with the issuance and use of
cards. Figure 9.2 presents a breakdown of costs for issuers' Visa and
MasterCard card programs in 1996. The cost of funds was the largest
expense, accounting for approximately 40 percent of total costs; cost of
funds includes the cost of financing outstanding balances as well as financing charges accumulated during the grace period. Net charge-offs
were the next-largest expense, comprising approximately 32 percent of
total cost. (As noted earlier, charge-offs are amounts judged to be uncollectable from a consumer who has defaulted.) Other costs included labor,
data processing, system development and maintenance, and new cardholder solicitations.

Not only are net charge-offs the second-largest cost of operating credit card programs, they are one of the most unpredictable costs and the downfall of many issuers. Lending money is always risky. But credit card lending is especially risky because the loans are not secured, in general, by any assets and do not have a fixed duration. (Based on the financial analysis by Carlos Lapuerta and Stewart Myers discussed in the following chapter, only about 4 percent of all industries included in Standard & Poor's industry surveys are actually riskier than credit card lending.)

When cardholders default, payment card issuers must undertake expensive collection procedures. Because collection costs are often high relative to the amount of the defaulted loan, charge-offs are a significant operating cost. In 1997, net charge-offs for bankcard issuers increased nearly 30 percent from the previous year to approximately $24 billion. Approximately 50 percent of all charge-offs result from cardholder bankruptcy. This high level of bankruptcy charge-offs makes recovery of such losses difficult, and only 7 percent of gross charge-offs were recovered in 1997.

Although the use of computerized credit scoring has increased the industry's ability to weed out potential deadbeats, it remains hard to predict which consumers will default. Computerized credit scoring uses statistical methods to estimate the likelihood of default based on the individual's demographic characteristics, financial profile, and credit record. As highly sophisticated as these techniques have become, they have yet to bring down the historically high delinquency rates on credit card loans. In 1996, for instance, the delinquency rate on bankcard loans was 3.34 percent. When compared to the rates on other types of loans, such as home equity and mortgage (1.41 percent), direct automobile (1.87 percent), or personal (2.12 percent), the delinquency rate on credit card loans is remarkably high.

As we discussed in chapter 5, increases in interest rates may discourage borrowing by those most likely to repay (those likely to repay will face higher total finance charges when interest rates rise, so they may compensate by reducing their balances). They may also make default more likely (by making it more difficult for a borrower with financial problems to repay the loan in full). For these reasons, credit rationing at the individual level is an important dimension of card program management—and a very difficult one.

Product Variety

Given the heterogeneity of consumer tastes and the costs of accommodating those tastes, it is not surprising that the payment card industry is characterized by enormous product variety, as we showed in chapter 7. Payment card issuers achieve this differentiation through their choices of fees, interest rates, criteria for issuing cards to consumers, credit lines, card features, and marketing and promotional strategies. Each payment card reflects trade-offs among these characteristics. To reduce the issuer's financial exposure, for example, low-interest-rate cards are generally offered solely to the most creditworthy consumers, and they often provide only modest credit lines. In Arkansas, where the usury ceiling limits interest rates to the federal discount rate plus five percentage points, several banks offer credit cards at 8 percent. However, these issuers may approve just 10 percent of the applicants for the cards, and they often limit the credit line to $1,000.

Issuers of high-interest-rate cards can offer their cards to a broader range of consumers. Mass-marketed cards generally have high interest rates and low credit lines. Cards with a combination of large credit lines and lower interest rates are generally offered only to consumers with a proven credit history.

It is also not surprising that payment card issuers are constantly searching for previously unidentified market niches. Entry and expansion in this industry have been fueled, in large part, by the invention of new combinations of fees and features. For example, as mentioned earlier, affinity programs were one of the major marketing innovations of the 1980s. By associating cards with particular groups or clubs, card issuers were able to target specific consumer groups with cards designed for their common needs. More recent entrants into the payment card business have also developed innovative pricing and feature strategies. GM, for example, gives cardholders points toward a new GM-produced car as consumers use the card.

Competitive Strategies

As we mentioned in the previous section, there are two major avenues of competition in the payment card industry: competition to place cards in the hands of consumers, and competition to get those consumers to

**"He didn't get into Country Day,
but he got a gold card."**

use their cards. Here we take a look at the economics behind some of the strategies card issuers have adopted to accomplish both of these competitive goals and then review the competitive strategies several issuers have implemented in recent years.

Prospecting for High-Margin Consumers

Successful card issuers are good at "prospecting" for consumers that will generate long-run profits for the issuer. For finance-oriented cards, that means finding consumers who will carry balances but have little likelihood of defaulting. For transaction-oriented cards, that means finding consumers who will charge a lot and pay their charges off in full and on time.

The economics of prospecting for new cardholders is simple. There is an initial investment in contacting prospective cardholders either directly through mailings or indirectly through advertisements. That initial investment results in some fraction of prospective cardholders' applying for the card. In 1995, new account marketing, on average, cost issuers $21 for every application they processed. Once the application is processed, a decision on whether to accept the applicant is made and, in the case of approval, a card is issued. The cost to complete this entire process averaged just over $50 per approved application in 1995.

The credit quality of a card portfolio created by an issuer's initial investment will improve over time, all else (including the unemployment rate) constant, because the uncertainty inherent in the initial offer of credit is eliminated and because cardholders found not to be good credit risks are dropped over time. Moreover, the issuer will learn about each cardholder's charge and credit habits and from this information, her profit potential. Roughly speaking, the issuer's cardholders will consist of transactors and revolvers along with inactive cardholders. The most successful issuers obtain a high yield of profitable cardholders—creditworthy revolvers—from their initial investment. They obtain a bonus, too: they acquire information about the spending habits and creditworthiness of each active cardholder that they can use themselves or sell.

Card portfolios—the result of this "prospecting" for customers—are valuable assets. In fact, there is an active market for buying and selling portfolios of cardholders. The buyer obtains a group of cardholders whose spending and payment patterns have been observed for some time. The buyer avoids the expense of having to invest his own money in prospecting for customers. The seller obtains a return on her investment in the portfolio. The fact that issuers can sell their portfolios enables them to recover at least part of their investment if they decide to exit the business. In 1997, there were 22 portfolio ownership changes involving a record $21 billion in credit card receivables, nearly tripling the previous record of just over $7 billion of portfolio sales in 1996. Among the larger deals were the Bank of New York's sale of its $4 billion portfolio to Chase Manhattan and the sale of Advanta's $11 billion portfolio to Fleet Bank. This record level of portfolio sales does not even include the $22 billion of receivables that Banc One obtained when taking over the monoline First USA in 1997, which was classified as a merger, nor the sale of the $14 billion AT&T Universal portfolio to Citibank (discussed in the following section), because that deal was finalized in 1998.

In searching for new customers, credit card issuers try to persuade people to switch their balances to the new card from one or more of their existing cards. As part of the application process, consumers enter information on their existing account(s) and the amount of balances they want to switch. The issuer then arranges to pay off the loan and enters the balance owed to the new account for the issuer's own card. This procedure makes it easy for consumers to switch among cards and enables issuers to compete not only for new balances but for old ones as well.

An estimated $16.5 billion of balances were transferred to new credit card accounts in 1996, a sharp decline from 1995, when balance transfers totaled $32.5 billion. Even with this decline, between 1992 and 1996 balance transfers grew at an annual rate of nearly 50 percent. The standard incentive provided by issuers for transferring balances to new cards is the offer of introductory interest rates significantly below those normally paid. This initial interest rate discount, typically lasting six months, may range anywhere from five to ten percentage points. Although it has become easier for consumers to transfer balances to new cards, such activity may be limited for credit card borrowers, because the new card applications of those who make heavy use of credit card debt may be rejected relatively frequently.

Marketing Strategies

AT&T Universal Card   AT&T entered the credit card market in March 1990 with the introduction of its Universal Card. In its first six months of existence, 5 million AT&T Universal Cards were issued, and they generated $1.8 billion of transaction volume. Technically the Universal Card was an affinity card agreement between AT&T and Universal Bank (headquartered in Columbus, Georgia); AT&T effectively ran Universal Bank's credit card operations without being subject to banking laws. Through a rather complicated program, Universal Bank financed new consumer credit purchases, then proceeded to sell the receivables to AT&T at face value each day. Although this form of operation is rather common today, it was unusual at the time. Offering perks that were usually only associated with gold cards at the time, AT&T gained consumer favor through enhancements such as a promise of no annual fee for life, a 10 percent discount on long-distance calling, purchase protection, and insurance coverage on travel and automobile rentals.

AT&T aggressively marketed its card as truly "universal"; it could be used to make purchases, obtain cash advances, and make calling card calls. AT&T spent $30 million on advertising in the first three months after the card's introduction. By comparison, Citibank spent $55 million on credit card advertising for that entire year. AT&T also made great strides by offering the card in the college segment with the same benefits described above (albeit with a lower credit line) and teaming up with dozens of merchants and retailers, offering discounts on goods and services aimed at young adults.

In addition, AT&T assembled a well-trained customer service team rivaling that of American Express (Universal had a 20-second hold limit as its goal for telephone inquiries). AT&T was one of the first issuers to implement a technology that allows customer service representatives to access a cardholder's account simply on the basis of the telephone number from which the call is made. This innovation reduced the average service call time; such technologies are now standard throughout the industry. AT&T Universal's devotion to enhanced customer service was rewarded in 1992, when it became the first financial services firm ever awarded the prestigious Malcolm Baldrige National Quality Award by the Department of Commerce in recognition of AT&T Universal's quality management programs.

More than 80 percent of AT&T Universal Card holders also used AT&T as their long-distance carrier. AT&T was successful in combining formerly unrelated products (credit cards with long-distance and calling-card telephone service) into a single product. By doing so, AT&T ultimately increased customer loyalty while carrying the AT&T brand name into new, untapped markets.

Though all of these elements made for an extremely appealing credit card for consumers, they did not produce corresponding benefits for AT&T, which sold its entire credit card portfolio to Citibank in early 1998. AT&T's initial stress on not charging an annual fee had attracted a disproportionate share of transactor cardholders, who generally paid off balances in full each month and thus generated low finance charge revenue. (As previously noted, finance charges constitute a majority of revenue for the average bankcard issuer.) Even with this large share of transactors, AT&T Universal was suffering major credit losses, increasing from $220 million at the end of 1993 to more than $800 million by the beginning of 1997. These losses likely stemmed from AT&T's aggressive marketing in late 1993 and early 1994 when it (along with many other issuers) attempted to increase transaction volume and finance charge revenue by extending cards to less creditworthy applicants.

MBNA   From its humble beginnings in a converted A&P supermarket in Delaware in 1982 to its wildly popular public stock offering in 1991 to its status as the market leader in affinity cards, the development of MBNA into the second-largest bankcard issuer has been rapid and highly profitable. MBNA is widely regarded as the king of affinity cards, which constituted more than 60 percent of its portfolio of nearly 30 million cards issued and $64 billion of annual charge volume in 1997. MBNA earned profits of $630 million in 1997, an increase of 29 percent over the previous year. Integral to its rapid growth has been its reliance on a unique marketing strategy that seeks to recruit "upper-market" customers (generally viewed to be safer credit risks) through the promotion of affinity cards. Many believe the key to MBNA's marketing savvy has been its ability to develop a series of cards that act as visual symbols of consumers' lifestyles and that offer benefits tailored to their cardholders' interests.

For example, holders of the MBNA Ralston Purina Pet Card are entitled to $50 of Purina pet product coupons annually, in addition to a free video of pet care tips (and ads for Purina products). MBNA offers credit cards representing more than 4,500 different groups, from professional sports teams (such as the New York Yankees) to colleges and universities (including Penn State and Georgetown) to Star Trek fans. To exploit economies of scale, MBNA also issues credit cards for smaller banks and thrifts that lack the resources and infrastructure to obtain and manage new accounts efficiently. Whatever the affinity, the vast majority of MBNA-issued credit cards offer many features in common: no annual fee, introductory periods at low interest rates followed by a competitive APR thereafter (traditionally below market averages), and some sort of reward for card usage.

Citibank   Citibank's latest marketing strategy can be summed up in a word: global. By providing consumers with a full range of financial and banking services, Citibank has become the one-stop-shopping bank of the financial world. Citicorp launched its first global advertising campaign in 1997 in an attempt to promote itself as a worldwide brand, as Coca-Cola and Nike have done, above and beyond its actual products and services. Citibank's switch from Visa to MasterCard was in part motivated by its desire to emphasize its brand over the system's brand. Citibank is building its image by employing a strategy that stresses broad themes, such as globalization and technology. Citibank also markets through more conventional methods such as cobranding, holding sweepstakes for its card members, and offering customers convenient high-tech banking and ways to save money.

Citibank has the strongest name recognition of any U.S. bank abroad and has been successful in expanding into countries many in the industry previously considered impenetrable. Its marketing strategy in India, for example, targets well-off professionals and offers them preapproved cards. In Indonesia, Citibank uses promotions, such as sweepstakes, to attract customers and offers incentives to cardholders who enlist others to apply. Many international customers are amazed at the consistent and reliable customer service they experience from Citibank, as opposed to the sometimes casual and erratic service their domestic banks offer. They also enjoy the prestige associated with an American credit card.

In addition to being in the forefront of the foreign market, Citibank has long led the way in the United States. It launched the first cobranded credit card, the Citibank AAdvantage Card, in 1987 with American Airlines. The card offers members one mile in the American Airlines frequent flyer program for each dollar charged on the card. It is one of the largest cobranded airline programs in the United States, with more than 2.5 million accounts. A more recent venture is the Jack Nicklaus Visa card, designed to attract golfers and fans of Nicklaus. The card features the

Nicklaus Reward Program, which gives members one point for every dollar charged. Members can redeem their points for free golf vacations. They also receive previews of new golf equipment and a golf tip "direct from Nicklaus" in each monthly statement.

Like AT&T, Citibank has also marketed heavily to college students. Beginning in 1991, it held the Citibank College Advertising Awards contest, which challenged students to create a multimedia ad campaign for a fictional Citibank credit card to be targeted at college students and their parents. Citibank gave away $36,000 in cash prizes, and members of the winning team had the opportunity to pursue a summer internship with a Citibank ad agency in New York.

BankBoston   In 1989, Bank of Boston sold its entire $780 million credit card portfolio to Chase Manhattan. As part of the deal, Bank of Boston was prohibited from issuing credit cards for five years, a measure designed to keep it from competing against Chase. In 1995, Bank of Boston reentered the credit card market. In July 1996, it acquired BayBanks, adding roughly 350,000 credit card accounts, and changed its name to BankBoston. By 1997, it was the thirty-sixth largest bankcard issuer with more than $2 billion of transaction volume.

Part of BankBoston's strategy has been to lure revolvers away from their existing cards. To do so, it has offered low introductory interest rates on its cards. Additionally, in September 1995, Bank of Boston Corp. announced its future "Starts Low, Stays Low" campaign, with interest rates that would start at 1.85 percent below prime for the first six months and then increase to a variable rate of 3.75 percent above prime. They also guaranteed that customers who carried balances would save money and pledged to refund the annual fee to any customer who found after one year that he or she hadn't saved money.

BankBoston also relied on cobranding programs to attract new customers both domestically and internationally. In 1995, for instance, it launched two cobranded cards in Brazil, one with General Motors and another with United Airlines. According to an article in the Brazilian business newspaper *Gazeta Mercantil Online*, the cobranded cards were "decisive in the bank's outstanding performance in the area."

Market Structure

Economists often look at an industry's structure to predict the nature and intensity of competition within. An extreme market structure is described by the textbook case of perfect competition, in which

- a large number of competing firms vie for the consumer's dollar,
- these sellers produce identical products,
- no seller is large enough to affect market price significantly by itself,
- firms can enter and exit the industry easily without substantial unrecoverable (i.e., sunk) costs,
- consumers have good information about the choices available to them, and
- consumers can switch vendors when better offers are available to them.

Almost all real industries depart from this ideal to some extent, most commonly because firms do not produce identical products. In most industries, firms try to distinguish themselves from their competitors by making their products different and by targeting particular consumer segments. Sometimes product uniqueness is the whole game (e.g., perfumes); in other industries differentiation is the result of innovation (e.g., pharmaceuticals).

As we discussed in chapter 7, payment cards are moderately differentiated compared with other products. All credit cards offer consumers the ability to make payments and to finance purchases. There are few differences among competing card issuers in how they provide these two basic services. Nevertheless, card issuers find other ways to compete. They embellish their cards' basic services with a variety of additional services and benefits that provide added value to their cardholders' wallets. These benefits include such offers as low introductory interest rates, rewards and rebates, low or no annual fees, and emergency credit. They also include benefits not related to the cards, including frequent flyer airline mileage, discounts on theater tickets and sporting events, and the philanthropic distribution of profits to organizations such as the U.S. Olympic Ski Team.

Cardholders appreciate these added benefits. A recent consumer survey commissioned by Faulkner & Gray found that an attractive introductory interest rate was the prime credit card selection criterion for more than a third of all respondents. Almost 20 percent of all respondents said that rewards and rebates were the prime selection criteria for their cards. Finally, 15 percent of respondents claimed that their main credit card selection criterion was the "no annual fee" offered by many issuers. Among credit card issuers, the development of attractive new features is crucial. The race to offer new services and benefits and to find consumer segments to whom these benefits appeal drives the day-to-day competition in the payment card industry.

But as we now argue, in almost every other way besides product differentiation, issuing payment cards conforms closely to the competitive ideal.

Large Number of Competing Firms

Competition takes place between the banks that issue MasterCard and Visa cards, most of whom issue both cards, and between Visa and MasterCard issuers and the other payment card brands: American Express charge cards, American Express Optima, and Discover. Each of these issuers sets interest rates, fees, features, and marketing strategy independently of all other issuers.

A 1998 Federal Reserve System survey of 148 of the largest credit card issuers in the United States found that seventy-two issuers distribute their cards nationally. The same survey reported that forty-five additional issuers distribute cards regionally in areas encompassing more than one state but do not issue them nationally. Moreover, the Federal Reserve System survey excluded many smaller, local banks that also issue credit cards, generally making them available at least to their good depository customers. Consumers in Chicago, for instance, can therefore obtain cards from more than seventy national issuers in addition to many more local and regional issuers. Consumers have more choice in their credit card issuer than they have for many other services. For example, in Chicago a typical consumer can choose among fifteen grocery store chains, twenty-seven health maintenance organizations, and eighty-two national or regional newspapers.

No Single Issuer Is Large Relative to the Industry

If a single issuer dominated the industry, it could perhaps act like a monopolist, raising charges above competitive levels, reducing output, and harming consumers. In fact, none of the numerous credit and charge card issuers dominate the industry. Table 9.1 reports the shares of the top ten payment card issuers according to charge volume, outstandings, and number of cards in 1997. American Express had the largest share based on transaction volume; Citibank and MBNA had the largest shares based on outstandings. Discover had the largest share based on number of cards. None of these shares, however, is large relative to shares of leading firms in many other industries.

Economists are also concerned that if a few leading firms together dominate an industry, they might be able to produce a monopoly outcome by reaching an understanding to compete less intensively. (An explicit agreement of this sort would be absolutely illegal, but U.S. merger policy is driven in large part by a belief that the fewer the leading firms, the more likely a tacit or implicit agreement becomes.) If many firms would have to be party to such an agreement in order for it to have a significant impact on the market, the risk of a monopoly outcome is greatly reduced, since stable anticompetitive agreements (explicit or implicit) involving many firms are rare. If a small number of firms account for most of an industry's sales, the industry is said to be "concentrated."

A common measure of industry concentration is the total share of sales accounted for by the four largest firms. (There is no magic in the number four, but it has become a convention.) The four largest credit and charge card issuers have a combined share of between 31 and 42 percent, depending on the measure used. In more than 40 percent of all manufacturing industries, the four largest firms account for more than 40 percent of the value of shipments in the industry. Thus, in terms of concentration, the payment card industry is about average relative to manufacturing. Less comprehensive data are available for other industries. But the largest eight property and casualty insurance companies have a 36.6 percent share and the largest eight securities brokerage firms have a 47.2 percent share.

Another common measure of industry concentration is the Herfindahl-Hirschman Index (HHI). The HHI is equal to the sum of the squared

Table 9.1
No single credit or charge card issuer was large relative to the industry in 1997.

		Top issuers ranked by share of:		
Rank	Total volume	Total outstandings	Total cards	
1	American Express	16.83%	Citibank	10.42%	Discover	9.88%
2	Citibank	11.50	MBNA America	9.62	Citibank	8.18
3	MBNA America	7.09	Banc One/First USA	8.32	Banc One/First USA	6.61
4	Discover	6.34	Discover	7.50	Chase Manhattan	6.22
5	First Chicago NBD	5.27	Chase Manhattan	7.03	American Express	6.12
6	Banc One/First USA	4.58	American Express	6.79	MBNA America	6.03
7	Chase Manhattan	4.45	First Chicago NBD	3.91	AT&T Universal	5.00
8	Household Bank	3.33	Household Bank	3.74	Household Bank	4.38
9	AT&T Universal	3.10	AT&T Universal	3.31	First Chicago NBD	4.36
10	US Bancorp	2.99	Capital One	2.95	Capital One	3.62

Source: The Nilson Report, no. 660, January 1998.

values of each seller's percentage market share. With n firms of equal size, each firm's percentage share is $(100/n)$, and the HHI is equal to $n(100/n)(100/n) = 10,000/n$. This measure of industry concentration can range from 0 (in the limit as n becomes large) to 10,000 ($n = 1$, a monopoly), with higher values indicating higher concentration. The Antitrust Division of the U.S. Department of Justice and the Federal Trade Commission consider industries with HHIs of less than 1,000 to be presumptively competitive. Based on the charge volume of the 100 largest card issuers in 1997, the HHI for the general-purpose payment card industry was 639. (Since the top 100 issuers account for approximately 93 percent of total U.S. charge volume, we conservatively assumed that the remaining 7 percent of transaction volume was equally distributed among issuers of size equal to that of the 100th largest issuer.) The payment card industry has an HHI well within the competitive range, especially when compared to industries such as breakfast cereals (2,253), automobiles (2,676), and greeting cards (2,922).

Table 9.2 reports the shares, based on transaction volume, of the twenty-five largest Visa and MasterCard issuers in 1997. Citibank was the largest issuer with 15.2 percent of Visa and MasterCard volume. The four largest bankcard issuers had a 38 percent share of this segment of the payment card industry based on transaction volume.

Entry and Exit Are Easy

Entering the payment card industry as an issuer is fairly easy. Over the years, for example, Visa has had a virtually open membership policy. From the mid-1970s, any financial institution eligible for FDIC insurance was also eligible for Visa membership. In the mid-1980s, Congress adopted legislation that allowed the creation of several new types of financial institutions, thus expanding the number of institutions eligible for Visa membership. As a result, financial institutions owned by or affiliated with nonbanks such as retailers, investment firms, insurance companies, and automakers issue Visa cards and MasterCards today. Only companies that issue cards that compete directly with Visa and Master-Card, namely Discover and American Express, have been precluded from issuing Visa cards or MasterCards. This rule has led to antitrust litigation that we discuss in chapter 11.

Table 9.2
No single bankcard issuer was large relative to the bankcard industry in 1997.

Rank	Top bankcard issuers ranked by share of:			
	Charge volume		Outstandings	
1	Citibank	15.16%	Citibank	12.16%
2	MBNA America	9.36	MBNA America	11.23
3	First Chicago NBD	6.94	Banc One/First USA	9.71
4	Banc One/First USA	6.17	Chase Manhattan	8.20
5	Chase Manhattan	5.87	First Chicago NBD	4.56
6	Household Bank	5.05	Household Bank	4.37
7	AT&T Universal	4.09	AT&T Universal	3.86
8	US Bancorp	3.94	Capital One	3.44
9	NationsBank	3.42	Advanta	2.84
10	Bank of America	3.22	Bank of America	2.63
11	Capital One	2.92	NationsBank	2.29
12	Advanta	1.81	Providian	1.97
13	Wells Fargo Bank	1.66	Wells Fargo Bank	1.85
14	Providian	1.28	First Union National	1.59
15	USAA Federal	1.21	US Bancorp	1.52
16	Wachovia Bank	1.17	Wachovia Bank	1.51
17	First Union National	1.01	Associates National	1.47
18	Associates National	0.94	GE Capital Consumer	1.36
19	Chevy Chase FSB	0.91	Chevy Chase FSB	1.29
20	PNC Bank	0.85	PNC Bank	0.97
21	GE Capital Consumer	0.85	USAA Federal	0.95
22	People's Bank	0.78	Direct Merchants	0.90
23	Marine Midland	0.64	First National of Nebraska	0.84
24	First National of Nebraska	0.57	People's Bank	0.81
25	Travelers Bank	0.52	Fleet Bank	0.69

Source: The Nilson Report, no. 660, January 1998.
Note: Shares are calculated as a percentage of all bankcard issuers.

Since 1992, to become a member of the Visa association, an institution must pay an initial service fee that depends on the type of membership applied for, the type of card(s) to be issued, and the number of accounts projected after three years. An institution can apply as a principal, associate, or participant member and can issue credit cards, debit cards, or both. Principal members are provided the most flexibility in issuing and acquiring, as they have no limit on account sales volume, may receive association dividends, and may sponsor other members. Associate members are required to have a principal member sponsor their card operations and are limited to quarterly sales volume of $7 million, but do have voting rights, and may have members on the board of directors. Participant members must join as either credit or debit members, but not both, may not have members on the board of directors, and have similar sales volume limits to those for associate members. Members must pay quarterly service fees based on sales volumes. MasterCard has similar initial membership fees and, like Visa, a quarterly fee structure based on transaction volumes.

To give some sense of the membership fees involved for new members, for a medium-sized Visa issuer with 80,000 accounts and $200 million of annual transaction volume after three years of operations, cumulative membership fees over the first five years of the card would total about $1.7 million. For a large issuer with 3.5 million accounts and $8.6 billion of annual sales volume, membership fees would be about $72 million for the first five years. With annual interest income averaging approximately $160 per bankcard account, the mid-sized firm would earn $64 million over the first five years from finance charges, and the large issuer would receive finance charge revenues of $2.7 billion. Clearly, the Visa membership fees are insignificant relative to the typical revenues from bankcard operations.

Visa established its current fee structure to reflect the value of membership and the costs of supporting new members. In adopting this fee structure, it recognized that the value that new members bring by expanding the cardholder and merchant base has declined substantially over time. As a result, new members obtain considerable value from the investments made by earlier members to establish the system and brand name. But new members do not, at this stage in the evolution of the system, help

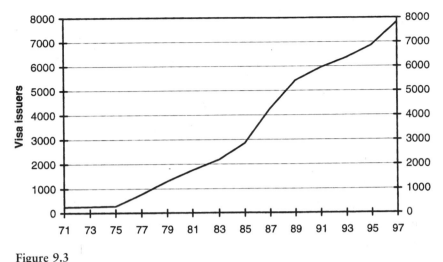

Figure 9.3
The number of Visa issuers has increased dramatically over time.
Source: Visa U.S.A.
Note: Figures include both credit and debit card issuers.

much to expand the system or to enhance the brand name. By charging
new members higher fees than earlier members had to pay, Visa reduces
the extent to which new members obtain a free ride on the investments
made and risks borne by earlier members.

Visa's and MasterCard's open membership policies and low entry
costs, together with the expansion of demand for payment cards, resulted
in a great deal of entry after the industry's early difficulties were behind
it. Figure 9.3 shows the number of Visa issuers from 1971 to 1997. Between 1981 and 1991, the Visa system had a net increase of about 4,200
issuer members, both small and large. Between 1991 and 1997, there was
a net increase of about another 1,800 issuers; more than two-thirds of
these joined to issue debit cards exclusively. (We discuss the growth of
debit cards in the 1990s in chapter 12.)

Some institutions' credit card programs have matured in a relatively
brief period. For example, one member joined the Visa system in the second quarter of 1982 with a reported quarterly volume of $2.7 million.
By the second quarter of 1997, that member had become one of the
largest Visa issuers, with a quarterly charge volume of approximately

$3 billion. Smaller banks and institutions have also entered the Visa system over time. In the second half of 1997, more than sixty financial institutions with less than $5 million in assets entered the Visa system.

As mentioned earlier, a number of financial institutions owned by or affiliated with large nonfinancial corporations joined the MasterCard and/or Visa associations in the early 1990s. The largest entrant by far was AT&T, which spent more than $130 million on advertising, acquisition, telemarketing, and sales promotion. AT&T entered in March 1990. By 1992, it was the fifth-largest issuer of Visa cards and MasterCards. In late 1992, GM rolled out its national MasterCard program with a reported initial marketing budget of nearly $80 million. Meanwhile, General Electric budgeted $23 million for promotion of its credit card, released in 1992.

Some entrants, of course, do not succeed in the payment card business and exit the industry entirely. The most dramatic examples of this took place in late 1997 and early 1998 when AT&T and Advanta sold off their portfolios to Citibank and Fleet Bank, respectively. As previously discussed, AT&T put its entire credit card business up for sale because of high default and charge-off rates that dramatically reduced profitability. In 1997, four of the top twenty credit card portfolios in the United States—those of Advanta, AT&T, First USA, and Bank of New York—were put up for sale or sold.

The development of markets for bankcard portfolios has made exit less painful. Members that wish to exit, for whatever reason, can sell their portfolios to other members. Indeed, many of the recent entrants into the payment card industry have purchased existing portfolios of cards. The sale of portfolios helps the owner recoup the cost of acquiring and nurturing cardholders and thereby reduces the amount of sunk and unrecoverable investment costs. That, in turn, makes entry into payment cards less risky and, other things being equal, increases the expected profitability of entry.

Not all entrants, however, choose to purchase a card portfolio to build a credit card program. In 1985, for instance, Sears chose to leverage its existing portfolio of retail cardholders to launch the Discover Card. According to some estimates, it took the program almost three years to generate positive after-tax net income, at a cost of about $330 million.

As explained above, one disadvantage of independently launching a card program as opposed to purchasing an existing portfolio is the high sunk and unrecoverable costs one incurs.

Information Is Widely Available to Consumers

Consumers have fairly extensive information about payment cards, largely because of issuers' advertising and marketing activities. During 1997, issuers sent out 3 billion direct-mail credit card solicitations, an increase of 26 percent over the previous year. This resulted in an average of approximately two-and-a-half solicitations per month for each household in the United States. With advertising spending by the card systems alone approaching three-quarters of a billion dollars, consumers are inundated with information for various cards. Other sources increase the availability of information to consumers. Newspapers publish lists of low-rate cards, and since 1990 the Federal Reserve has published a survey of credit card plans for about 150 issuers. Information is also readily available over the Internet, where one can locate information on the best credit cards available based on a variety of searchable criteria.

Consumer Switching Costs Seem Low

There has been a debate in the research literature over the cost to consumers of switching from one credit card to another to take advantage of lower interest rates or other features. At least in recent years, switching costs for most customers appear to have been quite low: credit card offers mailed to consumers have frequently included an option to roll over existing balances to a new card. With such offers readily available, taking advantage of lower interest rates or other card features seems quite easy for most cardholders. This suggests that both the search costs (What cards are available?) and switching costs (How much of a hassle is it to switch?) are low.

In a recent article, Paul Calem and Loretta Mester have estimated a statistical model that they claim demonstrates that switching costs matter. They found that current credit card balances had a positive (and statistically significant) correlation with past credit rejections. They interpreted this to mean that consumers face switching costs in the credit card market, because carrying balances will make consumers more likely to be rejected for future credit.

Even if one accepts their estimated results at face value, though, Calem and Mester have not demonstrated that this conclusion holds. At best, they have shown that consumers with currently high credit card balances are more likely than other consumers (all else equal) to have been turned down for credit at least once in the previous five years. One criticism (which Calem and Mester duly note but dismiss) is that the direction of causality may be reversed: having been turned down for some other form of credit, a consumer with a credit card may then be more likely than other consumers to load up on credit card debt. Such behavior seems quite possible and would explain Calem and Mester's estimated results. A second criticism is that the result may have little or nothing to do with the ability to roll over balances from one credit card account to a new account. The credit rejection variable that they analyze includes all types of credit, including, for instance, mortgage loans, not just credit cards. As a result, even if carrying high balances has an effect on future credit rejections, it does not necessarily have an effect on future credit card rejections.

Several authors have pointed out that even modest switching costs might inhibit switching to some extent. Consider a cardholder with balances of $2,160, approximately the average outstandings per Visa account in 1996 for those accounts incurring finance charges. If the cardholder paid finance charges at an annual rate of 13.8 percent, approximately the average credit card rate for Visa cardholders in 1996, total finance charges for a year would be about $300. Dropping the interest rate by a full percentage point, to 12.8 percent, would reduce the annual finance charges by only $22.

In general, however, the switching costs currently imposed on consumers seeking new credit card accounts seem minimal. With the average household receiving thirty direct-mail credit card solicitations each year, the search costs for credit offers have never been lower. The massive increases in balance transfers that have taken place this decade reveal just how easy it has become for consumers to switch from one issuer to another. The fact that borrowing users with good payment records are the most desirable customers for issuers because of revenues generated from interest payments on balances is likely to mitigate relatively higher switching costs for revolving customers resulting from credit rejections. Thus, the low costs imposed on consumers to switch credit card issuers enhance the arguments for strong competition in the bankcard industry.

Market Performance

The payment card industry's performance is consistent with its competitive structure. Consumers have benefited from the rapid expansion of payment card services as well as from numerous innovations. As a consequence, the prices of payment card services have not kept pace with the general rate of inflation. Finally, competition among issuers has dissipated most of the profits that could have been earned from the innovations that have made payment cards such a widely used method of payment and financing.

Output

By any measure, the payment card industry has experienced rapid growth in the last three decades. Figure 9.4 shows several key measures of total bankcard output over this period. The compound annual growth rate in transaction volume (in 1998 dollars, as always) was 17.9 percent in the 1970s, 11.9 percent in the 1980s, and 14.8 percent thus far in the 1990s. The number of cards increased at an average annual rate of 12.4 percent in the 1970s, 6.1 percent in the 1980s, and 11.7 percent thus far in the 1990s. The compounded growth rate of outstanding balances was 17.3 percent in the 1970s, 15.2 percent in the 1980s, and 11.7 percent thus far in the 1990s.

Consumers have obtained more cards over time, increased their usage of these cards (charging more per card), and increased the amount owed per card, as shown in figure 9.5. The average outstanding balance—the best available measure of the use of cards as sources of credit—and the annual transaction volume have increased for Visa cardholders over time. This growth has come about through the expansion of existing card issuers and through the entry of new issuers.

The output of the payment card industry has expanded more rapidly than the economy. Between 1971 and 1997, the number of cards in

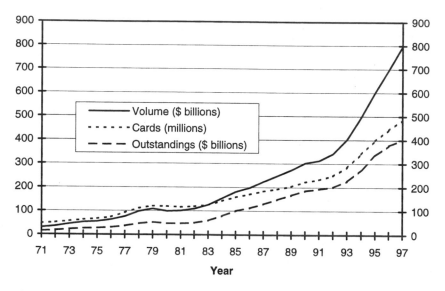

Figure 9.4
All measures of output for Visa and MasterCard have grown substantially over time.
Source: Visa U.S.A.

circulation increased by more than 900 percent, while the number of households increased by only 54 percent. The total dollar volume of credit card transactions increased by 2,630 percent in that same period while personal consumption expenditures increased by 125 percent. Finally, outstanding balances increased by 2,700 percent while total consumer credit outstanding increased by 140 percent. This is, of course, just another way of saying that payment cards have grown at the expense of other means of payment and other sources of credit.

Prices

As we have discussed, many factors besides finance charges affect the true price that consumers pay for payment card services, including annual and other fees, the rate of inflation, the tax deductibility of credit card interest, the nature of the grace period, and the method used for assessing finance charges. To see how payment card prices have changed over time, we have constructed a price index that accounts for these and other elements

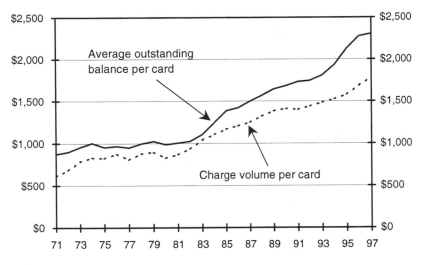

Figure 9.5
Use of cards as payment devices and sources of credit has increased significantly over time.
Source: Visa U.S.A.
Note: Average outstanding balance includes only accounts with outstanding balances.

as well as available data permit. The price index shows that the price of credit card services declined by 7 percent from 1984 to 1996. (This price index applies to MasterCard and Visa issuers, which account for 73 percent of all credit and charge card transaction volume, and includes only annual fees, service fees, and finance charges. The price index does not factor in card features such as frequent flyer mileage or insurance coverage.)

Because of data limitations, we focused on the period 1984–1996. During this period, the economy experienced a recession between 1990 and 1991. Inflation declined from an annual rate of about 4 percent in 1984 to about 2.75 percent in 1992 and had fallen to an annual rate of 1.9 percent by 1996.

Note that although the costs of providing credit cards to consumers and the price that consumers pay for credit cards should track each other in the long run, they do not do so in the short run. There is a lag between setting card prices and resulting charge-offs, for instance, and the charge-offs vary over time depending on economic conditions. Although finance charges are the major cost to consumers, the corresponding cost of funds accounts for only about 40 percent of the total cost issuers incur. Other major costs include processing transactions, advertising, and soliciting new accounts, as well as charge-offs.

In developing a price index, it is also necessary to consider how inflation affects consumers' real costs in financing their balances. Suppose, for example, that the finance charge was 10 percent during a period when the inflation rate was also 10 percent. A consumer who charged $100 at the beginning of the year and paid all balances off at the end of the year would have to pay back $100 plus approximately $10 in interest—a total of $110. However, with inflation of 10 percent, the $110 paid at the end of the year has about the same value as the $100 charged at the beginning of the year. In general, the real interest paid by the consumer equals the nominal interest rate minus the inflation rate over the period of time in which the consumer carries balances.

These prices also ignore several additional factors that affect the prices that consumers pay for credit cards and the prices that issuers receive for them. Both of these prices depend on the extent to which consumers actually pay their bills. If a consumer defaults on a credit card loan, the issuer loses not only the consumer's interest payments but the principal as well. The additional cost of these charge-offs decreases the effective price paid for credit. In the most recent recession, the charge-off rate increased from 3 percent to 4.4 percent, leading to a sharp decline in the effective finance rate consumers paid, on average, to issuers.

Tax deductions for consumer interest also influence the price of payment cards to the consumer. Until 1991, at least some portion of interest paid on credit cards was deductible from federal taxable income taxes for individuals who itemized deductions. The Tax Reform Act of 1986 gradually phased out the deductibility of credit card interest between 1987 and 1991, increasing the after-tax cost of credit card loans to consumers who itemized their deductions.

Figure 9.6 shows average real after-tax and before-tax credit card interest rates to the consumer. The real after-tax interest rate rose by 0.7 percentage points between the second quarter of 1986 and the first quarter of 1989, despite the decline in real before-tax interest rates. The sharp

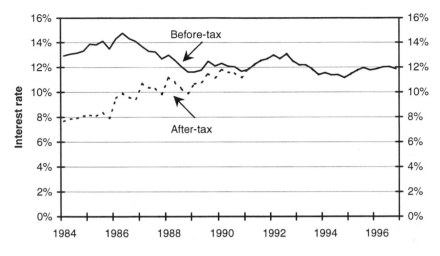

Figure 9.6
After-tax credit card interest rates increased after 1986 because of tax law changes.
Source: Visa U.S.A.
Note: Interest rates are net of inflation (or "real" interest rates).

increase in real after-tax interest rates during this period may help account for two related developments in the payment card industry. First, consumers reportedly became much more sensitive to interest rates than they had been in the first half of the 1980s; and second, by the early 1990s, issuers appeared to compete more aggressively on the basis of low interest rates rather than on other card dimensions.

Consumers end up paying the after tax/charge off-adjusted price on credit card balances. Issuers end up receiving the before-tax/charge-off-adjusted price. These two prices, which are critical for understanding issuer and consumer behavior, are shown in figure 9.7. The price that issuers actually received declined over the period we examined because charge-off rates increased. Prices declined by almost 35 percent between the first quarter of 1984 and the fourth quarter of 1996. The price that the typical consumer actually paid, however, decreased by 7 percent over this same period, and would have decreased significantly more had tax laws not been changed.

The fact that the average price issuers received declined by nearly 35 percent is not surprising, given the expansion of the credit card industry

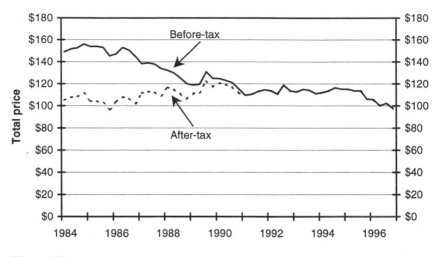

Figure 9.7
Price received by issuers declined significantly between 1984 and 1996 while after-tax price paid by cardholders remained roughly constant.
Source: Visa U.S.A.
Note: Total price equals the sum of service fees, finance charges, and annual fees less charge-offs.

during the 1980s. Credit card volume and outstandings expanded over the period in part because credit lines were increased (which always increases the issuer's risks) and in part because cards were issued to individuals who had previously not qualified. From 1983 to 1995, the percentage of the population above the age of 18 carrying at least one bankcard increased from 43 to 66 percent. The increase in credit lines was even more striking. From 1989 to 1995, the average credit line for credit cardholders increased by 65 percent, from $5,530 to $9,130.

Finally, it is important to emphasize that this price index does not reflect changes in the quality of credit cards. Though it is hard to quantify this, the quality of credit cards clearly increased over the period considered. Credit cards are more valuable to consumers if more merchants take them. Between 1985 and 1995, the number of merchants in the United States that accepted Visa cards increased from 2.2 million to 3.3 million. Because of system improvements, consumers did not have to wait as long for their transactions to be approved. Finally, credit cards had many more features, such as rebates, frequent flyer miles, and warranty programs, by the end of the period under consideration.

Innovations and Other Improvements in the Quality of Payment Cards
The value of payment cards to consumers has increased dramatically over the history of the industry. We discussed some of the major improvements in our earlier discussion of system competition. The number of merchants that accept payment cards from the various systems has increased dramatically over time, thereby increasing the usefulness of payment cards to consumers. The time it takes to process a transaction at a merchant has also declined dramatically over time. Credit card theft and fraud, which can be inconvenient for cardholders as well as merchants and issuers, has also become less of a problem because of improvements by the payment card systems. One such innovation is the Cardholder Risk Identification System (CRIS) developed by Visa. CRIS uses computer neural network technology to predict the probability that a particular transaction is fraudulent and prompts the issuer to contact the cardholder if a certain threshold is exceeded.

In addition to implementing these system-level innovations, the payment card issuers have introduced numerous innovative card features that make these cards more valuable to consumers. One major innovation was the Citibank and American Airlines cobranded card that awards frequent flyer mileage based on purchases made using the card. Subsequently, American Express included airline mileage in its Membership Rewards program as well as its cobranded card with Delta Airlines, and other bank issuers offered cobranded cards such as the First Chicago card with United Airlines. Citibank was also a pioneer in its use of the photograph of the cardholder on the front of the card for security purposes, an innovation that BankAmerica and other banks have subsequently copied. Affinity cards, such as the ones issued by MBNA, are yet another example of successful innovation; as discussed earlier, these cards allow consumers to choose an affiliation with their card, such as a favorite charity or football team.

Discover was innovative in the use of its cashback bonus award that provided a rebate to consumers based on purchases. Discover also offered its card without an annual fee, which was then relatively uncommon. Subsequently, many Visa and MasterCard banks and American Express followed with no-fee offerings.

Historic Profitability

The measurement of profitability for the payment card industry is complicated and controversial. The proper measurement of rates of return requires a careful determination of which cost items should be expensed and which capitalized as well as the proper depreciation rate for capital expenditures. Before the rate of return for the payment card industry can be compared with rates of return in other industries, the financial risks in these various industries must be assessed and compared. At this point, data limitations preclude a definitive treatment of these issues. Claims that the payment card industry makes exorbitant profits, however, are dubious because they are based on estimates that do not treat capital and depreciation properly and do not assess credit card lending risks. The next chapter deals with some of these complications and controversies. Here we confine ourselves to reporting historic accounting profitability data on the credit card portion of the payment card industry.

The Federal Reserve Board's *Functional Cost Analysis (FCA)*, based on data obtained from a sample of commercial banks, is one of the major sources of data on the profitability of credit cards over time. Figures from the *FCA* need to be viewed with some caution because the sample is not random and has changed over time and banks in the *FCA* tend to be small and medium-sized institutions. Thus, the largest issuers tend to be excluded. In addition, of course, the data are for credit cards and do not include information on charge cards.

Table 9.3 reports the rate of return on assets (net before-tax earnings divided by assets) on credit card lending and other forms of lending for 1974–1996. As we will discuss in detail in the next chapter, using these accounting rates of return to assess economic profitability presents a number of problems. Nevertheless, over a long time period, these data provide some indications of the relative profitability of credit card operations to other types of lending. The average historical rate of return on credit cards has been lower than that on other bank lending to consumers. Credit card lending has had an average return of 1.77 percent, about 0.40

Table 9.3
Accounting rates of return are lower for credit card lending than for other types of lending.

Year	Before-tax earnings as a percent of outstanding balances			
	Credit card	Installment	Real estate mortgage	Commercial and other
1974	0.77%	1.56%	2.21%	3.49%
1975	1.58	2.34	2.74	2.60
1976	2.73	2.45	2.85	1.84
1977	3.09	2.75	3.18	1.86
1978	2.55	2.82	2.70	2.86
1979	1.62	2.32	2.06	4.02
1980	−1.61	1.57	1.65	4.58
1981	1.00	1.69	0.73	5.38
1982	2.32	2.81	0.91	3.26
1983	2.36	3.17	2.16	1.49
1984	3.42	2.81	2.10	1.95
1985	3.97	2.70	2.86	1.40
1986	3.28	2.57	2.37	0.97
1987	3.38	2.31	3.05	1.34
1988	2.53	2.23	2.70	1.96
1989	1.20	2.21	2.67	2.43
1990	1.51	1.92	1.66	0.79
1991	3.12	1.72	2.72	1.12
1992	2.92	2.02	3.16	0.77
1993	4.22	2.14	3.20	1.35
1994	1.44	1.45	3.18	1.90
1995	−2.93	1.01	3.10	2.29
1996	−3.75	0.99	3.06	1.99
Average 1974–1986	1.77	2.15	2.48	2.25
Average 1980–1989	2.19	2.41	2.12	2.48
Average 1990–1996	0.93	1.61	2.87	1.46

Source: "The Profitability of Credit Card Operations of Depository Institutions," Board of Governors of the Federal Reserve System, August 1997, table 2. Available at <*http://www.bog.frb.fed.us/boarddocs/RptCongress/creditcard/CCPROFIT.htm*>.

percentage points below that for installment loans, such as automobile loans. Even though credit card operations have lower rates of return, credit card lending is substantially riskier than other bank lending because the loans are generally not secured. In table 9.3, it is apparent that the profitability of credit cards has been much more variable than that of other types of consumer lending.

During the mid-1980s, credit card profits were robust as a result of the decline in the cost of funds to banks (due to the decline in interest rates) and the increased demand for payment cards for both payment and finance (due to the economic expansion that began in 1982). Rates of return exceeded those in other kinds of lending in several years between 1983 and 1994.

There are many indications that profitability of credit cards has declined once again. Credit card charge-offs reached an all-time high in 1997, with 5.9 percent of outstandings being charged off. Large issuers such as Citibank reported 20 percent declines in profits from credit card operations between 1996 and 1997. Consumers have also increasingly been paying off their monthly balances in full. One reflection of diminished profitability is that prices of credit card portfolios have dropped significantly. From 1986 to 1990, the average weighted gross premium paid for these portfolios (relative to the value of the outstanding balances) was in the range of 19–20 percent. In 1997, the average premium was only 13 percent.

Consolidation in Banking and Cards

Although the record level of credit card portfolio sales in 1997 caused moderate shifts in the relative rankings of bankcard issuers, the massive bank merger wave of 1998 had more noticeable effects among the top issuers. In the first half of 1998 alone, the four largest proposed bank mergers represented merging assets of more than $1.7 trillion. These included the merger of the largest bankcard issuer, Citibank, with the Travelers Group; two of the ten largest issuers merging when Banc One/ First USA took over First Chicago; NationsBank merging with Bank of America; and Norwest Bank merging with Wells Fargo Bank. Including

Citibank's purchase of the AT&T portfolio, these eight banks combined accounted for more than $280 billion of total credit card volume in 1997, or more than 40 percent of all bankcard volume. With the combination of the First Chicago and Banc One/First USA portfolios, the resulting Bank One is likely to be the second largest bankcard issuer after Citibank/Travelers, and the combined NationsBank/Bank of America portfolio will presumably make it the fifth largest bankcard issuer.

Even after these mergers and the portfolio sales of 1998, however, the credit card industry remains a fiercely competitive marketplace. Incorporating the mergers mentioned above with the other bank mergers and portfolio acquisitions of the first ten months of 1998, we calculated a new HHI for this industry structure based on the likely market shares after the transactions are completed. Even with these sizeable acquisitions among the top issuers and other mergers and portfolio sales, the index increased by only 141 points, from 639 to 780, still well within the government's guidelines for a competitive industry.

This movement of mergers among the largest commercial bank issuers, combined with the purchases of the First USA, Advanta, and AT&T portfolios in 1997 and 1998, may signal difficulties for the remaining monoline banks: MBNA, Capital One, and Providian. As issues of scale become even more important for success in both credit card issuing and banking in general, relatively smaller monoline issuers like Capital One and Providian may face the same difficult decisions that caused Advanta to sell its portfolio. Although MBNA should remain among the three largest bankcard issuers even after the mergers are completed, the future of this largest of the monolines is anything but certain. The declining profit margins in the credit card industry, combined with a possible downturn in the economy after six years of sustained growth, could force pure-player issuers to capitulate to more diversified commercial bank issuers. However, the strong marketing efforts of Capital One have allowed it to expand its card base while maintaining high levels of profitability, and MBNA's targeting of specific affinity groups has resulted in lower levels of charge-offs and higher profit margins than those obtained by the commercial bank issuers. The resolution of this competition between the monoline issuers and the commercial banks in the late 1990s may have enormous implications in the market for credit cards in the beginning of the next century.

Credit and charge card issuing is a highly competitive industry populated by a large number of firms that vie for share by offering innovative and attractive combinations of fees, interest rates, credit lines, and a myriad of card features. (Recall again that we have excluded debit cards from this analysis; they are discussed in chapter 12.) The industry has expanded robustly in the past twenty years. Output, measured by the number of cards issued, the amount charged on cards, and the amount of charges that are financed, has risen dramatically. Prices, measured by the average revenue issuers receive after adjusting for charge-offs, have fallen. The quality of cards has increased, although this increase is difficult to quantify.

The expansion of this industry has taken place through both the continual entry of new issuers and the growth of existing ones. The industry has experienced periods of high profits and low profits. On average, credit card profitability has been somewhat lower than that of other bank lending activity. The industry's competitive structure naturally limits its profits. It is relatively easy to become a bankcard issuer and even easier for an existing issuer to expand. High profits, such as those that appear to have been earned in the mid-1980s, attract entry and expansion and thereby force prices down and maintain pressure to innovate.

Not all analysts and observers hold this sanguine view of the competitive performance of the payment card industry, however. The next chapter examines the contrary view of some economists.

10

Puzzles and Paradoxes

Despite the presence of 4,000 competitors, the bank credit card market behaved widely at variance with the predictions of a competitive model. . . .
—Lawrence Ausubel

In a provocative article in the *American Economic Review* Lawrence Ausubel concluded that the credit card industry is a "paradox": an industry that appears competitive but is not. Examining the credit card industry in the mid- to late 1980s, he made the following observations:

• Credit card interest rates were nearly constant (between 17.8 and 18.9 percent) from 1982 to 1989 while the cost of funds fluctuated substantially (between 7 and 15 percent).
• The banks were making about three to five times as much on credit card lending as they were overall. The average rate of return on equity for credit card lending was 60 to 100 percent, whereas the average rate of return on equity for banks was only 20 percent.

There were other signs in the early 1990s that competition was not as intense as economists would expect given the low concentration among issuers. When a large number of firms are competing with each other and none of these firms is dominant, we do not expect that adding another firm to the fray will have much of an effect on price. Yet some thought that AT&T increased competition significantly when it introduced its Universal Card in 1991. An article by Dennis Carlton and Alan Frankel stated that "many industry participants and analysts credited AT&T with igniting a price war." Their subsequent study appeared to confirm that view. They found that the entry by AT&T, and later by GM, resulted in a decrease in the annual fees consumers had to pay for their credit cards.

Indeed, they concluded that if MasterCard and Visa had also allowed Dean Witter to issue cards, consumers would have saved more than a billion dollars. (Both associations prohibited Dean Witter from issuing cards because it operated the competing Discover Card. We discuss the antitrust lawsuit over this prohibition in chapter 11.)

This chapter tries to explain these puzzles and to resolve Ausubel's paradox. We show that the solution to these puzzles depends on understanding the rather unusal economics of the credit card industry. It is not that competition does not work in this industry, as Ausubel concluded, but rather that competition works somewhat differently in this industry than it does in most industries, and a proper analysis must take these differences into account. We have discussed some of the economic reasons for these differences in earlier chapters, and we introduce a few others here.

High and Sticky Interest Rates

Credit card interest rates are usually higher than the interest rates on many other types of consumer loans. As of August 1998, the typical credit card had an interest rate of just under 16 percent. That same month the average forty-eight-month automobile loan had an annual interest rate of 8.7 percent, the average home mortgage loan had an annual interest rate of approximately 7 percent, and the average twenty-four-month personal loan had an annual interest rate of 13.5 percent. Credit card rates were also higher than rates on nonconsumer loans: the prime rate was only 8.5 percent, and the yield on three-month Treasury bills hovered around 5 percent.

Not only are credit card interest rates high, they do not always move as quickly as other interest rates in response to changes in the cost of the funds that banks raise to support their lending activities. According to one study, if the cost of funds changes, credit card rates will change by only about one-twentieth as much by the next quarter. The long-run impact on credit card rates is only about one-third of the cost change and is fully felt only after three or four years.

In the early 1990s, evidence of high and sticky credit card interest rates helped persuade some legislators that regulations were needed to lower

credit card interest rates and to tie them to other market rates. Several
bills to cap credit card interest rates were introduced in the U.S. Congress
and several state legislatures. (We discussed one such bill in chapter 1.)

High Interest Rates

Credit card loans have higher interest rates than other kinds of consumer
loans for several reasons. To begin with, they are riskier than other consumer loans and require a higher interest rate to compensate for this
higher risk. Unlike automobile loans, home equity loans, mortgages, and
most other consumer loans, credit card loans are not secured by assets
that could be seized if the consumer defaulted on the loan. Furthermore,
a consumer with an available credit card line of credit may be most inclined to borrow the maximum when his financial situation worsens—
precisely the riskiest time for a creditor to make him an additional loan.

Unlike other consumer loans, credit card loans are sold as part of a
bundle of services included in the credit card. Banks use the interest earnings on credit cards to recoup not only the cost of funds they lend to the
consumer, but also the costs of the other services they provide. As we
saw earlier, about 40 percent of consumers at any point in time are using
their credit cards as payment devices and are not taking out loans. Many
credit cards provide other costly benefits such as frequent flyer miles, purchase guarantees, and insurance. Some programs, such as GM's, will even
give cardholders rebates based on their annual purchases.

To see why the interest rate would have to be set several percentage
points above the cost of funds to the issuing bank, consider a typical card
program that charges a variable rate of interest and no annual fee. If a
bank can borrow money at a 6 percent annual rate to finance its cardholders' purchases, it must charge at least that rate if it expects to make any
money. However, as chapter 9 also noted, the bank incurs expenses to
service accounts, rent space, pay salaries, and so forth. These additional
operating expenses averaged 5.3 percent of outstandings in 1997. In addition, the bank incurs losses from accounts that do not repay. In 1997,
such charge-offs averaged 5.8 percent of average outstandings. These
costs would be partly offset by interchange revenue that averaged about
1.9 percent of outstandings. Thus, if the interest rate an issuer charges
to its cardholders is its primary source of card-related income, the average

issuer would have to set its rate at 15.2 (6.0 + 5.3 + 5.8 − 1.9) percent just to break even in 1997. In addition, even under perfect competition the issuer would earn an additional return as compensation for bearing the risk of even higher defaults.

Sticky Interest Rates

The fact that credit card interest rates help cover the many costs of offering credit card services also helps explain why issuers do not change rates in tandem with their costs of lending money. A related explanation involves defaults. A study by Alexander Raskovich and Luke Froeb looked at how quickly various loan rates changed in the 1980s when the net cost of providing those loans changed. They measured net costs by looking at the cost of borrowing the funds as well as the cost of loan principal that could not be collected (charge-offs). They found that the interest rate on credit card loans varied with changes in the net cost of providing credit card loans to about the same extent as the interest rate on other types of loans responded to the net cost of providing those loans.

The rates on all of these loans were sticky to some degree. That is, they tended to respond slowly to cost changes. Economists have developed explanations for this phenomenon. For example, when a lender lowers its interest rates, the potential borrowers most interested in increasing their loans are those who are least creditworthy, and the lender may be able to identify such borrowers only imperfectly. As a result, a reduction in interest rates could lead to higher default rates, raising the lender's costs. The lender can lessen this problem by reducing the interest rates for its loans only partially when market interest rates fall.

Interest rates are not the only consumer prices that are sticky, of course. You might have noticed that the cover price of *The Wall Street Journal* has been 75 cents since late 1990, even though the cost of newsprint has varied from as low as $430 a ton to as high as $800 a ton. When demand and costs change, businesses in many industries do not reflect those changes fully (or sometimes do not reflect them at all) in the prices they charge. Sometimes instead of changing price, businesses change the amount of the goods sold per unit: making candy bars larger or smaller, for instance, or adding features that increase overall quality or providing links to other products that have value to the consumer. Although economists are exploring the reasons why businesses adjust different aspects of their product offerings and prices, there is little evidence that the failure to adjust dollar prices signals a breakdown of competition.

Interestingly, though, credit card interest rates seem to have become more responsive to changes in the cost of funds in the 1990s. Variable-rate credit card plans were of minor importance through 1991. But by 1995 variable-rate plans outnumbered fixed-rate plans and accounted for more cards and outstandings. One possible explanation for this shift is that innovations in credit scoring have enabled issuers to better identify which cardholders are good or bad credit risks and to curtail the expansion of credit card loans to cardholders whose financial situations suddenly deteriorate. Issuers can fine-tune their credit card offerings to individual cardholders. With customer-specific interest rates and with the ability to prevent customers from taking out huge credit card loans when their financial situations deteriorate, issuers may be better able to avoid the adverse selection problem than they were in the past. Further research on this conjecture is clearly needed.

The Myth of Exorbitant Profits

In the 1970s, many banks fretted over the low profits their credit card portfolios earned. As we described in chapter 4, they were especially hard hit when the cost of funds skyrocketed in the late 1970s but state usury laws prevented them from raising interest rates to consumers. By the late 1980s, after nearly a decade of robust growth, observers commented instead on the high profits then being earned by credit card lenders. As we noted, Lawrence Ausubel found that rates of return for credit card operations were three to five times those for bank operations overall. These high profits attracted more firms into credit card lending. Another decade later, the credit card business did not seem quite as attractive, at least to the editors of *Credit Card Management:* "The credit card industry is on the defensive in the wake of rising credit card losses and what is expected to be another year of record consumer bankruptcy filings." AT&T, touted as one of the most successful entrants into the credit card business in the early 1990s, had sold its increasingly unprofitable credit card operation to Citibank by 1998. In fact, the worst of times were not as bad nor the best of times as good as the profit measures that bankers routinely calculate had suggested.

Biases in Accounting Rates of Return

Accounting rates of return are only slightly more useful for comparing profitability across companies in different industries as average grades are for comparing educational achievement across high school students in different countries. Accounting rates of return, like grades, mask important differences. Students of economics, corporate finance, and accounting now widely recognize the notoriously misleading nature of accounting rates of return. As one leading textbook noted, "investors and financial managers, having been burned by inflation and creative accounting, have learned not to take accounting profitability at face value."

Accountants have developed objective standards for evaluating and reporting company profitability. These standards are necessary for preventing companies from deceiving investors by manipulating their rates of return and for tracking profitability on a consistently measured basis for each company. Accounting standards are designed so that auditors can calculate company profitability from objective and verifiable data with a minimum of subjective judgments. There is great value to this.

Unfortunately, the standard accounting rate of return provides at best an approximation of the true rate of return earned by a company. It is well known that the accounting rate of return can only equal the true rate of return when

- accounting depreciation equals true economic depreciation, or
- the firm is steadily growing at a rate just equal to the true rate of return on its investments, or
- random events cancel out these and other biases.

In other words, hardly ever. To calculate the true rate of return, the analyst has to know the true economic rate of depreciation of assets and has to know the precise timing of investments and returns from those investments. That information is often hard to come by. (Although we find the concept of true economic depreciation endlessly fascinating, we have elected to spare you a (necessarily) technical exposition. The main point is that it equals accounting depreciation only under very special conditions.)

Even without this information, the accounting rate of return is useful for many purposes. For a particular business, the bias in the accounting rate of return may be roughly the same from year to year. If so, using the accounting rate of return to compare the business's performance this year with its performance last year would be entirely reasonable. Within an industry, it may be that companies are all subject to similar biases in the accounting rates of return. We could therefore use the accounting rate of return to compare the performance of these businesses.

The accounting rate of return can be highly misleading, however, when it is used to do something for which it was never designed: to compare the profitability of entirely different businesses for which the accounting biases may go in quite different directions. For historical reasons, *Fortune* magazine still ranks companies based on accounting rates of return, but those rankings are essentially meaningless and anyone who made their investments based primarily on those rankings would be essentially throwing dice. Nonetheless, comparisons among accounting rates of return are frequently made and frequently misused. For example, it is well known that the accounting rate of return tends to be much greater than the true rate of return in industries that engage in significant research and development or advertising. That has not prevented many commentators over the years from calling the pharmaceutical industry "the most profitable industry in America" despite extensive evidence now that its true profits are not extraordinary. At various times the oil industry, the computer industry, and the pharmaceutical industry, among others, have all been accused of making "high" profits based on misleading comparisons between their accounting rates of return and those of other industries—and often on examining only short-lived periods of rapid demand growth.

Credit card issuing is one of those industries. In 1991, New York Senator Alfonse D'Amato argued that "banks are making windfall profits from high interest rates they are charging consumers on credit cards. . . . The free market is not working." Industry commentators have also been exuberant from time to time about the high profitability of credit cards. A brochure entitled "More Profit Than Meets the Eye" obtained at the 1994 Credit Card Forum noted, "It's a fact. A well-managed, actively marketed credit card program can be your biggest money maker, often generating a return on assets four to six times greater than your average ROA."

To demonstrate that issuing credit cards is not a sure route to great wealth, we use a study by Carlos Lapuerta and Stewart Myers to show that one of the great credit card success stories of the 1980s, the Discover card, was far less profitable than its accounting returns indicated. Lapuerta and Myers focused on Discover not only because it was widely viewed as successful, but also because they could obtain complete data on the investments made in the development of the Discover card and on the returns from that development. It is therefore possible to calculate a true rate of return for the Discover card program. Most other credit card programs are parts of larger bank operations and do not report separate data (e.g., Citibank) or do not have data available from the inception of their programs (e.g., MBNA). The Discover card was issued through the Greenwood Trust. As a bank, Greenwood Trust has to produce financial reports known as "call reports." Credit card issuing is essentially all that Greenwood Trust has done since the inception of the Discover Card, so its call reports provide a complete history of Discover.

As with any credit card program, Greenwood Trust had to make considerable investments to persuade consumers to take the new card. It had to advertise the card and make direct-mail solicitations. It then had to screen the applicants for the card by conducting credit checks and other analyses to determine their creditworthiness. In its first three years of operation, Greenwood Trust had after-tax losses of nearly $350 million, primarily from the costs of acquiring new credit card accounts. Because of these initial expenses, the Discover Card was initially viewed with skepticism.

All of these acquisition costs were expensed according to the usual accounting conventions; they affected accounting profit only in the year they were incurred. As an economic and business matter, of course, that makes no sense. Credit card issuers invest in locating profitable cardholders. They do this by spending money on advertising and direct solicitation, processing applications, and then observing the resulting cardholders' credit behavior for some period of time. Some cardholders quickly fall into arrears and are eventually dropped, and others do not use the cards. Only a portion of the cardholders that initially sign up turn

Table 10.1
Economic and accounting rates of return for the Discover Card, 1985–95.

Year	Accounting	Capitalizing costs of new accounts
	Rates of return	
1985	−96%	22%
1986	−79	44
1987	−42	38
1988	5	36
1989	20	34
1990	22	27
1991	24	21
1992	27	7
1993	37	16
1994	53	22
1995	37	26
1989–95 average:	32	22

1985–95 internal rate of return: 22%

Source: Carlos Lapuerta and Stewart C. Myers, "Measuring Profitability in the Credit Card Business."

out to be profitable. Profitable accounts tend to remain for some time: they are the long-term reward for the up-front investment. Therefore, just as one would capitalize the up-front investment in a factory that enables one to produce shoes or computers at a profit for several years, one would want to capitalize up-front investments in cardholders that enable one to expand credit card outstandings over time. That is, investment in cardholders should be treated the same as the purchase of an asset, and profits should be affected only as that asset is depreciated over time.

The consequence of expensing Discover's startup costs is easy to see. If you built a factory and expensed it in the first few years of your manufacturing operation, you would show significant losses. Indeed, there are large accounting losses in Discover's first three years, as shown in table 10.1, which reproduces some results from the study by Lapuerta and Myers. Eventually you would show significant returns because your income statement would show the revenues produced by your initial investment in the factory, but you would not have any significant offsetting expenses because you wrote off all of the costs of building the factory years before. And that is exactly what happened to Greenwood Trust. Its accounting rates of return increase substantially from 1985 to 1995. By the early 1990s, the Discover Card was touted as one of the greatest business ideas of the 1980s. From 1989 to 1995, after the program had been established, the average accounting rate of return was 32 percent.

In reality, the Discover Card was neither the blunder it was thought to be in the late 1980s nor the money machine it was thought to be in the early 1990s. Lapuerta and Myers considered two ways of addressing the shortcomings of accounting estimates of the rate of return. First, they calculated an internal rate of return for Greenwood Trust, starting with the early years of Discover losses in 1985. An "internal rate of return" is the discount rate at which an investment has zero economic value. In other words, if the internal rate of return is greater than the cost of funds on a project, the firm undertaking the project earns more-than-competitive profits. The internal rate of return from 1985 to 1992 was 22 percent.

Second, Lapuerta and Myers calculated a true economic rate of return by capitalizing the investment costs of developing the Discover Card portfolio. They assumed that it cost about $100 to develop each account. (As it turns out, the results are similar if the acquisition cost is anywhere from approximately $50 to $150.) As shown in table 10.1, the average rate of return with costs capitalized was 22 percent for 1989 to 1995, the same as the 22 percent internal rate of return over the life of the Discover program, and considerably lower than the 32 percent average accounting rate of return.

How Risky Is Credit Card Lending?

Although we now know that Greenwood Trust did not really earn anything like the 53 percent rate of return its books showed in 1994, we still do not really know whether a 22 percent average rate of return makes it unusually profitable compared to other business investments. If credit card lending is a sure thing, like investing in Treasury bills, then 22 percent looks extremely high relative to the 5.4 percent average return on

Treasury bills between 1989 and 1995. If, on the other hand, credit card lending is extremely risky, like the biotech industry, then 22 percent looks like evidence of a very marginal business.

In fact, credit card lending is one of the riskier lines of business in the economy. It is not hard to see why. There is a fair amount of uncertainty over how profitable newly acquired cardholders will be. Credit card lending is unsecured. And default rates are highly sensitive to the state of the economy. As a result of this risk, it costs credit card lenders more than typical firms to obtain funds.

To determine the cost of equity capital to credit card lenders, Lapuerta and Myers have estimated values of beta, a common measure of risk, for three publicly traded monoline banks. The betas for these banks reflect the market assessment of the riskiness of credit card lending, since these banks engage almost entirely in credit card issuance. The average betas for these banks were 1.75 for 1991 to 1995, well above the 1.0 average for the market as a whole. These betas imply that the equity cost of capital for these banks equals the riskless rate plus 1.75 times the risk premium for the market as a whole, which is about 8.6 percent, according to Ausubel. The risk premium for these banks is therefore about 15 percentage points above a riskless interest rate. Using the Treasury-bill rate as a measure of the riskless interest rate gives an estimated after-tax cost of equity capital varying between 18 and 21 percent for 1991–1995, and somewhat higher in earlier years, when the risk-free rate was higher. These figures imply that the Discover Card was certainly a successful business venture, with an average estimated rate of return of 22 percent compared to an estimated risk-adjusted cost of capital of between 18 and 21 percent. But it was not the money machine that many observers claimed.

AT&T, GM, and Credit Card Prices

As we have already described, during the early 1990s, several large non-financial companies became members of the Visa and MasterCard associations and began to issue credit cards. Notably, AT&T launched its card in the spring of 1990, and General Motors (GM) entered in the fall of 1992. Dennis Carlton and Alan Frankel have argued that entry by AT&T

and GM caused credit card prices to fall substantially. We believe that a careful review of the AT&T and GM card programs and an inspection of the data on card prices shows that, although entry may have made life difficult for AT&T and GM's competitors, it did not have much effect on prices. That, of course, is what we would expect in a competitive industry.

AT&T and GM entered the credit card business with cobranded cards (technically issued by banks but with the AT&T and GM logos) carrying no annual fees and variable interest rates. The AT&T and GM card programs both grew quickly after their launches. From the end of 1993 through the end of 1995, the AT&T program had roughly twice as many accounts as the GM program; earlier it was even larger relative to the then-infant GM program. By the end of 1995, GM had more than 8 million accounts and AT&T had more than 17 million, amounting to approximately 3 percent and 6 percent, respectively, of total MasterCard and Visa accounts. Similarly, GM had $7.3 billion in outstandings and AT&T had $14.8 billion, accounting for approximately 2 percent and 4 percent, respectively, of total Visa and MasterCard outstandings. If entry by AT&T and GM did affect credit card pricing, then the effects of AT&T's entry should have been substantially greater than the effects of the later, smaller entry by GM.

Consumers signing up for the AT&T card (available as a Visa card or a MasterCard) within its first year were promised that they would never pay an annual fee and were charged a variable interest rate that at that time was the prime rate (then 10 percent) plus 8.9 percent. This rate was slightly above the 18.1 percent rate that the Federal Reserve found "typical" at that time, but the difference is small relative to the range of rates charged. The card offered some special features: it could be used as a telephone calling card, providing a discount on AT&T calling-card rates, and it provided insurance and extended warranty features generally found only on premium cards.

About two and a half years later, GM began to issue a MasterCard through Household International. This card also had no annual fee, and it provided rebates that could be applied to the purchase of GM products. Its interest rate, also variable, was also roughly comparable to interest rates on other cards. The GM rate at the time of its launch was 16.4

percent; the Federal Reserve Board's contemporaneous "typical" credit card rate was 17.4 percent.

According to some analysts, AT&T and GM began to issue credit cards in large part because of perceived profit opportunities in long-distance telephone and automotive products, respectively, not just in the credit card industry. For example, *Credit Card Management* noted that "[AT& T] boasts 22 million active calling card customers, but saw its [calling] card going the way of the dinosaur along with most other specialized credit cards. . . . Moreover, figure some experts, a new relationship opened up through the new card could give Ma Bell the tool it needs to keep customers without cutting its rates." And *Time* commented that "GM hopes the rebates will help it rebuild its once commanding but now eroded share of the U.S. car and truck market, which has slipped to 35 percent today, compared with 43 percent a decade ago."

At the time of AT&T's entry in 1990, and certainly by the time GM came along in 1992, there was nothing novel about credit cards with no annual fee. *Business Week,* for example, in an article discussing AT&T's then-new Universal Card, pointed out that "the no-fee option is hardly unique. Some issuers have been offering free Visas and MasterCards for years—and with lower interest rates." In fact, that same article estimated that "some 150 other issuers also offer no-fee cards" in addition to AT& T's Universal Card. Besides the Discover Card, which has never charged an annual fee since its inception in 1985, examples of issuers who also did not charge an annual fee before AT&T's entry include Manufacturers Bank and Amalgamated Trust & Savings Bank, which were offering standard no-annual-fee cards in 1986 and 1987, respectively.

Similarly, AT&T and GM were also far from the first to offer credit cards with a variable interest rate. In 1986, for example, Manufacturers Bank offered a variable interest rate in conjunction with its no-annual-fee credit card mentioned above, First Chicago and First Interstate Bank of California both began offering variable-interest-rate credit cards to their customers in 1987. By 1989, the year before AT&T's entry, 18.6 percent of credit cards, accounting for just under 15 percent of outstandings, had variable interest rates. Both fractions topped 80 percent by 1995. From simple statistics such as these, one cannot tell if AT&T and GM triggered a shift to variable-rate cards or simply participated in a shift caused by other factors. In any case, it is unclear whether consumer preferences or bank costs drove this shift.

As we noted above, service fees have become an increasingly important component of the cost to consumers of credit card usage. Comparing the net effect of these fees (and other terms and conditions for credit cards, such as grace periods) among cards is difficult, though individual items can sometimes be compared. For example, around the time that AT& T's card was introduced, some industry observers noted that the card's cash advance charges were higher than those of some other typical card programs, such as Citibank's. Additionally, AT&T imposed an over-limit fee (Citibank did not), and AT&T had a shorter grace period than did Citibank. It is certainly possible, in theory, that issuers who reduce their annual fees may raise other fees less visible to consumers. Available data on annual and service fees (discussed above) strongly suggest that, over time, issuers in the aggregate have done just this.

Overall, it is not apparent that the cards offered by AT&T and GM were significantly less expensive to cardholders than other widely available cards. They had certain features—the calling card in the case of AT&T and the credits toward buying a car in GM's case—that differentiated them from existing programs. But there is little evidence, based on the actual offerings, that either issuer chose to compete by lowering the price that consumers had to pay for having and using the card. There is also little reason to believe that AT&T and GM credit card programs had issuing costs substantially below those for other credit card programs; after all, both firms chose to use existing issuers for their programs.

In the previous chapter, we described an index of credit card prices that we calculated from comprehensive data on all MasterCard and Visa issuers. Figure 10.1 graphs credit card prices over time and notes when AT&T and GM entered. Credit card prices did not, in fact, decline with the entry by AT&T or GM. Although annual fees trended down before and after their entry, service fees trended upward. (We performed a statistical analysis of our quarterly index that controlled for the cost of funds to banks, lags in the setting of credit card prices, and possible annual and seasonal trends. Our analysis confirms the impression given by figure 10.1 and provides no evidence that entry by AT&T and GM made it less

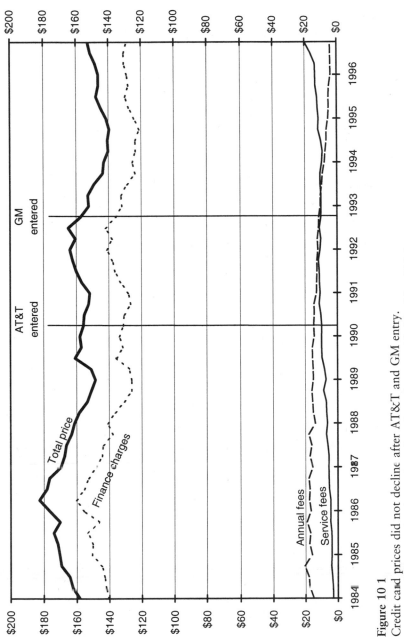

Figure 10 1
Credit card prices did not decline after AT&T and GM entry.
Source: Calculations by the authors based on data provided by Visa U.S.A.
Note: Total price equals the sum of finance charges, annual fees, and service fees. Year markers indicate observation from first quarter of year.

expensive for a consumer to have and use a credit card.) Carlton and Frankel reached a different conclusion in large part because they considered only annual fees. But annual fees accounted for less than 10 percent of the average price paid for a credit card at the time of AT&T's entry.

Payment card issuing looks competitive. It acts competitive. And despite recurring claims to the contrary, it really is competitive. Competition in payment card issuing results from hundreds of firms slugging it out on a national basis and many more doing so within particular regions. Each issuer competes on rates, fees, and features. Nonetheless, credit card issuers do cooperate along some dimensions in the Visa and MasterCard associations. And that cooperation has touched off the antitrust wars to which we next turn.

11

The Antitrust Wars

People of the same trade seldom meet together, even for merriment and diversion, but the conversation ends in a conspiracy against the public, or in some contrivance to raise prices.

—Adam Smith, *The Wealth of Nations*, 1776

What would Adam Smith have thought about MasterCard and Visa? Tens of thousands of bankers work together to provide services that have become essential to the daily economic lives of millions of consumers and merchants around the world. Representatives of these banks meet several times a year to talk business. Without knowing more, the cynical author of *The Wealth of Nations* might view the bankcard associations much as he viewed the local blacksmith club.

Of course, when Smith wrote his pathbreaking treatise on capitalism there were no important industries in which collaboration among competitors appeared necessary or desirable. Technology was simpler, as were economic relationships, and modern concerns about interconnection, compatibility, standardization, and network externalities—some of the key factors that make some collaboration worthwhile—were not important in Smith's day. In the next century, railroads raised some of these issues. But by early in this century it had been decided that U.S. railroad rates would be regulated, so that conversations between railroads were not likely to raise prices.

There were important scale economies for most of the other capital-intensive industries the Industrial Revolution created, including those producing textiles, refined sugar, iron and steel, machinery, and petroleum products. That is, unit costs decreased as firms became bigger. As railroads connected previously isolated local and regional markets, firms began to exploit these scale economies. As a result, many competitors were acquired or driven out of business, and most major U.S. industries came to be dominated by at most a few firms. (The reader should refer to chapter 7 for a discussion of the economic concepts in this paragraph.) The U.S. antitrust laws were a product of popular discontent with this process and its results.

Enduring principles of U.S. antitrust policy were established in the final years of the nineteenth century and the early years of the twentieth. After the passage of the Sherman Act in 1890, the U.S. Supreme Court promulgated a framework for distinguishing between permissible and impermissible competition. Congress then filled some perceived loopholes in the Sherman Act, and the Court's interpretation of it, with the passage of the Clayton Act and the Federal Trade Commission Act in 1914. Nonetheless, the Sherman Act defined the battlefield on which the bankcard associations have fought important antitrust battles over the last quarter century.

The Sherman Act has two key sections:

Section 1: Every contract, combination in the form of trust or otherwise, or conspiracy, in restraint of trade or commerce among the several States, or with foreign nations, is hereby declared to be illegal. . . .

Section 2: Every person who shall monopolize, or attempt to monopolize, or combine or conspire with any other person or persons, to monopolize any part of the trade or commerce among the several States, or with foreign nations, shall be deemed guilty of a misdemeanor.

After 1890, it was up to the courts, particularly the Supreme Court, to infuse meaning into this mess of words.

Smith's cynical view of collaboration among competitors is perhaps best reflected in what is now known as the "per se rule" against price fixing, which had its origins in Justice Peckham's 1897 majority decision for the Supreme Court in *United States v. Trans-Missouri Freight Assn.* In the *Trans-Missouri* case, a railroad association had agreed to fix rates. The railroads argued that they had set reasonable rates. Peckham would hear none of it. He found against the railroads without a trial, on the grounds that an agreement to fix prices is itself unreasonable, no matter what sort of prices the agreement produces. Any other rule of law, he argued, would force courts to regulate thousands of prices throughout the economy. He thus found that agreements to fix prices are illegal per se—illegal by their nature, regardless of their effects.

One year after *Trans-Missouri,* Judge (and later Chief Justice) Taft issued an opinion in *United States v. Addyston Pipe & Steel Co.,* which suggested an interesting dichotomy of business practices. Taft supported the application of the per se rule when an agreement serves no legitimate business purpose and only restrains competition. He argued, however, that "ancillary" restraints, restraints that are subordinate to a legitimate business purpose and exist to further that purpose, should not be subject to the per se rule. For example, members of a partnership would have a legitimate interest in agreeing not to compete with the partnership, because such competition would undermine the partnership's purpose. This restraint on the partners, Taft argued, is ancillary to the legitimate goal of forming a successful business venture.

Practices that do not fall under the per se rule, however, are not necessarily legal. Instead, the courts have treated these remaining practices on a case-by-case basis under what is now known as the "rule of reason." This approach had its origins in Chief Justice White's opinions in *Standard Oil v. United States* and *United States v. American Tobacco,* both handed down on the same day in 1911. According to White, certain practices may be harmful depending on their "inherent effect" and "evident purpose." Only practices that "unreasonably" restrain trade are to be found illegal. For business practices that are not per se illegal, courts must consider both why they were adopted and what effect they had. Although the details of the rule-of-reason inquiry have evolved considerably since *Standard Oil* and *American Tobacco,* the basic approach—a thorough examination of the competitive pros and cons of the practice at issue— has become the cornerstone of much modern antitrust analysis.

The suspicion that competitors are up to no good whenever they get together has influenced the antitrust analysis of collaboration between competitors in three ways. First, this suspicion influences which practices avoid per se condemnation. In the past, the courts have treated some efficiency-enhancing collaborations among competitors as per se illegal. Second, this suspicion influences the burden of proof that the courts impose on the parties to antitrust lawsuits. Competitors who have agreed to a particular business practice, perhaps through a trade association or joint venture, sometimes have the burden of showing that the practice results in efficiencies that could save consumers money. Because this is never an easy burden to meet, they are in effect guilty until proven innocent. Third, this suspicion has had the odd effect of forcing joint ventures to defend practices that would have been perfectly legal if the joint venture members had merged into a single firm.

During the early industrial era, in which many industries came to be dominated by a handful of firms and many industries went for decades without significant entry, this distrust of collaboration among competitors caused little harm. Indeed, it may have even helped send a strong message to businesses that all attempts to limit competition would be dealt with severely. And there is a lot to be said for clarity and simplicity.

During the current industrial (or postindustrial) era, however, declining computing and telecommunications costs have reduced the costs of collaboration, and many products produced by competing firms and different industries must work with each other. A strong suspicion of collaboration among competitors can now prevent the competitive process from advancing consumers' welfare. Technological change, especially since the end of World War II, has provided increasing opportunities for collaboration between competing firms that is sometimes in the public interest. Interconnection, compatibility, standardization, and network effects are central issues in industries in which communications and computers play important roles.

Joint ventures, such as MasterCard and Visa, have found the per se rule and the historic antipathy of the courts to collaborations among competitors particularly vexing. The courts and enforcement agencies have frequently attempted to apply case law aimed at ad hoc agreements among unintegrated competitors to a form of business organization that is usually a vehicle to facilitate innovation and increase competition. Plaintiffs have often argued that specific, individual joint venture practices or rules are per se violations of the antitrust laws, illegal regardless of their actual economic effects, because they amount to agreements among competitors to harmonize behavior or restrict output.

This chapter concerns three legal battles in which plaintiffs sought to use the antitrust law's hostility toward collaboration among competitors to get Visa to change its rules. In *Worthen Bank and Trust Co. v. National Bank Americard Inc.,* Visa sought to maintain a wall between itself and its arch rival MasterCard by keeping MasterCard members out of Visa and Visa members out of MasterCard. It won the battle, lost the war, and opened the door to duality to secure the peace. In *National Bancard Corp. (NaBanco) v. Visa, U.S.A.,* Visa was accused of fixing prices by adopting a systemwide interchange fee. It persuaded the Eighth Circuit Court of Appeals to treat the fee under the rule of reason and that, under that rule, the interchange fee was not anticompetitive. In *SCFC ILC, Inc. v. Visa U.S.A., Inc.,* Visa defended a rule that prohibited owners of competing systems from becoming Visa members. It persuaded the Tenth Circuit Court of Appeals to treat the exclusion under the rule of reason and that the exclusion was not anticompetitive. After reviewing these battles, we conclude this chapter by drawing some general lessons for the legal treatment of joint ventures.

Sleeping with the Enemy: *Worthen*

As of 1971 Visa (then NBI) and MasterCard (then Interbank) had two kinds of members. Class A members could issue cards and acquire merchants; Class B members could acquire merchants as agents of Class A members. Class A members of one bankcard association could not be members of the other association, but Class B members could handle both cards on behalf of two or more banks. (The A/B nomenclature is Visa's, but MasterCard's full and associate members had the same distinction.) Visa had 250 Class A members and 4,100 Class B members at the time. (Comparable data are not available for MasterCard.)

Worthen Bank & Trust Company, the largest bank in Arkansas, was a Class A member of Visa. It wanted to become a full member of Master-Card as well and gave three reasons in subsequent court filings. First, most merchants that accepted one of the national bankcards also accepted the other national bankcard. Because they could handle both cards, Class B members thus had a competitive advantage in acquiring merchants. Worthen claimed that it had lost some merchant customers to Union National Bank, a Class B member of both systems. Worthen wanted a level playing field with Class B members. Second, Worthen wanted to be able to provide its customers with another card they could use in parts of the country where Visa was not widely accepted. Third, Worthen wanted its agent banks in tourist areas in Arkansas to be able to offer MasterCards as well as Visa cards to merchants, since many tourists carried MasterCards.

Consequently, Worthen applied for Class A membership in Master-Card and was admitted in April 1971. In response, Visa enacted a rule— By-Law 2.16—that prohibited Class A and Class B Visa banks from issuing a competing card and Class A banks from acquiring for a competing card. Worthen would lose its Visa membership if it did not comply.

Visa Loses Ground

Worthen sued. It filed a complaint in November 1971 contending that By-Law 2.16 violated Sections 1 and 2 of the Sherman Act. Worthen described competition as taking place almost entirely at the bank level. Banks competed for cardholders, they competed for merchants, and they competed for relationships with other banks (Class As competed for Class Bs). The systems themselves were not important for competition.

Worthen argued that By-Law 2.16 harmed competition by limiting Worthen's (and other banks') ability to compete in the three ways described earlier. It also stifled incentives to start a competing system. According to Worthen, Visa members could not establish a competing system because they would have to leave Visa. By-Law 2.16 therefore helped maintain the existing duopoly in systems rather than promoting systems competition as Visa argued. Worthen, however, relied primarily on the law, not an economic analysis of competition, for its position that By-Law 2.16 was illegal per se. The *Sealy* and *Topco* cases were two key weapons in its arsenal.

In its 1967 decision in *United States v. Sealy, Inc.,* the Supreme Court found that carving up territories among licensees was a per se violation of the Sherman Act. Sealy licensed its mattress trademark to manufacturers who in turn owned most of the stock in Sealy. In the case at issue,

Sealy prohibited its licensees from selling outside of their assigned territories. The Court decided that these exclusive territories were anticompetitive even though Sealy sold less than 20 percent of the mattresses in the country. A combination of competitors who restricted competition among themselves was sufficient to find a per se violation.

In its 1972 decision in *United States v. Topco Associates, Inc.,* the Court also found that exclusive territories were a per se violation. Topco was an association of small and medium-sized supermarket chains with an average share of 6 percent of the grocery market in the regions in which they operated. Topco bought and distributed certain grocery items that were then sold under the Topco label. The Topco brand was designed to compete with the private-label brands offered by the larger supermarket chains. Topco restricted membership so that only one member could sell in each designated territory, and the Court condemned that restriction.

In response to Worthen, Visa said it was hardly a combination of competitors like those in *Topco* or *Sealy*. Its members simply could not produce nationally accepted general-purpose credit cards without collaboration. Visa's arguments focused on system competition. It contended that competition between MasterCard and Visa in innovation helped lower members' costs and, as a result, reduced charges paid by consumers and merchants. If banks belonged to both systems, these valuable incentives to compete would be blunted. It also contended that only one system would ultimately survive if banks were allowed to belong to both systems, and that was most likely to be MasterCard, whose members, at the time, had charge volume of $17.6 billion compared to $12 billion for Visa's members. Visa thus contended that By-Law 2.16 was essential for preserving intersystem competition.

In a July 1972 decision, the District Court for the Eastern District of Arkansas agreed with Worthen. The trial judge first considered whether By-Law 2.16 was an agreement among competitors. He concluded that Visa was "a combination of Class A member banks" and that By-Law 2.16 was an agreement by that combination of competing firms. The trial judge did not buy Visa's argument that it was like a single firm because it produced something that none of its individual members could produce on their own. He noted that Visa, like Sealy, owned the brand name and that Visa members could issue credit cards on their own just as Sealy licensees could sell mattresses on their own.

The trial judge then considered whether By-Law 2.16 restrained trade. He tried to fit the Visa by-law into one of the boxes that the Supreme Court had considered in previous cases. He agreed with Worthen that it was like a "group boycott" and a "refusal to deal" with competitors:

The rule imposed by the by-law results in a refusal to deal between the members of the NBI system with any of their Class A members who also desire to carry the Interbank Master Charge card. As [*Sealy, Topco, United States v. Associated Press*, and other previously cited cases] show, there can be no justification for a rule of this type, and the court has no choice but to strike down the by-law as a per-se violation of the Sherman Act.

He rejected Visa's argument that By-Law 2.16 would result in an anti-competitive merger of the two systems. In an earlier case, *United States v. Associated Press*, the Associated Press (AP) had made a similar argument and the Supreme Court had rejected it: "if AP were open to all who wished the service, could pay for it, and were fit to use it, it would be no longer a monopoly: a monopoly of all those interested in an activity is no monopoly at all, for no one is excluded and the essence of monopoly is exclusion." Indeed, the trial judge was persuaded that consumers and merchants would be better off if they could do business with banks that handled both cards.

Visa Regains Territory

Because the District Court's decision went to the heart of Visa's structure, Visa appealed that decision. It argued that the district court should have evaluated By-Law 2.16 after a full trial under the rule of reason. (Visa had a friend of sorts in its appeal. The U.S. Department of Justice filed a brief with the appeals court that explained why it agreed that a full trial should be held.)

In September 1973, the Eighth Circuit Court agreed with Visa. To get Visa out of the per se hole, it had to distinguish Visa and its by-law from the cases cited by Worthen and relied on by the trial court. The Eighth Circuit distinguished *Sealy* and *Topco* from *Worthen* on two grounds. The restraints by those two firms involved price and territories, not membership. More curiously, the Court said for *Sealy* and *Topco* "the association of members was *not* required by industry structure in terms of the ability to produce the product as is the case here." That was a stretch. It was no more possible for a small grocery store that belonged to Topco to produce private-label brands or for a member of Sealy to produce a nationally branded mattress than it was for a small bank that belonged to Visa to produce a general-purpose credit card. In each case, the product that the association could produce was very different from the product that any single member could produce.

The Eighth Circuit also noted that Visa did not restrict membership based on whether the applicants competed with current members. In fact, there were many areas in which competing banks belonged to Visa. It found that restraints of this sort were not so blatantly anticompetitive as to deserve condemnation per se. The Supreme Court declined to hear Worthen's appeal, and the case was sent back to the District Court for a full trial. That trial never happened. Worthen wanted to belong to both systems, in part, because it competed locally with Class B banks that belonged to both systems. Visa wanted to ensure the loyalty of its members. A deal was struck. Visa extended By-Law 2.16 to Class B banks; henceforth Visa Class B banks could not act as agents in the MasterCard system. That meant that Worthen would not face competition from banks that could offer both cards, and it dropped its lawsuit.

Visa won this battle. But it still risked lawsuits from other Class A banks and, as a result of the change in By-Law 2.16, from Class B banks as well. Although its revised by-law might not be per se illegal, no court had declared it legal under the rule of reason. Visa could face substantial costs if banks could show that it had violated the antitrust laws. In antitrust cases, plaintiffs get three times actual damages. Given the state of the law on joint ventures in the mid-1970s, Visa was understandably nervous.

Lacking an Ally, Visa Surrenders
To help buttress its legal position, in November 1974, Visa asked the Antitrust Division of the U.S. Department of Justice to agree that it would not challenge Visa's by-law. Then and now, businesses can get some assurance that the Justice Department will not sue them by obtaining a

"business review letter." Moreover, if the Department had agreed that By-Law 2.16 was procompetitive, Visa would have some assurance that it would have the government on its side in any private antitrust suits. Having the Department of Justice as a friend in *Worthen* had helped: the Court quoted and adopted the Department's position.

The Antitrust Division, however, even at the time it submitted its papers in *Worthen,* was not sure whether the by-law was on balance procompetitive or anticompetitive. That was one of their fundamental reasons for asking for a full trial: to find out. Indeed the Antitrust Division argued in its brief in *Worthen* that By-Law 2.16 reduced competition among banks:

> As the district court demonstrated in its careful opinion, the ability of a bank to handle both BankAmericard and Master Charge constitutes a significant competitive advantage. To this extent, dual membership may be said to enhance competition between banks. Accordingly, in the absence of countervailing competitive benefits, a flat bar against dual membership would appear to have anticompetitive consequences in almost every situation.

The Antitrust Division argued that there was not enough evidence in the record to weigh this effect against the increased intersystem competition claimed by Visa. The Division suggested that the card systems were primarily alternative service organizations for banks. Just as stores offer several brands of products, banks like Worthen might offer several brands of credit card services. A multibrand bank would want to maximize sales of both brands, and it would not want either system to "limit its advertisement, promotion, and enrollment of new members in other areas, since the more widespread each system becomes, the more attractive it is to consumers and merchants." (The Division's views were very much consistent with the Hausman-Leonard-Tirole model discussed in chapter 7.)

The Antitrust Division was also concerned that By-Law 2.16 erected a barrier to the creation of another national card system. Visa members could not join any new national system if they wanted to stay in Visa. Whereas repealing By-Law 2.16 might encourage a merger of the existing systems, preserving By-Law 2.16 might maintain the "existing duopoly at the national credit card level."

The division was skeptical of Visa's arguments that intersystem competition was important or that duality would harm intersystem competition.

It did not accept Visa's argument that duality would reduce local price competition among banks. The banks, not the system, set the prices to consumers and merchants. It was willing to entertain the possibility that further evidence would substantiate Visa's argument, and it suggested looking to see whether rates are less uniform in areas where competing banks belonged to different systems. It heard Visa's arguments that duality would reduce technology competition, but it demanded specifics.

When the Antitrust Division returned to this issue at Visa's request two years and four months later, what did it conclude? Maybe duality is a good idea, maybe it isn't. In its business review letter to Visa, the Antitrust Division pointed out three general areas of concern. First, it was concerned about the effects on the creation of other payment card systems:

[T]he proposed by-law flatly prohibits banks in the NBI system from any affiliation with any other national bank credit card system. The by-law . . . automatically precludes every NBI agent bank in any market from being an agent bank in any other credit card system. We believe such a restriction might well handicap efforts to create new bank credit card systems and may also diminish competition among the banks in various markets. The same pertains to the operation of the by-law to prevent an NBI card-issuing bank from becoming an agent bank in a competing bank credit card system and to prevent an NBI agent bank from becoming a card-issuing bank in another system.

Second, although the Antitrust Division was less troubled by the by-law's prohibition against dual issuance of credit cards, stating that "a prohibition of dual affiliation appears unobjectionable to the extent it is necessary to insure continued intersystem competition," it still declined to give full clearance to that aspect of the by-law.

It should be emphasized, however, that our views in this regard are based on an analysis of the bank credit card system as it presently exists and on the general impact of such a prohibition. We have not undertaken a detailed analysis of the impact of such a prohibition in particular markets. It is conceivable that unique competitive problems exist in particular markets which would be compounded by application of the prohibition of dual affiliation at the card-issuing bank level. As previously indicated, however, we have not undertaken the type of market by market analysis which would be necessary to determine if, in fact, any such situations presently exist.

Third, the Antitrust Division was concerned about the by-law's impact on the development of debit cards and electronic fund transfer systems (EFTSs) generally. It felt that those areas were so unformed as of 1975 that it would be "impossible . . . to reach any firm conclusions concerning the competitive implications of proposed By-Law 2.16 insofar as it relates to debit-card systems and EFTS."

The Antitrust Division thus declined to provide Visa with any reassurance that it would not challenge By-Law 2.16. It did not find this provision to be necessarily anticompetitive; it argued that there was not enough information to decide the issue. Faced with the specter of expensive antitrust litigation with no help from the Department of Justice, Visa reluctantly repealed its by-law. Banks stampeded to join both systems, and duality was born. It does not seem to have been a child that Visa management or the Antitrust Division really wanted.

What Next?

Are consumers better off when banks belong to just one association or to both? Dual membership enables banks to play one brand off the other, and it helps them keep the association managers in line. If Visa raised its fees, provided less reliable settlement and authorization services, or had an advertising campaign that bombed with consumers, banks would start pushing their MasterCard brand over their Visa brand. That constant threat instills fear in Visa's management. But dual membership comes with dual ownership and dual control over system strategies. The owners of Visa cannot help but think about the effects of their business strategies and investments on their MasterCard portfolios. And with single membership, Visa would still face the threat of banks switching their entire portfolios from Visa to MasterCard and of entrants joining MasterCard instead of Visa.

Economics does not provide a clear evaluation of duality. Dual membership has its competitive benefits, and it has its costs. Moreover, the impact of duality on the bankcard associations has changed markedly over time. MasterCard and Visa became more similar in the decade after dual membership was permitted in late 1975. They have become less similar since 1986, when Visa started its successful campaign to differentiate itself from its rival. MasterCard and Visa are complex organizations that must provide incentives for competitors to collaborate, and must discipline free-riding, moral hazard, externalities, and other social ills. Economists may be good at naming the diseases, but we are poor at devising the cures. We do not know enough about organizational design to determine whether cohesiveness and allegiance are important virtues of single membership, as Visa suggested in the *Worthen* case and its dealings with the Antitrust Division.

Visa reluctantly embraced duality in 1975 because it was apparent that the courts, perhaps even at the request of the Justice Department, would likely force it to do so. Visa had climbed out of the per se hole. But it was still faced with a case law that was hostile toward collaboration among competitors and that required collaborators to show that their agreements were essential and not harmful to competition. In the last section of this chapter, we will return to a fundamental question of antitrust policy—when should the courts second-guess the business decisions of joint ventures?—and argue that neither the courts nor the Justice Department should have made this particular call.

In October 1998, as this manuscript was nearing completion, the Justice Department sued MasterCard and Visa claiming that duality violated Section 1 of the Sherman Act. The Justice Department seeks to prohibit Visa members from having any role in the governance of MasterCard and vice versa. The lawsuit is ironic not only because of the Justice Department's role in delivering duality in the first place, but because it was filed at a time when MasterCard and Visa have increasingly divergent memberships and highly competitive management teams. (This lawsuit also challenges MasterCard and Visa rules that prohibit American Express and Discover from distributing those cards through MasterCard and Visa members. Chapter 8 discusses in more detail American Express' efforts to challenge this prohibition.)

Good Fix: *NaBanco*

Visa's next major antitrust battle was over the interchange fee. Setting a single fee centrally (as we discussed in chapter 7) eliminated opportunistic behavior by merchant banks and prevented what could have been enormously difficult and expensive bilateral negotiations among banks about payments and terms. Of course, no single fee could make all members of the association happy. Banks that specialized in issuing would generally like a high interchange fee, whereas banks that specialized in acquiring would generally like a low (or even negative) interchange fee. Merchants would always like a lower interchange fee because that would translate into lower merchant discounts they would have to pay. Cardholders, if they thought about it, would like a higher interchange fee because competition would likely force issuing banks to lower cardholder charges if they had another card-related revenue stream.

National Bancard Corporation (NaBanco) specialized in signing up merchants and processing card transactions. NaBanco wanted credit card receivables—the transactions it in effect bought from the merchant—to be sold at par just like check receivables were. That is equivalent to having an interchange fee of zero. Having a positive interchange fee put NaBanco at a disadvantage relative to large banks that issued cards. For example, NaBanco was competing to handle processing of credit card transactions for Carson Pirie Scott, a large department store in Chicago. First Chicago, a large Chicago bank that did both issuing and acquiring, offered Carson a better deal. In part, NaBanco argued, that First Chicago was able to offer a better deal because it did not have to pay an interchange fee on credit card transactions by its own cardholders, of whom there were many in Chicago.

A Large-Scale Assault . . .

NaBanco sued Visa in June 1979, claiming that Visa's interchange fee arrangements constituted a per se violation of the Sherman Act. The case went to trial before a judge in May 1982 in Ft. Lauderdale, Florida. Because the judge was juggling a heavy criminal caseload, the trial was held in segments as court time permitted through January 1984.

NaBanco portrayed the Visa association as an issuer cartel that imposed monopoly prices on acquirers. It argued that "[t]he merchant banks are selling cardholder receivables to the issuing banks, and the issuing banks, through their total control of the Visa Board, are directly fixing the discounted price of those sales." Visa could not deny that it had engaged in price fixing, but despite the general per se rule against such behavior, Visa had a possible defense. After deciding that the per se rule did not apply, the Supreme Court, in *Broadcast Music, Inc. v. CBS*, had recently allowed Broadcast Music, Inc. (BMI) to set the royalty fee for the broadcast of music by artists that belong to it. Its decision rested in important part on the finding that negotiating separate agreements with all of the music outlets in the country was not feasible for each artist separately. Thus, the court recognized that not all price fixing was per se illegal, and some price fixing was legal under the rule of reason.

NaBanco argued that the *BMI* decision did not apply because a fixed interchange fee was hardly essential for the provision of credit cards. The individual members of Visa could provide credit cards on their own, just as American Express, Carte Blanche, and Sears were providing credit or charge cards on their own. The interchange fee was simply a device to shift costs onto acquiring members. Even if the interchange fee were not per se illegal, NaBanco argued, it was clearly illegal under the rule of reason. The fee placed merchant banks at a competitive disadvantage. Issuing banks paid the interchange fee to themselves when the banks' own cardholders patronized a merchant that they also serviced. Consequently, issuing banks could offer merchants that were patronized by the banks' own cardholders a lower merchant discount. A merchant bank (or a third-party processor like NaBanco) could lose merchant accounts to an issuing bank even if the merchant bank was more efficient than the issuing bank. NaBanco implied that it lost the Carson account because of the competitive disadvantage caused by the interchange fee. (It is not obvious that NaBanco was right as a matter of economics. Both issuing and acquiring businesses are competitive, so that the interchange fees NaBanco paid simply helped cover issuers' costs; there are no excess profits to be squeezed out of the system. Because First Chicago also acted as an issuer, it had to cover the same sorts of costs. Even if all its transactions were "on us," First Chicago would have had to cover *its* total costs (of issuing and acquiring) with merchant discounts and fees paid by consumers, just as the Visa system as a whole had to do.)

On the other side of the battle, Visa portrayed itself as a joint venture of banks that wanted to maximize the use of Visa by both cardholders and merchants; increasing cardholders made it easier to attract merchants and increasing merchants made it easier to attract cardholders. Visa argued that the purpose of the interchange fee was to provide a "mechanism to distribute and share the costs of the joint venture [footnote omitted] in relation to prospective benefits, thereby encouraging members to provide the Visa service to a competitively maximum extent on both the cardholder and merchant 'sides' of the business." It further contended that the interchange fee was necessary for the joint venture to provide credit card services. Although there were proprietary systems like American Express (as a charge card), and although banks had in fact offered credit cards on their own, only a nationwide joint venture could provide the Visa service. The interchange fee was imposed to control opportunistic behavior by merchant banks (as described in chapter 7) and to avoid a chaotic system of bilateral negotiations between issuing and acquiring banks. As Visa put it, "Were there no advance agreement or understanding as to the 'price' (and other terms) upon which the card-issuing bank is to 'buy' its cardholder's paper from the merchant bank, self-interested behavior would quickly cause the system to collapse."

Visa argued that the interchange fee was procompetitive. Consequently, just as the Supreme Court had found in *BMI,* the collective decision by Visa members to fix the interchange fee should not be condemned as illegal per se, but should be evaluated under the rule of reason. And under the rule of reason, the fee was legal. First, Visa lacked market power. Visa competed with other payment systems such as cash and checks. It had only a small share of all transactions. (When Visa first set the interchange fee in 1971, only one in six households had a bankcard, and relatively few merchants accepted Visa cards. Visa could expand only by persuading merchants that took cash and checks to take credit cards as well.) Second, NaBanco had shown no evidence that the interchange fee harmed consumers. For example, banks such as First Chicago could offer lower merchant discount rates to Chicago merchants than could NaBanco because its costs were lower. First Chicago probably had lower credit and fraud losses resulting from acquiring transactions for cards that it had issued than NaBanco did for cards that it had not issued.

. . . Successfully Repulsed

The District Court for the Southern District of Florida refused to treat the interchange fee under the per se rule. It found that the interchange fee's principal purpose was not to fix prices, but rather to facilitate the provision of credit card services that no bank could provide on its own. The Court then turned to the rule-of-reason analysis. It embraced Visa's view that credit cards competed with many other forms of payment. That, together with the ease of entry of other payment mechanisms, eliminated the prospect that Visa could charge noncompetitive prices.

The Court went on to argue that the interchange fee helped rather than harmed consumers and was thus clearly legal under the rule of reason. The interchange fee made the Visa system operate more efficiently by eliminating costly negotiations among individual members. It also helped promote credit card services by solving imbalances between the costs and revenues on either side of the system. The District Court accepted Visa's argument that the interchange fee was the best available alternative for dealing with these imbalances. It rejected NaBanco's suggestion that banks could just negotiate with each other, and pointed to the problems that Visa members had dealing with each other before the imposition of the uniform interchange fee.

Finally, the District Court was impressed with several aspects of the interchange fee. It thought that Visa had incentives to establish the interchange fee so as to balance the two sides of the business. The Board that set the fees had both issuing and acquiring members; the fee provided no additional revenue for the system as a whole (one member's interchange revenue was another member's interchange cost); and setting too high an interchange fee would reduce merchant acceptance and thereby harm issuers.

NaBanco appealed to the Eleventh Circuit but was rebuffed again. To prevail, NaBanco would have had to convince the Eleventh Circuit that the District Court had made a clear error in the two principal factual findings supporting the lower court's opinion. To the contrary, the Appellate Court ruled that there was no clear error in either of the two findings made by the District Court: that Visa lacked market power in the relevant market of all payment systems and that the interchange fee was procompetitive.

In 1986, the Supreme Court declined to review the Eleventh Circuit's decision. Visa had won an important antitrust battle. For itself, it succeeded in continuing the interchange fee system. For others, it helped establish that joint ventures can set internal transfer prices just as a single firm can without being hauled off for a per se violation of the antitrust laws.

Battle Over?

As a matter of economics, NaBanco's antitrust case was weak. It had no coherent economic theory of how the interchange fee could enable issuers to make more money. As we explained in chapter 8, Visa issuers whittled away any profits they received from interchange revenue through competition, by giving cardholders cheaper cards—lower annual fees, more card features, and lower interest rates. In the early 1970s when the interchange fee was first imposed, issuers had strong incentives to increase the number of merchants that took Visa cards. Nor did NaBanco have any evidence that the interchange fees harmed consumers. It had evidence only that it, as a competitor, was disadvantaged. Not surprisingly, NaBanco tried to damn Visa with the per se label. Ten years earlier with the same facts, the courts might well have pinned that label on Visa. But the Supreme Court's 1981 decision in *BMI* made NaBanco's per se case a tough sell.

Would the Visa system have collapsed if NaBanco had won? If the courts had mandated a zero interchange fee (one of NaBanco's requested remedies), Visa issuers could have recouped their costs in several ways. They could have increased annual fees, made it harder for transactors to get or keep cards, or started charging interest on the date of the purchase rather than offering a grace period. Moreover, the interchange fee was part of a set of rules governing the relationships among members. Most likely, Visa would have changed these rules if the courts had forced issuers to take receivables from acquirers at par. For example, issuers bore the full risk of nonpayment. With zero interchange, Visa might have shifted some of the risks of nonpayment onto the acquirer to reduce a perceived imbalance between costs and revenues of the two sides of the system. So Visa would probably have survived with a zero interchange fee. But imposing that constraint could only have lowered system efficiency and raised overall cost. Moreover, unless the courts also regulated Visa rules for allocating risks, they could not ensure that NaBanco would be better off with a zero interchange fee and new rules than with the actual interchange fee and the actual rules for allocating risks.

The courts could have taken NaBanco's other suggestion and forced individual banks to negotiate interchange with each other. But that idea is nutty. Bilateral negotiations are at least feasible today because, as we discussed in chapter 6, consolidation has sharply reduced the number of acquirers. But during the first two decades of the Visa system, there were thousands of acquirers and issuers across the country. In many cases, acquirers and issuers who seldom did business with each other would have to enter into an agreement either in advance or the first time a particular issuer's cardholder shopped at a specific acquirer's merchant.

Under such a system, when acquirers and issuers could not reach an agreement, merchants would be unlikely to honor all Visa cards. Suppose a merchant was considering whether to accept a Visa transaction from a cardholder. The merchant would be willing to accept the transaction only if it believed the acquirer would guarantee payment. The acquirer would be willing to guarantee payment to the merchant only if it believed the issuer would in turn guarantee payment. Without an explicit agreement between acquirer and issuer, there would be no such guarantee. The issuer might try to keep an interchange fee of 1 percent or 100 percent. Without an agreed-upon interchange fee, the acquirer would have no claim to any portion of the transaction amount.

Someone's Knocking at My Door: *MountainWest*

As we discussed earlier, Dean Witter Financial Services Group (then owned by Sears, Roebuck and Co.) launched the Discover Card in 1985. (After the trial in this case, Sears spun off its Dean Witter subsidiary, which then merged with Morgan Stanley in 1997. Throughout this chapter, we refer to the plaintiff as Dean Witter for simplicity.) Dean Witter incurred substantial initial losses as it spent money prospecting for customers and building merchant acceptance. But the Discover Card soon became both popular and profitable, and it garnered 6.7 percent of all credit card outstandings five years after its introduction.

In late 1988, Dean Witter sought membership in Visa. Visa refused and then passed a rule—By-Law 2.06—that denied Visa membership to

any applicant which is issuing, directly or indirectly, Discover Cards or American Express cards, or any other cards deemed competitive by the Board of Directors; an applicant shall be deemed to be issuing such cards if its parent, subsidiary or affiliate issues such cards.

In May 1990, Dean Witter purchased the assets of an insolvent thrift institution, MountainWest Savings and Loan in Utah, from the Resolution Trust Corporation (RTC). Those assets included a Visa membership and a small payment card portfolio. Dean Witter intended to use this membership to launch Prime Option, a Visa card to be issued nationally. MountainWest requested the printing of 1.5 million Prime Option Visa cards without letting Visa know that Dean Witter had acquired it. A small Utah thrift preparing a major national launch piqued Visa's curiosity. When its investigation revealed Dean Witter's ownership, Visa refused to print the cards. In January 1991, Dean Witter filed a lawsuit in the Federal District Court for the District of Utah, complaining that Visa had violated Section 1 of the Sherman Act, and it sought damages and a permanent injunction ordering Visa to admit MountainWest as a member.

Attack and Defense

The key legal issue raised in this case was the conditions under which the antitrust laws compel a joint venture (e.g., Visa) to admit a direct competitor. Dean Witter thought the answer was

A joint venture that (a) has a large share of the relevant market and (b) cannot show that the exclusion is necessary for the efficient operation of the joint venture must admit any applicant for membership. Moreover, admission into an open joint venture or network joint venture is presumptively efficient.

Dean Witter argued that Visa had a large share of the relevant market and that Visa's efficiency justifications were mere pretexts for an anticompetitive exclusion.

Visa thought the answer was

A joint venture may have to admit a direct competitor only if its participation in the joint venture is essential for competition in the relevant market. Moreover, forced admission is presumptively bad because it is tantamount to the forced sharing of property with a competitor—a policy that would reduce the long-term incentives for the creation of property through investment and innovation.

Visa argued that Dean Witter had demonstrated its ability to compete in the relevant market through its successful Discover Card and that it should not get to use Visa's property just because it could compete better that way.

In addition to these polar views of the law, the two parties had very different views of the economic effects of exclusion on intrasystem and intersystem competition in the payment card market.

According to Dean Witter, the Visa joint venture has two important characteristics. First, it is a network in which firms work interdependently to provide a service and it is marked by the network externalities we discussed in chapter 7. Payment cards are more valuable to merchants if more consumers hold those cards and are more valuable to consumers if more merchants accept those cards. Second, Visa has been an open joint venture. Historically, virtually any financial institution could join the Visa system. It made sense that Visa was open because it was more efficient with more members: more members, more positive network externalities. Moreover, prior to passing By-Law 2.06, Visa did not demand exclusivity. It had allowed its members to issue MasterCards since 1976. And it continued to allow Citibank to own two competing payment card systems, Diners Club and Carte Blanche. By-Law 2.06 was thus clearly not required for Visa to operate efficiently.

Dean Witter further argued that it had been harmed by By-Law 2.06. Dean Witter executives testified that it had planned to enter the payment card industry by first introducing its proprietary Discover Card and then adding its own Visa and MasterCard. (Visa hotly disputed this claim.) Indeed, Dean Witter's president testified that it would not have launched the Discover Card had it known it could not later introduce a Visa card.

According to Dean Witter, a proper measure of the market power Visa exercised by excluding Dean Witter was the aggregate share of the relevant market held by the members who act together. Collectively, the members who adopted Visa By-Law 2.06 had a 45.6 percent share of the payment card market through their membership in Visa and an additional 26.4 percent share of the payment card market through their dual membership in MasterCard, for a total market share of 72 percent, all based on transaction volume. Visa therefore had market power because its members who adopted the exclusionary rule collectively had a 72 percent market share. This high market share gave Visa's members significant incentives to exclude important new competition, which Dean Witter claimed to be poised to provide.

Dean Witter also argued that By-Law 2.06 harmed competition and consumers by providing an "enormous disincentive for firms that might enter the market by developing new proprietary cards." The argument was that By-Law 2.06 reduced the incentives to start a new proprietary card because the entrant would then be unable to issue Visa cards. Existing Visa issuers were discouraged from starting their own proprietary systems because they would have to leave Visa (i.e., sell off their portfolios) to do so. Dean Witter argued that the fact that no proprietary system had been started since the enactment of By-Law 2.06 was evidence of this disincentive.

Visa argued that its members had engaged in significant innovation and investment to develop the Visa system. The Visa brand name, and the rights to use this brand name and the other Visa property associated with it, belonged to Visa. It argued that unless Visa were declared an "essential facility" under the antitrust law, something that occurs very rarely and only when a court is convinced that forcing an enterprise to share its property is essential to competition, Visa alone had the right to decide with whom it was going to share its property. Membership in Visa was not essential for Dean Witter to compete: it was already in the market with its Discover Card. And since the payment card market was highly competitive, granting Dean Witter membership was not essential to competition either. Thus, Visa was clearly not an essential facility.

Visa also argued that forcing it to share its property with a competitor would reduce the incentives for other firms to come together and engage in innovation and investment through the joint venture form of organization. Visa contended that the property of a joint venture should be treated no differently than that of a single firm. The District Court judge ruled that these broad arguments were irrelevant, but they nonetheless were the subtext for much of the Visa testimony and summations, and they were advanced on appeal.

Visa argued that By-Law 2.06 was not an exercise of market power in the first place because Dean Witter's Prime Option product was not excluded from the market. Dean Witter could not issue Prime Option under the Visa "brand," but it could issue Prime Option under the Discover "brand." Either way it was introduced, Prime Option would succeed or fail in the payment card market based on its merits. Dean Witter presented no evidence that access to the Visa brand was necessary for the success of Prime Option, only that it would have been helpful.

In the second place, Visa contended that the aggregate market share of Visa issuers did not establish market power in this case. By itself, aggregate share provides little economic information on whether the exclusion of a competitor would have a significant effect on price. For example, the exclusion of only a tiny potential competitor, no matter how large a share the excluding entity has, cannot possibly have any effect on price or output. These effects depend on what is added to or subtracted from a market, not on the aggregate share of the firms making the decisions. Aggregate market share would have been an appropriate measure of market power if Visa had agreed to fix prices. But it had not done this.

The entry of one more issuer into the highly unconcentrated and competitive payment card market would not result in a significant increase in price or reduction in output. Thus, even if Prime Option had been excluded from the market, this was unlikely to have had any discernible effect on prices even if, as claimed by Dean Witter, Prime Option would have been a low-cost card.

Visa argued that the primary effect of repealing By-Law 2.06 would be to reduce competition among payment card systems. The admission of Dean Witter into the Visa system would have resulted in a partial integration of Discover and Visa (and presumably MasterCard), and this would likely reduce the intensity of competition between Visa (and presumably MasterCard) and Discover (and potentially American Express). Visa also argued that letting Dean Witter into the tent would allow Discover to gain competitive intelligence on its system competitor, to free-ride on Visa investments and innovations, and to disrupt competitive decisionmaking.

Visa noted that there was no evidence that By-Law 2.06 was a disincentive for the entry of proprietary systems. No firm that had been deterred was identified, and no evidence was presented that any member of Visa had contemplated starting a proprietary system. Given that it was much easier to enter the payment card business through Visa or MasterCard than by starting a proprietary system, it is not surprising that with the sole exception of Discover, all of the massive post-1966 entry into this business has been through the bankcard associations. Moreover if the market problem were that there are too few proprietary systems, the solution should be to *close* the door at Visa, not to *open* the door more as desired by Dean Witter. Closing the door would encourage companies like AT&T and GM to start their own proprietary systems. (AT&T had in fact considered doing so.) Keeping the door largely open encouraged firms to enter as Visa issuers, not as proprietary systems.

Finally, Visa argued that the antitrust problem Dean Witter identified and the remedy it proposed were inconsistent with each other. The essential antitrust problem was that Visa allegedly had market power because it engaged in collective rule-making and had a large aggregate share of the market. Dean Witter's proposed remedy was the admission of Dean Witter and, if it wished, American Express to Visa. Under that remedy, Visa would be forced to raise the aggregate shares of its members to 100 percent of the market, thus increasing the system's market power and exacerbating the problem as defined by Dean Witter.

Decisions, Decisions

After a three-and-a-half-week trial, the jury found for Dean Witter. Visa asked the judge to overturn the jury verdict and had some grounds for optimism. In oral arguments after the verdict, the trial court judge had said, "I would have hung the jury before I would have come back with that verdict." Nonetheless, on April 1, 1993, deferring to the jury, the judge denied Visa's motions for a decision in its favor or for a new trial.

(In November 1993, MasterCard, which was facing charges similar to those plaguing Visa, reached a settlement with Dean Witter. The settlement provided that Dean Witter would be permitted to issue a cobranded Prime Option card through NationsBank. Furthermore, Dean Witter would be allowed to join MasterCard as an issuing member if Dean Witter ultimately prevailed in its litigation with Visa.)

Visa appealed to the Tenth Circuit. Both parties sought to frame the appeal in terms of the proper legal rule toward joint ventures. Visa argued that it should not have to admit Dean Witter unless Dean Witter could prove that it could not compete successfully without access to Visa's property. Dean Witter argued that joint ventures should not be allowed to impose membership conditions that have the purpose and effect of restraining competition and that are not ancillary to any legitimate purposes of the association.

In September 1994, a three-judge panel of the Tenth Circuit decided in Visa's favor. After summarizing the existing case law, the Appellate Court conducted a rule-of-reason analysis in which Dean Witter had the burden of proving that By-Law 2.06 would harm consumers.

It found that Dean Witter had not met that burden. The court found that "it is not the rule-making per se that should be the focus of the market power analysis, but the effect of those rules—whether they increase price, decrease output, or otherwise capitalize on barriers to entry that potential rivals cannot overcome." The Court noted that no evidence had been presented (other than the unconvincing aggregate market share analysis) that the Visa rule had any anticompetitive effects on consumers. The court went on to say,

Thus, without any eye on effect, the very exercise of rule-making became the factual basis for rule of reason condemnation of Bylaw 2.06. Consequently, rule-making was not only divorced from its functional analysis but also from the facts of the case. . . . We believe the evidence cited by the district court to conclude Visa USA possessed market power is insufficient as a matter of law.

The Court also found Dean Witter's arguments regarding the effect of By-Law 2.06 on the entry of new systems to be speculative and rejected Dean Witter's view that, in effect, Visa had to prove that By-Law 2.06 benefited consumers. They observed that the by-law did not bar Dean Witter from the payment card market and pointed out that there was no evidence that the by-law precluded Dean Witter from introducing Prime Option through Discover or through any other means. They did not believe that the Sherman Act required the admission of Dean Witter into Visa so that it could compete more effectively. But the Court stopped short of an explicit endorsement of Visa's "essential facility" standard for forced admission to a joint venture.

As is typical, this case ended with a whimper. The Tenth Circuit refused Dean Witter's motion for a rehearing, and the Supreme Court declined to hear Dean Witter's appeal.

Are We Done Yet?

The *MountainWest* case added fuel to debates regarding standards for evaluating the conduct of joint ventures and on the proper roles of evidence on efficiencies and on consumer harm in that context. It also illustrated the effects of legal hostility toward joint ventures. Suppose Business

A, which competes with Business B, decides that it could make more money if it could also sell B's product line in addition to its own. Business B says no. Can Business A make a claim under the antitrust laws? The general answer is clearly no. Businesses do not have to share their property with anyone, let alone direct competitors, except under very special circumstances.

Why then was Dean Witter's claim, which has almost exactly this fact pattern, taken so seriously? The answer lies in the courts' longstanding hostility to joint ventures. Even though the law on joint ventures had moved beyond *Sealy* and *Topco,* Dean Witter could fashion an antitrust claim because Visa was organized as a joint venture. This enabled Dean Witter to argue that Visa's exclusionary rule was enacted by a group of competitors acting together, and the law remains hostile to such agreements.

There is some irony in this. If Visa and MasterCard had organized themselves as proprietary systems (e.g., with member banks having equity shares) in which members did not compete with each other, there would have been far less competition in the payment card industry than there is today. There also would have been no *MountainWest* case.

Dean Witter argued on appeal that a joint venture with a large market share would have to admit all comers unless it could show that exclusion was necessary for efficiency. And if it was admitting other new members or had recently done so, the exclusion of any applicant was presumptively not efficient. Had the Tenth Circuit instead accepted Dean Witter's arguments, it would have made joint ventures, especially joint ventures that had admitted members in the past because of network externalities, a second-class form of business organization with attenuated property rights. Such a ruling would have discouraged the formation of joint ventures and would have encouraged resorting to mergers to exploit gains from cooperation.

Leveling the Battlefield

Over the space of less than twenty-five years, Visa fought three expensive legal battles concerning practices that would have been plainly lawful if it had been an ordinary, integrated firm. Except under very special circumstances, ordinary firms have the unquestioned right to require fealty from their employees and franchisees: AT&T employees cannot moonlight for MCI, Coca-Cola bottlers cannot bottle Pepsi, and you do not see McDonald's french fries sold at Burger King. Worthen National Bank was able to challenge Visa's rule against joining MasterCard without evidence that this rule had harmed competition only because Visa was organized as a joint venture. Ordinary firms can set internal prices for exchanges between their divisions with no risk of being hauled into court for an antitrust violation. Yet NaBanco could contend that setting an interchange fee between acquirers and issuers was illegal price fixing, even though the internal prices set within American Express and the Novus systems to balance the incentives for acquiring and issuing are completely immune to antitrust challenge. Single firms also have the unquestioned right to refuse to share their properties with anyone, and certainly competitors. Dean Witter, which operated the Discover Card, could seek to issue Visa cards—while being sure that Visa members could never assert a legal right to issue Discover Cards—only because Visa was a joint venture.

Visa's experience reflects the tortured treatment that joint ventures face at the hands of antitrust laws that have not quite figured out what to do with this type of business organization. The courts and enforcement agencies frequently attempt to apply case law devised to deal with ad hoc agreements among unintegrated competitors (stereotypically fashioned in smoky hotel rooms) to a form of business organization that is usually a vehicle to achieve efficiencies and increase competition. Plaintiffs have often argued that specific, individual joint venture practices or rules are per se violations of the antitrust laws because they are agreements among competitors, and such agreements tend to reduce competition. In many of these cases, the joint venture participants would have faced no antitrust issue if they had merged into a single firm, eliminating all competition between them, and engaged in the same practices.

Although, as the *BMI* case illustrates, the courts have become less likely to fall for such simplistic damnation through labeling, evading this trap takes hard judicial work, as Visa's legal battles demonstrate. Other associations and joint ventures have also found the need to defend their business practices. In *United States v. Realty Multi-List,* an association that shared real estate listings restricted membership to brokers maintaining "customary hours" because it argued that this would ensure that members would likely be in a position to contribute listings and would be available to conduct negotiations and service their listings; the Court was not persuaded by these arguments. In *Rothery Storage & Van Co. v. Atlas Van Lines, Inc.*, an association of long-distance moving companies with only a 5–6 percent market share had to defend rules that it argued were necessary to prevent free-riding among members. Although the association was ultimately successful on appeal, its insignificant market share suggests that the costs of litigation were almost pure waste.

In the remainder of this section, we present some principles that we believe should guide the antitrust treatment of joint ventures and describe how the courts should apply those principles.

Three Principles for Antitrust Analysis

Neutrality of Results   Antitrust policy should neither encourage nor discourage entrepreneurs and investors from choosing the joint venture form of business organization over other forms. Economists do not have any empirical or theoretical reasons to suggest that entrepreneurs generally start joint ventures to skirt the antitrust laws, so we would like entrepreneurs to choose the most efficient way to organize their businesses. That might be a closed joint venture, an open joint venture, an ordinary firm, a merger of firms, or some other type of organization.

To the extent that the courts condemn certain types of joint venture practices, the expected cost to actual or prospective joint ventures of adopting those practices—or practices that could be construed as similar—increases. For example, it is hard to imagine that *Topco* and *Sealy* did not discourage some efficient joint ventures. To keep the choice of organizational form unbiased, the courts should try to treat joint ventures like single firms as much as possible.

Sensitivity to Differences   Antitrust policy should recognize that joint ventures face different management and coordination problems than single firms and that they adopt practices to deal with these problems. Joint ventures have to solve complicated management, organizational, and incentive problems by adopting rules. Single firms either do not have these problems, or they solve them through internal policies that are not made public.

Joint ventures face at least four major problems:

1. Their members may have conflicting objectives. Members may want to push the joint venture in different directions.
2. Their members may attempt to free-ride on the efforts of other members, or they may impose negative externalities on each other.
3. The joint venture has to harness its members to generate positive externalities and to harvest scale, scope, or network economies.
4. The joint venture has to coordinate the actions of its independent members. That consideration is especially important in network industries.

Joint ventures adopt two kinds of rules to deal with these problems. "Structural rules" determine the membership and distribution of voting rights in the organization and help joint ventures maintain organizational cohesiveness. "Operational rules" determine how the joint venture and its partners work with each other and help joint ventures solve coordination problems. Both types of rules allow organizations to police free-rider problems and increase the realization of positive externalities.

Of course, the actual management problems a joint venture faces are often particular to its circumstances. These problems will depend on the industry in question, the joint venture's goals and structure, the personal dynamics of the venture members, and many other factors. We should therefore be careful about questioning whether particular practices chosen by a joint venture are necessary. It is easy for outsiders to think up alternative, apparently less anticompetitive means of solving a particular organizational or incentive problem. It is a quite different matter actually to show that these externally designed solutions will work well in the real world.

Actual joint venture practices at least have the appeal of having been designed by the people who run the businesses involved. That is at least one reason why it would be a bad idea to place the burden of proof on joint ventures to establish that any particular rule generates efficiencies, or to establish that *their* rule is the best way of achieving those efficiencies.

Hostility to Cartels   Antitrust policy should prevent joint ventures from circumventing the antitrust laws. Joint ventures provide an institution through which competitors meet and agree on matters of mutual interest.

Like trade associations, meetings in smoky hotel rooms, and plain old mergers, a joint venture can provide a vehicle for consumer harm. Antitrust laws should prevent joint ventures from engaging in anticompetitive activity that would have been prohibited if the entrepreneurs and investors in the joint venture had chosen some other way of organizing themselves. By the same token, the determination of whether a practice is anticompetitive usually should not turn on the fact that the entity under consideration is a joint venture; the touchstone should be impact on consumers.

Nonetheless, there are differences between a joint venture and, for example, a merger of the firms involved in the venture. For one, the joint venture may provide different efficiencies than a merger. At one extreme, if the joint venture partners do not consolidate production facilities, they may not realize some economies that a true merger would. At the other extreme, the joint venture partners may realize network economies from joint production without being saddled with diseconomies resulting from merging unrelated operations. To take another difference, the joint venture may adopt rules providing for extensive price competition among members. The joint venture may engage in joint production without necessarily engaging in joint pricing. In that case, the fact that there are efficiency benefits is the beginning and also the end of the story.

Rule-of-Reason Analysis

In our view, the courts should never strike down joint venture practices without at least considering whether these practices help solve management problems without causing harm to consumers. As the courts that have examined Visa's practices have all found, joint ventures are often too complicated to permit evaluating particular practices on the basis of a superficial exercise in labeling. It does not follow, however, that the courts need to embark on an open-ended rule-of-reason inquiry every time a joint venture gets sued under the antitrust laws. Instead, we would suggest a three-step investigation.

1. Does the joint venture rule raise price, reduce output, or otherwise harm consumers significantly? If not, it should be ruled legal because it can do no harm. If yes, we move to step 2.

2. Does the rule result in economies that the joint venture could not readily achieve through an alternative arrangement with no anticompetitive potential? If no, it should be ruled illegal because it offers no benefits that could offset the consumer harm identified in the first step. If yes, we to move to the third step.

3. Having reached this step, the finder of fact must balance anticompetitive costs found in the first step against procompetitive benefits found in the second step.

In conducting this inquiry, it is important to distinguish between operational rules that result in price fixing or market division and structural rules that define participation in the joint venture.

The general antitrust treatment of agreements between competitors that are ordinary firms provides a useful model for considering operational rules. For example, economic theory generally predicts that price-fixing or market-division rules will harm consumers. So the only justifications for these rules would be either that they are necessary for the joint venture to be formed in the first place, or that the joint venture has to fix prices to earn an adequate expected return on its risky investment. If competitors formed a joint venture and fixed the price of a product that these competitors were previously selling independently, we would have little trouble reaching a quick condemnation.

The antitrust treatment of mergers, refusals to deal, and essential facilities provides a useful model for considering structural rules. For example, consider membership restrictions. Economic theory suggests that there are sound reasons for limiting membership. Membership restrictions provide a way of policing free-rider problems and maintaining cohesiveness. Moreover, membership restrictions are intimately intertwined with the joint venture's definition and enforcement of property rights. At the same time, economic theory provides no basis for believing that membership restrictions will necessarily harm consumers. Importantly, membership restrictions differ from price-fixing in that regard. So we would generally allow joint ventures to refuse to admit new members. Doing otherwise would result in joint ventures' having more poorly defined property rights than single firms. We can see no reason for handicapping joint ventures in that way.

Our approach would result in several safe harbors for joint venture practices. In general, joint venture practices that do not harm consumers would be legal. This follows from the market power screen. Moreover, exclusionary joint venture practices that would be permitted by a single firm formed by a merger of the joint venture participants would also be presumptively legal. In particular, joint venture rules that prevent non-members from using the joint venture's property through membership or other affiliations would be presumptively legal. This safe harbor follows from the principle that antitrust should not arbitrarily handicap joint ventures relative to ordinary firms and from the principle that single firms are required to share property with rivals only under exceptional circumstances. The importance of property rights to the economy broadly implies that structural relief, which would alter the membership of a productive joint venture, should be employed only under the sort of conditions under which a court would dismember a single firm or force it to merge with a rival.

The advantage of these safe harbors is that they would provide joint ventures with some assurance that following efficient business practices—or just following business practices that imperfect managers happen to think are efficient—will not result in treble damages, legal expense, and endless depositions of top executives. Because showing that a practice falls into one of our safe harbors should enable the joint venture to prevail on summary judgment, unproductive lawsuits should be deterred. This sort of protection is particularly valuable for joint ventures because of the fragility of the joint venture form.

The antitrust laws have made joint ventures like MasterCard and Visa vulnerable to lawsuits from competitors acting in their own interest and against the interest of consumers. Fortunately, the courts are moving to correct this. Faced with increasingly complex business arrangements, the courts have recognized the error in extending the per se rule beyond naked cartel price-fixing. The courts have accepted that the very provision of a good or service to consumers may require that the joint venture fix prices (e.g., *BMI, NaBanco*) and have generally extended the scope of rule-of-reason analysis.

Still, there remains a tendency to apply the rule of reason more stringently to joint ventures than to ordinary firms. Several appellate courts and a few scholars have required joint ventures to show that challenged practices are efficient before even considering whether those practices harm consumers. As a matter of economic policy, that requirement is a mistake. It invites litigation from disgruntled competitors and handicaps the joint venture as a method for organizing a business. And just as Visa has been in almost constant antitrust wars, it is time to strap on helmets in other industries in which collaboration among competitors is necessary to realize network economies or other benefits. As we move into the next century, the courts should recognize the increasing importance of collaboration among competitors for consumer welfare. One only has to look at some of the recent developments in the payment card industry to see the crucial role that joint ventures will play in the years to come.

12

Debit Takes Off (Finally)

Faster than any but the most optimistic thought possible, electronic banking is sweeping the country.
—*Business Week,* August 1975

For three decades, experts on payment systems have forecast the imminent arrival of a completely electronic, paperless payment system. . . . While some parts of this payment revolution have arrived, in many respects the forecasts have proved to be overly optimistic. . . . The biggest disappointment, thus far, is the debit card.
—John P. Caskey and Gordon H. Sellon, Jr., 1994

As the century turns, the debit card is like an adolescent who has had a sudden growth spurt, has many internal conflicts, and is quite confusing to everyone. This chapter describes the recent growth of the debit card, discusses why it occurred after an infancy of almost twenty years, and examines the raging competition in the debit market between credit card systems and regional ATM networks for the allegiance of issuing banks, merchants, and consumers.

Awkward Growth, Complexity, and Confusion

Most debit cards are platforms that different providers of debit services employ to distribute those services to consumers and merchants. For example, BankBoston issues a debit card that provides debit services through MasterCard, BankBoston's own Xpress 24 ATM system, and the NYCE ATM system, to which BankBoston belongs. This is quite unlike credit cards, for which there is a one-to-one relationship between the credit card itself and the credit card system. The coexistence of different brands on the same platform is the source of considerable confusion for consumers and merchants.

The Emergence of the Multifunction, Multibrand Debit Card

First there was an ATM card. The first ATM in the United States was deployed in Philadelphia in 1969, and the machines were widespread by the mid-1980s. If you are like most Americans, your bank issued you an ATM card when you opened your checking account. To provide security, the bank assigned you a personal identification number (PIN)—or you might have picked it yourself—that you must enter before you can consummate transactions with your ATM card. The back of that card displays symbols for one or more ATM systems. In addition to conducting regular banking transactions at ATM machines affiliated with your bank, you can withdraw money at any ATM machine that displays one of these symbols. Most ATM cards have symbols for several regional systems plus one of the international systems: Cirrus, operated by MasterCard, or Plus, operated by Visa. You can therefore withdraw cash almost anywhere in the United States and at many ATM locations abroad that display the Cirrus or Plus symbols. In 1998, there were 187,000 ATMs in the United States generating nearly a billion transactions each month.

Then there were Visa check and MasterMoney. Visa and MasterCard first introduced off-line debit cards in the early 1970s. (We discuss the difference between off-line and on-line debit below.) They languished until the early 1990s, when banks started to add the systems' logos to more of their ATM cards. Visa and MasterCard made a concerted effort to persuade banks to issue debit cards and poured significant funds into persuading consumers to use them.

And then there were PIN pads. The regional ATM networks recognized that the ATM card could provide a convenient payment mechanism at stores. Beginning in the early 1980s, they began convincing supermarkets and other retailers to install PIN pad devices. Thus began the development of what today are known as "point-of-sale (POS) debit" transactions. After the cashier rings your order up, you can swipe your card through the PIN pad and enter your PIN. After you press the "Enter" key, a message is sent to your bank to debit the funds for the transaction from your checking account. (At many PIN pad locations, you can also get some cash back, thereby eliminating a trip to an ATM.) Approximately 700,000 retailers had installed PIN pads by 1998. PIN pads became common at supermarkets by the mid-1990s, and almost 80 percent of supermarkets had installed them by 1998.

Here is the beginning of the confusion. When we say "debit cards" we are generally not talking about banks issuing a debit card that is physically distinct from the ATM cards they are already issuing. Instead, the MasterCard or Visa symbol is just another symbol on what you had thought of as your ATM card. You can pay with this card at any location that displays the MasterCard or Visa logos. There were 88 million MasterMoney and Visa check cards in the hands of consumers in 1998. Approximately two of every five ATM cards also functioned as MasterMoney or Visa check cards that year. These cards received a further boost from a $11 million national advertising campaign by MasterCard in 1993 and a $105 million advertising campaign by Visa in 1995. The greater merchant acceptance coupled with the major advertising campaigns from the two systems resulted in a swift expansion of their off-line debit cards. Both systems continued to advertise their debit card programs heavily in following years.

Now the story becomes really complicated. You can use your debit card at three types of retailers (everything we say below is true for Visa merchants and Visa check cardholders as well as MasterCard merchants and MasterMoney cardholders):

1. *MasterCard merchants that do not have PIN pads.* If you use your MasterMoney card at a MasterCard merchant location that does not have PIN pads, your transaction will be processed through the MasterCard system. It may take up to two days before the funds are actually deducted from your checking account; it takes that long for MasterCard to settle the books between participating merchants and banks. (Your bank, though, learns almost immediately that you have made this transaction. It may freeze funds in your checking account at that point to make sure that you have the money when the MasterCard system settles accounts.)

2. *Non-MasterCard merchants that have PIN pads.* If you use your MasterMoney card at a merchant location that has PIN pads but does not accept MasterCards, your transaction will be processed through one

of the ATM networks just as we described above. In addition, Master Card has a separate card brand, Maestro (Visa's version is Interlink), that enables cardholders to pay at Maestro merchants with PIN pads.

3. *MasterCard merchants that have PIN pads.* If you use your Master-Money card at a MasterCard merchant location that has PIN pads, how your transaction gets processed depends on what you do at the checkout counter. If you swipe your card through the PIN pad and enter your PIN, your transaction will be processed through one of the regional ATM systems or Maestro. If you do not enter your PIN, the cashier will run the transaction through the MasterCard system and ask you to sign a charge slip.

Most merchants fall into the first category: they accept MasterCards but do not have PIN pads. There are a small number in the second category and a growing number in the third. Why would a MasterCard merchant spend the money to install PIN pads? A major reason is that the merchant discount is lower for on-line debit, at least as of 1998. On-line debit systems charge a flat interchange fee, around 8 cents per transaction, with some variation among systems. Interchange fees for off-line debit systems are about 1.0–1.4 percent of the transaction. Acquirers generally pass these fees on to the merchant, as part of the merchant discount for each type of transaction. On a typical $30 transaction, the on-line interchange fees would add about 8 cents to the merchant discount, whereas the off-line interchange fee would add about 38 cents, a difference of 30 cents. If a merchant would save 30 cents on enough transactions, it would find it worthwhile to install PIN pads. A PIN pad can cost as little as $100, so converting one $30 transaction per day from off-line to on-line debit would pay for the PIN pad in a year (although there are also training and other installation-related costs). It is interesting to note that of the PIN pad base in 1998, more than two-thirds had been installed after the beginning of the Visa check advertising campaign in 1995.

The story becomes yet more complicated as a result of Visa's introduction in late 1998 of a new debit card service, Visa check II, that processes transactions at PIN pad terminals through the Visa system. This will permit Visa merchants with PIN pads to process a Visa check transaction using a PIN rather than a signature for authorization. For the remainder of this chapter we will disregard Visa check II, since it has not been a major factor as of this writing.

On-Line vs. Off-Line Cards

To add to the confusion, people in the debit card industry refer to PIN-authorized transactions as "on-line" transactions and signature-based transactions as "off-line" transactions. The difference between these two types of transactions has nothing to do with whether the transactions are processed electronically. Almost all payment card transactions are processed electronically through telephone connections that convey the transaction information in seconds. Signatures are used only for security and verification purposes, and signed slips are not used at all in the settlement process except for those rare merchants that do not have electronic terminals.

On-line transactions differ from off-line transactions only in the process by which money is taken out of the cardholder's checking account and the time it takes to do this. When an issuer authorizes an on-line transaction, it sends back a message that also authorizes the immediate transfer of funds from the issuer to the acquirer for that transaction. By contrast, with an off-line transaction (which passes over the same lines as a credit card transaction), authorizing the transfer of funds takes place in a separate step; it may take up to two days to transfer the funds (although funds are ordinarily transferred in less than a day).

The ATM systems such as NYCE, Honor, MAC, and Star use only on-line technology for merchant transactions, and are thus limited to merchant acceptance at locations with PIN pads. MasterCard uses only off-line technology for processing debit transactions on its MasterMoney cards. Visa check also relied on off-line technology until the introduction of Visa check II, whose transactions can be processed both on line and off-line.

The Growth of the Debit Card

Six factors contributed to the growth of the debit card during the mid-1990s.

1. Most consumers had ATM cards. The growth of ATM cards resulted in millions of consumers' having a piece of plastic that could serve readily as a distribution vehicle for debit card services. It was a natural progression for the ATM networks that had developed to expand into debit.
2. Merchants installed PIN pads in increasing numbers. By successfully encouraging merchants to install PIN pads, the ATM systems provided

a convenient payment device for their cardholders. The higher inter-change fee for off-line debit also provided a significant incentive for PIN pad installation.

3. Most retailers and supermarkets took bankcards. Consumers could use their debit cards off-line at these locations. Importantly, several merchant segments, including supermarkets, in which consumers particularly like using debit cards had begun accepting bankcards in the early 1990s.

4. Many banks started putting MasterMoney and Visa check marks on their debit cards, thereby vastly expanding the range of merchants at which consumers could use their ATM/debit cards. The interchange fees available on debit cards made it economically attractive to banks to add these marks to their ATM/debit cards.

5. Visa and to a lesser extent MasterCard engaged in significant advertising and promotion to encourage consumers to use their Visa check and MasterMoney cards instead of checks. This advertising promoted the general use of ATM/debit cards with the MasterCard and Visa marks on them even when the transactions did not go through MasterCard and Visa. The increase in the number of cards together with the increasing use by consumers who had the cards stimulated merchants to install PIN pads.

6. Advances in technology have made transactions faster, cheaper, and more convenient for consumers, merchants, and banks alike. As documented in chapter 6, net merchant discounts charged by acquirers have declined substantially. Also, along with declines in the costs of computer processing and telephone rates documented in chapter 6, the price of PIN pads was cut in half between the mid-1980s and the late 1990s.

We discuss the first five factors in more detail in the rest of this chapter. These factors have reinforced each other. Indeed, it is likely that the confluence of a significant base of consumers with ATM/debit cards (resulting from the efforts of banks and the regional ATMs) and a significant base of merchants that accepted MasterCard and Visa cards (resulting from the efforts of banks and the bankcard systems) in the early 1990s was critical for the rapid rise of debit cards.

The Rise of ATMs

ATM Growth

Though ATMs and regional network logos are now as ubiquitous as McDonalds, this has not always been the case. Although the spread of credit cards in the mid-1960s spurred the move to electronic banking, the origin of debit cards has its roots in the early 1970s when the first ATMs were installed throughout the country. Bankers initially viewed ATMs as a means of reducing costs by replacing human tellers with electronic terminals that eliminated the need for brick-and-mortar branches. They also gave smaller banks the ability to provide services to customers in a much wider geographic radius. As ATMs became linked through regional networks, banks were able to promise customers a much broader range of cash access services and gain a competitive advantage in markets with limited ATM penetration.

The earliest ATMs were known awkwardly as customer bank communications terminals (CBCTs). These terminals provided only limited services compared to the ATMs of the 1990s. Customers were sometimes limited to cash withdrawals in only two denominations, such as $25 or $50. Even though ATMs were developed to eliminate the need for building extra branches, most of the first installments were in bank lobbies or elsewhere on the premises of banks. One of the first ATM deployments off the premises of a financial institution was in Nebraska, where the First Federal Savings and Loan Association of Lincoln issued debit cards for use at terminals installed at Hinky Dinky grocery stores in January 1974. In this period, it cost about $80,000 for the teller machine itself, and the necessary electronic and phone line connections added to the cost. The high cost of machines and initial consumer skepticism hindered the expansion of ATM placements, but by early 1977 there were more than 6,000 ATMs installed nationwide, and by late 1981, more than 20,000 ATMs had been installed. As figure 12.1 shows, the number of ATM cards in circulation grew more rapidly than the number of ATMs during the 1980s. By the early 1990s, there were more than 200 million ATM cards in the hands of consumers and about 80,000 ATMs. During the 1990s, the growth rate of ATMs has exceeded that for ATM cards.

ATM/EFT Network Structure

In the 1980s, ATMs not only increased in number, they became more interconnected. Early on, most ATMs were either stand-alone terminals or connected through proprietary networks owned and operated by a single bank. Citibank had the largest proprietary network by 1979, with more than 400 ATMs in use processing nearly 60 million transactions

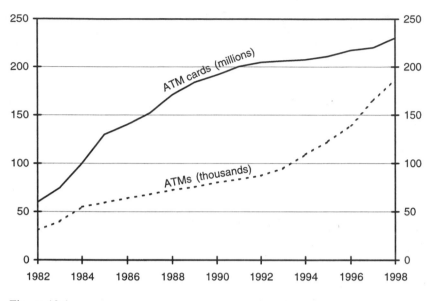

Figure 12.1
Significant growth in numbers of ATMs and ATM cards took place in the 1980s and 1990s.
Sources: Faulkner & Gray *Debit Card Directory,* 1999 and 1997; Steven D. Felgran, "From ATM to POS Networks: Branching, Access, and Pricing."

annually. These proprietary networks could be shared with other banks through franchising arrangements, but the proprietary bank provided the ATM processing and support. The other arrangement for a network of ATMs was linking proprietary networks through a joint venture among banks, which shared the ownership of the resulting ATM network. The percentage of shared ATMs grew dramatically in the 1980s from 16 percent in 1980 to 94 percent in 1990 and virtually 100 percent by 1996. We will refer to these networks more generally as EFT (electronic funds transfer) networks, because almost all have come to provide POS debit services as well as ATM services.

ATM sharing comes from the desire to distribute the costs of providing ATM services among several banks, to stimulate machine usage and thus cover fixed costs, and to provide all member banks' customers access to a large number of ATMs. An EFT network is a lot more attractive to a consumer if it includes most banks in her region rather than just her bank.

Some states required banks to allow smaller banks into proprietary or shared networks through mandatory sharing laws.

EFT network expansion and ATM sharing faced serious regulatory hurdles. As we described in chapter 3, since the 1930s interstate banking in the United States had been severely restricted. If ATMs were found to constitute a branch location, any system of EFT networks or multistate ATM placement could have been in violation of the McFadden Act. Early on, there was considerable debate and disagreement among the courts and the banking regulatory agencies as to whether ATMs were equivalent to branches. For example, in 1975 the Office of the Comptroller of Currency asserted that ATMs did not constitute bank branches, whereas some courts found that they did. Ultimately, legislative action and the courts resolved the issue in favor of ATM branching. The recommendations of the Commission on Electronic Fund Transfers in the late 1970s formed the basis for new legislation permitting interstate ATM networks. In addition, the Supreme Court's ruling in *Independent Bankers Association of New York State v. Marine Midland Bank* in 1986 allowed to stand a U.S. Court of Appeals decision in 1985 that ATMs did not constitute bank branches, thus allowing interstate EFT networks to thrive. In response, single-state networks crossed state lines, providing larger and more useful networks to their cardholders. In addition, massive consolidation occurred among the largest regional EFT networks. Although the twenty largest regional networks accounted for only 15 percent of all shared network transactions in 1982, this figure had increased to more than 90 percent by 1991.

Along with the growing prominence of regional EFT systems, there have also been attempts to develop national ATM networks. MasterCard and Visa were two of the first organizations to announce attempts to establish national networks in 1981. Shortly thereafter, several regional networks announced plans for establishing different national networks to compete with MasterTeller and Visa. Among these national network attempts were Exchange, Continet, Nationet, Cirrus, and Plus. MasterCard (with its acquisition of Cirrus) and Visa (through its Plus brand) both eventually established national ATM networks; the others either retreated to providing regional network service or disappeared.

The market for automated banking services has grown dramatically over the past thirty years, and the now ubiquitous ATM is the most obvious result. Of the 187,000 ATMs installed by late 1998, 84,000 (45 percent) were deployed off the premises of banks. As a result of consolidation among banks and regional networks, the five largest regional networks controlled 89 percent of all the ATMs in use in 1998. Although monthly ATM transactions more than tripled from 1986 to 1998, the number of transactions per ATM declined from a high of more than 6,800 each month in 1992 to less than 5,000 per month in 1998. This drop probably reflects the rapid increase in ATM placements after surcharging was permitted on ATM transactions, beginning in April 1996.

The Growth of PIN Pad Merchants

Whereas ATMs provide access to cash at a multitude of locations, the availability of debit at POS locations provides an attractive alternative to checks. As we discussed in chapter 3, America's intensive use of paper checks seems curious for a technologically advanced society in this era of electronic banking. Americans wrote more than 24 billion checks in 1971, soon after the advent of electronic banking, and this annual volume increased to 65 billion checks by 1997.

The growth of ATMs had created two conditions important to the growth of on-line debit. First, most consumers held an ATM card, and many had become comfortable using it. Second, banks had developed the infrastructure of ATMs that made it easy to use their ATM cards to withdraw cash from their checking accounts. It was then only a small step to envision consumers using these same cards at retail locations to pay for goods using money from their checking accounts. There was, however, one important obstacle. A consumer accessed her account at an ATM by entering her PIN. The only way for a consumer to enter her PIN at a store was if the store installed a PIN pad. To execute debit transactions, the store could use the same telephone lines it already had in place to execute credit transactions, but it had to add a PIN pad so that the on-line debit transaction could be authorized.

One of the first on-line POS debit experiments took place in Iowa in the early 1980s. Twenty-four PIN pad terminals were installed at two different grocery stores where shoppers could use their debit cards from any one of the more than 200 banks, S&Ls, and credit unions participating in the initial test. This and other early on-line debit experiments offered a couple of lessons. First, many of the most receptive merchants were grocery stores, which would prove to be the most important merchant category when on-line debit ultimately became successful. Consumers at grocery stores regularly used checks, and the stores saw on-line debit as a potential way of reducing their check-processing costs. The second lesson also was related to costs: the PIN pads and associated technology were still too expensive in the early 1980s. As the president of one of the Iowa test stores put it, "[t]he only problem is cost."

A variety of attempts at popularizing on-line debit continued throughout the 1980s. Aside from the concerns over equipment costs, two additional factors hindered the growth of on-line POS debit. First, many consumers were still reluctant to use debit as a means of payment. (Ironically, many associated the term "debit" with debt.) Second, there were a number of different competing EFT networks in many areas. As we noted above, the move to shared networks accelerated during the 1980s, but more than half of all ATMs were proprietary as late as 1984. In some cases, the different networks used different technologies, so that a store would need separate equipment to connect to each. As might be expected, on-line debit has been more successful in regions, such as California and Pennsylvania, that had established successful shared EFT networks by the mid-1980s.

The interchange arrangements for on-line POS debit have changed over time as banks have debated which party benefits more from on-line transactions. Debit card issuers argue that merchants benefit from on-line transactions and thus the interchange fee payment should go from the acquiring bank to the issuing bank, with the acquirer collecting a fee from the merchant, as in credit card systems. Merchants argue that issuing banks save money, since the use of on-line debit reduces paper check–processing costs and adds value to their debit cards, so that issuers should pay acquirers, as in ATM systems. Initially, the interchange fee flowed from issuers to acquirers, but that has reversed as acquirers now collect fees from merchants and pass some onto issuers. (As the discussion of interchange in chapter 7 indicates, this suggests interesting changes in the

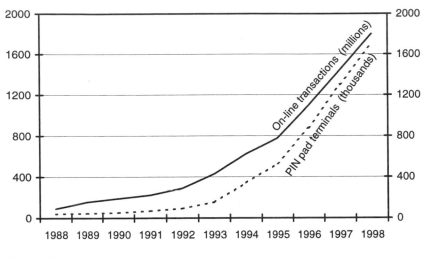

Figure 12.2
On-line debit grew quickly in the 1990s.
Source: 1999 Faulkner & Gray *Debit Card Directory.*

economics of these systems over time.) In 1998, interchange fees for on-line debit transactions ranged from 2 to 17 cents per transaction. In addition, transactions must be coordinated among issuers and acquirers. For most networks, both the acquirer and the issuer pay a fee for this service that may range from 1 cent to 9 cents per transaction.

Another fee issue is the charging of cardholders for the use of POS debit. This allows banks to recover switching fees and other costs to establish on-line POS networks but may discourage the use of on-line debit, particularly if banks do not impose similar charges for using paper checks or for off-line debit transactions. As the interchange arrangements for on-line debit have reversed to having the merchant and acquiring bank bear the interchange fee, all else equal, the cost to issuers of providing debit card services has effectively declined and reduced the need to impose on-line debit transaction fees on cardholders.

At the end of 1984, only 2,200 PIN pad–equipped terminals had been installed nationwide. By 1990, 53,000 PIN pads were in use. This did not represent an overwhelming number of merchants, since most on-line merchants need multiple terminals, but the number of PIN pads exploded in the 1990s. Figure 12.2 shows the growth in the number of PIN pads and on-line debit transactions. The number of installed PIN pads was 529,000 by 1995 when the Visa check advertising campaign started. As we have discussed, the success of off-line debit, coupled with the higher interchange rates for off-line than for on-line debit, created significant incentives for merchants to install PIN pads. In the following three years, the number of PIN pads tripled, to 1.7 million. And as we discussed earlier in this chapter, on-line debit transactions also took off starting in the mid-1990s.

But why did on-line debit take off when it did? Why did merchants install all these PIN pads? The higher interchange fee for off-line debit was one factor. In addition, as we described above, a number of the obstacles encountered in the 1980s had diminished significantly. First, the growth and consolidation of EFT networks allowed a network to offer potential merchants access to a large portion of the debit cardholders in a region. Standards had also developed among the EFT networks, as well as Visa and MasterCard, so that a merchant could process all cards using the same equipment. A second related factor was the penetration of Visa and MasterCard into supermarkets in the early to mid-1990s. A Visa or MasterCard supermarket would need only to add a PIN pad to accept on-line debit, since it would already have the magnetic stripe card reader and other equipment necessary for accepting payment cards. And third, consumers had become more familiar with the notion of using banking cards to debit their checking accounts as ATM usage became more commonplace and were also more comfortable with using the same cards at retailers.

Even with the tremendous growth of PIN pads in the 1990s, on-line debit had penetrated only a few merchant segments by late 1998. Merchants with relatively low profit margins, such as supermarkets and gas stations, quickly embraced the installation of PIN pad terminals, but few other retailers such as department stores and restaurants had accepted on-line debit in significant numbers. (One of the largest single deployments of on-line POS debit terminals occurred when the U.S. Postal Service installed more than 67,000 PIN pad–equipped terminals in its 33,000 offices in 1997.)

Most of the on-line POS debit networks have been regionally focused and developed by the same networks that switch ATM transactions. There have been attempts to create national on-line POS networks, but they have not met with great success. In the late 1980s, Visa and Master-Card attempted to launch a joint on-line debit system named Entrée. Fourteen state attorneys general filed an antitrust lawsuit alleging, among other things, that Entrée limited competition in debit. A settlement was reached: Visa and MasterCard agreed to go their separate ways.

Visa purchased the Interlink network, primarily based in California, in 1991 and has attempted to develop it into a viable national POS network. Although Interlink still handles a significant portion of on-line POS transactions in the western United States, it has not gained substantial volume outside of that region. MasterCard also developed a national on-line POS debit network, Maestro, in 1992. Maestro and Interlink have been reasonably successful in placing their logos on banking cards (the Interlink logo appeared on more than 17 percent of all debit cards in 1998, and Maestro appeared on 14 percent), but they tend to serve only as a POS system of last resort. Merchants and acquirers generally control transaction routing and route an on-line debit transaction to the regional systems if the cardholder has a logo on her card from one of those systems. These routing decisions reflect rules by some regional on-line systems that mandate routing to their systems if possible, as well as the slightly higher interchange fees charged by Interlink and Maestro. If Interlink were the least preferred on-line debit choice for the merchant, the transaction would be routed through Interlink only if the cardholder did not have a regional debit logo accepted by the merchant.

By 1997, consumers used on-line debit to complete approximately 1.4 billion transactions annually, with a value of about $49 billion. As shown in table 12.1, the ten largest on-line debit systems accounted for more than 90 percent of all on-line debit transactions, with the two largest networks, Star and Honor, providing more than 46 percent of all volume. (These two networks announced their intention to merge in 1998 following the merger of Bank of America with NationsBank, as we discuss later in this chapter.)

The Associations Finally Get It Right

A major development in POS debit was introduced by the two largest credit card systems, Visa and MasterCard, which devised plans to allow banks to issue debit cards that could be used for POS purchases at any

Table 12.1
The top ten on-line POS debit networks accounted for more than 90 percent of volume in 1997.

Network[a]	Transaction volume ($millions)	Number of transactions (millions)	Terminals (thousands)
Star	14,153	406	510
Honor	8,649	239	400
Interlink	6,672	213	831
MAC	5,467	116	400
NYCE	4,110	93	278
Pulse	2,749	88	104
TransAlliance	1,918	58	44
Xpress 24	761	18	25
Cash Station	672	18	14
Magic Line	648	28	154
Top ten	45,799	1,277	NA[b]
All systems	49,487	1,388	1,793

Source: The Nilson Report, no. 665, April 1998.
[a]The POS program for Pulse is Pulse Pay, the TransAlliance program is called Accel, and Magic Line offers POS services named ML Pay.
[b]Since many PIN pad terminals display the logo of more than one on-line system, the number of terminals controlled by the top ten systems cannot be precisely determined.

merchant that already accepted the systems' credit cards. After many years of development, the two cards have come to be known as Visa check and MasterMoney. Although these off-line debit cards are widely used today (with more than $50 billion of transaction volume in the first half of 1998, 88 million cards issued, and acceptance at nearly 4 million retailers), the two credit card associations had failed in several earlier attempts to develop an off-line debit product.

The bankcard associations launched their first attempt in the 1970s, with BankAmericard (Visa's previous name) issuing a national debit card called Entrée in October 1975 (the same name as the later attempted on-line joint venture between Visa and MasterCard) and Master Charge (now known as MasterCard) issuing one known as Signet in 1978. These cards were met with resistance both from merchants, who did not want to pay the same merchant discount rate for debit card purchases as they did for credit, and consumers, who didn't see the need for a debit card if they already had a credit card. By 1976, 80 million people carried either a BankAmericard or a Master Charge credit card. Five years after it launched Entrée, Visa had signed up only 140 banks to offer the debit card and about a million accounts had been issued cards. MasterCard's Signet attempt fared even worse and was phased out by the beginning of the 1980s.

The initial failure of Signet did not deter MasterCard from its goal of creating a viable debit card. In late 1980, MasterCard began issuing an off-line debit card dubbed MasterCard II. By late 1981, more than 200 financial institutions had signed up to issue MasterCard II, whereas Visa claimed to have more than 300 issuing institutions and 2.4 million Entrée cards in circulation.

In an incident foreshadowing future off-line debit battles, the retail chain Pay 'n Save filed suit in Seattle in late 1981 against a MasterCard II–issuing bank and the MasterCard association itself, contesting the merchant discount fees for MasterCard II, which were similar to those for MasterCard credit card transactions. A group of merchants in Seattle initially refused to accept the debit cards, even though they accepted MasterCard credit cards. The merchants felt they should be charged flat fees for off-line POS debit transactions, rather than the 2.5–5 percent of each transaction they were charged for transactions paid for with MasterCard II. The retailers viewed the debit transactions as replacing check transactions for which they paid no fees, whereas banks argued that retailers were benefiting from the acceptance of debit by not having to process collected checks (which were not guaranteed to clear) or to extend credit. The Pay 'n Save suit was settled out of court. The Nordstrom department store, which had filed similar litigation against Visa in 1983, dropped its suit but stopped accepting any Visa cards for a period in the mid-1980s. (In an ironic twist, Nordstrom began issuing a co-branded Visa card in 1993.)

Neither Visa's nor MasterCard's off-line debit program had much success in the 1980s, and the two associations were prevented from forming Entrée (which was for on-line debit) as a joint venture. But by the early

1990s, Visa (and subsequently MasterCard) was poised to make a splash in the debit card arena. Much as the strength of the ATM debit networks came from their existing ATM cardholder bases, the strength of Visa lay in its existing merchant base. As we described in chapter 6, by the mid-1990s Visa had substantially increased its penetration in several key retail segments, including supermarkets, a particularly important segment for debit card use. Visa's strength also came from its off-line technology, which did not require merchants to bear the costs of installing PIN pads, and from having significantly upgraded its processing capabilities in the early 1990s. However, Visa had its mark on only 10 percent of debit cards in 1994. Moreover, using debit cards to make retail purchases was still unfamiliar to most consumers, although they had become quite familiar with using credit cards. Visa had to overcome both of these problems.

Visa's solution was to invest heavily in marketing and to eliminate the use of the term "debit," which consumers often associated with debt. To increase consumer awareness of its debit products, Visa launched a campaign for "The New Shape of Checking" and developed brochures and held forums to let consumers know how to use the expanded capabilities of their debit cards. Visa came up with a new name for its debit card—Visa check—and developed an effective advertising campaign. The advertising told consumers that they could use Visa check cards anywhere Visa cards were accepted and in the same way as any other Visa card. In addition, the choice of Visa check as the name, as well as the advertising campaign ("The Card That Works Like a Check"), informed consumers that the value of transactions would be deducted from their checking accounts, much as with the use of paper checks. But unlike paper checks, as the advertising campaign emphasized, consumers did not need identification. The campaign made this point using well-known albeit diverse personalities such as former Senator and presidential candidate Bob Dole, Oscar winner and sometime New Age mystic Shirley MacLaine, premier NFL cornerback and part-time outfielder Deion Sanders, and the lovable but temperamental Daffy Duck. The advertisements were all set in stores where each personality was recognized and acclaimed but where their checks were not accepted without proof of identification.

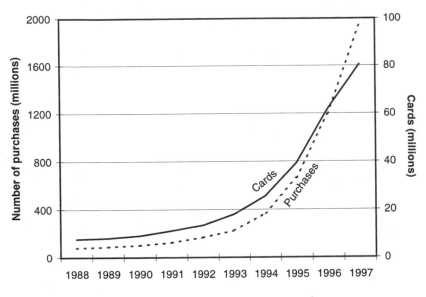

Figure 12.3
Off-line debit grew quickly in the 1990s.
Source: The Nilson Report, various issues, 1989–98.

Not only did consumers have to be persuaded of the advantages of debit, banks also had to be convinced to issue debit cards with Visa check functionality. Visa undertook a serious campaign to convince the top fifty banks to issue Visa check. As part of the sales pitch, Visa pointed to the massive advertising campaign it was going to undertake. Visa also invested in a processing facility in Denver that made it easier for issuers to operate their debit card programs by providing a single unified platform for processing both off-line and on-line transactions. Finally, Visa worked with the issuers to help programs encourage cardholders to activate and use their Visa check cards. All told, by late 1998, Visa had invested more than $250 million on advertising, marketing, and processing facilities.

Figure 12.3 shows the growth of off-line (total Visa check and Master-Money) cards and transactions in the 1990s. Visa check, in particular, experienced tremendous growth. Between 1990 and 1997, the number of Visa check cards in circulation increased from 7.6 million to 58.1 million. Purchase volume grew at an even faster rate, from 87 million purchases and $5.9 billion in 1991 to 1.53 billion purchases and $58 billion in

1997, with much of the growth taking place after 1995. MasterCard made its own successful push into off-line debit. By 1997, more than 22 million MasterMoney cards had been issued, and they generated $17 billion in volume on more than 400 million purchases. This represented phenomenal growth: only 1.4 million MasterMoney cards had been issued by 1991, and they generated $794 million of volume and only 14.5 million purchases that year.

Which Came First?

In the language of chapter 7, there are two different externality issues in the debit context. First, there is the ever-present chicken-and-egg problem. How does a potential debit card system attract both merchants and cardholders? The EFT systems solved the latter problem by relying on their already developed ATM cardholder bases. The EFT systems could use the same card, the same brand, and essentially the same technology for POS debit transactions. Because many networks required bank members to include their marks on all cards, they instantly had an issuer base. They simply had to persuade merchants to install the necessary PIN pads, which they did in part by setting merchant-friendly interchange fees. The credit card systems' solution to the chicken-and-egg problem was to rely on their merchant bases. To them a debit card was really just another Visa or MasterCard, accepted at the same merchants and processed the same way. Visa and MasterCard's interchange fees were, relatively speaking, more cardholder-friendly than those of the ATM systems.

The second major externality in the debit card world is between on-line and off-line transactions. This is not surprising given that 40 percent of consumers' banking cards carry both an on-line logo and an off-line logo. It is interesting to note from our discussion of on-line and off-line debit that both took off at about the same time. This is due in part to greater consumer comfort and interest in using debit to pay for retail transactions, making both types of debit more desirable. But the coincidence in timing is also due in part to externalities between the two debit types. As we have discussed, the tremendous growth of off-line transactions created greater incentives for merchants to install PIN pads, whose scarcity had been one of the major barriers to on-line debit use. In addition, consider a consumer who has seen a Visa check advertisement and, as a result, decides to use her Visa check card. Of course, her Visa check card is also her NYCE (or Honor, or MAC, etc.) ATM card. If she goes to a PIN pad merchant, she often will be asked to press either "Credit" or "Debit." If she (understandably) chooses "Debit," she will be asked for her PIN, thus authorizing a NYCE transaction, even if she thinks she is using her Visa check card. Her cost is usually the same either way, but her choice of "Debit" typically saves the merchant money.

With debit cards still developing and with the confusing presence of both on-line and off-line brands on the same card, both types of debit systems are more interested in promoting debit generally and are concerned about doing anything that might discourage either type of debit use. For example, even though issuers receive higher interchange fees on off-line debit than on on-line debit transactions, they do not generally charge different fees for the two types of transactions. Or consider the behavior of Magic Line, a Michigan-based EFT system, which has participated in advertisements that use its brand in conjunction with the Visa and MasterCard off-line debit programs. One of its executives stated, "We don't want to differentiate between products. The overall goal is to use the same card at the point of sale." Of course, since only one debit brand can be used for any given transaction, the logic behind this type of strategy must be that the on-line debit system would gain from this association with the Visa and MasterCard brands. In other words, Magic Line managers must think cardholders will end up using on-line debit frequently at PIN pad merchants.

The existence of off-line debit has also directly benefited some on-line debit systems by increasing their volume of processing traffic. The Honor network is the leading processor of off-line transactions among the regional debit systems, with more than 235 million off-line transactions in 1997, about one-quarter of its total switch volume. Off-line debit switch volume was about half of total on-line debit volume for ten major regional debit systems in 1997. To the extent that on-line debit systems still have increasing returns to scale, significant increases in volume from off-line debit transactions drive down average costs, as well as generating additional profits.

The Future of Debit Cards

Merchants

A variety of merchants, led by Wal-Mart, Sears & Roebuck, Circuit City, and Safeway, filed suit in late 1996 against Visa and MasterCard. The suit revolved around Visa's honor-all-cards rule, which requires all Visa merchants to accept all Visa cards for payment. (Here, we refer to Visa for simplicity; MasterCard had a similar rule and faced the same allegations. See chapter 6 for a more detailed discussion of these rules.) The plaintiffs wanted the option of accepting Visa credit cards but rejecting Visa check cards. Their stated rationale was that they felt that acceptance of Visa credit was valuable but that Visa check was not. They argued that Visa check consumers would still shop at their stores and would instead pay with on-line debit, cash, or checks, all of which they claimed were less expensive payment methods.

Visa asserted that its honor-all-cards rule was fundamental to its existence. It argued that the very purpose of Visa was to guarantee Visa cardholders that they could use their Visa cards at any Visa merchant, regardless of whether the particular Visa card was a platinum card or a classic card, used in Indiana or India, or issued by Citibank or the credit union next door. Visa also guaranteed merchants that they would be able to accept any type of Visa card and be guaranteed payment if proper authorization was obtained. Visa's position was that not only was the honor-all-cards rule fundamental to Visa, a similar rule was fundamental to all payment card systems. American Express requires its merchants to accept all American Express cards, and Discover/Novus requires its merchants to accept all Discover/Novus cards.

As of this writing the litigation is still pending. The results may affect not only the development of off-line debit but also the ability of payment card systems to enforce honor-all-cards rules. Besides filing suit, merchants are also exploring the possibility of setting up their own debit card network. If enough of them joined forces to do this, they would have automatically solved the merchant component of the chicken-and-egg problem. They would be able to produce cards either by convincing banks to issue them or by using automated clearing house (ACH) debit. ACH debit permits an issuer to debit a cardholder's account even if the issuer is not a bank or is not the bank where the cardholder has her checking account. The issuer, however, cannot directly verify the availability of funds in the account and must rely on an in-store negative file that keeps track of cardholders who have had insufficient funds in the past or have engaged in other suspicious activity.

Not So Regional

After a lull in the early 1990s, mergers between regional EFT networks increased rapidly during the mid-1990s, raising concentration substantially among the largest regional networks. The Honor network (based primarily in the Southeast) acquired six different regional networks between 1993 and 1997, in addition to merging with the Relay and Avail networks in 1991. However, the largest merger among EFT networks occurred in 1998 when Honor announced a merger with the Star network following the merger of two of their largest members, NationsBank (Honor) and Bank of America (Star). This trend of consolidation led some banking industry observers to raise antitrust concerns. As a result of mergers among EFT networks, Honor had the largest market share in the Southeast and Star ruled the West Coast, thus creating the first coast-to-coast "regional" network. MAC and NYCE together had a dominant share of the EFT networks in the Northeast, and Pulse stood almost alone in the Southwest.

Although EFT networks in the Midwest remained somewhat splintered, mergers among the large banks that owned various networks in the Midwest and elsewhere indicated the possibility of future mergers with the larger networks. The proposed merger of Banc One and First Chicago in 1998 led some to speculate that the MAC (Banc One) and Cash Station (First Chicago) networks, in which the two banks were dominant members, might be merger candidates. In late 1998, Magic Line, one of the larger networks in the Midwest, was put up for sale. This merger activity resulted in the largest on-line debit states having markets for POS debit with HHIs (based on the number of transactions) often well above 3,000, representing substantial concentration of EFT networks on a state-level basis. (The HHI measure of concentration was discussed in chapter 9.)

As we discussed, early attempts at national EFT systems were not tremendously successful. Plus and Cirrus survived, but they are ATM-only networks without POS capability. However, with the recent consolidation of the regional EFT networks and the wave of large-bank mergers, the potential for a new national ATM/POS debit network exists once again. Interlink, Visa's on-line-only brand, has also made progress, by gaining merchant acceptance at nearly three-quarters of PIN pad–capable merchants. The success of a national POS network, however, will necessarily be limited as long as multiple acceptance marks coexist on a banking card and individual merchants and acquirers make routing decisions. For a POS network to be truly national, it would have to be the only on-line mark on the card, or it would have to be the preferred on-line choice by most merchants who accept the card.

Though the transformation toward a cashless and checkless society may not have occurred as rapidly as some bankers of the early 1970s envisioned, the role of debit cards in society has changed dramatically over the past thirty years. With the advent of smart cards on the horizon and the possibility of POS debit's overtaking the use of credit cards or paper checks someday soon, it seems clear that Americans have overcome their fears of electronic banking and are becoming debit devotees.

13

And They Don't Take Cash

An economist is an expert who will know tomorrow why the things he predicted yesterday didn't happen today.

—Laurence J. Peter, author of *The Peter Principle*

Could you live without cash? You can order your groceries, get your dry-cleaning done, and obtain your videos from on-line supermarkets in many urban areas. As of late 1998, shoplink.com and peapod.com offered these services and more in the Boston area. You can order books and music from amazon.com and its several competitors. And you can buy a wide variety of other items, from modems to airline tickets, from other Internet-based retailers. Payment cards are the medium of exchange in this burgeoning electronic marketplace. What you cannot find on-line, you can obtain through mail order companies that take your order—and your payment card number—over the phone or through the mail. If you want to venture from home, your life without cash becomes more difficult but not impossible. Most grocery stores now take payment cards, as do many taxicabs and limousine services. To avoid handling coins, you can have the tolls on the Massachusetts Turnpike deducted automatically from your checking account. You can buy almost anything else you need—somewhere, not everywhere—with plastic. The trick in most cities is to avoid parking meters and laundromats.

Still, living without cash, even if possible, is somewhat inconvenient. Several new technologies may help. Smart cards (also known as stored-value cards) are payments cards with a small computer chip that keeps track of how much money is "on" the card and can transfer some of the money to pay for a transaction at a merchant with a card reader. As with most new payment technologies, these have had rocky beginnings. Visa launched one of the earliest trials in the United States at the 1996 Summer Olympics in Atlanta, with the hope that the system would continue to expand there. By late 1998, it had virtually shut down. These false starts are not unusual in the payment card business, of course, as we have seen. American Express was far from an instant success with its charge card: it almost gave it up in 1961. Bankcards in one form or another were around for almost twenty years before they took off in the 1970s. And industry observers had just about given up on debit cards before Visa check pushed this long dormant product out of bed.

As Internet commerce and electronic banking expand, there is a real prospect that cash and checks will decline in importance and that payment cards—Dee Hock's "guaranteed dots"—will become the real coin of the realm. Even if that does not happen until the centennial of the payment card industry in 2050, it will be remarkable nonetheless. In the space of a century, virtual money (bits of information that exist only on computer media and travel the world at the speed of light) would have supplanted physical money (coins, paper, and checks) after a 4,000-year reign.

That virtual money is even a contender for the throne is a testament to the suppleness of competitive markets in handling extraordinarily complex coordination problems through the development of novel business organizations and arrangements. The chicken-and-egg problem has bedeviled the payment card industry from the launch of the first charge card at midcentury in Manhattan to the disappointing test of the smart card at the century's end a few blocks away. Diners Club gave its card away to selected consumers who used it at restaurants. These consumers liked using the card, so more restaurants started taking it, so more consumers got the card, and even more restaurants started taking it. Nurturing these network externalities made Diners Club a success. In late 1997, Citibank and Chase Manhattan, using Visa and MasterCard smart-card technology, started a smart-card trial on the Upper West Side of Manhattan. But consumers had little interest in using the cards and few stores wanted to take them. Consumers and merchants had to be given rebates to participate. Both Citibank and Chase Manhattan decided to shut down their trials in late 1998. Whether the smart card will fail because it cannot solve the chicken-and-egg problem, like the local bankcard programs in the 1950s, or take a long time to solve it, like the debit card, remains to be seen.

Plastic cards did not experience explosive growth until a mechanism existed for signing up large numbers of consumers and merchants. Although other business arrangements are conceivable, in the United States and most other industrialized countries, competing banks developed associations for distributing payment cards widely to consumers and enlisting merchants. In the 1950s and early 1960s, Diners Club, American Express, the various local bank programs, and BankAmericard did not reach enough consumers or merchants to make payment cards much more than a partial substitute for cash and checks for some traveling businesspeople and a minor source of credit and convenience for some upper-income households. It took the development of the bankcard associations in the late 1960s to ignite growth in payment cards. The liftoff after that ignition has been spectacular: three decades later, most adults in the United States have at least one payment card that they can use at millions of merchants around the world and on the Internet.

The bankcard associations, like the product they were designed to produce, are unique in important respects. MasterCard and Visa are unusual mixtures of competition and collaboration, and of centralization and decentralization of business functions. The members collaborate through these associations on making MasterCard or Visa the card of choice for consumers and merchants and maintaining centralized authorization and settlement systems and other business functions for managing the card brand. Then they compete vigorously to persuade consumers to take and use their "flavor" of the brand instead of someone else's flavor, or another brand altogether. These members have fostered management teams at each association that compete intensely with each other, despite duality and the resulting overlap between the membership of the two associations. (Of course, these teams do collaborate sometimes, as they should in an industry in which standards are important. Moreover, as we discussed, duality provides incentives for attenuating brand competition along some dimensions.)

The complex business practices that have arisen to solve the chicken-and-egg problem and to balance the forces of competition and collab-

oration have been magnets for antitrust attacks by private parties and
federal enforcement agencies. Fortunately for the payment card industry,
the courts have applied somewhat more sophisticated economic analysis
to antitrust issues in the last quarter of the twentieth century than in
the first three quarters. Most importantly, as was the case on setting
interchange fees (*NaBanco*) and excluding competitors from membership (*MountainWest*), the courts have refused to strike down agreements
among competitors automatically and have been willing to look closely at
competitive and efficiency effects. Nonetheless, the bankcard associations
continue to face the risk that the courts will reject collectively set rules.
As of late 1998, the bankcard associations were facing an antitrust suit
filed by the U.S. Department of Justice seeking to end the same duality
that the Department of Justice declined to prevent in 1976. They were
also facing an antitrust suit brought by Wal-Mart and other retailers seeking to prevent the bankcard associations from enforcing their honor-all-
cards rule (see chapter 12), in particular as it requires merchants that
accept credit cards also to accept debit cards.

Payment cards have not flourished just because they provide a convenient alternative to cash and checks. Over time, entrepreneurs have discovered that they can integrate other products and services into payment
cards and thereby make these cards more valuable for consumers and
merchants. Combining payment and lending services on the same card
was by far the most important innovation along these lines. General-
purpose credit cards enabled consumers to take out instant loans to make
purchases. This innovation also helped the many merchants who lacked
the size or sophistication to extend consumers credit by themselves. And
it provided banks with a convenient method for lending money to an
ever-expanding set of households and small businesses. Combining cash
withdrawal services and payment services on the same card was another
important innovation. Debit cards, which do just this, have become popular because people can use the cards both to withdraw cash at ATMs
and to pay for purchases at millions of merchants. Of course, payment
cards provide a wide range of other services, from acting as a form of
identification to providing a convenient method for making security deposits at car rental companies, from conducting Internet transactions to

making clear to all that you back the local NFL team. Whether you think of payment cards as pieces of plastic, small computer platforms, lines of credit, or just sequences of numbers in banks' computers, they truly are much more than money. And because payment cards open up so many more possibilities than cash or checks, it is by no means implausible that the twenty-dollar bill will go the way of wampum before the middle of the next century.

Sources and Notes

We have prepared notes and source cites for each chapter, as well as a selected bibliography. Sources included in the bibliography are cited only in abbreviated form in this section, and the reader is referred to the bibliography for full information.

We start by making some general comments on definitions and conventions used in the book. First, all dollar figures in this book are adjusted (using the GDP implicit price deflator) to reflect purchasing power in 1998. Although this practice may seem unusual to noneconomists, it is a useful way of comparing dollar figures from different time periods and putting them in context for the reader, at least as of the late 1990s. We place occasional reminders about this convention throughout the book. Second, although we have defined payment cards to include debit and smart cards, this book has focused primarily on the development of credit and charge cards. For the sake of brevity, we have at times used "payment cards" to refer only to credit and charge cards and "bankcards" to refer only to credit cards even though both terms, strictly speaking, include debit cards.

Chapter 1

Dee Hock is quoted in Martin Meyer, *The Bankers: The Next Generation*, p.128, which also provides a good introduction to recent developments in payment devices. Payment card usage and acceptance is documented in the Faulkner & Gray 1999 *Debit Card Directory* and the fall 1997 and spring 1998 issues of *The Nilson Report*, an industry newsletter that includes payment card statistics commonly used within the industry. Data for the number of households and mean household income were provided by the U.S. Bureau of the Census, *Current Population Survey*, <http://www.census.gov/hhes/income/histinc/h05.html>. The scare to the payment card industry caused by the proposed credit card interest rate cap in 1991 is described in "The Price Vice," *Credit Card Management* (January 1992) and "Bank Stocks Drop on Moves to Cap Credit-Card Rates," *The Wall Street Journal* (November 15, 1991).

Current statistics on payment cards were found in *The Nilson Report*, nos. 663 (March 1998) and 673 (August 1998) and Faulkner & Gray's *1999 Card Industry Directory*.

As mentioned in "The Main Characters," John Friedman and John Meehan's *House of Cards: Inside the Troubled Empire of American Express* provides a history of American Express. In addition, we reviewed several articles in relation to the initial failure of the Optima Card, including "One Word: Plastic," *Barron's* (September 19, 1994); "What Went Wrong?" *Credit Card Management* (December 1991); and Artemis March, *Harvey Golub: Recharging American Express.* Information on the history of MasterCard was provided by Visa U.S.A. and "The Master Plan at MasterCard," *Credit Card Management* (February 1993). We supplemented this section with data from *The Nilson Report*, nos. 533 (October 1992) and 663 (March 1998), Visa U.S.A., and Faulkner & Gray's *1999 Card Industry Directory*.

The January 1998 (no. 660) and March 1991 (no. 496) issues of *The Nilson Report* provide information on the top fifty bankcard issuers in the United States. For the individual issuers discussed in "Other Members of the Cast," we also relied on the 1997 Annual Reports of Citicorp and MBNA.

The international information described in "The Foreign Cast" was gathered from several sources. Information on worldwide merchant acceptance was provided by Visa's home page (www.visa.com). The April 1998 issue (no. 666) of *The Nilson Report* should be consulted for current worldwide information on payment cards.

Other sources we relied on include "Acquiring's Pacesetter," *Credit Card Management* (August 1996); "JCB's Formula for Success," *Credit Card Management* (May 1993); "Stronger Foothold," *CardFAX* (March 18, 1997); the Bank for International Settlements, *Statistics on Payments in the Group of Ten Countries;* Visa's *Payment System Panel Study;* and Faulkner & Gray's *1998 Card Industry Directory.*

Chapter 2

See Antoine Augustin Cournot's *Researches into the Mathematical Principles of the Theory of Wealth* for a discussion of the nature of currency. The history of early mediums of exchange and barter and the quote on Lydian methods of exchange are provided by John Kenneth Galbraith, *Money: Whence It Came, Where It Went.* The development of metals as the standard medium of exchange in ancient Asia Minor, India, and China are traced in fine detail in the following works: John Maynard Keynes, *Essays in Persuasion;* Elgin Groseclose, *Money and Man;* and Simon Chen, *Coins of Ancient China.* The revolution resulting in the use of paper bills for exchange is discussed in Glyn Davies, *A History of Money from Ancient Times to the Present Day.* The progression toward the advent of paper money is summed up in Galbraith's book and in Ernest Ludlow Bogart's *Economic History of the American People,* as cited by Galbraith.

The history of the United States' early monetary policies is based on the Federal Reserve Bank of New York, *A Brief Summary of Coins and Currency;* Davies, *A History;* Milton Friedman and Anna Schwartz, *A Monetary History of the United States, 1867–1960;* and Board of Governors of the Federal Reserve System, *The Federal Reserve System: Purposes and Functions.*

The Nilson Report, no. 656 (November 1997), provides statistics on American consumption of goods and services and their methods of payment; see also "The Use of Cash and Transaction Accounts by American Families," *Federal Reserve Bulletin* (February 1986). As discussed in "Debit or Credit," fees and interest rates assessed by American Express were found on its Web site, <*http://www.americanexpress.com/apply/personal/card/docs/termsb0.shtml*> (visited Oct. 21, 1997). The statistics we gathered involving the use, cost, and transaction fees of payment cards were compiled from a variety of sources, including Visa U.S.A.; Faulkner & Gray's *1998 Card Industry Directory; The Nilson Report,* no. 663 (March 1998); and the Faulkner & Gray *1999 Debit Card Directory.*

The figure for the average credit card purchase as given in "The Role of Payment Cards in the U.S. Economy" was provided by *The Nilson Report,* no. 664 (March 1998). Crime statistics were based on Federal Bureau of Investigation, *Crime in the United States,* tables 23 and 24. Visa U.S.A. provided information on consumer attitudes toward different payment methods as revealed in the Gallup Payment Methods Attitude Study (September 1993). The Federal Reserve Board has compiled studies of merchant costs incurred in securing check payments. They can be found in Board of Governors of the Federal Reserve System, *Report to the Congress on Funds Availability Schedules and Check Fraud at Depository Institutions* and *82nd Annual Report. The Nilson Report,* no. 668 (May 1998), provides data on the cost to merchants to guarantee checks.

Merchant costs for customer usage of payment cards can be found in Bernstein Research, *The Future of the Credit Card Industry: Part II* (January 1996). The U.S. Bureau of the Census, *Measures of Value Produced, Capital Expenditures, Depreciable Assets and Operating Expenses,* tables 7 and 10, were used to determine average retail incremental margins. Examples of credit card use over the World Wide Web were furnished by "Gambling Online with Credit Cards," *CardFlash* (March 1997), and "Citibank Golf Card," *CardFlash* (July 1997).

Statistics regarding the use of credit cards as a line of credit were found in Faulkner & Gray's *1999 Card Industry Directory;* "Look Deep Into Your Wallet," *Fortune* (November 10, 1997); Council of Economic Advisors, *Economic Report of the President* (February 1998), table B-77; and Rebel Cole and John D. Wolken, "Financial Services Used by Small Businesses: Evidence from the 1993 National Survey of Small Business Finances." The data from the *Economic Report of the President* include store cards and thus differ from the payment card definition we use. Data on households were taken from the *Current Population Survey.* "Discover's Bearish Outlook," *Credit Card Management* (November 1992), discusses the success Sears has had with the Discover card. Finally, the details on Visa's computer system were provided by interviews with Visa personnel.

Chapter 3

Statistics from the following reports were used extensively throughout chapter 3: "Top 300 Commercial Banks in Deposits and Assets," *American Banker* (April 1997); Bank for International Settlements, *Statistics on Payments in the Group of Ten Countries;* and Datamonitor's *European Plastic Cards* (1996) publication. Additional information on America's usage of local banks was found in the *1996 American Banker & Gallup Consumer Survey* and Arthur B. Kennickell, Martha Starr-McCluer, and Annika E. Sunden, "Family Finances in the U.S.: Recent Evidence from the Survey of Consumer Finances." *BankSearch* by Sheshunoff Information Services, Inc., tracked the number of banks in Boston offering checking accounts, and the *Statistical Abstract of the United States: 1997* from the U.S. Bureau of the Census provided data on the number of U.S. banks. "Bank America's Profits Far Below Expectations," in *American Banker* (October 15, 1998), details the NationsBank-BankAmerica merger. For a more detailed history on the savings and loan crisis of the 1980s, see Meir Kohn's *Financial Institutions and Markets* (McGraw-Hill, Inc., 1994).

The data on the concentration of the banking industry were provided by "Top 100 Commercial Banks in Deposits and Assets" from *American Banker* (September 17, 1998). We compared banks to the brewing, steel, and tobacco industries based on data from the U.S. Bureau of the Census, *1992 Census of Manufactures*. See also Bank for International Settlements, *Statistics on Payments,* and James Barth, et al., "Commercial Banking Structure, Regulation, and Performance: An International Comparison," for more information on the U.S. banking industry in comparison to those in the rest of the world.

Further information for "Small Is Beautiful . . ." on the development of the American banking industry can be found in Peter S. Rose, *The Interstate Banking Revolution;* Harry D. Hutchinson, *Money, Banking, and the United States Economy;* and Kohn, *Financial Institutions and Markets*. For a discussion on U.S. government regulations on the banking industry, see Barth et al., "Commercial Banking Structures"; and Joseph Nocera, *A Piece of the Action: How the Middle Class Joined the Money Class*.

"In Midwest, Interstate Doesn't Mean Going Far" in *American Banker* (August 15, 1997) supplements the discussion of changing limitations in ". . . But Not Very Efficient . . . ." Details on the expansions and mergers in the banking industry were compiled from Federal Deposit Insurance Corporation, *1994* and *1998 Historical Statistics on Banking;* "Strength in Numbers: Credit Unions Seek Merger to Boost Services," *Anchorage Daily News* (July 23, 1996); and David E. Nolle, "Banking Industry Consolidation: Past Changes and Implications for the Future." We also relied on the following sources for the conclusion of "Banking in America": William Baxter's "Bank Interchange of Transactional Paper: Legal and Economic Perspectives" and Donald I. Baker and Roland E. Brandel, *The Law of Electronic Fund Transfer Systems*.

Data on payment card issuers and charge volume in "Banks, Nonbanks, and Payment Cards" were provided by *The Nilson Report,* nos. 660–662 (January–

February 1998), 664 (March 1998), and 666 (April 1998), and the FDIC *1997 Historical Statistics on Banking*. Information specific to credit unions was found in the following studies from the Credit Union National Association, *Operating Ratios & Spreads Year-End 1997* and *Credit Union Services Profile: December 1997*, and from the National Credit Union Association, *1997 Year-End Statistics for Federally Insured Credit Unions*. The 1997 Annual Reports of Citicorp and BankAmerica also provided a view into their credit card operations, and the American Express <www.americanexpress.com> and Discover Card <www.discovercard.com> Web pages (visited on July 27, 1998) provided information on the process of recruiting new cardholders. The changing relationship between customers and their credit card issuers is discussed in Board of Governors of the Federal Reserve System, "Remarks by Chairman Alan Greenspan." Other sources used in "Banks, Nonbanks, and Payment Cards" are Faulkner & Gray, *1999 Debit Card Directory*; Visa International, *International Country Overviews* (September 1997); Office of Thrift Supervision and Office of the Comptroller of the Currency, *Comparison of Powers of Federal Savings Associations to the Powers of National Banks*; "ISOs in Flux," *Credit Card Management* (November 1995); and "A Different Ballgame: A Survey; Frankfort the World Tomorrow," *The Economist* (March 14, 1981).

Chapter 4

We relied on Lewis Mandell's *The Credit Card Industry: A History* and *A History of Bank Credit Cards* by Gavin Spofford and Robert H. Grant throughout this chapter. We used the following sources for "Diners Club and the Birth of the Payment Card": Robert W. McLeod, *Bank Credit Cards for EFTS: A Cost-Benefit Analysis*; Board of Governors of the Federal Reserve System, *Bank Credit-Card and Check-Credit Plans*; John Friedman and John Meehan, *House of Cards: Inside the Troubled Empire of American Express*; information from Visa U.S.A.; Council of Economic Advisors, *Economic Report of the President* (February 1998); and the following articles found in *Business Week*. "Charge Accounts at the Chase," October 25, 1958; "Banks Take on the Consumer," March 7, 1959; and "New Shuffle in Credit Cards," November 3, 1962. The Diners Club lunch story comes from Mandell's book but a different version can be found in "Dining on the Cuff," *Newsweek* (January 29, 1951). News accounts from 1950 and 1951 place the lunch as taking place in January 1950 and the beginning of Diners Club in March or April 1950.

"The Infancy of the Card Associations" draws on Visa U.S.A.'s *Visa/Bankcard Industry Milestones* (September 1990) for some of the information on Bank of America's movement into the payment card industry. Three sources provided information on Visa and Mastercard's process of recruiting issuing banks: Donald M. T. Gibson, *The Strategic and Operational Significance of the Credit Card for Commercial Banks*; "What Lies Ahead in Consumer Credit," *Bankers Monthly* (March 15, 1968); and the transcript of a presentation given by Charles T. Russell and Dan Dougherty at the regional meetings of the Bank Public Relations and

Marketing Association in Columbus, Ohio, April 5, and in Montreal, Canada, April 22, 1966. Finally, we conclude the section with statistics from *Fortune* ("The Credit Card's Painful Coming-of-Age," October 1971) and *American Banker* ("Banks Reappraise Cards As Losses Mount," May 18, 1971; "Harvard Trust Drops Card Business," May 27, 1971; and "1970 Losses for Bank Cards Top $115.5 Mil., Over 50% Higher Than '69," March 29, 1971).

Inflation rates in "Early Policy Issues: Duality and Usury" are based on the Gross Domestic Product Implicit Price Deflator in the Bureau of Economic Analysis, *Survey of Current Business,* and the card issuers' cost of funds is based on proprietary data collected by the Visa system. Perspectives on the effects of that decision and usury laws in general were provided by Christopher DeMuth, "The Case against Credit Card Interest Rate Regulation," *Yale Journal on Regulation;* Glenn B. Canner and Charles A. Luckett, "Developments in the Pricing of Credit Card Services," *Federal Reserve Bulletin*; and "Regulating Credit Card Interest Rates: Does Anybody Benefit?" *Credit Card Management* (May/June 1988). There has been continuing litigation over whether the particular methods by which issuers imposed fees in response to usury limits illegally circumvented the usury laws. See, for example, the *Worthen* case and *Greenwood Trust Co. v. Commonwealth of Massachusetts.* The most recent cases, such as *Greenwood Trust,* confirm that the "exportation" of these fees from the state in which the card issuer is domiciled to the state in which the cardholder is located is legal. The following sources were also used in this section: Council of Economic Advisors, *Economic Report of the President* (February 1992); RAM Research, *Cardsearch* (1992); and Donald I. Baker and Roland E. Brandel, *The Law of Electronic Fund Transfer Systems.*

The statistics in "The 1980s Spending and Debt Spree" were compiled from a variety of sources. Consumer credit, debt, spending, and the number of households can be found in the U.S. Bureau of the Census, *Current Population Survey,* and Council of Economic Advisors, *Economic Report of the President* (February 1998), tables B-77 and B-16. Consumer credit outstanding extends beyond payment card debt but does not include mortgage or other debt secured by real estate. Restaurant expenditures are found in the *Consumer Expenditure Survey,* published by the Bureau of Labor Statistics. Visa U.S.A. provided information on the number of merchants accepting cards and the value of outstanding balances (Faulkner & Gray's *1999 Card Industry Directory* supplemented Visa's information). We found details regarding affinity card programs in Visa U.S.A.'s *Visa/ BankCard Industry Milestones* and "A Hard-Charging Driver for a Turbocharged Issuer" in *Credit Card Management* (August 1992). Finally, *The Nilson Report,* no. 510 (October 1991) was the source of transaction volume shares.

The data identifying the rise of nonbank issuers were found in *The Nilson Report,* nos. 496 (March 1991) and 660 (January 1998). For their methods and motivations, please see "U.S. Credit Card Industry—Competitive Developments Need to Be Closely Monitored," *GAO Report* (April 28, 1994); "Challenging the Credit Card Giants," *Institutional Investor* (August 1990); and "Business Q&A," *Gannett News Service* (June 28, 1990). "The Legacy of Card Bonds," in *Credit Card Management* (May 1998), discusses the increasing amounts of securitized card balances. See also *The Nilson Report*, no. 663 (March 1998), and "Charge!" *Time* (January 12, 1998) for more information discussing American Express and its road to increasing market share. Finally, we referred to Faulkner & Gray's *1999 Debit Card Directory* and "Turning Up the Volume on Debit's TV Advertising" from *Debit Card News* (September 16, 1997) for the sections on the rise of debit cards in the 1990s.

The failures of Datran and RCA are detailed in the following works: "A Shocking Failure in Communications," *Business Week* (September 6, 1976); and W. David Gardner, "Curtain Act at RCA." The mass-marketing approach to the credit card industry is discussed in "Planning and Control System for Bank Credit Card Operations," *Bankers Magazine* (Autumn 1971). An outline of the rules of success in the credit card industry can be found in "Size No Sure Road to Success in Card Field, Large Banks Learn," *American Banker* (July 21, 1966). Failures of certain marketing techniques are described in "The Credit Card's Painful Coming-of-Age" in *Fortune* (October 1971). Monitoring suspected credit card delinquents and other methods of preventing abuses are explained in "Credit Card Fraud," *Bankers Monthly Magazine* (June 15, 1967); "The Credit Card's Painful Coming-of-Age"; and Dwayne Krumme, *Banking and the Plastic Card*. The cost of theft to firms is examined in "Theft of Credit Cards Jumps Rapidly, Posing Big Problem for Firms," *The Wall Street Journal* (November 18, 1970); additional information can be found in "The Credit Card's Painful Coming-of-Age" and Mandell, *The Credit Card Industry*. Just as fraud complicated the payment industry's success, so too did interchange, as discussed in "Compatible Bank Credit Cards," *Bankers Monthly* (July 15, 1967), and "Exposure to Risk Is Increased as Credit Cards Go Nationwide," *American Banker* (July 27, 1966). The economic cycle's effect on the credit card industry is examined by "Credit Paradoxes: Tight Money Pinches Different People, Firms in Very Uneven Fashion," *The Wall Street Journal* (June 10, 1966); Gibson, *Strategic and Observational Significance;* and "A Banker's Pipe Dream?" *Forbes* (June 15, 1971).

Retailer rivalry, another impediment to the developing credit card industry, is described in "Stores Pay 30% of Charge Account Costs, Merchants Group Says Study Discloses," *The Wall Street Journal* (November 5, 1963); Mandell, *The Credit Card Industry;* and "Money Goes Electronic in the 1970s," *Business Week* (January 13, 1968). The Kaplan quote can be found in "Retailers Plan Test of Own Charge System to Counter Credit Inroads by Bank Cards," *American Banker* (January 13, 1971). We used *The Nilson Report*, no. 673 (August 1998) for the data on store card outstandings. Competition posed by charge card plans is examined in "Charge It! Bank Credit Cards Win Wide Usage, Bringing Both Benefits, Problems," *The Wall Street Journal* (December 22, 1969), and "Oil Firm Credit Cards Now Buy Other Goods, Rivals Aren't Upset," *The Wall Street Journal* (August 22, 1966). Franchise programs are discussed in "Bancardcheck Seeks to Provide Variation on Credit Card Theme," *American Banker* (July 26, 1966) and "Money Goes Electronic in the 1970s," *Business Week* (January 13, 1968). The check-credit plans are explored in Board of Governors of the Federal Reserve System, *Bank Credit-Card and Check-Credit Plans;* "A Quick Fix For the Bank Card," *The Bankers Magazine* (Spring 1972); "Credit-Card and Check-Credit

Plans at Commercial Banks," *Federal Reserve Bulletin* (September 1973); "Money Goes Electronic in the 1970s"; and "Bancardcheck Seeks to Provide Variation on Credit Card Theme." Risks to new ventures are considerable; see "Optima Backfires on American Express," *The Wall Street Journal* (October 3, 1992); "Plastics Go Pop," *The Economist* (September 12, 1992); "Fate Worse than Debt," *Barron's* (February 28, 1992); and David S. Evans and Richard Schmalensee, *The Economics of the Payment Card Industry.*

Chapter 5

We used data obtained from the Board of Governors of the Federal Reserve System's Survey of Consumer Finance throughout this chapter. See David S. Evans and Matthew Leder, "The Growth and Diffusion of Credit Cards in Society," for a detailed discussion of these data and their reliability. Evans and Leder also provide more details on the analysis in "The Growth and Diffusion of Credit Cards in the American Economy." The comparison of payment card usage to other methods is made based on data from *The Nilson Report,* no. 656 (November 1997). That same data for 1984 is provided by R. B. Avery et al., "The Use of Cash and Transaction Accounts by American Families."

Studies on payment cards and demand deposits include E. Marcus, "The Impact of Credit Cards on Demand Deposit Utilization," and Kenneth White, "The Effect of Bank Credit Cards on the Household Transactions Demand for Money." It is also cited in John V. Duca and William C. Whitesell, "Credit Cards and Money Demand: A Cross-Sectional Study."

"Credit Cards and Liquidity Constraints" is based on David G. Blanchflower, David S. Evans, and Andrew J. Oswald, "Credit Cards and Consumers." For an analysis of income growth over the life span, see Ronald G. Ehrenberg and Robert S. Smith, *Modern Labor Economics* and Jean Olivier Blanchard and Stanley Fischer, *Lectures on Macroeconomics.* The classic theoretical treatment of credit rationing is Joseph Stiglitz and Andrew Weiss, "Credit Rationing in Markets with Imperfect Information." A useful summary of the subsequent literature is provided by Xavier Freixas and Jean-Charles Rochet, *Microeconomics of Banking.* For examples of studies on liquidity constraint in households as mentioned in "Credit Cards and Liquidity Constraints," see Giovanni Ferri and Peter Simon, "Constrained Consumer Lending: Exploring Business Cycle Patterns Using the Survey of Consumer Finances"; Robert E. Hall and Frederic S. Mishkin, "The Sensitivity of Consumption to Transitory Income: Estimates from Panel Data on Households"; Tullio Jappelli, "Who Is Credit Constrained in the U.S. Economy?"; and Fumio Hayashi, "The Effect of Liquidity Constraints on Consumption: A Cross-Section Analysis." The data on charge-offs comes from "Fair, Isaac Finds Card Use Patterns Predict Bankruptcy," *American Banker* (August 19, 1997), and "Credit Scoring New Markets," *Bank Technology News* (July 1996). Some statements in the section are based on information provided by Visa U.S.A.

"Credit Cards and Entrepreneurships" is based in part on David S. Evans and Matthew Leder, "The Role of Credit Cards in Providing Financing for Small Businesses." The data on Sytel and other small businesses as used in "But Are Payment Cards Really a Good Deal?" were compiled from a variety of sources, including Dun & Bradstreet, *Business Background Report* (August 1998); "Don't Start a Business Without One," *Inc.* (February 1, 1998); Small Business Administration, *The State of Small Business: A Report of the President;* and *Summary Report to President Clinton* from the U.S. Small Business Administration. For a discussion of the measurement of job creation by small businesses, see J. Haltiwanger and S. Davis, "Gross Job Flows." Situations similar to that of the start up of Sytel are not rare. See "More Businesses Start Up on Plastic; Entrepreneurs Use Credit Cards to Get Set Up," *The Idaho Statesman* (December 28, 1997), and "Need Capital? Just Charge It," *Indianapolis Business Journal* (October 27, 1997). The 1997 value of venture capital expenditures comes from VentureOne: Venture Capital and Private Equity Research and Information, *Venture Capital Statistics,* <*http://www.ventureone.com/index.html*> (visited August 26, 1998). For a general piece on venture capital funding, see J. Lerner, "The Return to Investments in Innovative Activities: An Overview and an Analysis of the Software Industry." For an analysis of liquidity constraints and entrepreneurship see David S. Evans and Boyan Jovanovic, "An Estimated Model of Entrepreneurial Choice under Liquidity Constraints." Other papers on this issue include Douglas J. Holtz-Eakin, and Harvey Rosen, "Sticking It Out: Entrepreneurial Decisions and Liquidity Constraints," and David G. Blanchflower and Andrew J. Oswald, "What Makes an Entrepreneur?" Finally, data on the success rate of the self-employed applying for loans came from the Board of Governors of the Federal Reserve System, *Survey of Consumer Finances* (1995).

Chapter 6

Additional information on ISOs and their payment card policies can be found in the following articles from *Credit Card Management*: "Funny Thing About ISOs" (November 1994); "Instant Credit—for Merchants" (September 1997); and "A Big Boost from the ISOs" (May 1998). "The Rise and Sprawl of a Credit Services Empire" in the *ABA Banking Journal* (July 1998) gives a history of First Data Corporation. Details on its growth were provided by "First Data Strengthens Position in Card Processing" in *American Banker* (December 21, 1993); "The Fight for the No. 2 Spot," *Credit Card Management* (April 1998); and "Acquiring's Pacesetter," also in *Credit Card Management* (August 1996). Data on the number of accounts processed were found in "EDS Aims to Oust First Data As No. 1 Processor," *American Banker* (June 18, 1998), "Sears Roebuck Hires Total System as Processor for Its 60 Million Cards," also in *American Banker* (May 18, 1998), and *The Nilson Report*, no. 663 (March 1998). Additional information on First Data came from "Another Top Executive Is Leaving First Data Corp.," *Credit Card News* (August 1, 1998) and "Total System Dominates Commercial Card Processing," *American Banker* (October 21, 1997). Finally, the following articles from *American Banker* were also used in "Who Are the Players": "Banc One to Revamp Processing After 1st USA Deal" (April 15, 1997); "1st Data Said to Break Off Sears Talks" (March 16, 1998); and "Total System Has No. 1 First Data in Its Sights" (May 5, 1998).

For an overview of the POS terminal market, see "Why Terminal Makers Are Smiling," *Credit Card Management* (April 1996), and "New Directions for Terminal Resellers," also in *Credit Card Management* (March 1998). The Hewlett-Packard–Verifone merger is described in "Suddenly, Hewlett-Packard," from *Credit Card Management* (July 1997). Market share and rankings of the terminal manufacturers come from the following two *Credit Card Management* pieces: "The Terminal Vendors' Chip Shot" (April 1997) and "The Fight for the No. 2 Spot" (April 1998).

In "More and More Merchants Take Credit Cards," we relied generally on data and information supplied by Visa U.S.A. and Joseph Nocera, *A Piece of the Action: How the Middle Class Joined the Money Class*. The CPI and PPI indices at the beginning of this section were taken from <*http://stats.bls.gov/cpihome. htm*> and <*http://stats.bls.gov/ppihome.htm*> (visited October 1998). Information on J.C. Penney's decision to accept Visa cards came from "Penney to Honor Visa: 1st Big Retailer to Accept Bank Cards," *American Banker* (April 5, 1979), and "1% of Penney Sales on Visa," also from *American Banker* (March 24, 1980). Coverage of Montgomery Ward's decision can be found in "Ward, Penney Go All Out on Cards" (July 2, 1980) and "Wards Honors AmEx Card" (October 31, 1985), both from *American Banker*. A variety of sources provided information on Visa/MasterCard's marketing program targeted toward upscale retailers, including "MasterCard, Visa Break into Bloomingdale's," *American Banker* (November 14, 1986); "Bank Cards Crack Department Store Niche," *Member News* (March 1987); "Retail Credit Cards," *The Nilson Report*, no. 400 (March 1987); and "Saks Fifth Avenue Will Accept Visa, MasterCard at Its Stores," *American Banker* (October 15, 1987).

Industry articles, as well as our conversations with Visa personnel, have characterized the acquiring business as having high-volume firms with very small margins. See, for example, "United Airlines Pulls Out of National Processing's Acquiring Gate," *Credit Card News* (August 1, 1997); "Behind Chase's Re-Entry into Merchant Acquiring," *Credit Card News* (January 15, 1997); and "Many Major Players Join High-Stakes Card Game," *American Banker* (September 30, 1996). For information on credit card expansion into supermarkets, see "Priming the Supermarket Pump," *Credit Card Management* (March 1996). The section on American Express' External Sales Agent Program was compiled from many sources, including "AmEx Enlists ISOs and Banks to Find Small Merchants," *Credit Card News* (April 1, 1994); "AmEx Recruiters Strike Pay Dirt with Merchants," *Credit Card News* (January 15, 1995); "AmEx's Push for Merchants Begins to Pay Off," *Credit Card News* (May 1, 1996); "Call in the ISOs," *Credit Card Management* (December 1997); "Behind AmEx's Merchant Push," *Credit Card Management* (August 1998); and "Partnering with Rivals," *Credit Card Management* (August 1998). Finally, more information on credit card acceptance by gas stations can be found in these *Credit Card News* articles: "Hoping to Gas Up Its Card Program, Exxon Drops Its Discount-for-Cash Policy" (September 1, 1994); "Texaco Becomes the Latest Oil Marketer to Drop Its Gas-Card Discount

Fee" (December 1, 1994); and "A Lonely Amoco Abandons Two-Tier Pricing" (April 1, 1995).

Chapter 7

Information regarding the method of calculating interest charges for Citibank Visa and Discover Cards can be found on their respective Web pages (<*http://www.citibank.com*> and <*http://www.discovercard.com*>, visited July 1998). "Platinum Plastic on the Cheap" in *Credit Card Management* (April 1998) reveals the details behind the emergence of platinum credit cards. Joanna Stavins's "Can Demand Elasticities Explain Sticky Credit Card Rates?" and Visa U.S.A. provided data on credit card service fees; card features are discussed in "Amex Plays Its Cobranded Cards," *Credit Card Management* (February 1998). Data on advertising expenditures came from Faulkner & Gray's *1998 Credit Card Marketing Sourcebook*. Their estimates differ from internal data from Visa U.S.A., but they are used to compare advertising estimates across the different systems.

"Economics of Network Industries" draws heavily on David S. Evans and Richard Schmalensee, "A Guide to the Antitrust Economics of Networks." A good general introduction to the economics of network industries (and to some related ongoing controversies) is provided by the three essays in Symposium on Network Externalities, *Journal of Economic Perspectives*. Supplemental data are provided by Visa U.S.A., *1995 Credit Card Functional Cost Study*.

"Some Economics of Joint Ventures" draws on Howard H. Chang, David S. Evans, and Richard Schmalensee, "Some Economic Principles for Guiding Antitrust Policy Towards Joint Ventures." For one of the classic articles on antitrust policy and joint ventures, see Joseph F. Brodley, "Joint Ventures and Antitrust Policy." Additional details on the American Airlines/Citibank joint venture can be found in "American Express Applies for a New Line of Credit," *The New York Times* (July 30, 1995).

The discussion of the disadvantages of joint ventures is supplemented by the following published works: Caroline Ellis, "Making Strategic Alliances Succeed: The Importance of Trust," and Oliver E. Williamson, *Markets and Hierarchies: Analysis and Antitrust Implications*. Paul A. Allen's testimony before the Federal Trade Commission for the Joint Venture Project (July 24, 1997) elaborates on the effect on Visa of antitrust actions. The discussion of the interchange fee is based on Richard Schmalensee, "Payment Systems and Interchange Fees," and Jean-Charles Rochet and Jean Tirole, "Cooperation among Competitors: Interchange Fee Determination in the Credit Card Industry." One of the earliest discussions of interchange fees can be found in William F. Baxter, "Bank Interchange of Transactional Paper: Legal and Economic Perspectives." We also referred to "American Express: Service That Sells," in *Fortune* (November 20, 1989).

Some published works contribute to the discussion of organizational problems in joint ventures. They include James P. Johnson, "Procedural Justice Perceptions Among IJV Managers," and Mitrabarun Sarkar, S. Tamer Cavusgil, and Cuneyt Evirgen, "A Commitment-Trust Mediated Framework of International

Collaborative Venture Performance"; "Are Strategic Alliances Working?" *Fortune* (September 21, 1992); and Jordan D. Lewis, *Partnerships for Profit: Structuring and Managing Strategic Alliances.* Some of the data in this section came from *The Nilson Report,* no. 660 (January 1998).

We used the 1997 American Express Annual Report for much of the data in "Interdependent Pricing." The data on American Express' revenues include its charge and credit card operations, but credit cards constituted only about 13.6 percent of total American Express volume. The empirical study on the elasticity of demand in the credit card industry is Stavins, "Can Demand Elasticities Explain Sticky Credit Card Rates?"

Chapter 8

The Local Area Unemployment Statistics from the Bureau of Labor Statistics, the Regional Economic Information System at the University of Virginia <*http:// fisher.lib.virginia.edu/reis/*>, and the *New England Electronic Economic Data Center* <*http://www.bos.frb.org/economic/neei/neeidata/mp.txt*> (both visited December 1998), provided statistics on the economic conditions in the Boston area in 1991. Our discussion of the "Boston Fee Party" attempts to give, from the merchants' perspective, a picture of some of the economic issues confronting them at that time. It is not intended to provide a complete analysis of the relative costs and benefits to them from acceptance of American Express cards. The following sources provided information on the merchant discounts charged by American Express and its sources of revenue: "The Pressure Is Building on AmEx Discount Rates," *Credit Card News* (April 15, 1991); "Restaurateurs Take on American Express," *The Boston Globe* (March 29, 1991); "Peers Join Hub Restaurateur to Derail American Express," *The Boston Globe* (April 20, 1991); "American Express Keeps the Heat on Its Merchants," *Credit Card News* (February 1, 1992); and "American Express' Golub Takes Aim at Bank Cards," *American Banker* (October 7, 1992). We relied on a variety of sources for the details of American Express's relations with Boston area merchants, including John Friedman and John Meehan, *House of Cards: Inside the Troubled Empire of American Express,* and the following articles: "Visa's Legal Aid Program: Helping Restaurants Fight AmEx," *Credit Card News* (May 1, 1991); "Amex Fights to Discourage Defectors," *Business Week* (July 1, 1991); "The Bill is Due at American Express," *Fortune* (November 18, 1991); "Endangered Status Symbol," *The Boston Globe* (April 18, 1991); "Is a Wider Anti-AmEx Revolt Brewing?" *Credit Card Management* (November 1991); and "Charge!" *Time* (January 12, 1998). American Express' transaction dollar share at that time was provided by the Faulkner & Gray *1999 Credit Card Directory* and Visa U.S.A.

In "Who Are the Warriors?" we relied on *The Nilson Report,* nos. 401 (April 1987) and 664 (March 1998), and "Market Saturated, but Underused" from *Cards International* (August 16, 1996) for the data on charge volume of the top cards and issuers. For a discussion on television advertisements by the leading card companies, see the *1998 Credit Card Marketing Sourcebook* by Faulkner &

Gray. Merchant acceptance, as listed in "The Weapons of War," was provided by *The Nilson Report*, nos. 660 (January 1998) and 664 (March 1998). Finally, the promotional initiatives in supermarkets are described in "Visa Ends a Reprieve from Interchange Increases," *Credit Card News* (June 15, 1992); "Safeway First Taker of Visa's Supermarket Discount Program," *The American Banker* (April 8, 1991); "The credit boom . . . ," *Progressive Grocer* (October 1991); and "Amex Changes Its Stripes to Woo Customers," *American Banker* (February 23, 1995).

In "The Rise and Decline of American Express Cards," the information on the first hundred years of American Express is based on the discussion in Peter Z. Grossman's *American Express: The Unofficial History of the People Who Built the Great Financial Empire*. This section is supplemented with data from *The Nilson Report*, no. 660 (January 1998); the 1997 American Express Annual Report; the American Express WorldWide Consumer Directory Listing <*http://www.americanexpress.com/travelservices/?aexp_nav=hp_travelserv*> (visited August 19, 1997); and the following articles: "Travel Giant Makes Nice Profits," *Business Week* (July 20, 1957); "Hazards Down the Track for American Express," *Fortune* (November 6, 1978); "The Trick Is Managing Money," *Business Week* (June 6, 1970); and "Plastic Gaining on Traveler's Checks," *The New York Times* (May 17, 1998). American Express' financial situation at midcentury is described in *Time* magazine ("Private State Department," March 27, 1950, and "Host with the Most," April 9, 1956) and *Business Week* ("American Express Finds New Ways to Make Money," November 26, 1960, and "Travel Giant Makes Nice Profits," July 20, 1957). Diners Club and its origins as the first charge card are discussed in *The Nilson Report*, no. 310 (June 1983) and *Business Week* ("Credit Card Pays Entertainment Bills," November 11, 1950, and "On the Cuff Travel Speeds Up," August 16, 1958). "Credit Card for Anything?" in *Newsweek* (July 28, 1958) discusses American Express' entrance into the charge card industry. Additionally, its growth is discussed in the Grossman book; *Business Week*'s "The Trick Is Managing Money," (June 6, 1970); and Lewis Mandell, *The Credit Card Industry: A History*.

We used data from the U.S. Bureau of the Census, *Statistical Abstract of the United States: 1997* (table 854) for the statistics on retail failures and *Measures of Value Produced, Capital Expenditures, Depreciable Assets and Operating Expenses* from the same author for information on restaurant profit margins. Supermarket acceptance of American Express is explored in "Groceries on Credit," *Grocery Marketing* (November 1995), and "Amex Changes Its Stripes to Woo Customers." The remainder of the data on American Express usage came from the following sources: "Hazards Down the Track for American Express," *Fortune* (November 6, 1978); Visa U S A ; "Amexco Raising Gold Card Fee," *American Banker* (July 2, 1984); "The Great Plastic Card Fight Begins," *Fortune* (February 4, 1985); and "The Bill Is Due at American Express," *Fortune* (November 18, 1991).

The Nilson Report, nos. 663 and 664 (March 1998) and the *Statistical Abstract of the United States: 1997* from the U.S. Bureau of the Census provided data on the number of cards per household. "Visa Ups Budget in War Against Amex" in

Adweek (September 30, 1985) describes Visa's new line of commercials targeting American Express cardholders. Additional problems faced by American Express are described in Friedman and Meehan, *House of Cards,* and "American Express Applies for a New Line of Credit," *The New York Times* (July 30, 1995). Consumer perceptions of card acceptance were captured in Visa U.S.A.'s *Cardholder Tracking Study* (August 1996). Information regarding American Express' alliances with banks can be found in the following: "Visa Backs Down on European By-Law," *European Banker* (June 1, 1996); "Amex in Marketing Partnerships with 3 European Banks," *American Banker* (June 18, 1998); "Hapoalim Cuts Prime Interest Rate by 0.5%," *Israel Business Today* (February 14, 1997); and "A Steamy Mediterranean Saga," *Credit Card Management* (March 1997). Data on bankcard issuers were taken from *The Nilson Report,* nos. 660 (January 1998), 664 (March 1998), and 668 (May 1998), and the Board of Governors of the Federal Reserve System, *Remarks by Chairman Alan Greenspan.* Golub's speech concerning bankcards was presented at the Credit Card Forum, Atlanta, Georgia, on May 2, 1996. Finally, the data on American Express' current operations were taken from *The Nilson Report,* no. 663 (March 1998); information from Visa U.S.A.; and the 1997 American Express Annual Report.

Visa's competition with MasterCard, as discussed in "The Bankcard Battles," is mentioned in "Visa's Marketing Exploited Its Advantage in Ubiquity and Utility, Ad Architect Says," *American Banker* (July 7, 1997), and "Poll: Consumers Prefer Visa to MasterCard," *American Banker* (September 26, 1988). This is also confirmed through conversations with Visa personnel and Visa internal documents. Its advertising initiatives to this end are documented in the Minutes of Meeting of the Product Development and Marketing Committee of the Visa U.S.A. Board of Directors (June 16–17, 1985). Statistics for this section come from the Cardholder Tracking Studies conducted by Visa U.S.A. since 1985, and Faulkner & Gray's *1999 Card Industry Directory.* MasterCard's response to Visa's advertising is described in the following articles in *American Banker*: "Visa Outranks MasterCard, but MasterCard's Outlays for Ads Lead Competitors" (September 9, 1986); "Visa Ads Attack New American Express Card" (July 1, 1987); and "Advertising Blitz Planned for Gold MasterCard" (April 7, 1988). Citibank's spending on advertising can be found in the *1998 Credit Card Marketing Sourcebook* by Faulkner & Gray.

For a technical discussion of the principal-agent problem, see Jean Tirole, *The Theory of Industrial Organization.* A more accessible discussion can be found in David M. Kreps, *A Course in Microeconomic Theory.* In "The Impact of Duality on Productive Efficiency and Innovation," Jerry Hausman, Gregory Leonard, and Jean Tirole address the impact of duality on innovation in credit card associations.

Chapter 9

Data on the top fifty issuers and single-issuer networks can be found in *The Nilson Report,* no. 660 (January 1998). In our discussion of monoline issuers we included the estimated portion of the Banc One/First USA (which merged in 1997) volume attributable to First USA (a monoline) based on their respective pre-merger volumes. The estimate of the proportion of cardholders with depository relationships with their issuers comes from Board of Governors of the Federal Reserve System, *Remarks by Chairman Alan Greenspan*. Information on "transactors" came from discussions with Visa U.S.A. personnel and Payment Systems, Inc., *1991 Consumer Survey Crosstabulations*. The following articles provide data on fees and revenues: "Card Late Fees Have Risen 26% since '95," *American Banker* (July 28, 1997), and "The Profit Freefall Ends, But for How Long?" *Credit Card News* (April 1, 1998). For a discussion of the factors affecting the use of various payment methods across countries, see David B. Humphrey, "The Evolution of Payments in Europe, Japan, and the United States." Consumers' attitudes toward cash versus credit cards are revealed in Visa U.S.A.'s *Gallup Payment Methods Attitude Study*. Supplementary data for "Product Differentiation and Market Segmentation" also came from Visa U.S.A., *Profit Analysis Reports*. David S. Evans and Richard Schmalensee address net charge-offs/fraud in *The Economics of the Payment Card Industry*. Comparisons of risk within industries are calculated by Standard & Poor's Industry Survey's *Monthly Investment Review* (June 1997). More information on default and charge-offs can be found in Visa U.S.A., *Characteristics of Credit and Fraud Losses and Account Control* (1990); *The Nilson Report*, no. 664 (March 1998); and "Subprime's Dangerous Waters," *Credit Card Management* (March 1998). Loan rates were compiled from the U.S. Bureau of the Census, *Statistical Abstract of the United States: 1997*, table 797. Finally, we concluded the section with assistance from RAM Research Group, *CardData* (1997), and trial testimony of Robert McKinley in *MountainWest*.

The average cost to issuers for new applications was taken from Visa U.S.A., *1996 Credit Card Issuer Benchmark Study*. The data on portfolio ownership changes came from "Card Portfolio Sales Almost Tripled in '97," *American Banker* (January 9, 1998); information on balance transfers can be found in "Free Fall," *CardFax* (July 19, 1997). For an extended discussion on the costs of switching, see Paul S. Calem and Loretta J. Mester, "Consumer Behavior and the Stickiness of Credit Card Interest Rates," *American Economic Review*. The following published sources were essential in developing the section on the AT&T Universal Card: "One World. One Card. And a Lot of Worried Banks," *Credit Card Management* (November 1990); "Behind the Citibank Legend," *Credit Card Management* (August 1991); "How Technology Helped AT&T Win the Baldrige Award," *New Technology Week* (December 21, 1992); "AT&T Credit Card Receives Baldrige Award from President in Ceremony," *Card News* (December 14, 1992); "AT&T Puts Universal Credit Card on the Block," *The Wall Street Journal* (October 21, 1997); "An Irresistible Force?" *Credit Card Management* (January 1998); and "AT&T's Loss Bucks the Card-Industry Profit Trend," *Credit Card News* (November 1, 1996). In addition to information from the MBNA Web site <http://www.mbnainternational.com/this/index.htm> (visited August 1998), we used Orla O'Sullivan's "Profiting from the Ties that Bind"; *The Nilson Report*, no. 660 (January 1998); and "Industry Profits Dip, but 1998 Holds Promise," *Credit Card News* (February 1998) for the section on MBNA.

For additional information on Citibank, see *Retail Banker International* (January 28, 1997); "The King of Plastic" in *Forbes* (December 15, 1997); "The Ante Rises in East Asia" from *The New York Times* (July 14, 1996); and "Indonesia Stiff Competition in Credit Card Industry" in *International Market Insight Reports* (August 12, 1997). Its cobranded card is mentioned in "Citibank Relationship Account," *Cardtrak Online* (November 11, 1997) and its college competition is described in "Anderson University Students Share Grand Prize in 1996 Citibank College Advertising Awards," *PR Newswire* (June 17, 1996). Finally, the section discussing BankBoston's credit card efforts relied on the following sources: "Bank of Boston Is Poised for Big Move in Credit Card Market," *Boston Business Journal* (February 2, 1996); *The Nilson Report,* no. 660 (January 1998); "Two Major Offers Launched," *Cardtrack Online* (September 1995); and "Bank of Boston Intensifies Credit Card Activities," *Gazeta Mercantil Online* (February 21, 1996).

One textbook that we used to supplement "Market Structure" is F. M. Scherer and David Ross, *Industrial Market Structure and Economic Performance* (1990). The Faulkner & Gray study can be found in the *1998 Credit Card Marketing Sourcebook,* and the Federal Reserve survey was published as the Board of Governors of the Federal Reserve System, "Semiannual Credit Card Survey" (July 31, 1998), located at <*http://www.bog.frb.fed.us/pubs/shop/*>. The number of Chicago grocery chains was taken from PhoneDisk Business, v. 3.01, 1997 Edition 2. HMOs were found in the *Guide to Illinois Health Maintenance Organizations* from the Illinois State Medical Society (October 1997) and the number of newspapers can be found in *The Internet Press,* Newspaper Mania, <*http://www.club.innet.be/~year0230/link4.htm*>. These numbers were accurate as of October 1997. The data on industry concentration within the manufacturing industry are based on the U.S. Bureau of the Census, *Concentration Ratios in Manufacturing,* from the 1992 Census of Manufactures, <*http://www.census.gov/mcd/mancen/download/mc92cr.sum* > (visited November 1998). The paragraph on the HHI is based on Department of Justice and Federal Trade Commission, *1992 Horizontal Merger Guidelines,* <*http://www.usdoj.gov/atr/public/guidelines/horiz_book/hmg1.html*>, with April 8, 1997 revisions. See also *The Nilson Report,* no. 660 (January 1998).

Our discussion of Visa's fee structure is based on Visa U.S.A., Executive Summary, Board of Directors Meeting (February 10–11, 1992), and the illustrative examples of member fees comes from Visa U.S.A. The data on issuers affiliated with the Visa system were also provided by Visa U.S.A. Prior to 1993, Visa's data did not distinguish issuers that issued only debit cards because there were few such issuers. Consequently, the numbers we report include debit-only issuers. Information on large industrial corporations joining the Visa system can be found in the *1993 Credit Card Issuer's Guide* by Faulkner & Gray, and "Accounts in Review," *Adweek* (September 14, 1992). In addition to the $130 million AT&T spent on advertising for its new card, its total investment has been estimated at $675 million. See "Raising the Stakes in a War of Plastic," *The New York Times* (September 13, 1992). Carlos Lapuerta and Stewart C. Myers discuss Discover's road to profitability in "Measuring Profitability in the Credit Card Business." The number of credit card solicitations is mentioned in "Tough Times in Card Marketing," *Credit Card Management* (May 1998). For Internet sites on credit card information, see <*http://asque.com/credcard.htm*> and <*http://www.bankrate.com*> (accessed August 1998). Finally, we referred to the following two articles in the discussion on credit card switching: P. S. Calem, "The Strange Behavior of the Credit Card Market," and Calem and Mester, "Consumer Behavior."

Data for the beginning of "Market Performance" were provided by Visa U.S.A., the *Current Population Survey* by the U.S. Department of the Census, and the Council of Economic Advisors, *Economic Report of the President* (February 1997). The price index discussed is based on the assumption that 68 percent of the cardholders revolve balances, with average outstanding balances of about $1,400—which represent the values for those variables over the relevant time period. For further discussion of the index for payment card prices, see David S. Evans, Bernard J. Reddy, and Richard Schmalensee, "Did AT&T and GM Affect Credit Card Pricing?" Inflation rates were based on the GDP Implicit Price Deflator from the Bureau of Economic Analysis, *Survey of Current Business* (August 1998), table 3, located at <*http://www.bea.doc.gov/bea/dn1.htm*>. The cost of funds for issuers is addressed in Evans and Schmalensee, *Economics of the Payment Card Industry*. The policies discussing deductibility of interest payments are located in the Internal Revenue Service, Internal Revenue Code, 26 U.S.C. 163. Consumer responses to changing interest rates are described in "Consumers Finally Respond to High Credit Card Interest" in *The New York Times* (March 29, 1993) and "The Price Vise" in *Credit Card Management* (January 1992). Finally, the following data sources supplemented the conclusion of the section: Board of Governors of the Federal Reserve System, *Survey of Consumer Finances* (1983, 1989, and 1995); "Industry Profits Dip, but 1998 Holds Promise," *Credit Card News* (February 1, 1998); and "Card Portfolio Sales Almost Triple in '97," *Credit Card Management* (January 9, 1998).

The calculation for the HHI following the bank merger wave of 1998 incorporates the sizeable mergers and sale of the AT&T portfolio mentioned in the text, as well as Fleet Bank's purchase of the Advanta portfolio, the merger of First Union National with CoreStates Bank, the merger of Crestar Bank and SunTrust Bank, the merger of Firstar with Star Banc, and the purchase of a portion of First Union's portfolio by Providian. Four additional portfolio sales and two mergers among the fifty largest bankcard issuers documented in 1998 issues of *American Banker* were also used in the calculation.

Chapter 10

Lawrence M. Ausubel, "The Failure of Competition in the Credit Card Market," is discussed in the introduction. See also Ausubel's "The Credit Card Market Revisited." A number of studies by Dennis Carlton and Alan Frankel discuss competition in the credit card market. See "Antitrust and Payment Technologies" and "The Antitrust Economics of Credit Card Networks" as well as Dennis W. Carlton and Steven C. Salop, "You Keep on Knocking but You Can't Come In: Evaluating Restrictions on Access to Input Joint Ventures."

In "High and Sticky Interest Rates," credit card, forty-eight-month auto and twenty-four-month personal loan data came from the Board of Governors of the Federal Reserve System, *Statistical Release G.19*. Home mortgage loan data were supplied by a U.S. Department of Housing and Urban Development News Release (August 25, 1998). Prime rate and three-month Treasury bill data came from the Board of Governors of the Federal Reserve System's *Statistical Release G.13*. For more information on the relationship between cost of funds and credit card rates, see Alexander Raskovich and Luke Froeb, "Has Competition Failed in the Credit Card Market?" We supplemented the section on high interest rates with two articles from *Credit Card Management*: "Those Naughty Nonrevolvers" (December 1996) and "The Profit Freefall Ends, but for How Long?" (April 1, 1998).

We consulted a number of sources regarding sticky interest rates. See, for example, Raskovich and Froeb, "Has Competition Failed?"; Joseph Stiglitz and Andrew Weiss, "Credit Rationing in Markets with Imperfect Information"; Loretta Mester, "Why Are Credit Card Rates Sticky?"; and Dagobert Brito and Peter Hartley, "Consumer Rationality and Credit Cards." Dennis W. Carlton's "The Rigidity of Prices" discusses other "sticky" consumer prices. For a useful summary of the literature on this topic, see Carlton's "The Theory and Facts of How Markets Clear: Is Industrial Organization Useful for Understanding Macroeconomics?" The following sources provide more information about the changing responsiveness of credit card interest rates: Victor Stango, "Fixed Rates vs. Variable Rates: Competition and Pricing in the Credit Card Market," and Joanna Stavins, "Can Demand Elasticities Explain Sticky Credit Card Rates?"

"The Myth of Exorbitant Profits" is based on work by Carlos Lapuerta and Stewart Myers and on extensive discussions we have had with these authors. See their "Measuring Profitability in the Credit Card Market" as well as "Faulty Analysis Underlies Claims of Excess Card Profits," *American Banker* (October 10, 1995). The comment on credit card industry losses came from "Passing the Chargeoff Buck," *Credit Card Management* (March 1997). For more information on the state of the industry, see "Faulty Analysis Underlies Claims of Excess Card Profits"; David S. Evans and Richard Schmalensee, *The Economics of the Payment Card Industry;* and Raskovich and Froeb, "Has Competition Failed?" *Principles of Corporate Finance* by Richard Brealey and Stewart Myers and *Modern Industrial Organization* by Dennis W. Carlton and Jeffrey Perloff address the issue of biases in accounting rates of return. See also Thomas R. Stauffer, "The Measurement of Corporate Rates of Return: A Generalized Formulation," and Franklin M. Fisher and John J. McGowan, "On the Misuse of Accounting Rates of Return to Infer Monopoly Profits." Former Senator D'Amato's quote can be found in "Senate Votes to Slash Rates on Credit Cards in Bid to Stir Economy," *The Commercial Appeal* (November 14, 1991).

The discussion of Greenwood Trust is based on research conducted by Lapuerta and Myers in "Measuring Profitability in the Credit Card Market." Praise for the Discover Card is provided by "Sears Can Still Do Something Right,"

Credit Card Management (May 1991). Data for the average return on Treasury bills were found in the Council of Economic Advisors, *Economic Report of the President* (February 1998), table B-73.

We relied on David S. Evans, Bernard J. Reddy, and Richard Schmalensee, "Did AT&T and GM Affect Credit Card Pricing?" for most of "AT&T, GM, and Credit Card Prices." See Carlton and Frankel, "Antitrust and Payment Technologies" and "Antitrust Economics," and Carlton and Salop, "You Keep on Knocking" for their analysis of GM and AT&T entry into the credit card business. For a summary of the *MountainWest* case, see David S. Evans and Richard Schmalensee, "Joint Venture Membership: MountainWest." We consulted "Household Sells Bank Branches to Focus on Credit Cards," *Investor's Business Daily* (July 25, 1996), and *The Nilson Report*, nos. 612 (January 1996) and 617 (April 1996) for GM and AT&T outstandings and accounts. Quotes on GM and AT&T strategy came from "One World, One Card, and a Lot of Worried Banks" in *Credit Card Management* (October 1990) and "Muscle Card" in *Time* (September 21, 1992).

Other published sources used in "AT&T, GM, and Credit Card Prices" include "Picking a Path through the Plastic Jungle," *Business Week* (August 6, 1990); "Variable Rate Card," *American Banker* (September 24, 1986); "Amalgamated Bank Enters Credit Card Market," *PR Newswire* (February 17, 1987); "Bank Lowers Card Rate," *American Banker* (April 1, 1988); "Bank Offers Variable Rate," *American Banker* (July 13, 1987); "First Interstate of California Announces Variable Interest Rate on Credit Card Balances," *Business Wire* (January 22, 1987); and "Looking Behind the New AT&T Card," *Money* (September 1990). Some of the data used in this section were provided by RAM Research.

Chapter 11

The Adam Smith quote is taken from *An Inquiry into the Nature and Causes of the Wealth of Nations*. On the history of the U.S. antitrust laws and for a general discussion, see William Letwin, *Law and Economic Policy in America*; Alan D. Neale, *The Antitrust Laws of the United States;* and Robert H. Bork, *The Antitrust Paradox*.

In "Sleeping with the Enemy: *Worthen*," information on market share for Sealy was provided in Richard Posner, *Antitrust Law: An Economic Perspective*. The United States also submitted a brief as amicus curiae in *Worthen*. Finally, a letter by Thomas E. Kauper, Assistant Attorney General in the Antitrust Division of the U.S. Department of Justice, provided information on the Antitrust Division's position on Visa's request for a business clearance review letter (October 7, 1975). We used both of these documents (made available to us by Visa U.S.A.) throughout the section, and the latter two quotes in "Lacking an Ally, Visa Surrenders" come from this letter.

In "Good Fix: *NaBanco*," we relied on Appellant Brief of NaBanco, United States Court of Appeals for the 11th Circuit; and Appellee Brief of Visa, United States Court of Appeals for the 11th Circuit. An argument for a zero interchange fee is made by A. S. Frankel, "Monopoly and Competition in the Supply and Exchange of Money."

"Someone's Knocking at My Door: *MountainWest*" is based on David S. Evans and Richard Schmalensee, "Joint Venture Membership: MountainWest," as cited in the previous chapter. The authors consulted for Visa U.S.A. on this case, and Schmalensee testified as an expert witness for Visa at trial. The quote from Visa's By-Law 2.06 is located in Visa U.S.A., Inc., "By-Laws/Operating Regulations," May 1, 1992. The main documents relied upon in our discussion of *Mountain-West* are the Responding Brief of Appellee MountainWest, 10th Circuit Court of Appeals, and Opening Brief of Appellant Visa U.S.A., Inc., 10th Circuit Court of Appeals. See also, Dennis Carlton and Alan Frankel, "The Antitrust Economics of Credit Card Networks"; William H. Pratt, James D. Sonda, and Mark A. Racanelli, "Refusals to Deal in the Context of Network Joint Ventures"; and David S. Evans and Richard Schmalensee, "Economic Aspects of Payment Card Systems and Antitrust Policy Toward Joint Ventures." On the so-called essential facility doctrine, see Phillip Areeda, "Essential Facilities: An Epithet in Need of Limiting Principles."

"Leveling the Battlefield" is based heavily on Howard H. Chang, David S. Evans, and Richard Schmalensee, "Some Economic Principles for Guiding Antitrust Policy towards Joint Ventures" (as cited in chapter 7). Articles triggered by *MountainWest* include Herbert Hovenkamp, "Exclusive Joint Ventures and Antitrust Policy"; Dennis W. Carlton and Steven C. Salop, "You Keep on Knocking but You Can't Come In: Evaluating Restrictions on Access to Input Joint Ventures"; William H. Pratt, James. D. Sonda, and Mark A. Racanelli, "Refusals to Deal in the Context of Joint Ventures"; and David S. Evans and Richard Schmalensee, "Economic Aspects of Payment Card Systems" and "Joint Venture Membership."

Chapter 12

The opening quotations for chapter 12 can be found in "Bank Cards Take Over the Country," *Business Week* (August 4, 1975), and John P. Caskey and Gordon H. Sellon, Jr., "Is the Debit Card Revolution Finally Here?" The history of ATMs and PIN pads as discussed in "Awkward Growth, Complexity, and Confusion" was compiled with assistance from James J. McAndrews, "The Evolution of Shared ATM Networks"; "An Expanding World of ATM Opportunities," *Bank Network News* (September 11, 1998); and "Off-line or On-line?" *Bank Systems and Technology* (August 1998). The data on MasterMoney and Visa check cards came from a variety of sources, including "Online's Double-Digit Growth Loses Its Luster," *Bank Network News* (September 11, 1998); "MasterCard Goes on Debit Card Offensive," *American Banker* (November 16, 1993); and "Visa Launching Big Ad Campaign for Check Cards," *American Banker* (September 5, 1995). The interchange rates for off-line debit were taken from the June 25, 1998, issue of *Debit Card News* ("Interchange Fee Hikes Test Merchants' Muscle"). The interchange discussion in the text does not include details on the differences between Visa and MasterCard's interchange fees. In 1998, Visa's off-line debit interchange fee was 6 cents plus 1.04 percent of the transaction value; however, Visa had a flat supermarket interchange rate of 36 cents. MasterCard's interchange fee was the same as for its credit card transactions, with an average around 1.36 percent and a special supermarket rate of 1.15 percent.

Some information on the effect of credit cards on electronic banking comes from "Bank Cards Take Over the Country," *Business Week* (August 4, 1975). The increasing number of ATM machines in the United States is chronicled in the following articles: "A Retreat from the Cashless Society," *Business Week* (April 18, 1977); "Machines Provide 24-Hour Bank Service," *U.S. News and World Report* (January 29, 1972); "Electronic Shopping Builds a Base," *Business Week* (October 26, 1981); and McAndrews, "Evolution of Shared ATM Networks." The size of Citibank's ATM network in 1979 was estimated in "Customers Love Checking Balances on ATMs," *American Banker* (August 27, 1979). Data on the number of shared ATMs came from Elizabeth S. Laderman, "The Public Policy Implications of State Laws Pertaining to Automated Teller Machines." Recent data came from Faulkner & Gray's *1999 Debit Card Directory*. The new legislation on ATM networks is described in *EFT in the United States: Policy Recommendations and the Public Interest* from the National Commission on Electronic Fund Transfers (1977). The history of interchange networks is described in "MasterCard to Unveil National ATM Network in November," *American Banker* (April 22, 1981). Finally, the number of ATM transactions can be found in Faulkner & Gray's *1999 Debit Card Directory*, the Laderman article, and "Get Ready for Surcharges" in *Credit Card Management* (August 1996).

Data on check volume in "The Growth of PIN Pad Merchants" were compiled from "The Fed Tries to Push Checkless Banking," *Business Week* (May 20, 1972), and "N.Y. Clearing House Forms Small-Payment Unit," *American Banker* (April 24, 1998). For an explanation of the first POS debit experiments, see "Iowa, the Debit Card State," *Forbes* (August 29, 1983). See also Caskey and Sellon, "Is the Debit Card Revolution Finally Here?"; Steven D. Felgran, "From ATM to POS Networks: Branching, Access, and Pricing"; Steven D. Felgran and R. Edward Ferguson, "The Evolution of Retail EFT Networks"; and "Postal Service Delivers Consumers an On-Line Debit Package," *Debit Card News* (June 18, 1997).

A history of the early attempts by Visa and MasterCard to introduce debit cards was compiled based on information from "MasterCard II to Vie with Visa's Debit Card," *American Banker* (September 9, 1980); "The U.S. Has a Date with Electronic Banking," *Forbes* (July 1, 1976); "A Faltering Step Toward Electronic Banking," *Business Week* (August 23, 1976); and "Explosion in the Bank Card Cafeteria," *Fortune* (September 8, 1980). An interesting analysis of why consumers might prefer credit for some purchases and debit for others is provided by Drazen Prelec and George Loewenstein, "The Red and the Black: Mental Accounting of Savings and Debt." The competition between the new MasterCard II and Visa Debit is described by "Now It's the No-Credit Card," *Time* (September 29, 1980), and "The Debit Card Hits a Roadblock in Seattle," *Business Week* (December 7, 1981). "Visa Adds Marketing Muscle to Debit POS," *Bank Network News* (June 11, 1993), follows the introduction of Visa's new marketing campaign. We also relied on *Credit Card Management*'s "Debit Cards Bankers Can Shout About" (February 1991) for information on off-line debit programs. Finally, information obtained from Visa U.S.A. was used.

Two published sources supplement the discussion in "Which Came First?": "EFT Networks Go for the TV Advertising Spotlight," *Debit Card News* (September 16, 1997), and "Double Dose of Debit Volume Helps Keep EFT Networks Healthy," also in *Debit Card News* (February 17, 1998). The lawsuit described in "The Future of Debit Cards" can be found at *Wal-Mart Stores, Inc., The Limited, Inc., and All Similarly Situated Parties v. Visa U.S.A., Inc.,* United States District Court, E.D.N.Y., filed October 25, 1996. The entire November/December 1995 issue of the *Federal Reserve Bank of St. Louis Review* is devoted to the topic of antitrust issues in electronic payment networks. HHI calculations and regional market shares in this section are based on data from Faulkner & Gray's *1998 Debit Card Directory.* Other useful sources include "Star and Honor Redefine Regional Networks," *Bank Network News* (July 24, 1998); "Mergers and More Roil the EFT Waters," *Bank Network News* (April 23, 1998); and "Visa Launches Check Card II, but Stands Alone at Program Altar," *Debit Card News* (October 13, 1998).

Chapter 13

For more information on the smart-card experiment in New York City, see "A Disappointing West Side Story for Smart Cards," *Debit Card News* (November 11, 1998); "A Test in Cashless Spending Turns Out to Be a Hard Sell," *The New York Times* (July 27, 1998); and "Got a Dime? Citibank and Chase End Test of Electronic Cash," also in *The New York Times* (November 4, 1998). The rise of smart cards is chronicled in "Banking on Smart Cards," *Credit Card Management* (December 1997), and "Attack of the Smart Cards," *Bank Marketing* (February 1998).

Selected Bibliography

Books

Baker, D. I., and R. E. Brandel. *The Law of Electronic Fund Transfer Systems.* New York: Warren, Gorham & Lamont, 1988.

Blanchard, J. O., and S. Fischer. *Lectures on Macroeconomics.* Cambridge, MA: MIT Press, 1989.

Bogart, E. L. *Economic History of the American People.* New York: Longman's, Green and Co., 1930.

Bork, R. H. *The Antitrust Paradox.* New York: Basic Books, 1978.

Brealey, R., and S. Myers. *Principles of Corporate Finance.* New York: McGraw-Hill, Inc., 1996.

Carlton, D., and J. Perloff. *Modern Industrial Organization.* New York: HarperCollins College Publishers, 1994.

Chen, S. *Coins of Ancient China* (L. May, trans.), <*http://hanwei.com/culture/coin.html*>.

Cournot, A. A. *Researches into the Mathematical Principles of the Theory of Wealth.* Homewood, IL: R. D. Irwin, 1986.

Davies, G. *A History of Money from Ancient Times to the Present Day.* Cardiff, England, UK: University of Wales Press, 1994.

Ehrenberg, R. G., and R. S. Smith. *Modern Labor Economics.* New York: HarperCollins College Publishers, 1994.

Evans, D. S., and R. Schmalensee. *The Economics of the Payment Card Industry.* Cambridge, MA: National Economic Research Associates, 1993.

Freixas, X., and J-C. Rochet. *Microeconomics of Banking.* Cambridge, MA: MIT Press, 1997.

Friedman, J., and J. Meehan. *House of Cards: Inside the Troubled Empire of American Express.* New York: Kensington, 1992.

Friedman, M., and A. Schwartz. *A Monetary History of the United States, 1867–1960.* Princeton, NJ: Princeton University Press, 1963.

Galbraith, J. K. *Money: Whence It Came, Where It Went.* Boston, MA: Houghton Mifflin Co., 1995.

Gibson, D. M. T. *The Strategic and Operational Significance of the Credit Card for Commercial Banks.* Washington, DC: Federal Reserve Bank, 1968.

Groseclose, E. *Money and Man.* Norman, OK: University of Oklahoma Press, 1976.

Grossman, P. Z. *American Express: The Unofficial History of the People Who Built the Great Financial Empire.* New York: Crown Publishers, Inc., 1997.

Hutchinson, H. D. *Money, Banking, and the United States Economy.* Englewood Cliffs, NJ: Prentice Hall, 1988.

Keynes, J. M. *Essays in Persuasion.* New York: Norton, 1963.

Kohn, M. *Financial Institutions and Markets.* New York: McGraw-Hill, Inc., 1994.

Kreps, D. M. *A Course in Microeconomic Theory.* Princeton, NJ: Princeton University Press, 1990.

Krumme, D. *Banking and the Plastic Card.* Washington, DC: American Bankers Association, 1987.

Letwin, W. *Law and Economic Policy in America.* New York: Random House, 1965.

Lewis, J. D. *Partnerships for Profit: Structuring and Managing Strategic Alliances.* New York: Free Press, 1990.

Mandell, L. *The Credit Card Industry: A History.* Boston, MA: Twayne Publishers, 1990.

McLeod, R. W. *Bank Credit Cards for EFTs: A Cost-Benefit Analysis.* Ann Arbor, MI: UMI Research Press, 1979.

Meyer, M. *The Bankers: The Next Generation.* New York: Truman Talley Books, 1997.

Neale, A. D. *The Antitrust Laws of the United States.* Cambridge, England, UK: Cambridge University Press, 1980.

Nocera, J. *A Piece of the Action: How the Middle Class Joined the Money Class.* New York: Simon & Schuster, 1994.

Posner, R. *Antitrust Law: An Economic Perspective.* Chicago, IL: University of Chicago Press, 1976.

Rose, P. S. *The Interstate Banking Revolution.* Westport, CT: Greenwood Press, 1989.

Scherer, F. M., and D. Ross. *Industrial Market Structure and Economic Performance.* Boston, MA: Houghton Mifflin, 1990.

Smith, A. *An Inquiry into the Nature and Causes of the Wealth of Nations* (R. H. Campbell & A. S. Skinner, eds.). Oxford, England, U.K.: Clarendon Press, 1970.

Spofford, Gavin, and Robert H. Grant. *A History of Bank Credit Cards.* Washington, DC: Federal Home Loan Bank Board, 1975.

Sun Tzu. *The Art of War* (T. Cleary, trans.). Boston, MA: Shambhala Pocket Classics, 1991.

Tirole, J. *The Theory of Industrial Organization*. Cambridge, MA: MIT Press, 1988.

Williamson, O. E. *Markets and Hierarchies: Analysis and Antitrust Implications*. New York: Free Press, 1975.

Articles

Areeda, P. 1990. "Essential Facilities: An Epithet in Need of Limiting Principles." *Antitrust Law Journal* 58:841–853.

Ausubel, L. M. 1991. "The Failure of Competition in the Credit Card Market." *American Economic Review* 81:50–81.

Ausubel, L. M. "The Credit Card Market Revisited." Working Paper, Department of Economics, University of Maryland (July 20, 1995).

Avery, R. B. et al. 1986. "The Use of Cash and Transaction Accounts by American Families." *Federal Reserve Bulletin* 72:87–108.

Barth, J. et al. "Commercial Banking Structure, Regulation, and Performance: An International Comparison." OCC Economics Working Paper (February 1997).

Baxter, W. F. 1983. "Bank Interchange of Transactional Paper: Legal and Economic Perspectives." *Journal of Law and Economics* 26:541–588.

Blanchflower, D. G., and A. J. Oswald. 1998. "What Makes an Entrepreneur?" *Journal of Labor Economics* 16:26–60.

Blanchflower, D. G., D. S. Evans, and A. J. Oswald. "Credit Cards and Consumers." National Economic Research Associates Working Paper (December 1998).

Brito, D., and P. Hartley. 1995. "Consumer Rationality and Credit Cards." *Journal of Political Economy* 103:400–433.

Brodley, J. F. 1982. "Joint Ventures and Antitrust Policy." *Harvard Law Review* 95:1521–1590.

Calem, P. S. 1992. "The Strange Behavior of the Credit Card Market." *Business Review*, Federal Reserve Bank of Philadelphia, January:3–14.

Calem, P. S., and L. J. Mester. 1997. "Consumer Behavior and the Stickiness of Credit Card Interest Rates." *American Economic Review* 85:1327–1336.

Canner, G. B., and C. A. Luckett. 1992. "Developments in the Pricing of Credit Card Services." *Federal Reserve Bulletin* 78:652–666.

Carlton, D. W. 1986. "The Rigidity of Prices." *American Economic Review* 76: 637–658.

Carlton, D. W. "The Theory and Facts of How Markets Clear: Is Industrial Organization Useful for Understanding Macroeconomics?" In *The Handbook of Industrial Organization* (Richard Schmalensee and Robert Wilig, eds.). Amsterdam: North Holland Press, 1989, pp. 909–946.

Carlton, D. W., and A. Frankel. 1995. "Antitrust and Payment Technologies." *Federal Reserve Bank of St. Louis Review* 77:41–54.

Carlton, D. W., and A. Frankel. 1995. "The Antitrust Economics of Credit Card Networks." *Antitrust Law Journal* 63:643–668.

Carlton, D. W., and S. C. Salop. 1996. "You Keep on Knocking but You Can't Come In: Evaluating Restrictions on Access to Input Joint Ventures." *Harvard Journal of Law and Technology* 9:319–352.

Caskey, J. P., and G. H. Sellon, Jr. 1994. "Is the Debit Card Revolution Finally Here?" *Economic Review,* Federal Reserve Bank of Kansas City, 79:79–95.

Chang, H. H., D. S. Evans, and R. Schmalensee. 1998. "Some Economic Principles for Guiding Antitrust Policy towards Joint Ventures." *Columbia Business Law Review* 1998:223–329.

Cole, R., and J. Wolken. 1995. "Financial Services Used by Small Businesses: Evidence from the 1993 National Survey of Small Business Finances." *Federal Reserve Bulletin* 81:629–667.

DeMuth, C. 1986. "The Case against Credit Card Interest Rate Regulation." *Yale Journal on Regulation* 3:201–242.

Duca, J. V., and W. C. Whitesell. 1995. "Credit Cards and Money Demand: A Cross-Sectional Study." *Journal of Money, Credit and Banking* 27:604–623.

Ellis, C. 1996. "Making Strategic Alliances Succeed: The Importance of Trust." *Harvard Business Review* 74:8–9.

Evans, D. S., and B. Jovanovic. 1989. "An Estimated Model of Entrepreneurial Choice under Liquidity Constraints." *Journal of Political Economy* 97:808–827.

Evans, D. S., and M. Leder. "The Role of Credit Cards in Providing Financing for Small Businesses." National Economic Research Associates Working Paper (December 1998).

Evans, D. S., B. Reddy, and R. Schmalensee. "Did AT&T and GM Affect Credit Card Pricing?" National Economic Research Associates Working Paper, 1997.

Evans, D. S., and R. Schmalensee. 1995. "Economic Aspects of Payment Card Systems and Antitrust Policy toward Joint Ventures." *Antitrust Law Journal* 63:861–901.

Evans, D. S., and R. Schmalensee. 1996. "A Guide to the Antitrust Economics of Networks." *Antitrust* 10:36–40.

Evans, D. S., and R. Schmalensee. "Joint Venture Membership: MountainWest." In *Antitrust Revolution* (John Kwoka and Lawrence White, eds.). New York: Oxford University Press, 1999, pp. 286–309.

Evans, D. S., and M. Leder. "The Growth and Diffusion of Credit Cards in Society." National Economic Research Associates Working Paper (December 1998).

Felgran, S. D. 1985. "From ATM to POS Networks: Branching, Access, and Pricing." *New England Economic Review* May/June:44–61.

Felgran, S. D., and R. E. Ferguson. 1986. "The Evolution of Retail EFT Networks." *New England Economic Review* July/August:42–56.

Ferri, G., and P. Simon. "Constrained Consumer Lending: Exploring Business Cycle Patterns Using the Survey of Consumer Finances." Mimeograph, Princeton University, Princeton, NJ. (December 1997).

Fisher, F. M., and J. J. McGowan. 1983. "On the Misuse of Accounting Rates of Return to Infer Monopoly Profits." *American Economic Review* 73:82–97.

Frankel, A. S. 1998. "Monopoly and Competition in the Supply and Exchange of Money." *Antitrust Law Journal* 66:313–361.

Gardner, W. D. "Curtain Act at RCA." In *Great Business Disasters* (Isadore Barmash, ed.). Chicago, IL: Playboy Press, 1972, pp. 218–241.

Hall, R. E., and F. S. Mishkin. 1982. "The Sensitivity of Consumption to Transitory Income: Estimates from Panel Data on Households." *Econometrica* 50:461–481.

Haltiwanger, J., and S. Davis. "Gross Job Flows." In *Handbook of Labor Economics* (Elsevier Science, Ltd., forthcoming).

Hausman, J. A., G. K. Leonard, and J. Tirole. *The Impact of Duality on Productive Efficiency and Innovation.* Unpublished manuscript.

Hayashi, F. 1985. "The Effect of Liquidity Constraints on Consumption: A Cross-Section Analysis." *Quarterly Journal of Economics* 10:183–206.

Holtz-Eakin, D. J., and H. Rosen. 1994. "Sticking It Out: Entrepreneurial Survival and Liquidity Constraints." *Journal of Political Economy* 102:53–75.

Hovenkamp, H. 1995. "Exclusive Joint Ventures and Antitrust Policy." *Columbia Business Law Review* 1995:2–125.

Humphrey, D. B. "The Evolution of Payments in Europe, Japan, and the United States." Policy Research Working Paper 1676, The World Bank Financial Sector Development Department, Washington, DC.

Jappelli, T. 1990. "Who Is Credit Constrained in the U.S. Economy?" *Quarterly Journal of Economics* 105:219–234.

Johnson, J. P. "Procedural Justice Perceptions Among IJV Managers." In *Cooperative Strategies: North American Perspectives* (Paul Beamish & J. Peter Killing, eds.). San Francisco, CA: New Lexington Press, 1997, pp. 197–226.

Kennickell, A. B., M. Starr-McCluer, and A. E. Sunden. 1997. "Family Finances in the U.S.: Recent Evidence from the Survey of Consumer Finances." *Federal Reserve Bulletin* 83:1–24.

Laderman, E. S. 1990. "The Public Policy Implications of State Laws Pertaining to Automated Teller Machines." *Federal Reserve Bank of San Francisco Economic Review* Winter:43–58.

Lapuerta, C., and S. C. Myers. "Measuring Profitability in the Credit Card Business." Unpublished manuscript (January 7, 1997).

Lerner, J. "The Return to Investments in Innovative Activities: An Overview and an Analysis of the Software Industry." Working Paper, Harvard Business School, Boston (1998).

March, A. *Harvey Golub: Recharging American Express.* Case study no. 9-396-212, Harvard Business School (March 9, 1996).

Marcus, E. 1960. "The Impact of Credit Cards on Demand Deposit Utilization." *Southern Economic Journal* 26:314–316.

McAndrews, J. J. 1991. "The Evolution of Shared ATM Networks." *Business Review,* The Federal Reserve Bank of Philadelphia, May/June:3–16.

Mester, L. 1994. "Why Are Credit Card Rates Sticky?" *Economic Theory* 4: 505–530.

Nolle, D. E. "Banking Industry Consolidation: Past Changes and Implications for the Future." Economic & Policy Analysis Working Paper 95-1, OCC (1995).

O'Sullivan, O. 1997. "Profiting from the Ties that Bind." *ABA Banking Journal* 89:43–48.

Pratt, W. H., J. D. Sonda, and M. A. Racanelli. 1997. "Refusals to Deal in the Context of Network Joint Ventures." *The Business Lawyer* 52:531–557.

Prelec, D., and G. Lowenstein. 1998. "The Red and the Black: Mental Accounting of Savings and Debt," *Marketing Science* 17:4–28.

Raskovich, A., and L. Froeb. "Has Competition Failed in the Credit Card Market?" Economic Analysis Group Discussion Paper, U.S. Department of Justice, Washington, DC (June 1992).

Rochet, J-C., and J. Tirole. "Cooperation among Competitors: Interchange Fee Determination in the Credit Card Industry." Institut d'Economic Industrielle Working Paper, University of Toulouse (1998).

Sarkar, M., S. T. Cavusgil, and C. Evirgen. "A Commitment-Trust Mediated Framework of International Collaborative Venture Performance." In *Cooperative Strategies: North American Perspectives* (P. Beamish and J. Peter Killing, eds.). San Francisco, CA: New Lexington Press, 1997, pp. 255–285.

Schmalensee, R. "Payment Systems and Interchange Fees." Unpublished manuscript (December 1998).

Stango, V. "Fixed Rates vs. Variable Rates: Competition and Pricing in the Credit Card Market." In *Competition, Prices and Consumer Interest Rate Sensitivity in the Credit Card Market.* Unpublished doctoral dissertation, University of California-Davis, Department of Economics (1996).

Stauffer, T. R. 1971. "The Measurement of Corporate Rates of Return: A Generalized Formulation." *Bell Journal of Economics* 2:434–469.

Stavins, J. 1996. "Can Demand Elasticities Explain Sticky Credit Card Rates?" *New England Economic Review* July/August:43–54.

Stiglitz, J., and A. Weiss. 1981."Credit Rationing in Markets with Imperfect Information." *American Economic Review* 70:393–410.

Symposium on Network Externalities, *Journal of Economic Perspectives* (Spring 1994). Volume 8, no. 2.

Symposium on Antitrust Issues and Payment Systems Networks, *Federal Reserve Bank of St. Louis Review* (November/December 1995). Volume 77, no. 6.

White, K. 1976. "The Effect of Bank Credit Cards on the Household Transactions Demand for Money." *Journal of Money, Credit and Banking* 8:51–61.

Government Publications

Board of Governors of the Federal Reserve System. *Survey of Consumer Finances.* <www.bog.frb.fed.us/pubs/oss/oss2/scfindex. html>

Board of Governors of the Federal Reserve System. *Bank Credit-Card and Check-Credit Plans.* Washington, DC: Federal Reserve Bank, July 1968.

Board of Governors of the Federal Reserve System. *The Federal Reserve System: Purposes and Functions* (8th ed.). Washington, DC: Federal Reserve Bank, 1994.

Board of Governors of the Federal Reserve System. *82nd Annual Report.* Washington, DC: Federal Reserve Bank, 1995.

Board of Governors of the Federal Reserve System. *Report to the Congress on Funds Availability Schedules and Check Fraud at Depository Institutions.* <www.bog.frb.fed.us/boarddocs/RptCongress/> Federal Reserve Bank, October 1996.

Board of Governors of the Federal Reserve System. *Flow of Funds Accounts of the United States.* Washington, DC: Federal Reserve Bank, 1997.

Board of Governors of the Federal Reserve System. *Remarks by Chairman Alan Greenspan.* Chicago: Federal Reserve Bank of Chicago, May 1997.

Board of Governors of the Federal Reserve System. *Statistical Release G.13.* <www.bog.frb.fed.us/releases/G13> Federal Reserve Bank, June 1998.

Board of Governors of the Federal Reserve System. *Statistical Release G.19.* <www.bog.frb.fed.us/releases/G19> Federal Reserve Bank, November 1998.

Bureau of Economic Analysis. *Survey of Current Business.* <www.bea.doc.gov/bea/pub/0898cont.htm> (1998).

Bureau of Labor Statistics. *Consumer Expenditure Survey.* <*www.bls.gov/csxhome.htm*> (Various Dates).

Bureau of Labor Statistics. "Local Area Unemployment Statistics." <*www.bos.frb.org/economic/neei/neeidata/urma.txt*> (November 1998).

Bureau of Labor Statistics and the Bureau of the Census. *Current Population Survey.* <*www.bls.census.gov/cps/cpsmain.htm*> (November 1998).

Council of Economic Advisors. *Economic Report of the President.* Washington, DC: U.S. Government Printing Office, February 1992, February 1997, February 1998.

Department of Justice and Federal Trade Commission. *1992 Horizontal Merger Guidelines.* <*http://www.usdoj.gov/atr/public/guidelines/horiz_book/hmg1. html*> (April 1997).

Federal Bureau of Investigation. *Crime in the United States.* Washington, DC: FBI, 1995.

Federal Deposit Insurance Corporation. *Historical Statistics on Banking.* <www2.fdic.gov/hsob/> FDIC, various years.

Federal Reserve Bank of New York. *A Brief Summary of Coins and Currency.* New York: Federal Reserve Bank, 1953.

Humphrey, D. B. *Payment Systems: Principles, Practice, and Improvements.* Washington, DC: World Bank, 1995.

Internal Revenue Service. Internal Revenue Code 26 U.S.C. 163.

National Commission on Electronic Fund Transfers. *EFT in the United States: Policy Recommendations and the Public Interest.* (Washington, DC 1977).

Office of Thrift Supervision and Office of the Comptroller of the Currency. *Comparison of Powers of Federal Savings Associations to the Powers of National Banks.* (Washington, DC: OCC, January 1997).

U.S. Small Business Administration. *The State of Small Business: A Report of the President.* Washington, DC: U.S. Government Printing Office, 1997.

U.S. Bureau of the Census. *Measures of Value Produced, Capital Expenditures, Depreciable Assets and Operating Expenses.* From the 1992 Census of Retail Trade. *<http://www.census.gov/prod/www/titles.html#rt>* (November 1996).

U.S. Bureau of the Census. *Statistical Abstract of the United States: 1997.* Washington, DC: U.S. Government Printing Office, 1997.

U.S. Bureau of the Census. *Concentration Ratios in Manufacturing.* From the Census of Manufactures. *<http://www.census.gov/mcd/mancen/download/mc92cr.sum>* (November 1998).

U.S. Bureau of the Census, *Current Population Survey.* *<http://www.bls.census.gov/cps/cpsmain.htm>* (Various Dates).

U.S. Government Accounting office. "U.S. Credit Card Industry—Competitive Developments Need to Be Closely Monitored." In *GAO Report* (Washington, DC: GAO, April 1994).

U.S. Small Business Administration. *Summary Report to President Clinton.* *<http://www.sba.gov/regulations/clinton.html>* (June 1998).

Legal Cases

Broadcast Music, Inc. v. CBS, 441 U.S. 1 (1979).

Greenwood Trust Co. v. Commonwealth of Massachusetts, 776 F. Supp. 21 (D. Mass. 1991), *rev'd and remanded,* 971 F.2d 818 (1st Cir., 1992), *cert. denied,* 506 U.S. 1052 (1993).

Independent Bankers Association of New York State v. Marine Midland Bank, 583 F. Supp. 1042 (W.D.N.Y., 1984), *rev'd in part, vacated in part, and remanded,* 757 F.2d 453 (2nd Cir., 1985), *cert. denied,* 476 U.S. 1186 (1986).

Marquette National Bank of Minneapolis v. First of Omaha Service Corp. et al., 439 U.S. 299 (1978).

National Bancard Corp. (NaBanco) v. Visa, U.S.A., Inc., 596 F. Supp. 1231, 1265 (S.D. Fla., 1984), *aff'd*, 779 F.2d 592 (11th Cir., 1986), *cert. denied*, 479 U.S. 923 (1986).

Rothery Storage & Van Co. v. Atlas Van Lines, Inc., 792 F.2d 210 (D.C. Cir., 1986), *cert. denied*, 479 U.S. 1033 (1987).

SCFC ILC, Inc. v. Visa U.S.A., Inc., 819 F. Supp. 956 (D. Utah, 1993), *rev'd in part and aff'd in part*, 36 F.3d 958 (10th Cir. 1994), *cert. denied*, 515 U.S. 1152 (1995). (This case is generally referred to as the *MountainWest* case).

Standard Oil v. United States, 221 U.S. 1 (1911).

United States v. Addyston Pipe & Steel Co., 85 F.271 (6th Cir., 1898), *aff'd*, 175 U.S. 211 (1899).

United States v. American Tobacco Co., 221 U.S. 106 (1911).

United States v. Associated Press, 52 F. Supp. 362 (D.N.Y., 1943), *aff'd*, 326 U.S. 1 (1945).

United States v. Realty Multi-List, 629 F.2d 1351 (5th Cir., 1980).

United States v. Sealy, Inc., 388 U.S. 350 (1967).

United States v. Topco Associates, Inc., 405 U.S. 596 (1972).

United States v. Trans-Missouri Freight Assn., 166 U.S. 290 (1897).

Wal-Mart Stores, Inc., The Limited, Inc., and All Similarly Situated Parties v. Visa U.S.A., Inc. (E.D.N.Y., October 25, 1996).

Worthen Bank and Trust Co. v. National BankAmericard Inc., 345 F. Supp. 1309 (E. D. Ark., 1972), *rev'd*, 485 F.2d 119 (8th Cir., Ark. 1973).

Other Sources

American Banker. *1996 American Banker & Gallup Consumer Survey.* Princeton, NJ (1997).

American Express. *Annual Report, 1997.* <*www.americanexpress.com/corp/annual_report/annual97/index.shtml*>

BankAmerica. *Annual Report, 1997.* <www.bankamerica.com/batoday/annual97>

Bank for International Settlements. *Statistics on Payments in the Group of Ten Countries.* Basle, Switzerland: BIS, 1996.

Bernstein Research. *The Future of the Credit Card Industry: Part II.* New York: Bernstein Research, January 1996.

Citicorp. *Annual Report, 1997.* <*www.citibank.com/corporate_affairs/reports.htm*>

Credit Union National Association. *Operating Ratios and Spreads Year-End 1997*. Madison, WI: CUNA, 1998.

Credit Union National Association. *Credit Union Services Profile: December 1997*. Madison, WI: CUNA, 1998.

Datamonitor. *European Plastic Cards 1996*. London, England, UK: Datamonitor, 1996.

Dun & Bradstreet, Business Background Report: Sytel, Inc. MurrayHill, NJ: Dun & Bradstreet (1998).

Faulkner & Gray. *Credit Card Issuer's Guide*. New York: Faulkner & Gray (1993).

Faulkner & Gray. *Credit Card Marketing Sourcebook*. New York: Faulkner & Gray (1998).

Faulkner & Gray. *Card Industry Directory*. New York: Faulkner & Gray (1998, 1999).

Faulkner & Gray. *Debit Card Directory*. New York: Faulkner & Gray (1997, 1998, 1999).

Faulkner & Gray. *Card Industry Directory: European Plastic Cards*. New York: Faulkner & Gray (1996).

MBNA. *Annual Report,* 1997. <www.mbnainternational.com/stocks/index.htm>

National Credit Union Association. *1997 Year-End Statistics for Federally Insured Credit Unions*. Alexandria, VA: NCUA, 1998.

The Gallup Organization. *Payment Methods Attitude Study*. Princeton, NJ: The Gallup Organization, 1993.

HSN Consultants, Inc. *The Nilson Report* (various dates). Oxnard, CA: HSN,

RAM Research Group. *Cardsearch*. Frederick, MD: RAM Research (1992).

RAM Research Group. *CardData*. Frederick, MD: Ram Research (1997).

Standard & Poor. *Monthly Investment Review*. (New York, NY: June 1997).

Russell, Charles T., and Dan Dougherty. "Presentation at the Regional Meeting of the Bank Public Relations and Marketing Association, April 5 and April 22, 1966." Unpublished transcript obtained from VISA U.S.A.

Visa International. *International Country Overviews*. Foster City, CA (1997).

Visa U.S.A. *1995 Credit Card Functional Cost Study*. Foster City, CA (1996).

Visa U.S.A. *1996 Credit Card Issuer Benchmark Study*. Foster City, CA (1997).

Visa U.S.A. *Bylaws* (1997).

Visa U.S.A. *Cardholder Tracking Study*. Foster City, CA (various dates).

Visa U.S.A. *Characteristics of Credit and Fraud Losses and Account Control*. Foster City, CA (1990).

Visa U.S.A. "Executive Summary, Board of Directors Meeting, February 10–11, 1992." Unpublished notes.

Visa U.S.A. "Minutes of the Meeting of the Product Development and Marketing Committee of the Visa U.S.A. Board of Directors, June 16–17, 1985." Unpublished notes.

Visa U.S.A. *Payment System Panel Study.* Foster City, CA (1995).

Visa U.S.A. *Profit Analysis Reports.* Foster City, CA (1996).

Visa U.S.A. *Visa/Bankcard Industry Milestones.* Foster City, CA (1990).

Index